The Seven Fat Years

The Seven Fat Years

AND HOW TO DO IT AGAIN

Robert L. Bartley

THE FREE PRESS
A Division of Macmillan, Inc.
New York

Maxwell Macmillan Canada
Toronto

Maxwell Macmillan International
New York   Oxford   Singapore   Sydney

The Free Press
A Division of Macmillan, Inc.
866 Third Avenue, New York, N.Y. 10022

Maxwell Macmillan Canada, Inc.
1200 Eglinton Avenue East
Suite 200
Don Mills, Ontario M3C 3N1

Macmillan, Inc. is part of the Maxwell Communication
Group of Companies.

Printed in the United States of America

printing number
1   2   3   4   5   6   7   8   9   10

Library of Congress Cataloging-in-Publication Data

Bartley, Robert L.
The seven fat years—and how to do it again / Robert L. Bartley.
p.   cm.
Includes bibliographical references and index.
ISBN 0–02–901915–X
1. United States—Economic policy—1981–   2. Supply-side
economics—United States.   3. United States—Economic
conditions—1981—   I. Title.
HC106.8.B375   1992
338.973—dc20   92–1137
                                                          CIP

The author and the publisher gratefully acknowledge permission to quote from the following publications:

Editorial, "Why No One Wants Dollars." *The Times* (London), January 4, 1978.

Editorial, "Who's Selling the Snake Oil?" *The Sunday Times* (London), October 19, 1986.

Robert J. Barro, "Are Government Bonds Net Wealth?" *Journal of Political Economy*, 82 (November/December 1974), "The Ricardian Approach to Budget Deficits," *Journal of Economic Perspectives*, Volume 3, Number 2 (Spring 1989), and private correspondence with author.

Alan Greenspan, "Business Outlook: The Threat to Thrift Institutions," Townsend-Greenspan & Co. Inc., April 17, 1974.

F. A. Hayek, "The Austrian Critique," in "The Keynes Centenary," *Economist*, June 11, 1983, p. 45, U.S. edition.

Merton Miller, "Leverage," Nobel Memorial Prize Lecture, presented at the Royal Swedish Academy of Sciences, Stockholm, December 7, 1990. © The Nobel Foundation 1990.

Norman Ture, " 'Supply-Side' Analysis and Public Policy," The Lehrman Institute, Economic Policy Round Table, Nov. 12, 1980.

Paul Volcker, "The GATT Under Stress—Is There Life After 40?" Fortieth anniversary address to the General Agreement on Tariffs and Trade, Geneva, Nov. 30, 1987.

To my father and the memory of my mother;
they arranged their lives so that I might do this.

Contents

INTO THE NINETIES

Preface

In the 1990s the United States faces history's most magnificent opportunity. It surveys the world as the sole superpower. It provides the capstone and epitome of mankind's most successful economic system. It dominates technology at a time of breathtaking technological advance. Its political traditions embody the aspirations of peoples everywhere. Its opportunity is not to conquer the world but to free it, to lead it into a new era of freedom, cooperation and prosperity.

The United States *can* do this. In what should become the future's prelude, it just did.

In the years just before 1982, democratic capitalism was in retreat. Its economic order seemed unhinged, wracked by bewildering inflation, stagnant productivity and finally a deep recession. The diplomatic and military initiative lay with Communist totalitarianism, which proclaimed inevitable ideological victory and could send crowds into European streets to protest efforts to offset its own shiny new missiles and tanks. Economic confusions and a sense of futility sapped the morale of the Western people; leaders talked of "malaise" in America and "Europessimism" across the Atlantic.

In a remarkably short time, all of this has been totally reversed. Today mankind affirms democratic capitalism as its role model.

The First World forged this transformation with a series of related decisions—economic, military, diplomatic, moral. Some of them, such as the containment policy that changed Soviet society through patience rather than conquest, reach back two generations. But the keystone in so suddenly changing the world was the economic recovery that began in the United States as 1983 dawned. The trough of the recession was reached in November 1982; the expansion lasted through July 1990. From 1983 to 1990, we enjoyed Seven Fat Years.

"We" being the developed world, for the recovery that began in the United States was also the spark that lifted despond from Europe and contributed to the explosive economic growth of Asia. The recovery engendered the confidence for steadfast diplomacy, the wherewithal for military rearmament and the morale for initiatives such as the federation of Europe, the revival of Mexico and the taming of Iraq. None of this would have been likely, and much of it not even possible, without the Seven Fat Years.

If the United States accomplished this once, it can do it again. Except only, Americans do not understand *what* they did or *how* they did it.

Much of the American elite, indeed, seems to have persuaded itself that the Seven Fat Years were a failure and that their nation has declined. Wallowing neurotically in arcane and ill-understood statistics, a gaggle of declinists denies a reality evident to everyone else in the world. The rest of the world, though understandably nervous about a hesitant and unpredictable giant, knows in the end that only America can lead.

To reap its opportunity, American society needs above all to draw the lessons of its own success. The economic crisis of the 1970s was overcome by policies put into place at great effort and pain between 1978 and 1983. The specific steps were tight monetary policy, embodied in Paul Volcker, and incentive tax cuts, embodied in Ronald Reagan. But there was also a broad social movement fully evident as early as 1978, not only a "tax revolt" but a change in American feelings and understandings, a reassertion of American optimism and creativity.

The new policies and new mind-set unleashed the Seven Fat Years, a wave of sustained growth and a dynamic outburst of entrepreneurial creativity. As the nation drew away from these policies and lost its grip on this mind-set, the surging prosperity was interrupted; the string of fat years ended. But there need not be seven lean years. We only need to understand the policies that did work, and to apply and adapt them to the 1990s and the new century.

The danger lies in prosperity's discontents. American economic history is a story of booms fading into resentment. It is not so much a business cycle as a cycle of public sentiment, alternating between times of optimism and times of pessimism. Between, if you must, decades of greed and, if you will, decades of envy. One phase started in 1969 and ended in 1978; the risk is that the phase that started then has ended as the 1990s dawn. The declinist prophesy, if believed, could be self-fulfilling. If the nation allows itself to slip back to the failed policies and crabbed attitudes that led to crisis, it will stumble economically and wither spiritually. The United States will have forsaken the birthright of history.

• • •

I understand the history of the Seven Fat Years, of course, from my own perspective. In directing the editorial pages of *The Wall Street Journal* during the 1980s, I was a prominent advocate of the economic policy conducted by the Reagan administration. Even before there was a Reagan administration, indeed, I supervised the editorials and published the articles expounding what came to be called "supply-side economics." This movement was accurately and sympathetically described from inside the Reagan administration by Martin Anderson:

> When an idea's time has come, whether it's a new one or an old one polished up a bit, it's apt to occur to a lot of people at about the same time. Robert Mundell, Arthur Laffer, Paul Craig Roberts, Robert Bartley and Jude Wanniski all played important roles in spreading the essential idea that tax rates matter, that they can and do affect economic growth. There were others who also helped, writing and arguing the case—Jack Kemp, Norman Ture, Bruce Bartlett, Irving Kristol, Steven Entin, and Alan Reynolds. All together there were probably about a dozen people who propelled the effect of tax rates into a major plank of economic policy. All but Kemp were intellectuals, and Kemp was very close to being a politico-intellectual. They were like a many-linked chain. Perhaps the chain would have held without any one of them, or two of them, but we know it would not have been without all of them.[1]

Other commentators are less sympathetic. When they write that economic policy in the 1980s was captured by "a small band of ideologues," they mean my friends and myself. As a standard economics text, *Macroeconomics* by Rudiger Dornbusch and Stanley Fischer, puts it: "*Supply-side economics* became the fad of the early 1980s, promising an easy way out of the economic mess of the time by cutting taxes. But supply-side economics overpromised, and there was no easy way out."[2] In my own view, the lessons of the 1980s are misunderstood partly because what were called the supply-side policies have been widely caricatured and widely misunderstood. Beyond the catchy "Laffer curve," something intellectually important was happening.

We would understand better if the label "supply-side" were retired. It could be replaced by "the new classical economics," which while no one was looking became dominant among the younger generation of academic economists. "Classical" means before Keynes. It means that the "Keynesian revolution" was a detour, that the economic apparatus America's leadership generation learned back in college is now obsolete. The people Martin Anderson named did not see supply-side economics as something new on the face of the earth. As Art Laffer wrote at the time, "Supply-side economics is little more than a new label for standard neoclassical economics."[3]

Anyone who doubts my account of the evolution of academic economics should read "A Quick Refresher Course in Macroeconomics" by N. Gregory Mankiw of Harvard, an article reprinted in pamphlet form by the National Bureau of Economic Research. Mankiw ponders "the great disparity between academic and applied macroeconomics." Understandings of macroeconomics have undergone a "radical change" in the academy, he notes, but popular understandings "have not substantially changed." The old Keynesian formulas still dominate "discussions of economic policy in the press and among policy makers."[4]

The Keynesian universe collapsed with the "stagflation" of the 1970s. In policy terms, its proudest achievement was the "Phillips curve," which purported to depict a trade-off between unemployment and inflation. The cure for unemployment was a little more inflation, and the cure for inflation was a little more unemployment. When we experienced escalating inflation and escalating unemployment simultaneously in the 1970s the Phillips curve fell. It took along its graduate-school cousin the IS-LM model (the convoluted details of which are now of only historical interest), the conceit that "econometricians" can program an economy into computers, and the rest of an intellectual house of cards.

By 1990, Professor Mankiw writes, "The IS-LM model rarely finds its way into scholarly journals; some economists view the model as a relic of a bygone age and no longer bother to teach it. The large-scale macroeconometric models are mentioned only occasionally at academic conferences, often with derision."[5] The economists who have made their reputations in the last 20 years talk instead of "rational expectations" and look back beyond Keynes to Alfred Marshall, David

Ricardo and Jean-Baptiste Say. The new classical economists would not agree with everything that carried the "supply-side" label, of course, but the years in which it was starting to become a popular phenomenon were the same years when the academic journals carried the landmark new classical articles.

• • •

To reap its opportunity, the leadership generation of the 1990s will have to relearn some economics. To meet the challenge we, by which I mean the literate public for which journalists write, need to do some work. We can no longer delegate economics to the "experts'" and their computers. We can start, indeed, by understanding that an economy is a living, breathing animal with political and social dimensions. The advanced mathematics of contemporary economics surely has much to contribute in the right hands, but the nontechnical observer and the policymaker will do better to seek understanding through history.

What follows is the history of the Seven Fat Years as I understood it. Those who have advocated a policy have an obligation to defend or confess, to give the public the benefit of their own perspective in discerning what happened, what works and what does not. This personal emphasis will inevitably overemphasize the role of *The Wall Street Journal*, but sometimes a more personalized account can communicate in ways that an academic exposition cannot. While I hope the account will prove useful to the historical record, it is not intended as exhaustive. It is the experience as I lived it.

The economic history that follows, also, is directed at the problems of the 1990s. It is only incidentally a defense of Ronald Reagan or Paul Volcker or supply-side economics. It is intended to highlight recent experience as it bears on the problems of the 1990s, most of which have their roots in the crisis of the 1970s and the antidotes of the 1980s. It is intended, too, to show what was not done, what needs to be done next to fulfill the current decade's opportunity.

For if today the United States stands athwart the world, so it did at the end of World War II. The American society of that era proved itself capable of leadership and statesmanship; it led the world in creating institutions that last to this day. On today's record, NATO is a historic triumph. If the United Nations faltered, it can now perhaps be redeemed. The Marshall Plan helped reequip Europe's human capital. The Bretton Woods international monetary system and the

General Agreement on Tariffs and Trade set an international economic policy that led to an amazing burst of economic growth throughout the world.

"The years 1950 to 1973 were a 'golden age,' " writes Professor Angus Maddison in his OECD study of our century.[6] With the dismantling of trade barriers, new opportunities for cross-border investment and the development of international institutions and aid, he writes, "The golden age saw a growth of GDP and GDP per capita on an unprecedented scale in all parts of the world economy, a rapid growth of world trade, a reopening of world capital markets and the possibilities for international migration."

My grandest hope is that the United States can find similar creativity in the 1990s. We need to understand our history and our times, to hone our economics, to shake our pessimism and decide what we want to do. If only we try, we can not merely have another Seven Fat Years, but lead a new golden age.

THE PARADOX OF
THE EIGHTIES

1

The Man from Mars

In July 1990, the Seven Fat Years ended. An economic expansion of record peacetime duration ground to a close.

That summer, too, the Man from Mars landed in Kankakee and began to watch television programs, browse in bookstores and listen in on daily chatter. The shopping malls were air-conditioned; the parking lots were filled with cars shipped from far-off Japan; the movie house offered a choice of five attractions; what used to be record shops sold "music videos" by Madonna and Milli Vanilli; and kids in the mall wore $100 sneakers.

Yet everywhere he heard and read of economic decline. Everyone talked of "excesses." Best-selling books mocked recent history, depicting the follies of tycoons, elaborating on the poor sinking into deeper misery and bemoaning the decline of the nation. The impending recession was the start, everyone seemed to assume, of the collapse the Cassandras had predicted throughout the 92 months of economic expansion.

No one could see any economic statistic except the "deficit," a kind of black hole into which vanished the savings of all America and maybe the world. The corner savings and loan has somehow mutated into the eggplant that ate Kankakee, Tampa and Los Angeles. America had become a "debtor nation" and was declining as previous empires had. Whole companies had been financed on "junk." The financial genius of the preceding decade was headed for jail, and the huge financial firm built around him was bankrupt.

Most curiously of all, in all this the Man from Mars sensed a peculiar satisfaction. The country was leaving behind a "decade of greed." The time had come to atone our sins, his most fashionable interlocutors seemed to feel. Seven lean years would be good for us. It was as if part of the American soul *wanted* a recession. This was our nervous breakdown; we had earned it, and we were going to enjoy it.

Disoriented by the disjunction between the affluence he saw and the poor-mouthing he heard, the Man from Mars pulled out his hand-held Databoy, and started to query for some statistics.

ECONOMIC GROWTH?, he punched. In 1990, the Databoy screen said, the gross national product of America was 31 percent above 1982 in real, inflation-adjusted terms. During the Seven Fat Years, America had grown by nearly a third. At the beginning of the period, the German economy was about a third of America's; in its years of "excess" the American economic machine had in effect built a whole new West Germany.

LIVING STANDARDS?, the Man from Mars punched. Inevitably the economic expansion had affected individual Americans. The Databoy exhibited the best measure of standard of living, something economists called real disposable income per capita. As expansion ended in 1990, this was 18 percent above 1982. Over the Seven Fat Years, that is, the standard of living of the American people grew by nearly a fifth. At least, the Man from Mars thought, this explains the $100 sneakers.

HOW?, he punched, pressing for elaboration. The growth happened because the expansion was a long one, he learned, and powers of compound interest do wonders in a long run of uninterrupted growth. The Databoy said the expansion started at an economic trough in the final quarter of 1982 and reached its peak in the third quarter of 1990. Over this time, real gross national product grew by 32 percent.

DEINDUSTRIALIZATION?, the Man from Mars punched, picking something he'd heard. He found that manufacturing production grew even faster than GNP, rising by 48 percent over the expansion. And despite the deficit black hole, gross private investment grew by 32 percent, in line with GNP. And just as a demographic surge reached working age, enough jobs were created to boost civilian employment by 19.5 percent. Between 1982 and 1990, the U.S. economy added 18.4 million jobs.

PRODUCTIVITY?, he continued. During all that "excess," nonfarm productivity, the output of an hour of American labor, grew by 10.6 percent, though it had previously been stagnant for a decade. And while the interlocutors bemoaned "noncompetitive" industries, exports to the rest of the world grew by 92.6 percent.[1]

GREED, he typed, DECADE OF? No statistics on greed, the Databoy replied, reference CHARITY? Here he found that the 1980s were a remarkably generous decade, with charitable giving growing at 5.1 percent a year, compared with a rate of 3.5 percent over the previous 25 years. Giving increased faster than jewelry purchases, beauty parlor and health club spending and consumer debt.[2]

TAX REVENUES? This time the Man from Mars was sure he'd find a catch, having heard again and again of "irresponsible" tax cuts. The Databoy replied that between fiscal years 1980 and 1990, federal government receipts grew by 99 percent, against GNP growth of 102 percent. From the low point in 1983 to the high point in 1989, the figures showed, tax receipts actually grew faster than GNP.

CHART, U.S. ECONOMY, the Man from Mars punched into the Databoy, CRUDE. It told him that as the expansion began, the crudest measure of economic progress was something called a "misery index," offered by the late Arthur Okun, the Brookings Institution economist. It was simply the sum of the inflation rate and unemployment rate. The data base offered up a chart. It showed that the misery index had been at a peak when the Seven Fat Years started, and declined until they came to an end.

FIGURE 1–1

The Misery Index

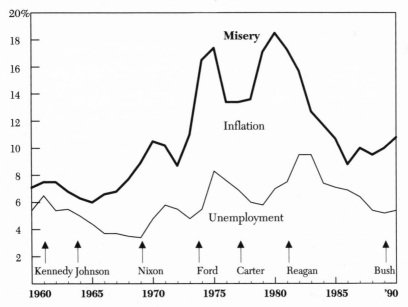

For sources and notes see Notes for Figures and Tables.

Taking one glance at the misery index, the Man from Mars punched, CHART, U.S. ECONOMY, INFLECTION POINTS. Yes, it told him, there had been a discontinuity in the growth path of the U.S. economy, but it had come before the years of "excess." From World War II until 1973, real economic growth averaged 3.6 percent a year. After 1973 the economy staggered, growing only 1.6 percent a year over the next nine years. But after 1982, growth returned, hitting a 3.5 percent path through 1990. From the beginning of 1983 through the end of 1989, growth hit 3.8 percent—The Seven Fat Years.

FIGURE 1–2

GNP Growth

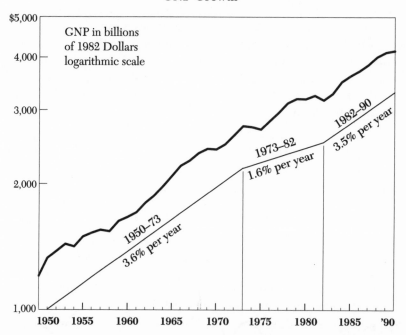

SEE FOOTNOTE, the Databoy screen flashed, INFLECTION POINTS. There is a convention among economists to measure different economic periods peak-to-peak or trough-to-trough. By their nature, inflection points measure peak-to-trough or trough-to-peak. The usual convention is "fair," but doesn't help much with the issue of what causes peaks and what causes troughs. Sometimes inflection points will help show when things changed.

Yes, the Man from Mars thought, to glance at these charts, something changed in 1973 and in 1983. While I know little about the partisan and ideological battles of Earthlings, something caused a flattening and something caused a revival. It probably takes a while to work out policies, and anyway economists talk of lags, so maybe the crucial times were a year or two before the chart's inflection points.

Marking this thought as something to return to, the Man from Mars punched, U.S. ECONOMY, RELATIVE POSITION? The United States, it told him, was the wealthiest society on earth, indeed the wealthiest society in the history of mankind.

SEE FOOTNOTE, the Databoy instructed, PURCHASING POWER PARITY. It's hard to compare the wealth of different societies on earth, he learned, because they all measure things in different monies. And these yardsticks keep changing size in relation to each other—and unfortunately, experience seems to show, not in line with any underlying economic fundamentals. Comparisons require something called Purchasing Power Parity, the exchange rate at which two currencies would each buy the same basket of goods. Fortunately, this figure is churned out in tedious work by something called the OECD, or Organisation for Economic Co-operation and Development.

Since about 1985, it turns out, market exchange rates for the dollar have been far below PPP rates, so that comparisons built on current exchange rates show America falling behind. But adjusting the comparisons to PPP, as economists agree must be done in comparing standards of living, makes the picture entirely different.

In a typical comparison using 1988 figures and contemporary exchange rates, the United States ranked only ninth in the world in gross domestic product per capita—behind Switzerland, Japan and the Scandinavian countries, for example. But if you use PPP exchange rates, the American standard of living is far above its main competitors. With the United States at 100, Canada rates 92.5 and Switzerland 87.0. Then come the Scandinavian nations and some small nations, in 1988 including Kuwait. West Germany rates tenth at 78.6, and Japan 12th at 71.5. Other developed nations trail. In short, the American standard of living is about 40 percent above that in Japan and most of Europe.[3]

This is confirmed by physical measures. Americans own an automobile, for example, for every 1.8 persons. Iceland has two people for each car, while Canada, New Zealand and West Germany have 2.2. France has 2.5, the United Kingdom 2.8 and Japan 4.2. Similarly, there are 1.2 Americans per television set, compared to 1.7 in Japan and 2.4 in Germany. The United States is also one of the world's great underdeveloped countries, with 26.3 persons per square mile, compared to 102.1 in France, 233.8 in the United Kingdom, 246.1 in West Germany, 324.5 in Japan, and 395.8 in the Netherlands. In terms of gross economic power, the United States economy was 70 percent larger than the second-place Japanese economy even at exchange rates current in 1988.

MILITARY POWER?, the Man from Mars queried, wondering if he had wandered into a Sybaris sinking in its own luxury and threatened by poorer but more vigorous rivals. Instead, he learned that a two-generation military rival had collapsed at a stroke, leaving the United States as the world's sole superpower. Shortly into his visit, he witnessed its warriors decimate the world's fifth-largest army in 100 hours of ground combat and at the cost of 124 Americans lost in action.

See, the computer instucted, related items:

IDEOLOGICAL POWER? The American ideas of democratic pluralism and market economies were spreading throughout South America, Eastern Europe and even Africa. America remains the favored destination of the world's refugees and immigrants.

TECHNOLOGICAL POWER? Despite challenges from the industrious Japanese, America still dominates scientific innovation. Its university system is unparalleled. While it educates many foreign nationals, many of them stay in the United States. Many transnational corporations, even if based in Germany or Switzerland, locate their research divisions in New Jersey or North Carolina. Japanese auto companies open design labs in Los Angeles. Above all, the United States utterly dominates the single capstone technology of the era, which despite the plethora of earth languages is in every country called "software."

The Man from Mars, by now at wits' end to understand, wants only the outcome. PROSPECTS?, he queries. The Databoy turns terse: Limitless. Theirs to grasp, and theirs to drop.

• • •

As the Man from Mars' computer suggests, today we live in one of the great, exciting moments in mankind's economic history. Not since the Industrial Revolution has technological advance been so breathtaking, or more pregnant with changes in the way mankind lives and thinks of itself.

More breathtaking now, probably, than even then. James Watt's steam engine pales beside what our generation has already seen: the splitting of the atom, the decoding of the gene, and the invention of the transistor and the computers it spawned. These are not only magnificent leaps of the technological imagination, they are potential precursors of unimaginable economic advance. Atomic power, unless cold fusion turns out to be real after all, has perhaps not realized what we thought of as its potential. The first fruits of biotechnology are just now entering the markets. But already the transistor and the rest are changing the world.

For we live every day with the electronic revolution. As the First Industrial Revolution changed an agricultural economy into an industrial economy, a Second Industrial Revolution is changing an industrial economy into a service economy. More specifically, into an information economy, in which the predominant activity is collecting, processing and communicating information. We are headed toward a world in which everyone on the globe is in instant communication with everyone else, and this evolution is changing world society in a myriad of ways.

Economically, the web of instant communication has stitched the world into a web of increasing interdependence. In fact, throughout this century the world economy has been more interdependent than anyone realized; the Great Depression, for example, was preeminently a world event, and its origins lie in disturbances in the international economy. But today, with 24-hour financial markets spanning the globe, and with the transnational corporations of the United States, Japan and Europe becoming nearly indistinguishable, economic interdependence is hard to miss.

This too has an effect on governments. In an interdependent world the costs of autarky are enormous, in the case of developed countries practically intolerable. A government simply cannot afford economic policies that are too far out of step with other nations. In François Mitterand's first year as prime minister of France, we saw a dedicated socialist experiment, starting with nationalization of banks. But as the franc plunged, the external costs were too great; within a year socialism had to be abandoned for market-oriented policies like those of other nations. Similarly, even the United States found that it could not maintain a stoutly proclaimed policy of benign neglect of the dollar.

The global information network renders almost instant verdicts on changes in government policy. We are moving toward a world ruled not by politicians but by markets. National governments will evolve toward something like state governments today: Each will have its own industrial development program to show why it has the best business and investment climate. The real competition will not be between nations, but between their various regions, and between different world-spanning corporations.[4]

For the individual citizen, this world will be, at least should be, a liberating one. It is the onslaught of the information age that already has liberated Eastern Europe and spread democratic currents through the Soviet Union, Latin America and more recently even Africa. Orwell, in *1984*, saw information technology as an instrument of Big Brother. We're now seeing clearly that it is quite the opposite. A censor can tell what books are being brought through customs, but he'll never be able to keep track of all the computer disks. Big Brother can of course build a society without computers, but that society will not be able to compete in the modern world. China can still suppress students in Tiananmen Square, but the whole world will instantly know and express its outrage. I doubt that the suppression, already exacting high costs on Chinese development, can be often repeated.

Likewise in the economic sphere. As instant information and instant markets erode the power of governments, so too they erode the power of corporate chieftains and labor bosses. We can now all watch the poor chairman of Exxon writhing because of an oil spill in Alaska. Many chief executives find themselves displaced, albeit with golden parachutes. Under the force of industrial competition and information on wages and working conditions, labor unions find their private-sector membership declining. But the individual entrepreneur, the guy with the good idea, is likely to find easier access to capital and markets.

Our century has been a beastly one, with two world wars and the rise of modern totalitarianism an epoch of suffering. But as we move toward its end we can see that era setting before our eyes. The pieces are falling into place for a new era of material advance and individual freedom. The whole world can participate and contribute to the dawning age. But its epitome, the font of both its technological breakthroughs and its political inspiration, lies preeminently in the United States of America.

• • •

Yet in the midst of these achievements and opportunities, the fashionable talk in America has been of decay and decline.

As the 1980s opened, decline of America, indeed decline of the

West was a theme of conservatives, expressed most notably but far from solely by Jean-François Revel.[5] The conservatives looked at a United States falling behind in the military competition with the Soviet Sparta, wracked by inflation and stagnant productivity at home, manipulated by Soviet campaigns like the one against the neutron bomb, preoccupied with hostages held by a primitive cleric and unable even to fly six helicopters across the desert. They worried that the American-led West lacked the will to use its superior economic resources even to defend itself.

But these fears faded as Ronald Reagan started to fill the military spare-parts bins, frankly labeled the Soviet Union an "evil empire," invaded Grenada, bombed Libya and revived the option of missile defense. The turning point was 1983, when the West withstood a determined Soviet campaign, including street demonstrations in Europe and the suspension of arms negotiations, to stop the deployment of Pershing missiles in Europe. M. Revel continued to worry, but the changing world eroded decline as a theme of the right.

Only, lo and behold, to see it become a theme of the left. While there are earlier precursors, the theme came to its fruition with Paul Kennedy's *The Rise and Fall of the Great Powers*. In 1988, as voters were rewarding a platform of "read my lips" and Willie Horton, book buyers were handsomely rewarding Professor Kennedy's thesis of "imperial overstretch." The filling of the spare parts bins and the reassertion of American military power abroad was not the cure for decline, it was the cause of decline. It was decline itself.

Though it topped the lists for 24 weeks, *The Rise and Fall of the Great Powers* was no doubt an example of the contemporary phenomenon of the unread best-seller. Few readers could have been interested in his view of the Habsburgs or Ming China, and Professor Kennedy covered the predicament of the United States on pages 514–35. But in op-ed pages and seminar rooms these pages triggered a national debate that centered squarely on the economy. Excessive military spending undermined the economy, the critique went, and the slackening economy could not support the military commitments. And the United States was in "relative decline," still first in importance but with a shrinking lead. Professor Kennedy sounded a common theme, "the only way the United States can pay its way in the world is by importing ever-larger sums of capital, which has transformed it from being the world's largest creditor to the world's largest debtor nation *in the space of a few years*."[6] In the ensuing debate, few even mentioned the other logically consistent interpretation of the capital flows—that the world's investors found the United States the most promising place to put their money.

The left naturally found great appeal in this double-barreled critique of the Reagan administration: The evident economic prosperity was marred by hidden flaws, and the root of the flaws lay in the military build-up. The fat years are only a dream— *Our Long National Daydream* in the title of Sidney Blumenthal's book on the 1980s, or in the title of Haynes Johnson's book on the period, *Sleepwalking Through History*.

Eventually we would awake, the wish seemed to be, and through the mists Camelot would reappear. As Democratic vice-presidential nominee Lloyd Bentsen put it in his acceptance speech, "My friends, America has just passed through the ultimate epoch of illusion: An eight-year coma in which slogans were confused with solutions, and rhetoric passed for reality; a time when America tried to borrow its way to prosperity and became the largest debtor nation in the history of mankind. . . . At long last, the epoch of illusion is drawing to a close. America is ready for the honest, proven, hands-on, real-world leadership of Michael Dukakis."[7]

The voters seemed to have different ideas about the status of their nation and their recent experience. The decline discussion among the elites only haltingly permeated public opinion. In February of 1989, the CBS/New York Times poll found that 48 percent of respondents either strongly agreed or somewhat agreed with the assertion that the U.S. is in decline as a world power. By March of 1991, after the Gulf War, this figure plunged to 22 percent. (After the Gulf victory, Professor Kennedy wrote that this is just what you would expect from a declining power.[8]) The polls generally find that Japan is a formidable economic competitor, but tend to rate their own economy at least among the best.[9]

Among the elites, however, the liberal prophets of decline did find allies on the right. Not least, they could count on rhetorical support from the likes of Motorola and Chrysler, transnational corporations headquartered in the United States, who found they couldn't keep up with Sony and Toyota, transnational corporations headquartered in Japan. They were understandably eager to blame their predicament on anything but the shortcomings of their own management. They and their labor union allies belabored the trade deficit and debtor nation in their campaign to erect walls athwart history's march to an integrated world economy.

Then too, there was a species of financial conservative that found debt worse than taxes. This preference is far from self-evident, as will be explored in later chapters. Bond traders and central bankers have a natural tendency to focus on the supply and demand for credit (to whatever extent it can be measured). And though growing corporations add debt every year as a matter of course, the executives running them were taught in their childhood to judge government finance solely by whether current income matches current outgo. And some conservatives who correctly identify government spending as the true issue take a worse-the-better attitude, hoping that high immediate taxes will force their treasured confrontation with the welfare state.

So the liberal declinists were joined by a chorus of financial-market conservatives predicting an imminent collapse. *The Great Depression of 1990* by Ravi Batra, inspired by an Indian swami, became a best-seller in 1988. My colleague Alfred L. Malabre, Jr. contributed *Beyond Our Means: How America's Long Years of Debt, Deficits and Reckless Borrowing Threaten to Overwhelm Us* (1987) and *Within our Means: The Struggle for Economic Recovery After a Reckless Decade* (1991). Investment banker and one-time commerce secretary Peter G. Peterson exercised the same theme with his prodigious energy, culminating in a 1987 *Atlantic* article, "The Morning After."[10] Then too, the critique of American business as short-sighted found an initially surprising resonance among those running American business. Corporate CEOs chaffed under the discipline of their stock price, and all the more under the threat of takeovers.

Given these various roots of support, it is perhaps not surprising that the notion of decline proved surprisingly resilient in the face of both self-evident prosperity and intellectual refutation. I thought the matter had been laid to rest in *The Wall Street Journal* by May 1988, when RAND Corporation sage Charles Wolf took his usual beady aim: Yes, the U.S. share of world product had declined from 45 percent in 1950, "a manifestly atypical year." But against the mid-1960s or 1938, the U.S. share remained at 22 percent to 24 percent. "Japan's central-government debt is a larger fraction of its GNP than is that of the U.S., while the foreign indebtedness of the U.S. has been grossly overestimated in the official statistics." Somehow statist politics and economics had spread internationally in the 1960s and 1970s, while market economies and democracy had advanced in the 1980s. "The rhetoric of decline is wrong because it portrays a past that wasn't, a present that isn't and a future that probably won't be."[11]

There followed similar refutations from assorted centrist scholars. Economist Francis Bator of Harvard wrote in *Foreign Affairs,* for example, "The air is full of warnings against overestimating America's economic strength. The more likely error, I think, is the opposite."[12] Samuel Huntington and Joseph S. Nye, both also of Harvard, set out to make the case for maintaining American leadership.[13] By 1990, Mr. Nye had published *Bound to Lead: The Changing Nature of American Power.*[14]

My colleague Karen Elliot House spent months interviewing hundreds of leaders around the world, finding *they* didn't think America was threatened by decline. Jean François-Poncet, a former foreign minister of France, told her, "It's hard to take seriously that a nation has deep problems if they can be fixed with a 50-cent-a-gallon gasoline tax." Seizaburo Sato, a sometime adviser to the Japanese prime minister, recalled Henry Luce. "The 20th century was the American century," he said, "And the 21st century will be the American century."[15]

Yet the decline thesis not only remained steady, it infected even those who supported—even those who made—the policies that created the Seven Fat Years. David Stockman, by 1990 a business partner of Mr. Peterson, had jumped ship as early as 1981, in his famous comments to *Atlantic* author William Greider. Kevin Phillips, a self-styled conservative, albeit one who had made a career of criticizing office-holding conservatives, authored *The Politics of Rich and Poor.* His thesis that in the fat years the rich prospered at the expense of the poor found an appetite that created another best-seller. [16]

Most amazing of all, consider Richard Darman, who under President Bush held the same post Mr. Stockman had in 1981.

Mr. Darman had stuck with Ronald Reagan through the end, and indeed had been point man on the 1986 tax legislation slashing the top marginal tax rate to 28 percent. Mr. Darman had the option of celebrating his accomplishments. Instead, in a remarkable address to the Washington Press Club in July of 1989, he chose to castigate the "cultural now-nowism" of American society. "Now-nowism is a shorthand label for our collective shortsightedness, our obsession with the here and now, our reluctance adequately to address the future."

"Like the spoiled fifties' child in the recently revived commercial, we seem on the verge of a collective now-nowscream: 'I want my Maypo! I want it now!' " The deficit, Mr. Darman elaborated, is one symptom. Interest payments had doubled as a percentage of the federal budget, to 15 percent in 1990 from 7.5 percent in 1960. Transfer payments had also doubled, to 50 percent of the budget from 25 percent. "Some of our most creative and energetic private sector talents are motivated to invent paper transactions that merely reward financial manipulators rather than expand private productive capacity. And in the world of fast-moving deals, institutions responsible for longer-term investment feel obligated to chase near-term financial plays."

Mr. Darman had some useful and instructive things to say about the tax code's bias against investment, and about the need to consider all future obligations of the government, not merely the recorded deficit. During the question period he was asked, "In faulting now-nowism of recent years, does a lot of blame belong on a failure of leadership from the Reagan administration in which you served?" He stammered that at least President Reagan helped the nation regain some of its confidence, and "it's got to be looked at over a much longer time period than merely one administration, to the extent that you buy the argument in the first place that there is this more fundamental cultural problem."[17]

• • •

What accounts for the mood of pessimism in what would seem so promising an age? In particular, as the Seven Fat Years ended, you can sense a change in mood, in economic ebullience, in the willingness to take risks on which economic progress depends.

Why should the nay-sayers, held at bay through the Seven Fat Years, suddenly gain the upper hand?

A great part of the answer is that progress is unsettling, as rapid change always is. Looking back over history, indeed, ages of economic advance have often been ages of pessimism. In particular, history's all-time champion economic pessimist, Thomas Malthus, published his first essay on population in 1798; this was 29 years after James Watt's first patent in connection with the steam engine.

The First Industrial Revolution, in other words, was the venue for Malthus's gloomy theorizing. He was explaining why economic progress was impossible just as mankind was taking the greatest economic leap in history.

Not surprisingly, the Malthus paradox attracted the attention of Joseph A. Schumpeter, our century's greatest economic historian and one of its greatest economists. One chapter in his massive *History of Economic Analysis* relates how ancient societies were worried about overpopulation, but that after about 1600 this changed completely. The prevailing attitude was "increasing population was the most important symptom of wealth; it was the chief cause of wealth; it was wealth itself."

"It is quite a problem to explain why the opposite attitude," Schumpeter wrote, "should have asserted itself among economists from the middle of the eighteenth century on. Why was it that economists took fright at a scarecrow!" The pessimism associated with Malthus did not develop despite the progress of the Industrial Revolution, Schumpeter concluded. It developed because of the progress.

Rapid progress means rapid change, and rapid change is unsettling. Long-run progress causes short-run problems. Schumpeter wrote, "in the Industrial Revolution of the last decades of the eighteenth century, these short-run vicissitudes grew more serious than they had been before, precisely because the pace of economic development quickened."[18]

To be fair, this is not to say the short-run problems were imaginary. In the short run, technological advance destroyed agricultural jobs faster than it created manufacturing jobs, especially since guilds and the like created bottlenecks. A type of mass unemployment arose that had been unknown in the Middle Ages, and with it came urban slums, gin mills and great social debates over the poor laws. Malthus's pessimism was echoed a few decades later by Dickens. But we now know that during the lives of both men, humankind was rapidly building wealth.

If we are currently experiencing a Second Industrial Revolution, then, it is not surprising to hear Malthus's themes echoing through our public discourse. Overpopulation, the exhaustion of resources, are indeed the common coin of our discourse. From the primitive technology of a wooden sailing ship, the earth's forces look overwhelming. Now that we have the technological prowess to put men on the moon, the earth looks like a tiny jewel set against a vast blackness—a fragile flower puny beside our own powers.

Nor is it surprising, if progress is limited by man's capacity to absorb rapid change, that a decade of progress should dissolve into pessimism. Indeed, you can find this kind of cycle in American economic history. In the last 100 years, we have seen four decades of rapid progress: the gay 1890s, the roaring 1920s, the go-go 1960s and the greedy 1980s. Each of the earlier ones dissolved into the kind of acrimony we are now starting to taste. Each was in its way derided as a "decade of greed."

The 1890s were the decade in which we became a continental nation. The frontier was closed; five great transcontinental railroads had been slashed through the Rocky Mountains. Today, these monumental achievements are taken for granted; what we remember are the "Robber Barons."

In the 1920s, we forged the continent into an integrated economy. We still honor Henry Ford and Thomas Edison, but Franklin Roosevelt derided Edison's disciple Samuel Insull with the phrase "the Insulls and the Ishmaels." Today's conventional wisdom still holds that the Great Depression was caused, not by the Smoot-Hawley Tariff, but by the "excesses" of the fat years that came before.

The 1960s dissolved into a different kind of acrimony, centered on the nation's role in the world. But it had an economic component as well. For like the 1890s, the 1920s and now perhaps the 1980s, the 1960s ended with a definite break in the direction of tax policy.

The level of the income tax, indeed, is a good index of the beginning and end of the boom decades. Booms come when it is low, but

FIGURE 1–3

Marginal Tax Rates

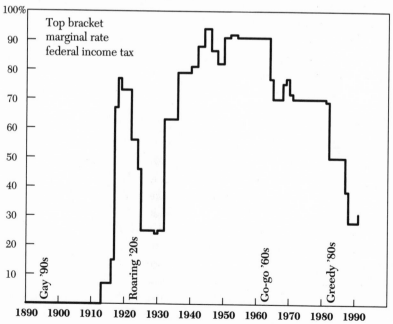

generate social pressures to tax "greed." The contemporary income tax has its roots in the 1890s; the income tax passed in 1894 was overturned by the Supreme Court in 1895. It was finally reinstated by the 16th Amendment in 1913.

During World War I, the top marginal rate of income tax reached 77 percent, along with excess profits taxes on corporations and so on. With the end of the war it dropped to 73 percent, and during the 1920s, Treasury Secretary Andrew Mellon was point man in cutting the rate progressively, to 24 percent in 1929. The Twenties roared.

Then, starting with the Smoot-Hawley Tariff, taxes started to rise. Hoover boosted the top rate to 63 percent in 1932, and Franklin Roosevelt had it up to 79 percent before the war began. In the last years of the war, the top rate was a record 94 percent, and with some wiggles it was still 91 percent when John F. Kennedy was elected president. The Kennedy tax cuts, passed after the martyred president's death, cut the top rate to 70 percent. The 1960s expansion ensued.

As the Johnson presidency wound down, Treasury Secretary Henry Fowler wanted to leave a bit early, and Joseph W. Barr served as Treasury Secretary for 30 days under a recess appointment. On January 19, 1969, Secretary Barr testified before the Joint Economic Committee, and predicted a "taxpayer revolt," though not one based on "the level or amount of taxes." The revolt, he predicted "will come not from the poor, but from the tens of millions of middle-class families and individuals with incomes of $7,000 to $20,000." Such citizens are "angered," he said, because of wealthy persons who "pay little or no Federal income taxes."[19]

In 1967, Secretary Barr reported, there were 155 tax returns reporting incomes above $200,000 and no federal tax liabilities. Indeed, he added, 21 persons had avoided all taxes despite incomes of a million dollars. Secretary Barr, he told me himself in 1978, did not realize what he was starting. It remained true that the top 5 percent of taxpayers paid some 40 percent of the income tax, twice their share of all income. No matter, U.S. tax policy spent the next decade chasing Joe Barr's 21 millionaires, with "minimum taxes" and "alternative minimum taxes" of various colors and shapes.

If Joe Barr's 1969 testimony was one turning-point between eras of taxation, the next was the Steiger amendment in 1978. The minimum taxes had raised the capital gains tax to nearly 50 percent, and Congressman Bill Steiger succeeded in cutting it back to the old rate in the face of the threat of a presidential veto. Barr had set a mood that lasted until Steiger, and Steiger set a mood that lasted through the Seven Fat Years. The question now is what mood will prevail in the 1990s and beyond.

For there seems to be something of a cycle, of boom and bust, of optimism and pessimism, of tax cuts and tax boosts. No doubt the cycle expresses some deep social and even psychological roots, and as we shall see, economic policy itself has many facets, fiscal and monetary, foreign and domestic. But a simple proxy for the cycle seems to be the top tax rate. The rate started up with Joe Barr, and the result was stagflation. It started down with Bill Steiger, and in due course Seven Fat Years ensued.

The fat years ended with the recession that started in 1990. The Bush administration initially told itself that the problem was a temporary result of the Persian Gulf war and the shock from the spike in oil prices. But a year after the rout of Saddam Hussein, the economy was still faltering. It became increasingly obvious that something more had happened.

The war, indeed, had obscured the course of economic policy. The National Bureau of Economic Research officially dated the peak of the expansion as July, just before the August 2 invasion of Kuwait. But the real plunge did not come until October and November, well after the rise in oil prices. The October plunge corresponded with the budget deal between the President and Congressional leaders, announced on September 30. Initially defeated in Congress but quickly put back together, the agreement excluded the capital gains cut the president had sought, and instead raised the top marginal tax rate, both explicitly and still further through gimmicks with deductions and exemptions.

The agreement, in short, committed a classic fiscal blunder, boosting taxes as the economy entered a recession. The policy was the result of agreement between the administration and congressional leaders, a consensus among the Remocrats and Depublicans, as we christened them at the Journal. The initial economic downturn in July, for that matter, came just after the president recanted his "read-my-lips" pledge of no new taxes. The October deal was struck in the name of fighting the deficit, of course, and the deficit promptly soared as the economy sank.

It became evident, too, that something had changed in the nation's mood, something that reached beyond the mechanics of the economy. Entrepreneurial vigor turned feeble, consumer confidence turned sour, bankers talked of a "regulatory credit crunch," with bank examiners overly strict and bankers too frightened to lend. The economy suffered a lack of what John Maynard Keynes had called "animal spirits." The development had various roots: the psychological toll of the 1987 stock market crash, the prosecution of prominent Wall Street figures and the bankruptcy of Drexel Burnham Lambert, the collapse of much of the savings and loan industry and passage of an ill-designed remedy. But a decisive turning-point came late in 1989, over the issue of the capital gains tax.

The administration had proposed to reduce the tax. It had been boosted as part of the 1986 tax package, and during the 1988 election President Bush campaigned on reducing it. With this election mandate, his proposal passed the House and was obviously favored by a majority of the Senate. But Senate Majority leader George Mitchell turned it back single-handedly with a series of parliamentary maneuvers; the votes of 51 senators were not enough to turn back the filibuster he ultimately mounted. Mitchell won, with his "fairness" issue and his filibuster, and then went on to dominate the tax debate in succeeding years.

The economy of the 1990s, and much that depends on the economy, will turn on whether the Mitchell capital gains victory marks another turning point, like the Steiger amendment or the Barr testimony. Has it ushered in a new era of rising tax rates and other policies that suppress economic vigor? As the concluding chapters of this book elaborate, the tumult of the fat years has taken a psychological toll; perhaps the social fabric cannot stand too much change, too much success. It seems that prosperity may bring discontents, real and imagined, that in turn consume the prosperity.

In the new decade, then, the United States will pass a crossroads; one way or another it will resolve the paradox of the 1980s. During the last decade America overcame an economic crisis and led the global economy back to the path of prosperity. During the Seven Fat Years, its historic foreign policy won resoundingly and its political ideas became the model for the world. It stands as the richest nation in history. Its technology beckons with the economic and political promise of a Second Industrial Revolution. Given all this, its economy has an inevitable momentum.

As the 1990s dawned, though, the economic thrust was momentarily checked by curious political and psychological forces. In the midst of success, American elites were infatuated with failure. Economic progress was denied and its lessons derided. Any setback was exaggerated and even celebrated. As the decade progresses the economy will repeatedly strain at the reins of pessimism, and bids ultimately to prevail as economic forces shaped the First Industrial Revolution. But for the 1990s there is a danger. Over the short run of a decade or so, a kind of pessimism can become self-realizing.

The original "seven fat years" were described in the Book of Genesis. The pharaoh had dreamed of seven fat cows coming from the Nile and grazing on the marsh, and seven lean cows coming after to devour them, though remaining as gaunt as ever. He dreamed too of seven withered ears of grain sprouting from seven fat ears. Joseph, sold into Egypt by his brothers, prophesied seven fat years followed by seven years of famine. The pharaoh made him overlord of all Egypt.

Through the fat years, Joseph gathered the food Egypt produced, storing it in the cities under authority of the pharaoh, accumulating grain "in great abundance, like the sand of the sea, until he ceased to measure it, for it could not be measured."[20] When famine arrived, he consented to sell from this hoard. His brothers came to buy, and ultimately he brought his family out of Canaan into Egypt. He also sold to the people of Egypt, in return first for all their money, then all their cattle, then their land and finally themselves. Once he had made slaves of them, "from one end of Egypt to the other," he gave them seed to sow.[21] The next king, Exodus tells us, "did not know Joseph," and persecuted his kin until Moses led them away.[22]

Joseph, of course, saw his prophecy vindicated. The seven fat years were indeed followed by seven lean years. Genesis does not say why. Perhaps for seven years the Nile failed. Then again, perhaps the advent of the lean years had something to do with what Genesis does describe, Joseph's confiscatory tax policy.

LEAVING THE SEVENTIES

2

The Malaise Decade

Though the 1980s have but recently passed, their identity is stamped in our national memory. You may or may not have enjoyed the 1980s; you may think it a decade of excess, or a decade when America rediscovered its self-confidence. But the identity is clear; this was the decade of Ronald Reagan, with whatever that brings to your mind.

So too the 1960s are clear, the decade of heartbreak, starting with the glamour of JFK and ending in the mud of the Mekong. Clear, for that matter, are the 1950s with Eisenhower and McCarthy, the 1940s with the war, the 1930s with depression and the 1920s with their boom—and Calvin Coolidge cast as the Gipper. The 1970s was the decade we skipped; its identity is a blur in our national consciousness.

Memory is often merciful. It's understandable that we may have repressed the 1970s, the decade of the bombing of Hanoi, George McGovern's 1000 percent, Watergate, the flight from Saigon, the hostages in Iran, and—to come to the immediate point—double-digit inflation.

However understandable, forgetfulness about the 1970s precludes an understanding of the economic issues of the 1990s. To get any sense of contemporary economic issues, you have to start with the inflection points the Man from Mars discovered. What happened to Angus Maddison's "golden age?" Why did the economy start to stagger after 1973, and how did it recover after 1982? Unless we can answer these questions, we are trying to navigate the 1990s without a map.

This much is clear: the decline in growth after 1973 was a worldwide phenomenon. Across 32 countries, Maddison found, growth from 1950 to 1973 averaged 5.1 percent a year; from 1973 to 1987 it fell to an average of 3.4 percent. In Japan the annual real growth rate fell to 3.7 percent in the latter period from 9.3 percent in the former. In West Germany it fell to 1.8 percent from 5.9 percent. In these same periods U.S. growth in U.S. gross domestic product fell to 2.5 percent from 3.7 percent.

During the Seven Fat Years, as the Man from Mars found, the United States recovered its pre-1973 growth path. Seven years is too short a period to pretend to a new golden age, of course. And growth has sputtered again as we entered the 1990s; it is not clear the lessons have been learned. Still, the fat years were a striking contrast with the nine years between 1973 and 1982, when the economy grew at a rate of only 1.6 percent a year. That miserable period saw four years with actual declines in real GNP; productivity stagnated and poverty grew. By the way, inflation raged, with the consumer price index leaping by more then 10 percent in each of four years—1974, 1979, 1980 and 1981.

What caused this extraordinary jolt? The obvious event of 1973, of course, was the "oil shock"—the OPEC price increases and the Arab embargo against the United States. This was followed by a second shock and the Latin American debt crisis. "However, the shocks are far from the whole story," Maddison concluded. An inflation unprecedented in peacetime was already under way by the time of the oil shock, and "a major cause of the worldwide inflation was the breakdown of the Bretton Woods arrangements which had provided a fixed exchange rate, dollar based, international monetary system."[1]

In the 1970s, remember, we coined the word "stagflation." The nation's most prominent economists had neither explanation of nor answer to the problem of simultaneous inflation and stagnation. The conventional wisdom settled on the explanation of an "energy crisis"; it held that our problems were rooted in the hydrocarbon content of the earth's crust. Various administrations, Republican and Democratic, tried to cope by controlling wages and prices. The problems only seemed to multiply; it was the Malaise Decade.

Somehow it ended. In trying to understand what happened during the 1980s and what it portends for the 1990s, it's essential to remember that the Seven Fat Years were born in a period of acute economic crisis. If the golden years have not returned, the crisis is somehow over. To understand how the crisis ended, you have to understand how it started.

• • •

If anyone doubts that there has been a sea change in economic thinking since the 1970s, remember the emergency economic meeting in August 1971. The personnel helicoptering to Camp David on Friday the 13th included Richard Nixon, John Connally, George Shultz, Peter Peterson, Paul McCracken, Arthur Burns, Herbert Stein, Paul Volcker and William Safire. These were the folks who, in the swamps of the 1970s, decided that what the U.S. economy needed was wage and price controls.

"In this discussion, nobody is bound by past positions," President Nixon told his advisers before their meeting, Safire reports. He adds that on the way to Camp David, Mr. Stein told him, "This could be the most important weekend in the history of economics since March 4, 1933." That was the date President Franklin Roosevelt was inaugurated; the next day he closed the nation's banks.

Indeed, on August 15, the president descended from the Catoctin Mountains to decree his New Economic Policy: a 90-day freeze of all wages and prices under standby authority legislated earlier. He promised a study of what kind of controls would be necessary after the freeze, and proposed a potpourri of other sweeping steps: cutting taxes on individuals by increasing exemptions and on businesses through an investment tax credit, repeal of a 7 percent excise tax on American-built automobiles. In defiance of treaty obligations, he also imposed a 10 percent surcharge on all imports, and unilaterally revoked the U.S. pledge to sell other central banks gold at $35 an ounce.

"Short of an emergency of a kind which does not exist, mandatory comprehensive price and wage controls are undesirable, unnecessary and probably unworkable," the president's Council of Economic Advisers had written in its annual economic report earlier in the year. In mid-July, Chief Economic Adviser McCracken had written that the notion of a wage-price freeze was "illusory," and in June Treasury Undersecretary Volcker had testified that suspending gold redemption of dollars was not a "way out at all."[2]

But "the rules of economics are not working quite the way they used to," Federal Reserve Chairman Burns also testified in July. In particular, wage demands did not moderate despite unemployment, and commodity prices continued to increase despite "much idle plant capacity."[3] This was a description of what later came to be called stagflation.

Yet when President Nixon and his advisers reversed their economic policies, inflation was running about 4 percent, measured on a six-month moving average of the consumer price index, and by the same measure had actually declined from more than 6 percent early in 1970. Growth had resumed, though unemployment remained sticky at around 6 percent. Interest rates had declined somewhat from their record levels in 1970, when 10-year Treasury bonds yielded 7.35 percent. If these numbers seemed scary by what came before, they seem placid by what we have seen since.

As has often been the case, though, the real driving events were those of the international economy. The August 15 meeting was convened because of inquiries made by the Bank of England, which under Bretton Woods rules had been rapidly accumulating dollars. It wanted $2 billion protected against devaluation, in effect and as it was understood at Camp David a demand for gold. Though there were lingering attempts to revive the system until the institution of generalized floating exchange rates in 1973, with the gold window closed the Bretton Woods era was over.

Domestically, the August 15 initiative was a popular success. It played in the press as a bold policy, not a desperate one. Democrats in Congress had already been calling for controls and had legislated the standby authority. Telephone sampling disclosed a surge in consumer confidence. Business was supportive. Even *The Wall Street Journal* reacted mildly, noting that the freeze, "while no remedy for the underlying causes of inflation, should at least provide a breathing spell in which the country can make a renewed effort to deal with those causes."[4]

The remaining stalwart of the free market was organized labor. A month earlier, AFL-CIO President George Meany had said that if he were in the president's position he would impose controls. But there had also been much talk about wage-push inflation, that inflation was caused by excessive wage increases, which had run at 8 percent a year in the first six months of 1971. So in the event labor hotly dissented, with Mr. Meany complaining that "the entire burden is likely to fall on workers covered by highly visible collective bargaining contracts."[5]

No doubt for the same reason, big business was supportive, even as the freeze slid toward Phase II. In September, the board of directors of the National Association of Manufacturers voted strong support, officially but "temporarily" suspending its long-standing opposition to controls. C. William Verity, Jr., president of the Armco

Steel Corporation, said in a November speech that on August 15 President Nixon "lighted the way for us as businessmen and has turned all Americans away from despair and ding-a-lingism to hope and renewed dedication to our system."[6]

For others, though, disillusion started to creep. The Cost of Living Council soon found itself issuing Q&A lists:

Q: Can a municipality increase a utility franchise fee?
A: No. This is a charge for service and not a tax.
Q: What is the ceiling price for a long-term purchase contract calling for delivery during the freeze period?
A: . . . If the item is a standardized item such as a commercial aircraft, the ceiling is calculated using the substantial-volume-of-transactions rule . . . If the product is a unique product . . . the contractor may use the mark-up received during the base period on the most nearly similar product or service applied to the net direct cost or net invoice cost.
Q: If an agreement has been reached between a company and an employee specifying that part of the employee's salary will be held by the company until the end of the company's fiscal year as a binder, may the employee receive this held pay if the end of the fiscal year falls during the freeze?
A: Yes. The binder does not constitute increased compensation, but is a return of previously earned salary.[7]

Phase II, announced October 7, divided all commerce into three parts: Large, medium and small employers and unions had different reporting rules. The Price Commission, seven members from the public, would oversee a price guideline of 2.5 percent a year. The Pay Board, five members each from labor, business and the public, would oversee a wage guideline of 5.5 percent (with productivity increases to finance the extra wage increments).

The notion of "annual" reports suggested no temporary expedient, but a structural change in the economy. Similarly, Treasury Secretary Connally pledged a return to a free-market economy "if it can possibly be done." Housing Secretary George Romney declared unions and big business had accrued so much power "our economy is no longer predominantly based on a policy of free competitive enterprise." In setting prices and wages, companies could ignore all market factors, including "the impact of imports," the former American Motors chairman said.[8]

As Phase II descended, doubts were already growing. Later and larger consumer confidence surveys showed no surge, for example. Herb Stein, who became economic adviser when McCracken honorably fled, was greeted with brickbats explaining Phase II to GOP conservatives; they feared controls would become permanent. *The Wall Street Journal* recovered its tongue. Barely a week before his untimely death, Editorial Page Editor Joseph E. Evans wrote an editorial named "Weimar, U.S.A.?" It cited Professor Murray Rothbard's view that fascism came to America on August 15. While suggesting this was hyperbole, the *Journal* nonetheless worried about the docile acceptance of the New Economic Policy. "Irony of ironies, after having seen the mess the State makes of almost all of its economic and social interventions, many people, sheep-like, are content to permit it to assume still more power in these areas. Specifically at the moment, to try to run the economy—and what a mess it is making of that."[9]

Labor's four representatives resigned from the Pay Board when it rolled back pay increases won in a longshoreman's strike. By December, the University of Michigan consumer confidence survey found that the president's program was not helping. Anomalies continued to appear; the government of Puerto Rico, for example, inquired whether it had to keep the island's poorly paid workers at wage increases of 5.5 percent when their productivity gains were much larger. Congress seethed, but extended the president's authority into 1973. In November, with the economy growing and controls suppressing inflation, Mr. Nixon won a landslide reelection.

On January 11, a few days before inauguration, the president suddenly terminated controls, except in health, processed foods and construction. He instituted Phase III, voluntary restraint. The suppressed inflation suddenly appeared, concentrated in food costs. On March 29, the president reimposed controls on meat; he took to a national radio and television speech, branding meat "the major weak spot in our fight against inflation."[10]

Congress extended control authority for one year, to April 30, 1974. In June came Phase IV, a new 60-day freeze, but with industry-by-industry decontrol. By 1974, Congress's patience was exhausted, worn down by labor opposition and by the president's apparent success in using this broad authority for political manipulation. The administration proposed to extend control authority in the health and construction industries, and monitoring authority for what had by then become the Cost of Living Council. Congress refused even this, and the experiment with price control expired. The only exception was oil.

. . .

The Conference,

having considered the report of the Secretary General concerning the recent international monetary developments and their adverse effect on the purchasing power of the oil revenues of Member Countries;

noting that these developments have resulted in a de facto devaluation of the United States dollar, the currency in which posted prices are established, vis-a-vis the currencies of the major industrialized countries;

recalling Resolution XXI.122 which calls, inter alia, for adjustment in posted or tax-reference prices so as to offset any adverse effect resulting from de facto or de jure changes in the parity of monies of major industrialized countries:

resolves

1. that Member Countries shall take necessary action and/or shall establish negotiations, individually or in groups, with the oil companies with a view to adopting ways and means to offset any adverse effects on the per barrel real income of Member Countries resulting from the international monetary developments as of 15th August 1971.

2. that the results of negotiations shall be submitted to the next Conference. In case such negotiations fail to achieve their purpose, the Conference shall determine such action as necessary for the implementation of this Resolution.[11]

So reads Conference Resolution XXV.140 of the Organization of Petroleum Exporting Countries, adopted in extraordinary session in Beirut five weeks after the closing of the gold window. Throughout the world, oil is sold in dollars. The Japanese use yen to buy dollars, for example, and use the dollars to buy oil. Since the oil exporters end up with dollars, the health of the dollar is of some moment to them. They did not like what they heard on August 15, 1971.

There the "energy crisis" was born.

At the Beirut meeting itself, the oil nations moved to take equity interests in oil concessions, instead of merely collecting royalties from foreign oil companies. *The Wall Street Journal* reported at the time "Several oil sources said they regard the new OPEC demands as breaking the agreements signed last spring, which supposedly fixed financial terms on foreign oil production for the next five years. At the time, the oil companies had hailed the agreements as guaranteeing a semblance of stability in oil prices to consumers despite the agreed increases."[12] From OPEC's standpoint, of course, the bargain was struck when the dollar was redeemable in gold, and broken on August 15.

The heyday of the London gold pool, which redeemed dollars for gold under Bretton Woods, was also the heyday of the Texas Railroad Commission, which established the price of oil in East Texas and therefore the world. When the gold pool dissolved in 1969, a barrel of oil was worth almost 1/12 of an ounce of gold. At world prices in 1972, a barrel of oil was worth 1/16 of an ounce of gold. On the eve of "the first oil shock" a barrel of oil was worth 1/26 of an ounce of gold. In the first half of 1974, after "the shock," a barrel of oil was worth almost 1/12 of an ounce of gold.

The real shock was that the dollar was depreciating against oil, against gold, against foreign currencies and against nearly everything else. But no one understood this except a few gold bugs, a very few economists such as Robert Triffin and France's Jacques Rueff and, apparently, the Arab sheiks. As Triffin warned, a great inflation was coming, fueled by an explosion in monetary reserves held by central banks. An inflation always creates winners and losers, redistributing wealth. The OPEC cartel let oil producers corner a good share of inflation's gains in a wealth transfer from the developed world. But the price boosts were spurred by devaluation; without the inflation to validate them, their price increases would simply have caused a recession and broken the price.

In the United States, those most devoted to letting prices work, including the U.S. Treasury, were preoccupied with the notion of replacing Bretton Woods with a system in which exchange rates would float, supposedly smoothly. When the price of oil shot up, the most fashionable sectors of American opinion persuaded themselves the world was running out of energy. For a time in the 1970s, indeed, the worry was not merely that the earth's crust would run out of hydrocarbons, but that the earth's crust would run out of everything. A group at the Massachusetts Institute of Technology, with funding from the Volkswagen Foundation and the sponsorship of The Club of Rome, conducted a study, modestly entitled, "The MIT–Club of Rome Project on the Predicament of Mankind." It eventually resulted in a book, *The Limits to Growth*, which reported that Dennis

Meadows et al. had peered into their computers and discovered that Malthus was right after all.

Economists, predictably, rushed to differ; their conclusions are recorded in a caustic entry by Wilfred Buckerman in the widely acclaimed *The New Palgrave: a Dictionary of Economics*. The study ignored the effect of prices, he wrote, and by definition computer simulations collapse if fed assumptions about supplies.

Never mind, given the 1970s, *everyone knew* the Club of Rome was right. After all, the oil price exploded, just as the MIT computer predicted. Obviously the world was running out of oil, and if oil, why not everything else? In the confusion of the 1970s, no one noticed that OPEC told us plainly what was going to happen after the closing of the gold window. One of the few observers alert to the implications of August 15 at the time was John Brooks, whose urbane writing on economics graces *The New Yorker* and several popular books. Writing in *The New York Times*, he voiced "a suspicion that the president and his advisers, in making their Draconian move, did not understand what they were doing."[13]

• • •

The Nixon administration left a second economic legacy that is still being felt today. This time, though, President Nixon understood entirely what he was trying to do. Unfortunately, he lost, leaving us with the Congressional Budget and Impoundment Control Act of 1974. That is when, as the Man from Mars saw so clearly in his deficit chart, federal spending spun out of control.

As the title suggests, the act grew out of battles over "impoundment," which is to say, the president refusing to spend money the Congress had voted. In principle, the practice dates from the earliest days of the Republic. Treasury Secretary Alexander Hamilton shifted money from one account to another, and while some in Congress complained, no one seemed to doubt that this was proper so long as approved by President Washington. Similarly, Jefferson announced that he was refusing to spend a $50,000 appropriation for gunboats, the danger for which they were planned having passed.[14]

After World War II, presidents stepped up use of the impoundment power, using it as a fiscal policy tool. Presidents Truman, Eisenhower and Kennedy all drew congressional complaints for refusing to spend defense appropriations. In 1966, President Johnson impounded $5.3 billion to curb inflation. This included withholding $1.1 billion in highway funds and $760 million for housing and urban development.[15]

With Congress already restive over the practice, President Nixon upped the ante, especially after his landslide reelection in 1972. He set out to use impoundments, along with vetoes, to impose his budget priorities on a Democratic Congress. In the most notable case, he refused to spend $6 billion of the $11 billion in water-treatment funds Congress had passed over his veto. Congress rebelled, with Senator Sam Ervin leading the charge. He contended that impoundment amounted to "an item or line veto." It could be used "to modify, reshape or nullify completely laws passed by the legislative branch," and was therefore an unconstitutional invasion of the legislative power by the executive.

The water funds case ultimately reached the Supreme Court, which ruled 9-0 in favor of Congress in February 1975. The constitutional issue, however, was never reached. Solicitor General Robert Bork had based his case merely on statutory language. He contended that the water funds act sanctioned impoundment; in conference committee the word "all" had been deleted from the phrase in an earlier version directing the allotment of "all sums" authorized. And the act authorized appropriations "not to exceed" specified amounts. Justices including Burger and Rehnquist agreed that these words did not mean Congress had intended to permit the president to impound half the money. The opinion said that the 1974 budget legislation did not make the case moot, but that "Other than as they bear on the possible mootness in the litigation before us, no issues as to the reach of the Impoundment Act are before us."[16]

Congress had spent 1973 debating legislation to curb impoundments, but grew sensitive to the charge that *someone* needed to control the budget. Congress considered appropriations for each program individually, and didn't even have the procedures to consider the total budget and its impact on fiscal policy. So it designed the 1974 act, the promise of which was, *let us do it*.

The act created the now-familiar budget procedures. Working under a series of deadlines, Congress is to vote an initial budget resolution setting out budget totals and broad totals by spending categories. The resolution provides guidance but does not bind the Congress as it works on the 13 appropriation bills covering its spending. Later in the year Congress would move to "reconciliation," a new budget that approved or rejected totals reached in the appropriations process.

To give Congress more time, the bill also moved the start of the Federal fiscal year from July 1 to Oct 1, leaving the historical statistics with an awkward "transition quarter." It also established the Congressional Budget Office, to give Congress the expertise with which to do battle with the Office of Management and Budget. And it established a "current services budget," a required estimate of the funds necessary to maintain government programs at existing levels in the coming year. In the parlance of Congress, a budget "cut" became any reduction from the current services budget, even if total spending went up.

Congress, which is of course a committee of 535 members, could be expected to have trouble maintaining the disciplines the 1974 act suggests. This situation was aggravated by a simultaneous effort to "reform" Congress's internal procedures. The thrust of the effort, led by Rep. Richard Bolling (D., Mo.), was to make the Congress more democratic, with more power for junior members and less for an entrenched leadership. While Representative Bolling's plan was watered down, substantial measures were passed and a climate was created. The power of the congressional leadership declined, to the benefit of individual subcommittee chairmen and the majority party caucus. Inevitably, this further eroded the discipline the 1974 act assumed.

As for impoundment, the 1974 act permitted the president to send Congress a message asking that individual spending items be rescinded or deferred. In the case of rescissions, the president was required to spend the money after 45 days if Congress ignored his request. In the case of deferrals, his request could be rejected by a resolution of either of the two houses of Congress—a procedure increasingly used in other bills as the "legislative veto."

The political context of this legislation was of course the Watergate scandal; the prestige and power of the president was lower than it had been since the impeachment of Andrew Johnson. The Congress had already passed the War Powers Resolution over President Nixon's veto. Now, with the promise to make itself more responsible, Congress was reaching for a far larger share of budget-making power. The Budget and Impoundment Control Act passed the House by a vote of 401–6, and the Senate by 75–0. Bowing to the inevitable, President Nixon signed it on July 12, 1974. On August 9, he resigned.

• • •

If President Nixon felt he'd seen stagflation in 1971, it was nothing compared to what he left President Ford. In the year of the August 15 bombshell, inflation ran 4.4 percent and real GNP grew 2.8 percent. In the year of the Nixon-Ford transition, real GNP declined 0.5 percent, while the nation saw its first double-digit inflation, 11.0 percent.

Bewildered, the new president called a summit, inviting experts from various walks of life to give advice; they duly convened on September 27 and 28, 1974. The only consensus was in the review of the meetings. *The Wall Street Journal* editorial was as good as any:

> If you don't look closely, all you will see is a Tower of Babel. Cut taxes, raise taxes, leave taxes alone, cut some taxes while raising other taxes. Allocate credit. Don't allocate credit. Ease money. Tighten money. Cut the budget hard, cut it a little, don't cut it at all. Impose controls, impose guidelines, leave wages and prices alone. Can all these people be talking about fighting inflation?
>
> Yet underlying these varied prescriptions we can detect a thread of consistency, a bleak awareness that what is at stake here is not the division of the golden eggs, but the salvation of the goose. Far more than the politicians, who yearn for the quick fix that will see them through the next election, the summit participants seem to grasp that the very foundation of the economic system is cracking.[17]

Closing the meeting, President Ford asked each American to send him a list of ten suggestions on how to conserve energy and bring down prices. He urged that every American become an "inflation fighter," an "energy saver," and to help "bring balance and vitality to our economy." He made a number of appointments, including the coup of engaging financial columnist Sylvia Porter to head an effort to enlist consumers. On October 8, he announced his "Whip Inflation Now" program, distributing WIN buttons to the White House staff. The program was based on voluntary effort and a 5 percent tax surcharge. In 1975, the economy's plunge deepened, with real GNP falling 1.5 percent. The recession pushed inflation back into single digits, 9.1 percent.

In perhaps the worst mistake of his term, President Ford signed an energy bill passed by the Congress, providing for the extension of price controls, a plethora of powers over the import and use of energy products, fuel economy standards for autos and federal audits of oil companies and related enterprises. William Simon, his treasury secretary, was later to write in the *Journal*, "The only sensible answer is to begin dismantling existing controls, beginning with price controls over oil and natural gas and including repeal of the energy bill that President Ford, in a tragic error, signed in December 1975."[18]

To be fair to the Ford administration, by 1976 it had managed to produce 4.9 percent real growth and a decline in inflation to 5.8 percent, the lowest figure in the decade starting with 1973. Mr. Simon, Chief Economic Adviser Alan Greenspan and Budget Director James Lynn followed a course of patient budget restraint. In particular, they looked for what Mr. Greenspan called "reverse wedges"—small savings now that would grow to larger savings in the out years. In its final year, too, the Ford administration had proposed to index the tax brackets for inflation, ending "bracket creep" that meant inflation resulted in increased real government revenue. When President Ford failed at reelection, reverse wedges and indexing were the first to go. Growth held for two years—4.7 percent in 1977 and 5.3 percent in 1978. But inflation started to rise—6.5 percent in 1977, 7.6 percent in 1978, then double digits in 1979, 1980 and 1981.

• • •

James Earl Carter, Jr., opened his presidency with the $50 rebate. Mr. Carter shouldn't be blamed if this sounds silly from the perspective of 1990; he acted on the best economic advice the 1970s had to offer. In January 1977 Walter Heller reviewed the economy, remarking on "the flabbiness of the economy" and the extent of unused capacity. He proposed to reverse a "spending slowdown," which is to say Greenspan's reverse wedges. He proposed the tax policy of "a rebate-like cut of $12 billion for individuals," with the interesting wrinkle of "not only taxpayers but non-taxpayers getting a full share."[19]

At the *Journal*, we stressed that since the government had to borrow the $50 it would distribute, the source of the stimulus was not obvious. "The Carter program is no sort of tax cut; it is merely 1/20 of George McGovern's $1,000 'demogrant.' If the government kept its books honestly, the handout would be treated as a new expenditure."[20] The plan met increasing skepticism in Congress; someone branded it an attempt to stimulate the economy by scattering money from airplanes.

Mr. Heller had promised that the rebate "won't come within a country mile of generating excess-minded inflation," though the economy did face "a self-propelling wage-price spiral," for which the appropriate answer was "persuasion, jawboning, deregulation and stockpiling." But in March the wholesale price index jumped 13.2 percent, and the recovery seemed increasingly durable. Mr. Carter dropped his rebate, moving on to energy policy.

• • •

In a curious twist of fate, I spent nearly a month of the Ford-Carter presidential campaign in the Far East. James Schlesinger had invited me on a small junket in 1976; the Chinese had invited the deposed defense secretary to express their displeasure with Henry Kissinger and detente. Idling away the time during 23 days in China, Jim and I tilted over energy policy in the back seat of limousines bouncing over dusty rural roads. It was great fun, but obviously Jim was not a man to believe that a mere market could be smarter than he was. Lo and behold, Jim Schlesinger became energy czar under Jimmy Carter.

The president proclaimed "the moral equivalent of war," proposing a big tax on gasoline, a tax on crude oil (both defeated by Congress) and various measures for energy conversion. Defending it in a commencement speech at the University of Virginia, Jim Schlesinger obviously also remembered the conversations in China, for he noted that it was important to use the price mechanism.

> I mention the matter since that seems to be the gist of the policy recommended by ideologues of the market mechanism—who can discern the unfettered forces of competition where they do not exist. Who, in addition, believe in instantaneous adjustment—that we can go skittering over the edge of a cliff, and that, given such demand, suppliers of parachutes will miraculously and suddenly appear. . . .
>
> One can question whether a market, which historically has had its supply determined by such anti-competitive devices as the Standard Oil trust or by the Texas Railroad Commission, ever behaved in the prescribed textbook fashion. But surely the present price in no way resembles a market price. It is simply one administered by an international cartel, bearing no relation to production costs. . . .
>
> I trust therefore that you will not be bemused in your consideration of the nation's energy problem by such beguiling beliefs that the solu-

tion can be attained simply because there are supply and demand curves or that there is some price somewhere that will clear any market.

I trust also that you will not be beguiled by false analogies between today's conditions—in which an enormous stock of capital equipment, fueled in the main by oil, has overwhelmingly replaced human and animal labor as the driving force behind production—and the ability of the 19th Century economy to cope with a shortage of whale oil in an entirely different social and economic context.[21]

The mention of whale oil was a specific reference to a *Wall Street Journal* article. It said that when whale oil was the prime source of lighting, the world started to run out of whales. The price went up until it was profitable to discover kerosene. "The whale oil crisis is a case study of how the free-market system solves a scarcity problem," wrote an obscure economics professor at Texas A&M, Dr. W. Philip Gramm. Later he became Senator Phil Gramm of the Gramm-Rudman Resolution and other claims to fame.[22]

MEOW, he wrote on the first anniversary of the program's introduction. The moral equivalent of war had stalled in Congress, but the energy crisis was vanishing anyway. Oil imports were down 14 percent in the first three months of the year. The International Energy Agency predicted a "temporary" surplus of oil lasting into the 1980s. With higher prices, oil consumption per unit of GNP plunged, and even niggling price increases brought forth new production.

If parachutes appeared, perhaps it was because the problem did not lie in the earth's crust. In the depths of the Energy Research and Development Administration, someone made the mistake of drawing a cost curve. It was an innocent act, labeled the Market Oriented Program Planning Study, intended to help the bureaucrats decide which source of energy was the best bet to subsidize. Anguished bureaucrats protested to us that they didn't want to be part of the national debate, but the news that an official cost curve existed fell into the hands of Jude Wanniski, then associate editor of the *Journal*.

"1,001 Years of Natural Gas," the headline on Jude's editorial proclaimed. The Carter administration proposals would have put a ceiling on the price of gas at $1.75 per thousand cubic feet. But the MOPPS study had estimated that a price of $2.25 would bring out "inferred reserves" of ordinary gas, as well as the Devonian shale deposits in Appalachia, the Western "tight sands" and coal-stream methane. The numbers attached to these deposits would leave the nation "awash in natural gas." At a price of $3.00 or less, "industry could tap the big deposit—geopressurized methane that exists at depths of 15,000 feet, both onshore and offshore, in the Gulf region." Estimates of this resource—natural gas dissolved in ground water— were mind-boggling.[23]

The MOPPS bureaucrats were sent back twice more for lower estimates, but while they were less optimistic they were equally embarassing to the Carter program. For it didn't matter where the cost curve was drawn. Not that the MOPPS estimates were necessarily right, or that any geopressurized methane was produced. But with the MOPPS study the intellectual debate was over. It didn't matter whether you drew an optimistic supply curve or a pessimistic one, once you drew the curve, the energy crisis was over. The world was not running out of resources; we could start to move out of the 1970s.

In 1980 economist Julian Simon offered a $1,000 wager to any taker. Name any five natural resources, he suggested, and I will bet that in ten years their price is lower, rather than higher as shortages would dictate. Environmentalist Paul Ehrlich, author of *The Population Bomb*, took up the wager, specifying copper, chrome, nickel, tin and tungsten. By 1990, the price of all had dropped, and Ehrlich was honorable enough to mail Simon a check for $1,000.[24]

• • •

The year 1979, too, saw a final burst of wage and price controls. Congress had repeated the authorization for controls, but President Carter proclaimed "voluntary guidelines" enforced by the denial of government contracts to nonvolunteers.

As with the Nixon price-wage controls of 1971, President Carter's 1979 voluntary wage-price controls found their most prominent support among the very biggest corporations. Thomas Murphy, chairman of General Motors and head of the Business Roundtable, wrote the chief executives of the other Fortune 500 companies to urge compliance with the president's guidelines, which of course could not otherwise be enforced for want of legal authority. GM took out newspaper ads to the same effect, adding, "We have written to our suppliers, informing them of GM's commitment and asking them all to make the same commitment."

In other words, the *Journal* wrote in an editorial "Down With Big Business,"[25] GM was browbeating its suppliers into charging GM lower prices. Mr. Murphy protested in a letter to the editor, but another letter from a former GM supplier said the editorial "brought home some vivid memories of when I was vice president of sales for a small steel foundry." GM, his major customer, had simply advised how much of a price increase it would accept, under threat of taking its business elsewhere. The foundry was now bankrupt, but "When I read their advertisement, it made me cringe to remember, and I am sure most of their suppliers feel the same."[26]

Peter Bommarito, president of the United Rubber Workers, charged that intervention by the wage-price enforcers upset his labor settlement with Uniroyal, and voiced the suspicion that GM had backed them. While everyone denied everything, the suspicion remained. A West Coast union started a lawsuit against the program. It was far from clear that either the government or GM could refuse a low bid from a supplier on the grounds that the supplier paid too much for labor. Ultimately Mr. Murphy wrote to deny that his intention was to deny GM business to the lowest bidder.

The episode, though, shows a lot about the attitudes of the business community, especially the schism between big business and businesses that want to become big. This schism played an important role in the Seven Fat Years and is in its way a key to the economy of the 1990s. For the economy will slog if big business gets government help to keep little business from expanding.

• • •

Exhausted by confusion and defeat, in the summer of 1979, President Carter went to the Catoctin Mountains like President Nixon before him. He summoned a succession of people to Camp David trying to determine "Why have we not been able to get together as a nation to resolve our serious energy problem?" What, he asked his visitors, is wrong with America?

> The threat is nearly invisible in ordinary ways, it is a crisis of confidence. It is a crisis that strikes at the very heart and soul and spirit of our national will. We can see this crisis in the growing doubt about the meaning of our own lives and in the loss of a unity of purpose for our Nation. The erosion of confidence in the future is threatening to destroy the social and the political fabric of America. . . .
>
> The symptoms of this crisis of the American spirit are all around us. For the first time in the history of our country a majority of our people believe that the next 5 years will be worse than the past 5 years. Two-thirds of the people do not even vote. The productivity of Amer-

ican workers is actually dropping, and the willingness of Americans to save for the future has fallen below that of all other people in the Western World. . . .

Looking for a way out of this crisis, our people have turned to the Federal Government and found it isolated from the mainstream of our Nation's life. Washington, D.C. has become an island. The gap between our citizens and our Government has never been so wide. The people are looking for honest answers, not easy answers; clear leadership, not false claims and evasiveness and politics as usual.[27]

The cure for malaise, the president proclaimed, was a six-point energy program, including quotas on imports, government subsidies for oil shale and gasohol, and authority for standby gasoline rationing. The stakes were more than economic, he proclaimed. "On the battlefield of energy we can win for our Nation a new confidence, and we can seize control again of our common destiny."

• • •

Carter's pronouncement somehow epitomized the 1970s, the decade of the New Economic Policy, the WIN campaign and the Moral Equivalent of War. If it was a time of economic stagflation, it was a time of intellectual confusion. As Arthur Burns said early on, the old rules weren't working anymore. The nation went from one ad hoc response to another, stumbling deeper and deeper into a morass it didn't understand. As the decade dissolved into malaise, it was a time for new policies, which could only be built on new understandings.

3

Michael 1

Michael 1 is a restaurant for Wall Street wannabees. Nestled on Trinity Place thirty steps south of the American Stock Exchange, it draws the financial world's young and maybe rising. You can settle into the tufted leather armchairs, lean back with a drink or pitch forward into a porterhouse, look out over brown wood panels, brown Mexican tile on pedestals bathed in indirect lighting, and virtually see the deals of future years.

On some nights in the mid-1970s, it was also the site of extraordinary seminars in economics. The next table might talk Biomedical Instruments or other hot stocks, but this table talked about Poincaré's stabilization program in France, and British depression and American boom in the 1920s. These discussions spawned, at least in my mind, what later became known as supply-side economics—if not indeed what later became the Reagan administration's economic policy.

If the conversation was improbable, so were the participants. There was Arthur Laffer, bright and bubbly. Only 35 in 1975, he had already been chief economist for the Office of Management and Budget. The controversy that seemed to follow him everywhere had followed him there; in 1971, he offered OMB director George Shultz a GNP prediction—$1,065 billion for the year—that quickly became notorious for its excessive optimism. By 1976, the revised actual result came in at $1,063.4; as Daniel Seligman of *Fortune* wrote, this "might have made Laffer look like a genius if anyone had by then remembered the original controversy."[1] One of the fastest-talking and most entertaining people alive, Laffer kept his turtles as a hobby and after a foreign trip once showed up at his wife's door having shed 40 pounds of his customary bulge.

43

For contrast there was Robert Mundell, who had won academic renown as an international economist, but who wore shoulder-length hair and spoke with a slow slur—two habits that have both vanished by the 1990s. Laffer and Mundell had been colleagues at the University of Chicago, until one day the latter suddenly decamped to McGill University in his native Canada, later returning to Columbia. Mundell dabbles in painting and keeps a castle in Sienna. Today he publishes in *Rivista di Politica Economica*, published (albeit in English) in Rome by SIPI, the Servizio Italiano Pubblicazioni Internazionali.

Then there was my colleague Jude Wanniski, as impossible as the other two. His dark shirts and light ties were a holdover from his days as a newshound in Las Vegas. He moved to Washington with the *National Observer*, and met Laffer there. When I took over the editorial page of the *Journal* in 1972, he was the second person I tried to hire, succeeding with him though failing with the first, a then-unknown Congressional aide named George Will. St. Jude is the patron saint of lost causes, and Jude would often devote his manic energy to redeeming his namesake's reputation. He also had a brazen bent as a publicist; only Jude would entitle his book *The Way the World Works*.

On March 26, 1976 Herb Stein coined a label, the "supply-side fiscalists," telling a conference at the Homestead resort in Virginia that it consisted of "maybe two" economists. Alan Reynolds passed this along to Jude, who promptly appropriated the label, though dropping "fiscalists" as awkward and misleading. "Supply-side economics" it became.[2]

Beside the luminous plumage of the Mundell-Laffer-Wanniski trio, the rest of us were drab. Charlie Parker, then of H. C. Wainwright, played host. I came and went, as did others. At times the seminar left Michael 1 for the 71st Street elegance of the Lehrman Institute, a salon endowed by Lewis Lehrman in the years between winning his fortune with Rite Aid Corporation, and running for governor of New York. Lehrman, a disciple of Jacques Rueff, could and still can tilt monetary policy with anyone.

In the same years or shortly later, we were gradually to learn, parallel seminars were running in Washington, where Norman Ture and Paul Craig Roberts also invented tax cutting, and indeed in far-off California, where young John Rutledge was founding Claremont Economics.

The Washington group gathered around Congressman Jack Kemp,

the former professional quarterback who did bizarre things like sit down and read *The General Theory*. Roberts became Kemp's staff economist, drafted the Kemp-Roth bill and fought congressional battles with help from Steve Entin of the Joint Economic Committee staff and Bruce Bartlett, another Kemp aide. Roberts was later to serve as associate editor of the *Journal*, and still later as assistant secretary in the Reagan Treasury. Ture had been an adviser on the Kennedy tax cuts. In the mid-1970s he ran his own consulting firm, a rigorous economist in a political town. In the Reagan years he became an undersecretary of the Treasury.

The Michael 1 seminars did not arise from accidents of personality. They were a product of their time; their roots lay in the economic and intellectual turmoil of the 1970s. For as stagflation of the 1970s had upset the political universe, so it had overturned intellectual orthodoxy. We needed a new economics, and the assumptions and insights flowing from those discussions constitute an economic world-view, removed in important ways from the pop-Keynesian consensus that still informs most commentary on economic subjects. Perhaps the best way to understand is with examples. So from the perspective of the 1990s, take a few cross-sections of the economic worldview. Let's make the rubric, what I learned at Michael 1:

Keynes Is Dead

This was in fact the title of a *Journal* editorial in January 1977. It opened with a remarkable summary by Prime Minister James Callaghan, head of Britain's Labor government:

> We used to think that you could spend your way out of a recession and increase employment by cutting taxes and boosting government spending. I tell you, in all candor, that that option no longer exists, and that insofar as it ever did exist, it only worked by injecting bigger doses of inflation into the economy followed by higher levels of unemployment as the next step. That is the history of the last twenty years.[3]

The simultaneous stagnation and inflation of the 1970s had not only bewildered policymakers, but had ruptured the prevailing consensus of the economics profession. Since Keynes, the centerpiece of economics was "the multiplier." By running a deficit, the government "injected" money into the economy, and as this injection rippled through the economy it produced a far larger boost in Gross National Product. So if the economy needed a boost, run a bigger deficit, even if that meant hiring workers to dig holes and fill them back up.

Indeed, basic economics texts taught about a mythical creature called the "balanced budget multiplier," with magical powers to transmute a bigger government into a healthier economy. If the government spent an extra $20 billion and raised taxes $20 billion, all of the spending would be consumed, and some of the taxing would come out of savings rather than consumption. So on net, consumption would increase, and be multiplied into a bigger GNP. This was solemnly taught to innocent sophomores by professors who later ridiculed the Laffer curve.

The question, everyone at Michael 1 understood, was: Where does the government get this money it "injects" into the economy? Well, it borrows it. But if you borrow from Peter to pay Paul, what is there to be multiplied? And anyway, if someone "saves" by stuffing dollar bills into a mattress, the Federal Reserve can simply print up some more dollar bills. And if, more likely, someone "saves" by putting money in a bank, the bank will lend it to someone to "consume." What is it that Lord Keynes was trying to say, anyway?

This was supposed to be explained by Sir John Hicks's IS-LM model, and augmented in practice by the inflation-unemployment trade-off of the Phillips curve. But when the 1970s dealt more inflation and more unemployment simultaneously, the whole Keynesian universe imploded.

None of this should be taken as disparagement of Lord Keynes; the diners felt reverence was due. In the midst of a Great Depression, it was plausible to believe that there were pools of idle savings that might be tapped by government borrowings. But in the inflationary climate of the 1970s, idle money would waste away. Savers, banks, borrowers all rushed to convert it into interest-bearing instruments, or better, real assets such as gold or real estate.

"If Lord Keynes were alive today, he would no doubt be back at the drawing boards," our January 1977 editorial said. "As Oxford economist Walter Eltis has pointed out, through most of Keynes' life the gold value of the pound was precisely where Sir Isaac Newton had fixed it a century and a half before. If we had Lord Keynes today, surely he would have something instructive to say about an age of inflation."

In 1983, *The Economist* ran a centenary edition on Keynes. The contribution from F. A. Hayek read in part:

It will not be easy for future historians to account for the fact that, for a generation after the untimely death of Maynard Keynes, opinion was so completely under the sway of what was regarded as Keynesianism, in a way that no single man had ever before dominated economic policy and development. Nor will it be easy to explain why these ideas rather suddenly went out of fashion, leaving behind a somewhat bewildered community of economists who had forgotten much that had been fairly well understood before the "Keynesian Revolution." . . .

During this crucial period I could watch much of this development and occasionally discuss the decisive issues with Keynes, whom I in many ways much admired and still regard as one of the most remarkable men I have known. He was certainly one of the most powerful thinkers and expositors of his generation. But, paradoxical as this may sound, he was neither a highly trained economist nor even centrally concerned with the development of economics as a science, tending to regard his superior capacity for providing theoretical justifications as a legitimate tool for persuading the public to pursue the policies which his intuition told him were required at the moment. . . .

Keynes never recognized that progressive inflation was needed in order that any growth in monetary demand could lastingly increase the employment of labour. He was thoroughly aware of the danger of growing monetary demand degenerating into progressive inflation, and toward the end of his life greatly concerned that this might happen. It was not the living Keynes but the continuing influence of his theories that determined what did happen. I can report from first-hand knowledge that, on the last occasion I discussed these matters with him, he was seriously alarmed by the agitation for credit expansion by some of his closest associates. He went so far as to assure me that if his theories, which had been badly needed in the deflation of the 1930s, should ever produce dangerous effects he would rapidly change public opinion in the right direction. A few weeks later he was dead and could not do it.[4]

The Only Closed Economy

From the first, the diners at Michael 1 were preoccupied with the international economy, exchange rates, and the breakdown of Bretton Woods. Mundell's international work was recognized under such academic code words as "the monetary approach to the balance of payments" and "optimum currency areas." The first article that Laffer wrote for *The Wall Street Journal* had nothing to do with the Laffer curve or even tax policy. It was "The Bitter Fruits of Devaluation,"[5] blaming the 1973 inflation rate—nearly 9 percent in consumer prices and 18.2 percent in wholesale prices—on the devaluation of the dollar in 1971 and again early in 1973.

All economists agree that a devaluation had some inflationary impact. But Laffer noted, "If you view the domestic economy as basically a closed system with a few international inputs, as most economists traditionally have, then you will see this effect as slight." In the traditional view, a 10 percent devaluation would add 10 percent to the price of imports or, if 10 percent of all goods were imported, only 1 percent to the price level. "But if you conceive of the U.S. as but a part of a relatively unified world market, the inflationary effect of devaluation must be seen as far more dramatic." That is, if the international economy is "a relatively efficient market," nominal prices in a devalued currency would simply rise to restore the original prices of the good traded. Money is a veil, and will not change the relative value of a jug of wine and a loaf of bread.

These are the terms in which the heirs of Michael 1 see the world: There is one real price. There is one real interest rate. Idealistic and visionary perhaps, but surely a starting-point for analysis. Critics will argue that this merely expresses a long-run equilibrium not relevant in a realistic time horizon, as Marina v.N. Whitman did in labeling the view "global monetarism."[6]

The monetary approach to the balance of payments was widely recognized within the profession as the most advanced view. This argues that exchange rates are best seen as a monetary phenomenon; if a central bank supplies more money than demanded, this excess shows up as depreciation of the currency under floating rates, or a balance of payments deficit under fixed rates. A falling currency is a symptom of excessive money growth; to stabilize it the central bank should restrain money creation.

The monetary approach does not dictate the choice between fixed or floating exchange rates. Harry Johnson, the other leading light of the monetary approach, died a floater. But Mundell stressed fixed rates; an integrated world economy ideally should have one money so that real price signals could be transmitted throughout the economy. A fixed rate system simulated this; if rates were truly fixed, the world would have one money called different names in different countries. With exchange rates floating, price signals in the real economy would be subject to repeated disturbances that would detract from efficiency and growth.

Such disturbances would also be likely to upset plans for the domestic economy. Mundell's aphorism was, "The only closed economy is the world economy."

Markets Clear

I remember Art Laffer telling me I had to learn about Say's law. "That's what I believe in," he professed. "That's what you believe in too."

Jean-Baptiste Say (1767–1832) lent his name to the bedrock proposition of classical economics: Supply creates its own demand. That is, manufacturers pay workers to make widgets, and workers use their pay to buy widgets. Savers lend their money to investors who build widget factories, and the factories' profits go to repay principal and interest. A higher price will call forth more widgets, higher wages will call forth more widgetmakers, and higher returns will call forth more investment. Unless the government gets in the way, for example by fixing prices, markets will clear and everyone will live happily ever after.

Whether a free economy functions in this self-regulating fashion has been and remains the great issue of macroeconomics. It was at the heart of the differences between Ricardo and Malthus, and of a general 19th-century debate called "the general glut controversy."[7] In the 1930s, Say's law fell before the Keynesian onslaught; the massive unemployment showed the labor market had not cleared. Henceforth, governments were expected to correct "market failures."

In the 1970s, of course, the great proxy for Say's law was energy policy, Ricardo and Malthus redux. The energy issue was our generation's great battle between the free market and industrial policy (as already described in Chapter 2, "The Malaise Decade"). At Michael 1 these events were not seen as an oil problem but a monetary problem. As Mundell put it, the Arabs managed to corner the gains produced by an inflation that was coming anyway, unleashed by the lack of international monetary discipline. To the extent there was an oil problem, the answer was Ricardo's, was Say's, was, let the market clear.

From Chicago

Inevitably, the discussions at Michael 1 bore a heavy imprint from the University of Chicago. By long tradition, its economists were the leading champions of Say's law. And of course, the modern assault on Keynesianism had been led by Milton Friedman, Chicago's leading light. In 1968, Friedman and Edmund Phelps at Penn had each published papers demonstrating that the Phillips curve failed at the level of microeconomics: in making wage demands, workers will incorporate the expectation of inflation. It was no accident that both Mundell and Laffer had gravitated to Chicago and its free-market tradition.

The Chicago tradition, and all of neoclassical economics, owed much to Irving Fisher of Yale, the most prominent American economist of the first half of the century. In particular, it was Fisher who first separated the interest rate into theoretical components of a "real" rate and an inflationary premium, a distinction particularly relevant to the inflationary 1970s. Both borrowers and lenders anticipated that the principal of a loan would be repaid in less valuable dollars, and this was reflected in the interest rate.

In the markets that set interest rates, of course, it was not actual inflation that mattered but *expected* inflation. In inflationary times, this gave us heady interest rates, with market participants hypersensitive to blips in inflation and the monetary policy that affects it. And inevitably, when the inflation went away, the loans anticipating it turned sour—loans for Third World nations, for the energy states, for farmers who had borrowed to buy land, and for financial institutions like savings and loans.

Another Chicago imprint was efficient markets, developed at Chicago theoretically by Eugene Fama and empirically by James Lorie. The stock market, the theory holds, incorporates all available information. The thousands or millions of collective decisions incorporated in a market-determined price cannot be duplicated or even understood by one mind. You can't beat the market because it's smarter than you are. Intellectually, the only task is trying to determine what the market is telling you.

Laffer was a true-blue believer in efficient markets. Mundell was not. This was why Great Britain in the 1920s was a subject of debate. Mundell held the conventional view that the problem was Churchill's decision to repeg the pound sterling to gold at the prewar parities. Laffer said the economy would have adjusted to this choice, but the problem was failure to repeal the wartime tax rates.

Similarly, Mundell now dissents from Wanniski's "efficient markets" view of the 1929 market crash, which attributed it to the political progress of the Smoot-Hawley Tariff. Efficient markets research has demonstrated that the price of an individual share rises before a split rather than after, so the market would anticipate rather than follow a catastrophic market interference. In other words, the stock market crash on October 29, 1929 can after all plausibly be associated with the Smoot-Hawley Tariff that finally passed eight months later. Wanniski argued that the crash came when a break in the congressional coalition made it apparent that a new tariff would not be limited to agriculture, and traces subsequent market movements in light of the tariff debate. After dropping from 298 to 230 in the crash and hitting a November low of 198, the Dow Jones industrials recovered to 294 on talk of a veto and stood at 244 when Hoover announced he would sign the bill. With Smoot-Hawley in effect, the average fell to 41 a few months before the election of Franklin D. Roosevelt.

Mundell was initially impressed, but now stresses international monetary disturbances. "Sixty years after its beginning there is no general agreement on the causes of the great depression," he has recently written. In his own view, "The disequilibrium in the 1920s was *systemic,* and the problem lay not—or not only—with the dollar-pound exchange rate but with the price of all currencies in terms of gold."[8]

I Used To Be a Monetarist

If it was also no accident that Mundell and Laffer came to Chicago, it was also no accident that they both left, Mundell before the Michael 1 dinners and Laffer a bit later. Both Laffer and Mundell dissented from Milton Friedman's monetarist orthodoxy. Milton Friedman is a commanding figure in the history of economics and a marvelous human being. On most issues—Say's law, price controls, energy, efficient markets, deficits, Keynes or whatever—he would be entirely at home at Michael 1. But not on his centerpiece, controlling "the money supply."

Laffer would draw a tiny black box in the corner of a sheet of paper; "this is M-1," currency and checking deposits. A bigger box was M-2, including savings deposits. Still bigger boxes included money-market funds, then various credit lines. Finally, the whole page was filled with a box called "unutilized trade credit"—that is, whatever you can charge on the credit cards in your pocket. Do you really think, he asked, this little black box controls all the others. The money supply, he insisted, was "demand determined." What the big boxes demanded the little one supplied.

Beyond unutilized trade credit, indeed, there was the Eurodollar market. Mundell insisted that dollars were also created in London, and that if the Fed tried to squeeze the U.S. aggregates, Eurodollars would grow faster to meet demand and make up the difference. Fed officials heatedly denied that money is created in London, and spent lunches trying to persuade us. They hold the same position today. Mundell is right.

But if not M-1, how do you calibrate monetary policy? Well, Irving Fisher developed the idea of a basket of commodities. If an index of sensitive commodity prices starts to rise, it would suggest a central bank was supplying too much money. To the same end but more simply, there had been the gold standard; if a central bank gained gold it was to issue more currency, if it lost gold it was to issue less. Crude but workable.

"It doesn't have to be gold," Bob Mundell was fond of saying in the mid-1970s. Gold may be a barbarous relic, as Keynes had called it, or merely a device for searing politicians, as Hayek called it. But its traditional place as a monetary standard was not entirely an accident. For except in extraordinary conditions such as the Spanish opening of the New World, the supply of gold changes only slowly. So movement in the "exchange rate" between gold and money suggests that the supply of money is changing. Or more accurately, that the supply of money is changing *relative to the demand for money*. As a market-determined price rather than a statistically collected aggregate, sensitive commodity prices balance the supply and demand for money.

At the turn of the century and even under Bretton Woods, the price of gold had been at the center of a system of fixed exchange rates. Simply fixing rates will not stabilize the price level, for all monies could inflate together. The system needs an "anchor," some method of judging how much money the world needs. If all nations use their monetary policy to fix to the currency of nation n, the nth nation can use its monetary policy to anchor the whole system, to gold or some other indicator.

The monetarists, Milton Friedman and Harry Johnson, were the biggest proponents of floating exchange rates. They sought to free monetary policy from international interference, the better to target the Ms and control domestic inflation. We learned, I think, that it doesn't work. After 1981, when M-1 said money growth was too slow and M-2 said it was too fast, I met a prominent bank economist who described his economic philosophy as "Well, I used to be a monetarist."[9]

You Become What You Measure

The National Income Accounts, the familiar numbers used in all economic analyses and discussion, were formulated in a Keynesian era and often reflect Keynesian assumptions. It is almost as if they were designed to measure the amount of money the government "injects" into the economy. The heirs of Michael 1 don't necessarily believe.

If you pick a stock that shoots up, for example, you will no doubt feel wealthier and behave accordingly. Knowing of your gain, you may even draw down your savings account and buy a new car. Your net worth is higher, and you have a car that will last five years. But in the national income accounts, you are a naughty dissaver.

The unrealized gain on the stock is not reflected in the accounts. The purchase of the car is counted as consumption, though if a *Fortune* 500 company buys the same car it counts as investment. So the money you took out of savings will shrink any other additions to savings made out of your salary. If your stock gained enough that you don't need to save more, your "consumption" will exceed your "income." If you worry about the statistics, you will think you have a big problem.

The savings rate, the object of much concern during the 1980s, has to be taken with a grain of salt. So, too, investment. An engineering degree doesn't count as investment, but Octopus Enterprises' 20th Lear Jet does. Gross investment has been strong during the eighties, but net investment weak; in other words, there has been a big jump in depreciation schedules. What does this mean? Does it really mean we were eating the seed corn?

By now concern with the statistics is shared by many professional economists, in particular Robert Eisner, Northwestern University's noted Keynesian. He used his presidential address to the American Economic Association in 1988 to warn that economic statistics often do not measure what economic theory pretends they do. "Somehow, econometricians, theorists, and economic analysts of all stripes have lost essential communication with the compilers and synthesizers of their data," he wrote. "To put matters bluntly, many of us have literally not known what we are talking about, or have confused our listeners—and ourselves—into thinking that what we are talking about is directly relevant to the matters with which we are concerned."[10]

Nowhere is this difficulty more pronounced than on the balance of trade. In fact, international transactions are always in balance, by definition. They are an accounting identity, reflecting a great circle of transactions in which for every buyer there is a seller. But different items in the great circle carry different labels. The export of an airliner is called trade. The export of a share of stock is called foreign investment, as is the export of a deed to an office building. A loan between central banks is called official financing. With allowance for errors and omissions, in the end all these items *must* balance.

For many years the government published a plethora of different balances, reflecting different cross-sections of the circle of transactions. There was the merchandise trade balance, the balance on current account, the "basic" balance, the "net liquidity" balance and the official reserve transaction balance. In 1976, an advisory committee of prominent economists looked at these statistics, and was moved to wonder whether any of them meant anything.

The committee suggested that "the words 'surplus' and 'deficit' be avoided insofar as possible." For "these words are frequently taken to mean that the developments are 'good' or 'bad' respectively. Since that interpretation is often incorrect, the terms may be widely misunderstood and used in lieu of analysis."[11]

Following the committee's recommendations, the Commerce Department stopped publishing most of the balances. Because it had to publish something it kept the trade balance, which has been bedeviling us ever since. The "trade deficit" has been enthroned as a kind of economic black hole from which nothing escapes.

In fact, the United States ran a trade deficit in nearly all of its first 100 years, and ran surpluses in the midst of the Great Depression. A trade deficit is typical of rapidly growing economies, which require a disproportionate share of the world's resources, and provide investment opportunities to balance the equation. Indeed, under the accounting identity, investment inflows *must* be balanced with a deficit on the trade account. The mystery is why we even collect these figures; if we kept similar statistics for Manhattan Island, Park Avenue could lay awake at night worrying about its trade deficit.

Crowding Out

I first met Jack Kemp in a discussion of "crowding out." In the midst of the 1975 recession, I visited a Washington think-tank to expound on the theory that government borrowing merely soaks up the supply of credit, "crowding out" private borrowing for private investment.

Treasury Secretary William Simon had popularized the term to keep
the Democratic Congress from opening the spending gates during the
recession. The debate had reverberated throughout the financial community, and I had written a series of editorials with a lot of figures on
"the flow of funds," or projections for supply and demand in the
credit markets. So despite recession, a higher deficit was not a good
thing.

Well, would you increase taxes to cut the borrowing? The question
came from the handsome and youngish congressman who turned out
to be a former football quarterback. My answer was no, we're more
likely to get rid of the deficits than of taxes, but the question struck
me as penetrating. In retrospect, it was prescient, an acorn from
which Kemp-Roth and the rest grew, for if there is no reason to
increase taxes to fight the deficit, perhaps it's possible to cut them if
the right formula can be found.

In the ensuing years the "crowding out" theme has repeatedly
emerged as a rationale for opposition even to the best-designed tax
cuts. Art Laffer could foresee this, and was nearly apoplectic over my
crowding-out editorials.

I liked the argument because it was a coffin nail for Keynesianism.
During this debate, I put to Herb Stein, who went through various
careers as Chicago's token Keynesian, economic adviser to President
Ford, and a member of the *Journal*'s Board of Contributors, the
question of where the government gets the money it "injects" to be
"multiplied." He wrote back, "The question you ask has been answered at so many different levels of sophistication in the past forty
years that I hardly know where to begin." If a deficit crowds out an
equal amount of savings, it cannot stimulate. But if it does not crowd
out, incomes and savings will grow, boosting the economy and financing some of the deficit. "What determines in which of these economic
universes we live? It seems to be a little pituitary gland of the economic system called the interest elasticity of the demand for money."
So much, I thought, for Keynesianism.

While I thought "crowding out" a big leap in my own thinking,
Laffer kept asking, "Don't you see that it happens on the real side,"
as opposed to the financial side represented by the bond markets. In
other words, what counts is government control over real economic
resources, whether it commandeers the resources by taxing or buys
them with bonds. Or, it's not government borrowing that crowds out
the private sector, but government spending.

In the 1980s, opponents of tax cuts kept talking about "crowding

out" in the bond markets, as Art had foreseen. Having helped pop-
ularize the term in 1975, I felt a kind of a proprietary interest in it,
and wondered why *they* were explaining it to *me*.

As Jack Kemp sensed in his 1975 question, the whole crowding-out
argument brings you back to where you started: How do you boost
the economy in the first place? The essential point is that the supply
of credit is not fixed. The savings pool available for borrowing expands
and contracts with the fortunes of the economy. That is, total savings
depend on the success of economic policies.

If deficits actually succeed in stimulating the economy, whether
because Keynes was right to begin with or because new incentive-
enhancing tax cuts had been invented, savings would increase. If
the savings pool grew by enough to finance the deficits, interest
rates would not have to increase, and nothing would be crowded
out.

Incentives Matter

"We are all Keynesians now," Richard Nixon declared in 1971. He
was right, in the sense that Keynesianism *was* macroeconomics. But
Keynesianism was collapsing as President Nixon spoke, and macroeconomics was collapsing with it. By necessity, economists fell back
on microeconomics, the study of the individual consumer or pro-
ducer. This trend was further encouraged by the Friedman-Phelps
demonstration that Keynesianism fell from the flaws in its microeconomic foundation.

At the heart of microeconomics is the concept of incentives. Individual producers and consumers respond to incentives, expressed as
prices. They will buy more at a low price than a high one, and
produce more at a high price than a low one. The diners at Michael
1 saw the implications for macroeconomics: You could expand GNP
not by boosting demand, but by providing incentives for supply.

The most rigorous microeconomic analysis was not done at Michael
1, though, but by Norman Ture and Paul Craig Roberts in Washington. In a paper presented at the Lehrman Institute in 1980, Ture
wrote " 'Supply-side' economics is merely the application of price
theory—widely and tastelessly labeled 'microeconomics'—in analysis
of problems concerning economic aggregates—widely and tastelessly
labeled as 'macroeconomics.' " Its antecedents, he said, lay in Adam
Smith, J. B. Say and Alfred Marshall. "Its newness is to be found only

in its applications to the public economic policy issues of contemporary American society."[12]

Government economic action, Ture argued, should be judged by how it changes relative prices confronting households and businesses, not by its effects on aggregate demand. Since aggregate demand—the sum of all purchases—by definition equals output, demand can only grow if output grows first, and "changes in output occur only as a result of changes in the amount of production inputs or in the intensity or efficiency of their use."

The main instrument the government has to change incentives is the tax system. In the broadest case, Ture explained, there is a microeconomic trade-off between work and leisure. An extra hour of effort is balanced against an extra hour of leisure; on the margin, a tax on the returns for effort changes the relative price in favor of leisure. So lowering the tax will produce additional labor inputs, more output, more aggregate demand and more prosperity.

In the same vein, the talk at Michael 1 was always of *marginal* tax rates. That is, the tax on the last dollar of income—this is where the incentive lies. The kind of tax "cut" epitomized in Jimmy Carter's $50 rebate was designed merely to change aggregate demand. It would change the average or *effective* tax rate, but it changed no incentives, except perhaps for the worse. It was better seen as an expenditure.

If lower marginal rates meant more production, there would be more production to tax, a broader tax base. There would be some revenue gain from the broader tax base to offset some part of the revenue loss from the lower rate. There would be some "reflow," the government would not lose as much revenue as simple-minded "static analysis" would predict. The size of this reflow would depend on the amount of additional production, which would depend on the increase in incentives.

The Laffer Curve

The reflow notion leads to the Laffer curve. A tax of zero obviously raises no revenue, while a tax of 100 percent would extinguish the taxed activity and thus also raise no revenue. There must be a curve connecting these two extremes, and the curve must peak somewhere. Below the peak a higher tax will raise more government revenue, but beyond the peak it a tax cut would actually increase revenue. Laffer called this "the prohibitive range." In extreme cases, that is, a lower

FIGURE 3–1

The Laffer Curve

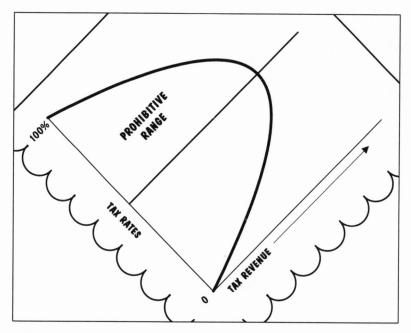

rate could expand the tax base so rapidly that the "reflow" could exceed 100 percent.

Laffer has said his curve was a pedagogical device. It is tautologically true, but contains no empirical information. No theory could say where the prohibitive range lay, and empirical data was lacking. On its face, the curve is not an assertion that all tax cuts will produce more revenue, only that some tax cuts might. The extreme example used at Michael 1 was a 300 percent tariff on, say, cashews. At this level, no cashews would be imported, at least not legally, so revenue would be zero. A more reasonable rate would allow imports, and start to raise revenues.

Wanniski says Laffer first drew the curve on a paper napkin in a meeting with Dick Cheney, then White House deputy chief of staff, at the Two Continents Restaurant in Washington. Neither Laffer nor Cheney remembers the incident, and Martin Anderson has noted that the restaurant used cloth napkins. Mundell thinks it was first drawn at Michael 1. I believe Wanniski; the napkin was in the bar, not the restaurant itself, he says, and it is precisely the kind of detail a good journalist would remember.

Goals and Levers

"For every policy goal, you need a policy lever" was another Mundell aphorism.

If you use monetary policy to fix exchange rates, or to follow a commodity price, you cannot use it to fix interest rates. For that matter, if you use it to fix one interest rate, you can't use it to fix other interest rates, as generations of central bankers have found to their sorrow. Whatever intermediate target you use, if ultimately you use monetary policy to fix the price level, you cannot use it to change the unemployment rate. Laying aside the considerable issue of the extent to which monetary policy can affect the real sector in the first place, this was the dilemma of stagflation.

With the Phillips curve, the Keynesians found themselves trying to hit two birds with one stone. To fight inflation, you needed one lever. And to fight stagflation, you need a second one.

To the diners at Michael 1, the answer was clear: You fight inflation with monetary policy, preferably international and preferably with a commodity link, but in any event with tight money. And you fight stagnation, you stimulate the economy, with incentive-directed tax cuts. You find the highest marginal rates and cut them.

With these understandings, the diners left Michael 1 to face the 1980s. In many ways they were on the forefront of what is now seen as the intellectual cutting-edge of economics, the new post-Keynesian classicism, efficient markets, the emphasis on microeconomics, a skepticism about numbers. Their globalism has not won the mainstream, but may yet.

Their policy mix was controversial, and has if anything become more so. The separation between monetary and fiscal policy, the very idea of a policy "mix," was nearly unthinkable in the Keynesian universe. Everyone understood that monetary policy was to complement fiscal policy. And, of course, unless you could find taxes in the prohibitive range of the Laffer curve, a tax cut would produce a deficit. With the Federal Reserve tied up keeping money tight to fight inflation, wouldn't it "crowd out" investment? How could it be financed?

Mundell, always internationally minded, brushed away the issue, "The Saudis will finance that." In the event, they did.

4

Turning Point

One morning it all started to come true. On April 20, 1978, a *Wall Street Journal* article on the House Ways and Means Committee's doubts about the Carter administration's tax proposals included the following paragraphs:

A major cause for worry on the part of liberals and the administration is a proposal by Rep. William Steiger (R. Wis.) to reduce the tax on capital gains. Rep. Steiger claims to be close to the 19 votes he needs to win approval for his amendment from the 37-member committee.

Under current law, taxpayers can exclude half their long-term capital gains from income, which has the effect of taxing gains at rates ranging from 7% to 35%. But for some top-bracket taxpayers, the interaction of the 15% minimum tax on preference income with the 50% maximum on "earned" income raises the capital gains rate close to 50%.

Rep. Steiger's amendment would roll back the maximum rates on capital gains—for both individuals and corporations—to 25%, the top rate in effect prior to the Tax Reform Act of 1969.

While Rep. Steiger argues that this tax cut would stimulate enough business activity and tax revenue to pay for itself, committee sources estimate the net annual revenue loss to the Treasury at between $2 billion and $3 billion.[1]

This was the moment at which a decade of envy came to its close, and the search for a growth formula started in earnest. The year 1978 was a remarkable turning point. Almost unconsciously, it seemed, the body politic rejected the gestalt that had dominated tax policy since

Joe Barr hoisted his 21 millionaires. The Democratic Congress gave the back of its hand to President Carter's three-martini tax proposals, and instead followed Bill Steiger, a minority Congressman from Wisconsin. The people of California rejected their establishment for Howard Jarvis's Proposition 13. And Jack Kemp, with Sen. William Roth, tabled the Kemp-Roth bill, an across-the-board income tax cut. After what in the 1990s we might call the mother of all tax debates, Kemp-Roth came within one anecdote of passing in that year's closing congressional hours, before Ronald Reagan had even declared himself a candidate for president.

This was not entirely a bolt out of the blue, of course, since the rites of Michael 1 were not exactly kept within the cloister. The participants, Jude in particular, were proclaiming to the world. "It's Time to Cut Taxes" was the title of the first Wanniski report on the full Mundell prescription: tight money to fight inflation, a $30 billion tax cut to spur growth.

"The national economy is being choked by taxes—asphyxiated," Mundell was quoted. He added, "It is simply absurd to argue that increasing unemployment will stop inflation. To stop inflation you need more goods, not less."[2] A $30 billion tax cut would imply a deficit, but perhaps no larger than would result from simply letting recession continue. Recovery would mean a bigger savings pool to finance government borrowing. Also, financing would come from abroad, Mundell predicted. With a tight-money, tax-cut combination, the United States would show a large inflow of foreign capital and a substantial trade deficit. The U.S. tax cut would pull the whole industrial world out of a slump.

It's hard from the perspective of the early 1990s to understand how unconventional these views seemed in the mid-1970s, before the words "policy mix" were common economic jargon. But whether or not they were fully understood, they did put talk of tax cuts in the air.

In any event, the themes were developed in the *Journal* and seemed to spread. "The Mundell-Laffer Hypothesis—A New View of the World Economy" by Jude Wanniski appeared in Irving Kristol's *The Public Interest* in the spring of 1975.[3] In his own *Journal* column, Kristol wrote about the need to develop a new economics, as later did Peter Drucker.[4] Both Kristol and *Journal* editorials elaborated the Keynes-is-Dead theme and proclaimed the futility of tax rebates instead of marginal rate cuts.

At the congressional staff level, Paul Craig Roberts led an assault on the large econometric models used by the Congressional Budget

Office, asking why they predicted a corporate tax cut would lower GNP. This battle was explained in his "Breakdown of the Keynesian Model," in *The Public Interest* in the summer of 1978.[5] The Washington circle—Roberts, Ture, Bruce Bartlett, Steve Entin—were enormously successful in Capitol Hill infighting, among Democrats as well as Republicans.

Laffer, at the time on the faculty of the University of Southern California, lent some shred of academic respectability to the outbreak of the California tax revolt, though of course the leader in collecting 1.5 million signatures for his Proposition 13 was the 75-year-old Howard Jarvis. Property taxes had been escalating in California as property values soared, driven in part by inflation. The state government had accumulated a surplus, also partly caused by the impact of inflation on an income tax with brackets fixed in nominal dollars. By early June, California voters had rejected a "moderate" alternative, and put a 65 percent majority behind the Jarvis constitutional amendment to roll back property taxes and erect impediments to future tax increases.

Proposition 13 was truly a "revolt," not merely a tax reduction measure. Kristol, who happened to be in California during the weeks of its passage, wrote, "For the first time one could witness a direct confrontation between middle-class Americans and the politicians who preside over the ever-expanding public sector." He noted the threats of teacher firings and library closings that marked the anti-Jarvis campaign: "Rarely has there been such a disgusting episode in American state politics—one in which politicians, fighting for control over their constituents' money, lied and threatened and lobbied without scruple. It was a new kind of class war—the people as citizens versus the politicians and their clients in the public sector."[6]

• • •

As 1978 opened, President Carter believed he'd won a mandate to make the tax system "fair." In particular he'd campaigned against "the three-martini lunch." Businessmen were able to buy lunch with "tax deductible dollars." That is, business taxes were levied on profits—gross income minus expenses—and business entertaining was considered an expense. Joe Lunchbucket, the apostles of envy pointed out, had to pay for his own lunch. The 1978 Carter proposals mostly restricted themselves to symbolic nastiness. In computing taxes, businesses could claim an expense only for coach air fares, for example, and only half the cost of business meals. This wouldn't end business entertainment or First Class travel, of course, since businesses would still be allowed to dispose of after-tax profit as they saw fit.

In the midst of this, Mr. Carter's treasury secretary, former Bendix chairman W. Michael Blumenthal, gave a curious speech to a financial analysts' convention in Bal Harbor. He complained that "capital formation often gets shoved to one side" and said that something should be done about "the shortage of equity finance." He proposed to study not only capital gains, but the taxation of dividends and the distinction between "earned and unearned income." After the martinis were taken care of, it seemed, we needed new incentives for investment.

As for Joe Lunchbucket, the Carter proposals would have cost him the tax deduction for state sales tax, gasoline taxes and so on. Medical and casualty losses would be deductible only if they exceeded 10 percent of income. While the 1978 proposals didn't go this far, tax reformers also had their eyes on the tax-free status of the value of his health insurance and other fringe benefits. Maybe even his pension, since pension contributions in his name are allowed to compound tax free and taxed only on when paid out. This tax break allowed Joe Lunchbucket's pension funds to buy up the public companies, making workers beneficial owners of the means of production. Pension-fund socialism, Peter Drucker called it.

Some of these proposals have since crept into tax law, and in the 1990s we seem to be returning to the theme that the overriding priority of a tax system is "fairness." In 1978, though, the Ways and Means Committee bashed one reform after another. Its leaders called on the president to throw in the towel. "He can't win on these reforms," said Rep. Joe Waggonner Jr. (D. La.). "There is no constituency in the Congress or the country for them."[1]

• • •

With all of this under way, the heirs of Michael 1 at once recognized the import of Bill Steiger's 19 votes. By the afternoon of the *Journal* article Jude Wanniski was in the congressman's office and returned to write an editorial "Stupendous Steiger." It announced that the "slight, youthful 39-year-old Republican has shaken the earth." It concluded, "Everyone should know that the Steiger amendment is not one tax provision among many, but the cutting edge of an important intellectual and financial breakthrough."[8]

It was entirely appropriate, indeed especially instructive, that the capital gains tax became the fulcrum for tilting from a decade of envy to a decade of "greed" and also a decade of growth. For the capital gains issue throws the fairness/incentive issue into stark focus. You can only make a capital gain if you have capital. That is, capital gains go to "the rich." It does make a difference whether you envision a stock-trader with gains year after year or a dry-cleaning shop owner cashing out to retire, but in the usual income statistics and the usual stump speeches, both are among "the rich."

At the same time, the prospect of capital gains almost certainly provides an especially important incentive; it is the big jackpot that attracts entrepreneurial vigor. In this society there are basically two ways to get rich—not the dry cleaning proprietor rich, or even the doctor-lawyer-corporate executive rich, but really rich. One is to be an entertainer—television, movies, sports or music. The other is to start your own company and sell it. If you sell it at a public offering, you get rich and keep the company too. It is the prospect of this capital gain that makes young engineers and scientists take the chance of leaving Bosom Industries Inc., mortgaging the family home and working 80 hours a week to form Nextrend Ltd.

Then too, the tax philosophers have never found the right pigeon-hole for capital gains. The tax-all-income-the-same slogan would have all taxpayers tot up their net worth each year, taxing them on the increase. Since this is obviously infeasible, taxpayers are taxed only on realized gains; that is, when they sell a capital asset, they're taxed on the difference between what they sell it for and what they paid for it. Inevitably, this means they have discretion on when to realize the gain, and their decisions are likely to have a heavy tax component.

This introduces further complications: First, what do you do with capital losses? In the depression, I've been told, millionaires followed the standard advice of cashing in losers and letting winners run. Big deductions for capital losses meant they paid no tax even if they had considerable income.

On the other hand, what about inflation? If all prices went up 10 percent, and you sold stock at $11 when you paid $10, do you really have a gain at all? The Internal Revenue Service says you do, which under 1970s-style inflation means you may end up owing tax on economic losses.

Yet the tax "reformers" say you have a terrific deal. Since you don't pay tax until a gain is realized, that means your year-to-year gains get compound interest. If you put the same money in a savings account, the taxman takes a whack at it every year, even if a large part of interest you receive is eaten up by inflation. Also, what if you haven't realized the gain by the time you die? Does your estate have to cash out and pay the tax? If your heirs sell, do they get taxed on the gain before they owned the asset? Do they have to pay an inheritance tax too?

Finally, some of us curmudgeons would add, there is an issue of whether returns to capital should be taxed to begin with. After all, you already paid income tax on the money you used to buy the stock. Why should you be taxed again at all? If you scraped up $100,000 and used it to buy a Rolls-Royce, you don't get taxed per luxury-driving mile. But if you use it to buy stock, providing the economy with investment funds, and then want to sell it to buy another stock, you only have paper to show for your $100,000, yet you still have to pay a tax.

Then too, don't we hear constant complaints about the need for more savings and capital? Did we ever hear them more loudly than during the Reagan boom, when American investment was fueled by Japanese and Saudi savings? Historically most European nations have not considered capital gains as income, taxing them not at all or very lightly. In the 1970s, some European nations had a pro forma tax on investment returns, but had rules prohibiting banks from reporting interest and dividends—a Latin (and Germanic) way of balancing the demands of incentives and fairness. By contrast, in the 1970s the U.S. tax code considered interest as "unearned" income, subject to a 70 percent rate instead of the 50 percent rate due on income "earned" in the form of wages and salaries.

Over the years prior to Joe Barr, the United States had evolved a different approach to the morass of capital gains taxation. Half of a capital gain would be excluded, and the other half taxed as ordinary income. Capital losses could be deducted against any realized gains, but only to a small extent—historically $1,000 but more recently $3,000 a year—against other income. Capital gains were not taxable at death; after paying inheritance taxes (if the deceased hadn't been clever enough to avoid it), heirs took current asset values as the basis for any future gain. Finally, everything was calculated in nominal dollars; no allowance was made for inflation between the purchase and sale of an asset.

The pursuit of Secretary Barr's 21 millionaires upset this bargain. Tax "reformers" had always fretted about the capital gains exclusion, and worried that clever tax lawyers would be able to "convert" ordinary income into capital gains. Those offering these schemes were often better at selling them to dentists than actually avoiding taxes. The best strategy, commodity "straddles," did succeed in converting short-term gains taxed at ordinary rates to long-term gains taxed at lower rates; it was closed in the 1981 tax bill, and by IRS rulings and litigation. But in the worry over the 21 millionaires, the "minimum tax" was made to apply to the "excluded" portion of capital gains. This pushed the top marginal rate on capital gains to 49.1 percent, against 25 percent in 1967. Since these were nominal rates, the raging inflation of the 1970s pushed the real rate even higher.

Representative Steiger proposed to go back to the 1960s treatment, on the simple argument that things were better then. His best argument was that a lower rate would collect more revenues. Even if you didn't believe a lower rate would stimulate entrepreneurs and the rest, you had to believe that a high rate discouraged asset-holders from exercising their discretion to realize their gains and pay the tax. The capital gains tax, in other words, is Exhibit A on the prohibitive range of the Laffer curve.

Unlike the Carter reforms, though, the capital gains cut had a definite constituency. In particular, it had Ed Zschau, then head of a task force of the American Electronics Association, and later himself congressman from Silicon Valley. He and his colleagues said the high capital gains tax was hampering their budding business; that he himself had to turn to Japan for capital. He even lobbied with a ditty, "The Old Risk Capital Blues."

Perhaps more persuasively, Theodore Levitt of the Harvard Business School testified that there were no high-tech startup companies founded in 1976, while more than 300 had been founded in 1968, when the old capital gains provisions applied. And Oscar S. Pollock, who followed the issue for the Securities Industry Association, produced Treasury figures showing actual capital gains receipts before and after the increase, most of which became effective in 1970. They showed receipts little changed by the higher rates, with the peak year in fact at the lower rates.

Raw experience seemed to suggest, in other words, that the Steiger proposal was costless to the Treasury; if Ed Zschau's Silicon Valley entrepreneurs thought it would help them, why not?

The Securities Industry Association also hired Data Resources Inc. to do an econometric study of various tax proposals. The DRI model, of course, was one of the large Keynesian contraptions against which Craig Roberts had railed. But even it found that total elimination of the capital gains tax would boost GNP by $200 billion over five years,

TABLE 4–1

Revenues on Federal Capital Gains Tax on Individuals
(reported as of 1978, in billions)

Old rates	New rates
(top marginal rate on capital gains)	
(25% to 27.5%)	(32.3% to 45.5%)
1965–$4.1	1970–$3.6
1966– 4.0	1971– 5.3
1967– 5.5	1972– 6.9
1968– 7.2	1973– 6.9
1969– 5.9	1974– 5.6-p
	1975– 5.5-p

increase capital formation by $81 billion and add over 3 million man-years of employment. Even though there would be no collections on the capital gains tax, this economic activity would be taxed through corporate and personal income taxes; the proposal was projected to yield the government a net revenue gain of $38 billion over the five years.

In the SIA study, the DRI model was fed three assumptions about how the tax cut would change the behavior of economic agents: That an end to the taxation of stock market gains would bid share prices up 20 percent, that there would also be a 20 percent increase in capital gains realizations as asset holders cashed in gains instead of holding them, and that as capital gains became more important, corporations would cut their dividend payout ratios by 10 percent. While there is always room for debate, these assumptions are not outlandish.[9]

Indeed, Chase Econometric Associates, under Michael K. Evans, had become even more supply-side oriented, and predicted that the Steiger proposal would produce a 40 percent rise in the stock market from its depressed 1978 levels, and enough revenue to reduce the federal deficit by $16 billion by 1985.[10]

A study by Joel Slemrod and Martin S. Feldstein at the National Bureau of Economic Research found that the upper-income individuals most affected by the 1969 changes quite clearly reduced their realizations of capital gains. The resulting lock-in effect, they wrote, "may be so large that a cut in the capital gains tax would actually increase revenue from this type of capital gain."[11]

When it came to the capital gains tax, in short, supporters of the Laffer curve included DRI, Chase and the NBER.

The Treasury came back with its usual static analysis. Since we can't be sure what effect a tax change will have, we assume it has none. So if you collect $50 from a 50 percent tax rate, you will collect $60 at 60 percent, $75 at 75 percent, $90 at 90 percent, and by inference, $100 at 100 percent. On this basis, the Treasury estimated that the Steiger proposal would reduce revenues by $2.4 billion. A White House fact sheet was honest enough to say this was based on " 'first-order' estimates (assuming no behavioral changes and no 'feed-back revenues')." It went on to argue that "there is no reason to believe that it would create more offsetting tax revenue over the long term than other forms of tax cuts that are vastly more equitable." Secretary Blumenthal said projections of revenue gains were "based on extremely unrealistic economic assumptions."

Secretary Blumenthal agreed that capital formation was important, asserting "the President has placed a substantial increase in the rate of real capital formation at the heart of his strategy." However, this was to come not from capital gains reductions, but from a reduction in rates, up to 10 percent for small businesses, and a liberalization of the investment tax credit. "Rolling back the capital gains tax rate would steal much of the revenue needed for this balanced program of investment incentives. That trade-off would be very bad for capital formation."

Most of all, however, the Carter administration argued against the Steiger proposal on grounds of "fairness." The Joe Barr millionaires tax, the White House argued, "addressed some of the worst inequities in the tax system." It asserted that "over 80 percent of the benefits for individuals would go to persons with incomes exceeding $100,000, or less than one half of 1 percent of all taxpayers." And "3,000 millionaire taxpayers would receive cuts averaging $214,000. . . . Few taxpayers with incomes under $50,000 would receive any tax savings at all."

Or as Secretary Blumenthal's letter to Congress said,

Rolling back the tax treatment of capital gains would sharply erode the progressivity and horizontal equity of the income tax system. The resultant tax system could not be squared with the notion that each citizen should pay a fair share of the nation's tax burden, according to ability to pay.

Over four-fifths of the benefits would go to persons with incomes over $100,000.

The changes since 1969 scarcely affected lower and middle-income taxpayers. Hence, they would get virtually no relief on their capital gains, but those in the 70 percent bracket would receive a one-third reduction in their effective capital gains tax rate.

Rolling back capital gains treatment to pre-1969 rules would recreate at high levels of income a perverse relationship between income and taxes. In 1969, income tax liabilities as a percentage of income actually began to decline as income rose over the $100,000 to $200,000 level.

The major components of a capital gains rollback would directly contradict elementary notions of tax fairness. Almost 97 percent of the benefits from extending the alternative tax would go to those with incomes of over $200,000. Over 56 percent of the benefits from eliminating capital gains as an item of tax preference would go to the same group. Two-thirds of the combined benefits go to the over $200,000 class, and 81 percent go to those with expanded incomes of $100,000 or more. These two measures would together reduce the overall tax burden of the over $200,000 income class by 8 percent.[12]

Arguments like these sound familiar in the 1990s, and before 1978 had swept aside all opposition for a decade. What tax reform was about was redistributing income. "The rich" were not paying a "fair" share. They must pay a higher share of their income. They must pay a larger share of every tax increase. They must receive a smaller share of the benefit of any tax reduction. Definitions of "income" must be expanded, "loopholes" must be closed. And after all, the "three martini lunch" was dynamite on the stump. The president had a mandate.

But by 1978, fairness was no longer the issue. Looking out through the malaise, society was searching for incentives and growth. With only 12 Republicans on the Ways and Means Committee, Representative Steiger held his 19 votes. Attempt after attempt to dilute his proposal was rejected. The final bill including the capital gains reductions garnered a majority of the Democrats as well, sweeping in 25–12. It passed the Senate with only pro forma opposition. Despite an earlier veto threat, President Carter signed the bill without comment on November 6.

"This bill reverses over 10 years of tax reform efforts," said the director of the Ralph Nader Tax Reform Research Group, complaining especially about the end of "the long effort to eliminate the special treatment of capital gains—the biggest loophole in the tax system for the wealthy." Retiring Republican senator Clifford Hansen agreed on the facts if not the judgment "We've turned around the whole thrust of what tax reform was two years ago."

"This obviously is not a tax reform bill," summarized Ways and Means Chairman Al Ullman. "It is an economic tax package."[13]

• • •

The Steiger amendment was not nearly as controversial, though, as the Kemp-Roth tax bill, which proposed to slash personal income tax rates by 30 percent over three years. After a stormy debate, the proposal was defeated in conference committee in 1978. It was endorsed by Ronald Reagan in his 1980 campaign and pretty much enacted as the 1981 Reagan tax cut. Intellectually, it broke ground that shaped the 1980s and casts a shadow over the 1990s. It also made Jack Kemp a national figure.

The Kemp-Roth argument was that a tax cut would stimulate the economy by boosting incentives. A lower tax rate would increase the after-tax returns for both labor and capital. If you pay more for something, economics teaches, you call forth a greater supply of it. If this is true, a lower tax rate will produce more labor and more capital, and harder work and more investment will give you more production. If government spending is unchanged this might be offset by "crowding out," of course, but then again it might not. It depends on the magnitudes of the incentive.

Keynesian-trained economists, especially politically liberal ones, denied first of all that it was clear that workers respond to incentives. They argued that lower taxes, or by implication higher wages, had two competing effects. Yes, they agreed, there was a "substitution effect" in which higher incentives produce more work. But this is offset by an "income effect," in which workers withdrew labor once they reached a set target income. The two effects were offsetting and indeterminate, they argued, so that you couldn't be sure even of the direction, let alone the magnitude, of the supply effects of lower taxes.

In other words, if you pay people more, they don't work any harder. As economists would say, the supply of labor is inelastic with respect to price. Since labor is needed to produce everything, the supply curve doesn't exist; and in that case, neither does economics, at least as it is commonly taught and understood. The rusty microeconomic underpinnings of popular Keynesianism was on embarrassing display.

Second, the Keynesian opponents of Kemp-Roth argued it would be inflationary. If you analyze Kemp-Roth with the "multiplier," the concept of "capacity" and the "Phillips curve," your answer is clear. As Walter Heller put it, "A $114 billion tax cut in three years would simply overwhelm our existing capacity with a tidal wave of increased demand and sweep away all hopes of curbing deficits and containing inflation. It would soon generate soaring deficits and roaring inflation."[14]

The third prong of the Keynesian counterattack was to leap on the Laffer curve. "The Kemp-Roth-Laffer Free Lunch," Heller entitled his *Wall Street Journal* article. Opponents of the proposal were altogether eager to spread the good news that its proponents believed it would "pay for itself" in increased revenues. The image that the Kemp-Roth bill was based on a curve drawn on a napkin proved irresistible, and Art Laffer's critics did as much as his friends to drive his speaking fees upward.

Laffer, Wanniski and other proponents were not averse to the publicity, but what they argued in serious debate was a bit more complicated. They certainly believed that the biggest bottleneck in the economy was personal income tax rates reaching up to 70 percent, with state income taxes in addition. "The Tax Brake," Craig Roberts called it.[15] They certainly believed that relieving this bottleneck would result in a healthier economy, and that a healthy economy produced more tax revenues than a sick one. Further, over some indefinite period of time the government would get more revenue if their proposal passed than if it were defeated.

And they certainly believed, as the Laffer curve depicted, that at some level of tax rates, lowering the tax will produce more revenue, even immediately. They certainly believed that such rates existed in the U.S. code. A rate of nearly 50 percent on capital gains, when taxpayers had discretion over whether and when to expose their paper gains to taxation, made no sense from the standpoint of maximizing tax revenues. So the Steiger amendment would have an immediate payback, plus a positive incentive for new business formation today that would lead to still more revenues over future years.

Similarly, there would be a quick payback from cutting the highest marginal rates, those farthest out of the Laffer curve. These were, of course, taxes on "the rich," those the Carter administration and liberals traditionally have been the most eager to increase. Michael K. Evans of Chase Econometric Associates did a little empirical research, and found that tax revenues from the highest income classes did indeed increase after both the Mellon and Kennedy tax cuts.

As Andrew Mellon cut the top marginal rate of 73 percent to 55 percent in 1922 and 25 percent in 1926, the rich paid more. Taxpayers reporting incomes of more than $300,000—a proxy for millionaires in 1978 dollars—paid $77 million in taxes in 1922. In 1927, the same group paid taxes of $230 million. The same thing happened with the tax cuts of the 1960s. Evans produced the following table:

TABLE 4–2

Tax Revenue from the Rich

Year	Maximum tax rate	Taxes collected from income classes of		
		over $1,000,000	500,000–1,000,000	100,000–500,000
1961	91%	342	297	1970
1962	91%	311	243	1740
1963	91%	326	243	1890
1964	77%	427	306	2220
1965	70%	603	408	2752
1966	70%	590	457	3176

Kemp-Roth, however, was an across-the-board tax cut. The initial bracket of the income tax, for example, would be cut to 8 percent from 14 percent.

A 14 percent marginal rate doesn't look very far out on the Laffer curve. Worse, in the structure of the tax brackets, even those paying the highest marginal rates paid only 14 percent on the first tranche of their income; for most taxpayers a reduction in the initial bracket rate would be a non-marginal cut with no change in incentives, a dead loss for revenues. So even using the Laffer Curve as the tool for analysis, immediate, first-year payback on a proposal like Kemp-Roth would be a stiff order. The image to the contrary, this is not a claim supply-siders seriously advanced. This will be elaborated in Chapter 11, but one particularly significant exchange should be related here.

Paul Craig Roberts, then on the Senate staff and an important author of Kemp-Roth, replied to Heller's "Kemp-Roth-Laffer Free Lunch" and a similar analysis by Herb Stein. With their "free lunch" rhetoric, he wrote, "they are demolishing a straw man. This is not what the bill's proponents mean when they said it would pay for itself. Part of the projected deficit will indeed by eliminated by revenue from the larger GNP. The remaining deficit will not be inflationary because it will be self-financing." That is, the increase in economic activity would also increase the savings pool sufficiently to finance the extra borrowing.

He also cited econometric estimates by Evans's Chase Econometrics that the federal government would recover 41 percent of static-analysis revenues in the first year, rising to 72 percent in the seventh year. Moreover "the remaining deficit is more than covered by the increase in personal savings, retained earnings, and state and local government surplus. Thus, the deficit puts no pressure on credit markets. The tax cut generates enough new savings to finance the deficit plus an increase in private investment."

Roberts also found some 1977 Walter Heller testimony on the Kennedy tax cut, saying it helped generate a budget surplus in 1965 before the Vietnam escalation. "It was a $12 billion tax cut which would be about $33 or $34 billion in today's terms, and within one year the revenues into the federal Treasury were already above what they had been before the tax cut." Heller had concluded, "Did it pay for itself in increased revenues? I think the evidence is very strong that it did."[16]

In a reply, Heller dismissed this as "a real howler." In saying that the Kennedy tax cuts paid for themselves, "I was at pains to demonstrate that this was a *demand-side* response (that is, stepping up consumer and business demand to take up existing slack in labor and product markets)—exactly the opposite of Laffer's implausible supply-side theory." And he took issue with whether the size of the savings response would be enough to finance the extra borrowings. Roberts had cited high savings-response estimates by Michael Boskin of Stanford (later chairman of the Council of Economic Advisers), but Heller said even these would not be sufficient.[17]

Henry Fowler, undersecretary of the treasury when the Kennedy cuts passed and later secretary, later told me that in lobbying for them he carried around a letter on how the Mellon tax cuts had boosted revenues. In any event, by the middle of 1978, then, the principle of incentive tax cuts had been extensively debated, and a number of points seemed to be resolved. Yes, it was possible for a tax cut to recoup revenues. The Kennedy tax cuts had; the argument was over why. (Keynesianism works half the time, when the "deficit" comes from tax cuts instead of spending increases.) Yes, some part of the deficit could be financed through increased savings; the argument was over the magnitude of the response. Kemp-Roth was larger in relation to GNP than the Kennedy tax cuts, but not enormously so—less than twice.

As the political debates of 1978 proceeded, the Keynesians had the prestige, but the upstart supply-siders had momentum, and made a surprisingly good showing, especially after the Heller-Roberts exchange. And the Keynesians were still hung with their albatross; they had no answer to inflation. They kept coming back to wage and price controls in one form or another. The Laffer curve didn't look quite so silly when the alternative was something called "Tax-Based Incomes Policies," or TIP.

In the Congress, the Republicans united behind Kemp-Roth, and started picking up some Democratic support. The House leadership allowed a floor vote, with Ways and Means Chairman Ullman saying "it is a political issue in every congressional district." On the floor it was rejected by a 240 to 177 vote, with only three Republicans deserting the ranks and 37 Democrats joining the Republicans.

In the Senate, Kemp-Roth was rejected, but one of its supporters, Democrat Sam Nunn, revived it by combining its future rate cuts with expenditure targets—anticipating the combination of Reagan rate cuts and the Gramm-Rudman deficit ceilings. The Nunn amendment passed the Senate by a vote of 65–20. On October 12, the House voted 268–135 to instruct their conferees to accept the Nunn provision. What was later to be the Reagan program had passed both houses of Congress.

Sometime later I had the pleasure of hearing Senator Daniel Patrick Moynihan describe what happened in the House-Senate Conference Committee. The Nunn amendment and the House vote were never mentioned until the wee small hours of October 15. When it could no longer be avoided, conference cochairman Sen. Russell Long started to talk about Uncle Earl, the always flamboyant sometime governor of Louisiana.

In one campaign, Uncle Earl had a problem running against Ralph Smith (on the name I vouch for neither my recollection or the senator's). The problem was that Smith, a Ford dealer, was an honest man, and no one in Louisiana politics had any experience with that. But Uncle Earl finally found a solution.

He set up a sound truck outside of the Ford dealership, and started to give a speech about Smith's honesty. "If you want to buy a Ford car, you go right in there and get an honest price from Ralph Smith," Uncle Earl said. But he added, "If you want to buy two Ford cars, you'd better go somewhere else. For Ralph Smith that is *too big a deal.*"

So much for the Senate vote and the instructions of House conferees. Kemp-Roth-Nunn was too big a deal for 1978. Still, it was a remarkable political and intellectual turning-point. The year opened with the national administration taking aim at the three-martini lunch. It ended with a big cut in the capital gains tax becoming law, and with the principle of incentive tax cuts not only on the table but dominating discussion. The nation was looking again for lessons understood by Andrew Mellon and at least some of John F. Kennedy's braintrust, but lost in the chase after Joe Barr's 21 millionaires.

The tax side of Bob Mundell's policy mix, that is, was on the national agenda by the end of 1978, before Ronald Reagan had even declared his presidential candidacy. The monetary side still seemed far away, with stagflation mounting and the Carter administration writhing over the dollar.

5

Meanwhile, Money

I've spent a lot of time studying about the American dollar, its value in international monetary markets, the causes for the recent deterioration as it relates to other major currencies. I can say with complete assurance that the basic principles of monetary values are not being adequately assessed on the current international monetary market.
President Jimmy Carter, March 2, 1978[1]

So Jimmy Carter lectured the financial markets; President Canute, we called him at *The Wall Street Journal*. Just as Bill Steiger was lining up the votes to break the jam on tax policy, the other half of the policy mix Bob Mundell outlined at Michael 1 was hitting a boil in the foreign exchange markets. The Carter administration found that despite its fervent wishes and incessant flailing, it could never escape from the dollar. When President Carter gave his lecture to the markets, the dollar had fallen to 2.01 marks and 238 yen, while the price of gold was $184.75. When he had been inaugurated a bit over a year earlier, the dollar stood at 2.40 marks and 290 yen, and gold sold for $133.10.

President Canute found that even the biggest economy around can't stop the globe and get off, but in this particular, the Carter administration was not notably incompetent. *All* our administrations have been just as bad, through the 1970s, the 1980s and, so far, the 1990s. American economic policymakers, not to mention members of the American literate public, are congenitally unable to digest Bob Mundell's aphorism that the only closed economy is the world economy.

Only the United States would ever conceive that it could simply ignore the international economy. European nations simply take for granted that they live in a trading world, and must take explicit

77

account of economic policies of other nations. Japan and the Asian tigers see themselves as exporters, primarily dependent on world markets. A large nation—the Soviet Union or India—can mount a determined effort at autarky, walling itself off from the world behind insurmountable trade barriers and inconvertible currencies. But only the United States would presume to follow its own domestic economic agenda oblivious to the rest of the globe.

This is of course because the United States is the world's dominant economy. It is by far the most productive. It is the largest unified market, and has a large and skilled work force. It is the world technological leader, and its agricultural prowess is even more awesome. It spans a continent, with vast natural resources, including energy resources. Until recent decades, the oil capital of the world was in East Texas; oil and natural gas reserves are still impressive, and coal reserves are vast.

Most important of all, the U.S. Federal Reserve is the world's banker—or at least, the dollar is the world's reserve currency.

To begin with, the dollar is the principal vehicle of world trade and finance. Most international shipments, including all international oil trade, are calculated in dollars. This is also true of most financial transactions—the multitude of sales and purchases of bonds and foreign exchange that regulate investment flows and link the world economy into a unified whole. In economists' terms, the dollar fills the vital function of the world's unit of account.

In the second classical monetary function, the dollar is also the world's principal store of value. Of all U.S. currency outstanding, more than half is in $100 bills; no one knows for sure where these bills are, but presumably many of them are hoarded in safe deposit boxes around the world. The dollar is not only a private store of value, it is a store of value for other central banks. The world's central banks may hold other currencies as a convenience, but only the dollar serves as a reserve currency, ranking alongside gold among central bank assets.

A reserve currency is a dangerous blessing, as the British found with the decline of sterling. The final "sterling balances" were "funded"—replaced by dollars—as recently as 1976. The big advantage of a reserve currency is a seemingly unlimited line of credit from the world's largest central banks. But the Faustian bargain lies in the store of value function; use as a store of value means that huge blocs of a reserve currency constantly overhang the market. When the currency starts to teeter, it begins to look untrustworthy as a store of value. Everyone will try to liquidate at once, greatly accelerating the decline.

At the same time the dollar is vital to world commerce. If it were suddenly to vanish, it's unlikely that any other currency could quickly be instituted as a worldwide unit of account. Trade would be clogged by the cumbersome process of barter. Cross-border investment would collapse until new financial instruments were invented. Great wads of central bank reserves would gyrate in value, with unpredictable effects on monetary creation in other currencies. These are the sorts of confusions associated with the world-wide Great Depression of the 1930s.

Yet with its nearly automatic credit line, ironically, the reserve currency role of the dollar is what permits the United States to ignore the rest of the world. Veterans of years of Federal Reserve deliberations testify that international implications were discussed only tangentially. When the dollar is devalued, foreign central banks suffer a loss on their reserve holdings. I've heard that when Valery Giscard d'Estaing started to complain about devaluation losses suffered by the Bank of France, John Connally replied, "Hell, Giscard, we got more dollars than you do!" (This is something treasury secretaries ought to remember when thinking a lower dollar would solve their problems.)

Given the understandable habit of focusing on our own continental economy, even Americans attentive to economic issues are only now in the 1990s grappling with international issues. They still tend to think in terms of the U.S. economy, connected by pipes and valves to other "domestic" economies. They have trouble envisioning the world economy as an integrated whole.

• • •

Certainly the Carter administration didn't have the world in mind with its economic policies; it merely wanted to stimulate the domestic economy. As it offered its $50 rebate proposal to end the recession, it wanted easy monetary policy for the same purpose. But in April, money growth spurted at a rate of 20 percent a year, and the Fed tightened. Long-term corporate bonds held steady, a good sign for investment and growth. But the banks raised their prime rate, and the administration complained.

Unhappily for the administration image, the point man in this complaint was Budget Director Bert Lance, who personally held millions in loans pegged to the prime. (After leaving office, he paid off these loans with the proceeds of the sale of his Georgia Bank to Ghaith Pharaon, a Syrian/Saudi investor closely associated with the rogue international bank, BCCI)

The main complaints about the administration posture, though, came from abroad. For the rapid money creation of course hammered the value of the dollar in the foreign exchange markets—all the more so since other nations were moving toward restraint and slower creation of their currencies. The Treasury maintained it didn't care about the foreign exchange value of the dollar, proclaiming a policy of "benign neglect." At a June OECD meeting in Paris, indeed, Treasury Secretary Blumenthal urged the Germans and Japanese to stop intervening in the exchange markets and let their currencies rise; that is, the secretary of the treasury was urging a lower dollar.

The dollar was falling, the official and conventional wisdom went, because of oil imports. Yet the United States imported only 19 percent of its energy needs; Japan imported 73 percent, but the yen was rising. Surely oil was not the whole problem. As recently as 1975, for that matter, the United States had run a trade surplus despite the oil shock. This had occasioned little comment since it was routinely offset by investment outflows. The 1975 balances reflected the classic position of a mature and developed economy; it exports capital to more promising investment opportunities abroad and correspondingly exports finished goods to turn a trade surplus.

Under the Carter administration, though, the U.S. trade account and investment account both fell apart at once. The trade deficit was no doubt swelled because the United States kept price controls on energy, thus boosting consumption above the levels the world price would dictate. And at the same time, investors fled, fearing a falling dollar would wipe out whatever gains they might make. As Dr. Jelle Zijlstra, chairman of the Bank for International Settlements, said of the United States, "Capital flows were in the wrong direction." In its official review of the year, the BIS remarked that at least part of the U.S. trade deficit would have been offset "had confidence in the dollar been maintained."[2]

Because there were no voluntary capital inflows, central banks had to step into the breach, buying more than $30 billion in dollars. The trade deficit was offset by "official financing." These purchases are largely made in the markets in the course of "support" operations for the dollar. That is, even with the United States pursuing a policy of "benign neglect," other nations were willing to stem the rise of their own currencies by selling them for dollars, which they accumulated in central bank reserves. Policymakers abroad accepted the common belief that too high a currency would make it hard for them to compete in the U.S. market. But they were even more fearful, given the dollar's role as an international unit of account and international store of value, of a precipitous drop in the dollar more-or-less closing down international trade and investment.

Perhaps most pertinent of all, the dollar's slide was complicating their own problems of monetary management. As the dollar became less trustworthy as a store of value, holders of dollar assets of course wanted to diversify. Someone calculated that if holders of dollars drew down their assets by 10 percent, and invested half in German marks and half in Swiss francs, they would buy up the entire money supply of Switzerland.

By December of 1977, Fritz Leutwiler, head of the Swiss Central Bank, was saying, "You can no longer say that what the United States is doing is benign neglect for the dollar. It is now malign neglect on the part of the United States. The United States has good reason to worry about its currency. If the dollar continues to go down it will incite the oil producers to raise their prices. There is a risk of less economic growth in countries like West Germany and Switzerland."[3]

These feelings became even more acute later that month, when the administration announced that Chairman Burns would be replaced by G. William Miller, the former Textron chairman with no discernible credentials in international finance. In January, *The Times* of London summed up what much of the world felt:

The confusion that is apparent about economic policy in Washington is at least one important factor in undermining confidence in the dollar. In that sense we are all suffering from what is happening, or not happening, in Washington. . . .

To be fair to the President, the confusion in the apparent actions of the administration is no more than a reflection of the confusion, many would say the bankruptcy of ideas, which pervades the economic establishment of the United States, as of all other developed industrial countries. . . . [I]t is perhaps not surprising that the President is confining himself to verbal and practical compromises. . . .

For American domestic policy is open to the charge of irresponsibility in its failure to come to terms with energy . . . The truth is that any energy package which does not use the full rigor of the price mechanism to reduce consumption and increase domestic supply will not be facing up to the magnitude of the problem. . . . [I]t is keeping up the price of energy unnecessarily for the rest of the world, while at the same time flooding it with increasingly unwanted dollars.[4]

The day *The Times* editorial appeared was the same day the Carter administration dropped benign neglect. It announced it would intervene in the foreign exchange markets to support the dollar. At the *Journal* we remarked that this was a step in the right direction, in that policymakers finally recognized that the United States had interests in and responsibilities to the global economy, but predicted the experiment was "utterly doomed to failure if they persist in their old ideas on interest rates and monetary growth."

But this proved not to be the road to Damascus. The dollar blipped up in early 1978, then resumed its fall as the Carter administration continued in its old ways. The Council of Economic Advisers criticized the Fed for "unsettling" interest rate increases and urged more rapid monetary growth. It also argued that since imports were only 10 percent of production, a 10 percent decline in the dollar increased domestic prices by only 1 percent—the precise argument Arthur Laffer had tackled in his first *Wall Street Journal* article.

Throughout the year, the administration went back and forth between worrying about keeping interest rates low and keeping the dollar from sliding. After an energy bill without price decontrol and a presidential speech in October, the foreign exchange market pretty much dried up. No one wanted dollars. In his excellent *The Fate of the Dollar*, Martin Mayer reports that "Washington was flooded with terrifying reports from embassies in all the major trading countries," and describes a meeting between President Carter and Secretary Blumenthal:

> The President asked Blumenthal to give him a description of what might happen, and Blumenthal did so. Domestic inflation would soar as the price of imports rose uncontrollably (this included oil) and foreigners bought heavily with their appreciated currencies in American commodity markets. Other nations would hastily erect import barriers against American exports, to protect themselves from the flood of goods made cheap only by the cheap dollar. International trade would diminish drastically, with losses for all participants. Third World countries, which still held most of their reserves in dollars, would be bankrupted, and interest rates on the dollar abroad—and thus, soon, at home—would fly into the high teens and maybe worse. American influence abroad, whatever triumphs might be achieved with Sadat and Begin, would plummet. Blumenthal is reported to have added, as

an afterthought, that the President would have to face these problems with a new Secretary of the Treasury.[5]

On November 1, with the dollar down to 1.87 marks and 187 yen and gold up to $227, the president personally announced a new package to support the dollar. The United States arranged huge lines of loans and swaps to buy dollars in the foreign exchange markets and arrest its slide. By mid-1979, when the President came down from the Catocin mountaintop for his speech on malaise, the dollar was at 1.83 marks and 216 yen, but gold continued up to $291.

It would strain credulity, of course, to suggest that President Carter went to Camp David to reflect on monetary policy. It's doubtful that he understood, or even understands today, how much monetary policy had to do with the malaise he felt and attributed to his countrymen. The gradual erosion of Bretton Woods, the August 1971 decision to close the gold window, the subsequent OPEC reaction, the wage–price experiment still lingering in the energy sector, the inflation and its social discontents—all these were a skein that wound the technical problem of the dollar into the spiritual problem of malaise.

By habit and background, of course, the president tended to moralize about the problem. But the answer to his question—why haven't we been able to pull together as a society to solve the energy problem—did not lie in moral failings but in intellectual ones. We as a society simply didn't understand. The problem was not energy, the problem was money.

Yet for all that, at Camp David President Carter stumbled toward the right answer, the key decision of his presidency. It was scarcely what he had in mind; his call for the resignation of his whole cabinet was intended to remove Secretary Blumenthal and Energy Secretary James Schlesinger, the two members of the cabinet with some understanding of market principles. Yet at the end of the process, he had named Paul Volcker chairman of the Federal Reserve.

Volcker was a central banker's central banker. He'd been at Camp David with Nixon, but was a practitioner of the old-time financial religion. I knew him slightly when he was undersecretary and president of the New York Fed, where they had to raise the dining room chandelier to avoid collisions with his six-foot-seven frame. I got to know him much better as we both served as trustees of the Mayo Clinic, and have come to regard him as a kind of saint. He could have commanded far more money in the private sector, and needed it, with an ailing wife and physically handicapped son. They stayed in

New York during his service as chairman, and he kept a small apartment in the capital. His only fault is his unrealism in expecting others to live up to his own standards. He was, in short, the perfect man to take charge of a world financial crisis.

Somehow the system worked. In his memoirs, President Carter mentions Volcker only once, noting that the new Fed chairman also opposed the Kemp-Roth bill. In his biography of Volcker, William Neikirk reports that the president responded, "Who's Paul Volcker?" when Treasury Undersecretary Anthony Solomon suggested the name.[6] The president evidently offered the job to David Rockefeller, whom he knew from the Trilateral Commission. But everyone seemed to point him back to Volcker.

Nor, on the record, did the president seem to understand the importance of the job. After dismissing Blumenthal, he felt he needed a strong treasury secretary, and plucked Miller out of the Fed, leaving a vacancy to fill. But with its control over credit, its choice of inflation rate and supervision of commercial banks, a central bank is an enormous font of economic and political power. Speaking of Émile Moreau's memoirs as governor of the Bank of France, Charles Kindleberger has related:

> One of the most interesting passages in Moreau's memoirs records a report of a visit by Quesnay to London where he saw not only Norman but also Niemeyer, Salter, Strakosch and Kindersley. As reported by Moreau, Quesnay observed that the grand British design was not only to stabilize currencies, even without the support of the Bank of France, but to link up central banks into a cooperative network which could, independent of political considerations, and even of governments, regulate the questions essential for prosperity, viz. monetary security, distribution of credit and movement of prices. Moreau characterizes these views as "surely doctrinaire, no doubt somewhat utopian, even perhaps Machiavellian, but possible!"[7]

• • •

Presumably the administration had at least some inkling of Volcker's views. As president of the New York Fed, he had been a leading force against easy money policies on the Fed's Open Market Committee. Only three months earlier Fed Chairman Miller had taken the extraordinary step of publicly proclaiming a "steady as you go" course just before the Open Market Committee met; in its previous meeting he'd had to face a bloc of four dissenters voting to tighten, including

Volcker. Less than two weeks after the Miller announcement, the Fed was forced to tighten by new statistics showing huge money growth.

Neikirk reports that in meeting the president, Volcker said he thought tighter money might be needed, and came away feeling he wouldn't get the job. But somehow he did. At the *Journal* we called it "a bright spot in what has otherwise been a rather dismal month for those looking to the White House for leadership." The markets rallied.

It was clear enough where Paul Volcker's heart was; his every instinct would be for a sound dollar, domestically and internationally. But central banking is also a political art. Central banks around the world are to varying degrees "independent," able to set their own policies or at least available for politicians to blame for credit policies unpopular in the short term but necessary in the long term. The Federal Reserve, with 14-year terms for governors for instance, is toward the more-independent end of the spectrum. But even the most independent central bank seldom feels it can afford a showdown confrontation with an elected administration; for one thing, in such showdowns other central banks have lost their independence.

Given such constraints, the first thing a strong-willed central bank chairman needs is unity in his own institution. In the Fed's Board of Governors or Open Market Committee, no dissent is taken lightly. And 4–3 victories are seen as the next thing to a disaster. So as Volcker took the helm of the Fed, it remained to be seen how persuasive he would be with his own board, and whether he'd be able to keep a modicum of cooperation with the incumbent administration.

In the throes of 1979, Volcker succeeded in winning a unanimous board vote for one increase in the largely symbolic discount rate; but in September, prevailed by only 4–3. The dollar sank; the Volcker symbolism was no longer a help. The immediate outcome was overwhelmed by the suggestion of future irresolution. The kind of collapse Secretary Blumenthal had sketched for the president once again seemed a possibility.

In an atmosphere of crises, Volcker, Treasury Secretary Miller and other policymakers headed for the annual meeting of the International Monetary Fund and World Bank in Belgrade. They stopped in Bonn for a lecture from their German counterparts, and encountered a nonstop earful from the central bankers and finance ministers of the world congregated in the Yugoslav capital.

Volcker broke away from the meeting early, and markets trembled on the rumor that he was about to resign. That Friday, the dollar was worth 1.76 marks and 223 yen, and gold had soared to $384. With the sense of crisis providing the political formula, Volcker convened an emergency meeting of the Open Market Committee. He called a Saturday night press conference to announce new Federal Reserve procedures, and a discount rate increase by unanimous vote. While the administration harbored doubts, it felt compelled to express support. Volcker was not only in office but in control.

Not everything went smoothly henceforth, to say the least. The momentum of events was strong, and the new procedures introduced their own confusions; they were certainly not the ones anyone at Michael 1 would have chosen (see Chapter 7, "The Perils of Paul"). Gold continued up, spiking at the incredible price of $875 an ounce in January, a month in which consumer prices also boiled at a 1.4 percent, one-month increase. The new procedures were ultimately dropped, but not until after recession arrived, in fact twice. The gold price was to subside during the 1980s, but the dollar was to continue an uneven course, soaring to 3.43 marks and 263 yen in 1985 and dipping to lows of 121 yen in 1988 and 1.44 marks in 1991.

Still, at Belgrade a corner was turned. The era of easy money was over, and with it the nightmare scenario of a precipitous collapse of the dollar, an implosion of world trade and a prolonged world stagnation. At Belgrade this outcome may have been only a few stumbles away. A painful course lay ahead, but the main corner had been turned.

On October 6, 1979, the 1980s began. It would stretch things to say that the monetary side of Mundell's policy mix was in place, but surely Belgrade represented a major step toward it. Monetary policy entered three years of creative turmoil, while tax policy surged toward a breakthrough.

6

Ronald Reagan

For too long, we have focused on short-run policies to stimulate spending, or demand, while neglecting supply—labor, savings, investment and production.

Consequently, demand has been overstimulated and supply has been strangled in a noose of disincentives woven of unnecessary regulation, taxation, inflation and codes of conduct not respected by our foreign competitors. Only recently have some computer models of the nation's economy been adapted to take those disincentives into consideration.

But we must quicken the pace if we are serious about controlling stagflation instead of having it control us.

I am convinced that we don't have to put people out of work to control inflation. The goal of the next decade should be to fight inflation and unemployment through supply side incentives to put more goods on the shelves. That's the way to cut prices and boost employment.

A recent JEC study demonstrates that supply incentives—even those which do not stimulate demand or widen the deficit—can lead to job creation, productivity gains and reduced inflation.[1]

These words were uttered in May 1980, in the midst of the presidential primaries. But they do not come from a stump speech by presidential aspirant Ronald Reagan. Rather, they come from a press release issued by the congressional Joint Economic Committee, relating the words of its Democratic chairman, Sen. Lloyd Bentsen.

Yes, this was the same Lloyd Bentsen who eight years later complained of the "ultimate epoch of illusion," who summed up the Reagan years as "a time when America tried to borrow its way to prosperity."[2] To judge by the rhetoric, by the time he became a vice-presidential candidate, the senator had forgotten a lot of what he'd learned in 1979 and 1980, when his Joint Economic Committee issued reports that unified Republicans and Democrats. In releasing the 1980 report, Senator Bentsen bragged, "The JEC is on the cutting edge of a new approach to economic policy. In 1979, we were a pioneer of the concept of supply side economics."[3]

To be fair, what "supply-side economics" meant to some members of the committee, say Sen. William Roth of Kemp-Roth fame, is not necessarily precisely what it meant to others. Senator Bentsen had in mind tinkering with the corporate tax structure by increasing the investment tax credit and accelerating depreciation schedules. It's true that such modest cuts would not have been expensive in foregone revenue, though one can doubt whether their economic effects would have been powerful enough to break the momentum of stagflation.

It was one of the ironies of the tax debates of 1980 and 1981 that the Republicans became populists while the Democrats sought to favor corporate interests, and even investors directly. Democrats instinctively sought to shape tax cuts into industrial planning, believing in the government's ability to direct money to its best uses. Republicans, fighting against the politician's natural instinct to hold on to power, sought to return money to the private sector and trust market forces to find the best outlets.

Yet whatever the differences, Senator Bentsen's supply-side rhetoric showed that, in 1980, much was agreed. That is to say, the Reagan economic program by no means came out of the blue. The language of the Joint Economic Committee reports of 1979 and 1980 is remarkably similar to the Reagan Campaign Policy Memorandum No. 1, discussed below. In 1980, Senator Bentsen and Ronald Reagan spoke the same language. This language grew directly out of the intellectual ferment of the decade; it was a response to the economic crisis of the 1970s.

This is not to take anything away from Ronald Reagan, a remarkable figure. Given the popular image of a detached role-playing president, few noticed that Ronald Reagan held a degree in economics. As it happens, his successor as president also had been an economics major as an undergraduate. But where George Bush was graduated from Yale in 1945, Reagan had the advantage of having been graduated from Eureka College in 1932. That is to say, the economics he was taught was untouched by the Keynesian revolution, and thus appropriate to the problems of the 1980s. It was also leavened by

personal experience; in his autobiography, the president describes
his curriculum:

> At Eureka College, my major was economics, but I think my own
> experience with our tax laws in Hollywood probably taught me more
> about practical economic theory than I ever learned in a classroom or
> from an economist, and my views on tax reform did not spring from
> what people called supply-side economics.
>
> At the peak of my career at Warner Bros., I was in the ninety-four
> percent tax bracket; that meant that after a certain point, I received
> only six cents of each dollar I earned and that the government got the
> rest. The IRS took such a big chunk of my earnings that after a while
> I began asking myself whether it was worth it to keep on taking
> work. . . . If I decided to do one less picture, that meant other people
> at the studio in lower tax brackets wouldn't work as much either; the
> effect filtered down, and there were fewer jobs available.[4]

While at another point the president says he was accused of ma-
joring in extra-curricular activities, the imprint of his education kept
popping up during his presidency. He didn't learn about the monetary implications of gold, for example, from his economic advisers. At
one point a prominent econometrician branded him a dunce for saying a trade deficit can sometimes be a sign of a healthy economy; the
econometrician was simply wrong and the Eureka College economist
right. Then there is the extraordinary matter of Ibn Khaldūn, who
popped up in a presidential press conference in October 1981:

> When we say "cutting taxes" we're really leaving a word off. There is
> a difference between reducing rates and reducing tax revenues; and we
> only have to look back just shortly before Lyndon Johnson's term to
> when John F. Kennedy was President, and when he followed the
> policy across the board against the same kind of economic advice that
> we've been getting—that he couldn't do that. But he cut those tax
> rates, and the government ended up getting more revenues because of
> the almost instant stimula to the economy.
>
> Now, that's what's being called today—they didn't use the term
> then—supply-side economics. And you don't even have to stop at that
> point. If you look at our reductions in capital gains tax, if you go back
> to the twenties when Mellon was the secretary of the treasury under
> Coolidge and was doing this every time; that kind of a tax cut brings us
> back, I've told, I think, some of you before, to a principle that goes
> back, at least I know, as far as the 14th Century when a Moslem

philosopher named Ibn Khaldūn said: In the beginning of the dynasty great tax revenues were gained from small assessments. At the end of the dynasty, small revenues were gained from large assessments. And we're trying to get down to the small assessments and the great revenues.[5]

We'd also discovered Ibn Khaldūn at the *Journal*; his views were brought to our attention in a letter to the editor from Stanley Ungar of Valley Stream, New York, and we published a 500-word extract from *The Mugaddimah*, which clearly does presage the Laffer curve. But I am entirely disposed to believe the president when he says he didn't learn tax policy from supply-side economics but from Ibn Khaldūn. Where else but at Eureka College in 1932 would he have learned to spell it Khaldoon, as he does in his autobiography?

This mixture of modern and ancient influences worked its way into the Reagan campaign. At the Reagan for President office, Martin Anderson pulled together the discussions among the candidate and his advisers to draft Policy Memorandum No. 1 in August 1979. "For many years it has been an article of faith among academic economists, and especially so among Republican politicians, that any attempt to increase employment would lead to more inflation," he wrote. "The consequence has been political paralysis in regard to the development of a powerful economic policy by Republicans."

The Phillips curve was not "an iron law," however. "If we look carefully at the experience of the last two decades—from 1960 to now—we can see that there has been no trade-off between inflation and unemployment. What everyone believed was happening simply was not happening. . . . It is thus possible to reduce inflation and stimulate economic growth without having an economic bellyache, recession or depression."

In particular, "the level of taxation in the United States has now become so high that it is stifling the incentive for individuals to earn, save and invest. We must have a program—of at least three years duration—of across-the-board tax cuts. The personal income tax rate must be cut by a specific percentage every year for three years, especially the higher, incentive-destroying marginal rates. The capital gains tax, and the corporate income tax must be cut by a commensurate amount. Tax rates that are too high destroy incentives to earn, cripple productivity, lead to deficit financing and inflation, and create unemployment. We can go a long way toward restoring the economic health of this country by moving toward reasonable, more fair levels of taxation."

Policy Memorandum No. 1 also offered a number of other proposals: indexing of income tax brackets to prevent "bracket creep", a hidden tax increase as inflation pushed everyone into higher brackets with no gain in real income. A drastic reduction in federal regulation to free the economy. The return of some programs to state levels. Except in a section warning against abrupt changes in economic policy, monetary policy was not mentioned.

The memorandum also noted, "The budget deficit must be reduced and eventually eliminated, but in doing so it is important to remember that every deficit is a function of both revenue and expenditures. The most effective way to eliminate the deficit is to reduce the rate of growth of federal expenditures and to simultaneously stimulate the economy so as to increase revenues in such a way that the private share grows proportionately more than the government share."

Spending control contemplated procedural reforms, at least some of which would require constitutional amendment: a two-thirds majority in Congress to pass spending bills, a line-item veto allowing the president to delete specific items in appropriations bills, a limit on the amount of income that could be taken in taxes, and a constitutional amendment requiring a balanced budget.[6]

Obviously large hunks of this program, especially those pertaining to spending control, remain unrealized even in the 1990s. But of course, Reagan was only president; there are two other branches of government. In particular, the House of Representatives remained under control of the opposition party through the eight years of his tenure. If he failed spectacularly at balancing the budget, it is far from clear whether this was a failure of economic philosophy or political authority.

In any event, Policy Memorandum No. 1 proved to be a remarkably consistent basis for the Reagan campaign and the Reagan presidency. As the campaign developed, the proposal for a phased tax rate reduction became an explicit endorsement of the Kemp-Roth bill; this by-name credit was a price the Reagan campaign was glad to pay to avoid Kemp entering the race and draining votes from Reagan in his battle with George Bush.

Mr. Bush of course denounced the Reagan plan as "voodoo economics." Independent candidate John Anderson said the only way

Reagan could cut taxes, increase defense spending, and balance the budget was with "blue smoke and mirrors." Skepticism abounded among many Wall Street economists with their flow-of-funds deficit preoccupation, central bankers including Paul Volcker, and even some economists willing to support Reagan, in particular former Council of Economic Advisers head Herbert Stein.

This issue came to a head on September 9, 1980, when candidate Reagan gave a major economic policy speech to the International Business Council in Chicago. In conjunction with that speech, the Reagan campaign issued a page of numbers, publicly endorsed by Alan Greenspan, widely trusted not to be a wide-eyed supply-sider. Anderson describes how this document was reached: At one point in the deliberations, he states, "We decided that the importance of increasing defense spending and going ahead with the full tax program was more important than balancing the federal budget quickly." But this decision was vetoed politically, especially by campaign manager Jim Baker. Whatever the economic realities, Reagan could not propose a higher deficit than Carter had promised in his administration's own blue-smoke-and-mirrors exercise.

Reagan's numbers were bailed out when the Democratic Senate Budget Committee happened to come up with new economic estimates, showing higher growth and more revenues to distribute. With this help, Anderson and Greenspan could offer numbers showing that with tax cuts, reasonable economic growth, modest budget restraint and a reasonable defense buildup, the budget could indeed be balanced by 1983. In the event, of course, spending continued to rise, economic growth faltered in 1982 and the early defense buildup proved larger than the estimate. But in the campaign, the Chicago figures were striking not for their boldness, but for their modesty. They demonstrated that the problems were not arithmetic, but political choice.

The key to this was the government's ongoing tax *increases*. Bracket creep alone insured that government revenues would grow faster than the taxpayers' incomes. In addition, the Carter administration had mandated a series of increases in the payroll tax to "fix" the social security system. Under the usual static analysis—which assumes the tax increases won't slow the economy—this spews out a stream of revenue to be divided among new spending, deficit reduction and tax increases. Consider, for example, the Carter administration budget for 1980.

In this paper exercise, government receipts were projected to

TABLE 6–1

**Carter Administration 1980 Budget
(in Billions Current Dollars)**

	1978	1984	increase	%
Gross National Product	2,106	3,546	1,440	68
Total Receipts	402.0	780.2	378.2	94
percent	19.1	22.0	26.3	
Personal Income	1,707	2,872	1,165	68
Ind. Income Tax Receipts	181.0	392.1	211.1	117
percent	10.6	13.6	18.1	

nearly double over six years. By 1984, the government would have an extra $378 billion a year to be distributed among tax reduction, deficit reduction and new military spending, not to mention new domestic spending. The only blue smoke and mirrors necessary to find "room" for the Reagan program was to believe that domestic spending could be restrained, and that the economy would follow the course sketched above despite being burdened with tax increases.

For under the administration scenario, government receipts would grow by 94 percent while the economy grew by 68 percent. Taxes would increase by nearly 3 percent of GNP. Taxes—federal taxes alone—would eat up over a quarter of all the additional revenue the economy was projected to produce. The burden of individual income taxes was to go up 117 percent, as against growth of 68 percent in income. And the Carter budgeteers were surprised by the outbreak of a tax revolt.

By the time of the 1980 election campaign, of course, the Carter administration had abandoned its assault on the three-martini lunch and was offering its own program of tax "cuts." On the personal income tax, it proposed a tax credit to offset the social security payroll tax and a credit for families with two wage earners. Neither would affect marginal tax rates, at least not above the $30,000 cap on the two-wage credit. On the business side, it offered a "refundable investment tax credit," which is to say a device to increase investment in money-losing businesses, and a "targeted investment tax credit," for investment in geographic areas approved by a government bureaucracy.

On economic issues, then, the voters in 1980 had a clear choice of philosophies. While both candidates advocated tax cuts, the two plans were of dramatically different shapes. President Carter proposed cuts aimed at income redistribution and industrial planning. Candidate Reagan offered an across-the-board tax cut, intended to spur the economy, and faith in market mechanisms. One candidate proposed to protect the losers, while the other proposed to reward the winners. The issue was growth versus fairness.

Economics, of course, was not the only issue in the 1980 elections. The big drama was the hostage crisis in Iran, the most memorable debate line was "there you go again," a cryptic slight everyone in the country immediately understood as a reference to a "mean streak" mixed with Jimmy Carter's personal piety. The decisive issue, I have no doubt, was a generalized sense of crisis that surrounded Mr. Carter and his administration. Yet beneath the hostages, the dealings with the Soviets, the fistfights on gasoline lines, that crisis was profoundly an economic one.

On election day, after all, the latest reports showed inflation accelerating to 15 percent a year. In early 1980, the economy sputtered into a short recession. Unable to solve its economic perplexities, stumbling since August of 1971 from one economic crisis to another, the country lost its sense of balance in foreign affairs as well as domestic ones. Reagan offered a change. But the program he articulated was not drawn on a napkin, but was drawn from the temper of the times and the cutting edge of intellectual debate. It should have been no surprise that he carried 45 states.

• • •

While the politicians traded sallies on taxes, deficits and hostages, the intellectual debate of 1980 delved into the ethereal issue of expectations—another intellectual issue that was to have profound effects on the real events of the next few years, and will need to be understood to follow the events of the 1990s.

The basic notion of expectations is simple: Economics being a branch of human behavior, reality is often less important than perception. The behavior of consumers and investors will depend on the economic conditions of the moment only as the present shapes what conditions they *expect* to pertain in the future. If this is a truism, the surging inflation of the 1970s made it manifest and unmistakable.

Interest rates, everyone came to understand, had to include Irving Fisher's inflation premium. If borrowers and lenders all expected that inflation would be 10 percent a year, the interest rate had to be,

say, 13 percent to provide any net return. It followed that if, overnight, borrowers and lenders all decided inflation would be only 5
percent, interest rates would fall to 8 percent. (Or as financial types
would put it, bond prices would soar. Since existing bonds pay a set
nominal rate of interest, their price in today's trading rises when
interest rates fall; their market prices vary so they "yield" the same
payment as new bonds issued at current rates of interest.)

So too with wages. Employees know that to improve their standard
of living they need wage increases that exceed inflation. In collective
bargaining, unions will negotiate for wage increases above the inflation rate they expect over the life of the contract. If they expect more
inflation they will demand larger settlements. And since wages are a
large component of prices, to same extent this expectation is self-
fulfilling. Larger wage increases in the expectation of inflation will
push up product prices and cause inflation. Keynesians saw this as the
heart of the inflation problem; thus their recurrent resort to various
types of wage–price controls.

Monetarists, by contrast, believed that wage–push could cause
inflation only if it were *accommodated* by the central bank supplying
more money. But monetarists also focused on expectations in trying
to explain the effect of money growth on the real economy, that is, in
debating whether faster growth of the money supply would have a
purely financial effect of higher inflation, or whether it could be used
to fight recession, boosting the production of real goods and employment in real jobs.

As the 1970s wore on, monetary policy seemed to have less and less
effect on the real economy. What stagflation meant was that faster
growth in the money supply would simply be dissipated in inflation.
Consumers and investors had been sensitized, and when they saw or
felt faster money growth they boosted their inflationary expectations.
The answer economists arrived at was that monetary growth can boost
production only if it catches the public by surprise; anticipated money
growth will only cause inflation.

This gave birth to an entirely new branch of economics, the "rational expectations school." The key paper, by Thomas Sargent and
Neil Wallace, was published only in 1975.[7] But it quickly made its
way into the public discourse. In April of 1979 it was elaborated in
The Wall Street Journal, for example, by Mark Willes, then president
of the Federal Reserve Bank of Minneapolis.[8]

These insights raise the intriguing possibility of affecting expectations *directly*. If you could somehow hypnotize the public into *be-*

lieving that inflation will go away, inflation *would* go away. More realistically, if you announced a big change in economic policy and the public actually believed it would happen, an important part of the effect would take place immediately—upon the announcement rather than its actual implementation.

These thoughts, heavy in the intellectual air of 1980, were to have an important bearing on the Reagan tax policies. Martin Feldstein, president of the National Bureau of Economic Research and later Ronald Reagan's chief economic adviser, constructed an expectation-based argument:

> [I]f it is done in the right way, a multi-year tax cut could bring immediate increases in investment, savings and individual effort, without any increases in the government deficit now or in the future.
>
> The most important thing to consider in a tax-cut strategy is that all important economic decisions are based on expectations. What matters for *current* actions—investment, saving, the choice of jobs—is not the current tax rates but the rates that are *expected*.
>
> Congress can therefore improve current incentives without any increase in the current deficit by enacting *now* a schedule of *future* tax cuts. These precommitted tax cuts can be financed as they occur out of the automatic revenue increases produced by inflation and out of the savings that could result from a slowdown in the growth of government spending. The commitment to a schedule of future tax cuts would give Congress and the government agencies time to shape their spending plans to the lower level of available revenue. Thus, while an immediate tax cut generally means an increased deficit, precommitted future tax cuts can change incentives without any deficits.[9]

Unfortunately, the future-tax-cut scenario could also be interpreted in an opposite way. From his temporary perch at the *Journal*, Paul Craig Roberts answered the Feldstein argument.

> What we have here is the responsible economist's version of the "Laffer curve." Instead of getting the revenues back after you cut taxes, you get them back before you cut taxes. Politicians are always attracted by the prospect of something for nothing, and they will find the "Feldstein curve" enticing as it allows all of the benefits of tax cuts before they go into effect. But the question is, Will it work?
>
> Professor Feldstein is right that people's current actions will be affected if they expect their tax rates to be lower in the future, but the effect may be the opposite of what he supposes. Remember, a reduc-

tion in marginal tax rates changes relative prices. It makes both leisure and current consumption more expensive in terms of forgone income, causing people to shift into work out of leisure and into investment out of current consumption.

However, if you know that the prices of leisure and current consumption are not going to rise now but at a future date, you might decide to enjoy them while they are still cheap and wait until the price (tax rate) actually changes before you work harder and save more. If people respond in this way, then the promise of lower tax rates in the future would cause GNP and tax revenues to be lower in the present. . . .

The key to a successful tax cut is one that raises the price of leisure and current consumption right now, not in some future year. Announcing a future tax cut can produce the opposite of the desired results as people withhold income until the future period when its after-tax value is greater. . . . That's why we need a tax cut that doesn't dawdle before it goes into effect.[10]

Expectational arguments also ran heavily through "Avoiding a GOP Economic Dunkirk," a paper written just after the election by Rep. Jack Kemp and Rep. David Stockman, later Reagan's OMB director. It began:

President Reagan will inherit thoroughly disordered credit and capital markets, punishingly high interest rates, and a hair-trigger market psychology poised to respond strongly to early economic policy signals in either favorable or unfavorable ways. . . .

Thatcherization can be avoided only if the initial economic policy package simultaneously spurs the output side of the economy and also elicits a swift downward revision of inflationary expectations in the financial markets. . . .

High, permanent inflation expectations have killed the long-term bond and equity markets that are required to fuel a capital spending boom and regeneration of economic growth . . . Again, the primary aim must be to shift long-term inflation expectations downward and restore bond and equity markets.[11]

The "Dunkirk Memo," echoing earlier statements by Rep. Stockman, asserted that "the federal budget has now become an automatic 'coast-to-coast soup line' that dispenses remedial aid with almost reckless abandon, converting the traditional notion of automatic stabilizers into multitudinous outlay spasms throughout the budget." It warned,

[T]he first hard look at the unvarnished FY 81 and 82 budget posture by our own OMB people is likely to elicit coronary contractions among some, and produce an intense polarization between supply-side tax cuts and the more fiscally orthodox. An internecine struggle over deferral or temporary abandonment of the tax program could ensue. The result would be a severe demoralization and factionalization of GOP ranks and an erosion of our capacity to govern successfully and revive the economy before November 1982.

• • •

"Hey, I'm thirty years old, and I thought these guys had discovered I was a genius and they were going to let me take over the U.S. government," remembers John Rutledge, who showed up as the new supply-sider between Ronald Reagan's election and inauguration. Way out in Claremont, California, separate from both Mundell-Laffer and Ture-Roberts brands of supply side economics, he had come to parallel conclusions. Upon being designated director of the Office of Management and Budget, David Stockman had installed Rutledge and his "rational expectations" model in the transition offices in the New Executive Office Building, to churn out some numbers on the effects of the Reagan tax policies.

Rutledge's numbers basically showed that with tax cuts growth would resume, that with restrained money growth inflation would rapidly subside, and that therefore interest rates would break. But various members of the economic transition team quarreled with various aspects of the prediction. Some monetarists noticed too sharp a drop in monetary "velocity," some argued that inflation could come down only with long lags. And many argued that, whatever else, the Reagan forecast could not show large deficits.

There are two standard arguments against deficits: (1) They are inflationary, and (2) the government borrowing they represent adds to demand for funds, pushes up interest rates and thus "crowds out" private investment. Since his forecasts showed both lower inflation and lower interest rates, Rutledge puzzled over why deficits should be so important. The answer was that they mattered politically; showing a low deficit projection was essential to preserving the political coalition.

At a definitive dinner meeting dubbed "the last supper," participants came armed with numbers cranked out in the basements of the

OMB and Treasury, showing "hellacious" deficits. So the Rutledge numbers were unacceptable, and the consensus, he says, was "let's make up what we want and use the model to prove it." After the meeting, he was reduced to a "mechanic" turning out numbers driven by the various demands of the political coalition to show growth, low inflation, a defense buildup and low deficits. The 30-year-old Rutledge packed his bags and left Washington never to return.

More worldly diners at the last supper remember this as merely the usual pushing and shoving in an inherently political process. And in fact, the Rosy Scenario of 1981 did offer defensible, internally consistent economics that conceivably might have happened. The main difficulty was, as Craig Roberts has repeatedly stressed, that it assumed a less stringent monetary policy than the Federal Reserve actually delivered. "Instead of evenly spreading the reduction in money growth over a six-year period, the Federal Reserve delivered 75 percent of the reduction in the first year."[12]

In many respects, the arguments at the last supper were arguments over the power of expectations. Take velocity, the rate of turnover of the money stock. If it is stable, inflation must be ground out of the system slowly and mechanically. If inflation can be quenched quickly, by affecting expectations directly, velocity must by definition be volatile. Despite these differences, though, the participants agreed on the need for tax cuts. Rutledge says a decade later, "If Rosy Scenario played a part in passing the tax cut, maybe it was worth it." And Roberts reports that when he saw the actual monetary policy developing, he wrote Treasury Secretary Regan that the turndown in money numbers made it "imperative" that the Reagan economic policy be passed with "an early due date."

When the Reagan tax cut reached Capitol Hill, Ways and Means Chairman Danny Rostenkowski inaugurated an annual ritual. He had not developed the "dead on arrival" lyric, but already had the melody: "The strategy would be to get Kemp-Roth out of the way so we can start working from concepts." He wanted a "consensus" bill "that the whole committee can be proud of."[13]

In fact, the main Democratic initiative in 1981 was a massive reduction in marginal tax rates for the richest taxpayers. Under the then-existing law, taxes on wages and salaries were capped at 50 percent of income, making this the top marginal rate. The higher marginal rates, up to 70 percent, applied only to "unearned income"—an "unearned income" rate is a penalty on savings and investment that makes no economic sense whatever, especially if you believe that the same stream of returns is also "double taxed" through the corporate income tax. However, people with a lot of investment income tend to be wealthy. The rich are different, as Hemingway said, they have money.

Whether through fear or guile, the initial Reagan proposals took no special effort to obliterate the whole concept of "unearned income." Under the concept of a 30 percent reduction over three years, the 70 percent rate would come down to 50 percent, making the distinction obsolete. But the Democrats raised the ante, in an amendment named after Rep. William Brodhead (D., Mich.), dropping the 70 percent rate to 50 percent in the first year of the program.

The idea was to stimulate investment and thus economic growth. Chairman Rostenkowski did not ask the Congressional Budget Office or the Joint Tax Committee to estimate how much of the benefit of Brodhead would go to the top 20 percent of the income distribution and how much to the bottom 20 percent. Instead, he offered the Brodhead amendment as part of the Rostenkowski package, remarking, "I guess it would be pretty hard for the Republicans to vote against that, wouldn't it?"[14] The Brodhead amendment also had a big effect on the tax on capital gains, which was applied after a 60 percent "exclusion." With the tax applied to 40 percent of the gain, the 70 percent top rate dropped to 50 percent. The Rostenkowski-led Democrats slashed the top rate on capital gains to 20 percent.

The tax cut was repeatedly diluted, though, by the congenital fear of deficits, and by OMB director Stockman's efforts to exploit this fear to curb the "coast-to-coast soup line." To reduce the deficit, or at least static estimates of future deficits, the tax cut was postponed. The original Kemp proposal had been for an immediate 30 percent cut in marginal rates. In Kemp-Roth this became 10 percent a year over three years. In the final bill this was compromised to 25 percent over four years. Similar compromises delayed the timing of the cut. During the Reagan campaign, the initial tranche was to have been retroactive to January 1, 1981, but this date was postponed first to July and then to October.

In the administration proposals, too, there had been no effort to index the tax brackets to stop bracket creep; this proposal was too "expensive" in foregone revenues. Another way to look at Rosy Scenario was as a plan to bring inflation down only slowly so that bracket creep would continue to provide revenues to keep deficits falling. Thanks to Sen. Robert Dole, the ultimate bill did index the tax brackets, but from fear of deficits not until the 1985 tax year. As the bill neared passage, economists at W. R. Grace and Company calculated that if inflation remained at 8 percent over four years, the 25 percent cut would merely offset 98 percent of bracket creep. In addition, there were previously enacted increases in the social security payroll tax.

"Remember, the 'effective' date for the personal income tax cut is important only from the point of view of an accountant. For the economy, what is important is the change in tax rates applicable to income earned in 1981. Since only one-quarter of the calendar year remains after the effective date of the cut, in general only one-fourth of the 5 percent rate reduction—1.25 percent—will be applicable to income earned in 1981," Art Laffer and Charles Kadlec wrote in their September investment letter. Similarly with the other two mid-year tranches of the cut: "The so-called 5-10-10 tax cut covering 33 months is in reality 1.25-8.75-10-5 extending over 48 months."

The tax cut had been pared in size and delayed because of the fear that it would add to the deficit; and of course, other taxes were rising. "After adjustment for a 10 percent increase in the price level that now appears all but assured for 1981, the vast majority of taxpayers have been pushed into a higher tax bracket even with the personal income tax."[15]

Unless you believed that expectation alone would turn the trick, there would be no help from the tax cut in 1981. And with Volcker's tight money already in effect, signs of an economic slowdown were appearing. We mused on this in the *Journal* under the title, "Taxes and Recession," as the tax cut neared passage. Brodhead would help, we said, and the cuts will break the momentum of ongoing tax increases. If the inflation abated more rapidly than the Grace estimate, tax cuts would become real. Still, "the tenuous nature of any real tax cut and the signs of economic softness certainly carry their warnings. . . . If the current slowdown proves more severe than we now expect, surely the answer is to move marginal tax rates down faster, to give the economy not a nominal tax cut but a real one."[16]

"What we passed was the Feldstein bill," Craig Roberts told me just after passage of the tax cuts he'd worked for since drafting the first Kemp-Roth bill. Craig does not have a reputation as an optimist, but the point was clear. Unless you were a big believer in a purely expectational effect, the tax cuts were not coming soon enough or forcefully enough to curb the recession already gathering as they were enacted.

A Michael 1 tax cut was legislated, all right, but from fear of the dread deficit taking effect slowly and grudgingly. A recession was coming quickly and forcefully. To understand why you had to look to the monetary side of the policy mix, to back up to 1979 and follow what had happened to monetary policy.

7

The Perils of Paul

By the time the Reagan tax cut passed in August 1981, Paul Volcker had been chairman of the Federal Reserve for two years. For all that time, he had been trying to apply the monetary brake to curb inflation domestically and protect the dollar internationally. The tight-money side of the prescription Bob Mundell had sketched at Michael 1 came into effect a year and a half before the tax-cut side was even legislated. Well, the monetary side had *sort of* come into effect. Volcker clearly *wanted* tight money to control inflation and protect the dollar, but how do you *tell* if money is tight?

These two issues—the timing and methodology of monetary policy—are the keys to understanding the 1982 recession. This downturn set the stage for the economics of the Seven Fat Years. And also, in the sense of panic it spread, for the misinterpretation of those years.

For when Paul Volcker came back from Belgrade, his big announcement was that the Fed would stop targeting interest rates and start targeting bank reserves and monetary aggregates, popularly understood as "the money supply." To those who understood, this was big news indeed.

It is not entirely clear, to say the least, that on the road to Belgrade Chairman Volcker became a born-again monetarist. One should always be suspicious about methodological protestations from those who deal in markets, whether central bankers or pit traders. They understand the intellectual arguments and can brilliantly expound their methodology of the moment. But over time they tend to pick and choose among methodologies as their mood changes; they want the explanation that gives them the result their instinct says they should reach. Volcker's imperative, understandably enough, was to end inflation.

It is clear, however, that the Fed did have serious procedural problems; it had to learn again how to run monetary policy. This learning process had a great impact on the economic events of the early 1980s, puzzling everyone including policymakers and our top economists. Volcker did get inflation under control, but as he learned how to accomplish this, the economy stumbled through two recessions. When he figured it out, the Seven Fat Years started.

• • •

Understanding this—and much of the subsequent debate—requires a plunge into the lore of central banking, which happily is not quite as mysterious as central bankers like to pretend.

A central bank runs monetary policy by buying and selling assets, usually government bonds but technically also foreign exchange or gold. If it buys, it pays out money and expands bank reserves. If it sells, it takes in money and contracts reserves. Bank reserves control how much banks can lend to their customers, and thus financial variables such as the money supply, interest rates and the availability of credit.

A central bank tries to use monetary policy to nudge the real economy; readily available credit and low interest rates will tend to spur borrowing for office buildings and cars, for example. But monetary policy naturally has a more direct effect on the financial sector. In particular, a central bank pretty much sets the rate of inflation, the general increase in the price level. It can't do this, however, on the basis of month-old price indexes; it has to decide today whether to buy assets or sell. Debates over monetary policy are basically debates over what immediate yardstick to follow: What should the central bank "target" in deciding when to sell assets and when to buy.

Usually a central bank will target interest rates, or more precisely an interest rate. The Federal Reserve uses the Federal Funds rate, or the rate at which banks lend to each other on an overnight basis. The principal reason this rate is used is that the Fed knows it can readily control it. Whether or not the overnight rate has much economic significance, at least the Fed knows what it has done.

The problem is that one interest rate may not have much to do with other interest rates, let alone everything else in the economy. There is an unpredictable animal economists and financial-market types call the "yield curve," a graph of interest rates for notes and bonds of different maturities. Even if the Fed can hit the Fed Funds rate it wants, the yield curve will simply change if other rates march to a different drummer.

The chief alternative target, much publicized by Milton Friedman and his disciples, is "the money supply." The money supply is an aggregate of financial statistics, available far more quickly than consumer price indexes. A central bank can use monetary aggregates as today's (or at least this week's) compass, on the assumption that there is a reasonable relationship between the aggregates and prices or economic growth.

As with interest rates, the central bank can only target one statistical aggregate closely, whether—in ascending order of size—bank reserves, the monetary base, M-1, M-2, and still others. The monetarist economists had long argued that the various aggregates moved generally together and any one would do, but by 1979 this no longer seemed self-evident. The high inflation had given birth to a variety of new financial instruments that blurred the distinction between ready cash and savings. No one was sure whether money market funds and the like were "transaction balances" the aggregates are designed to include or "investment balances" they are designed to exclude. Defining "the money supply" became a problem and was to become a bigger one.

These perplexities led to a new interest in an old target, gold. The long association of gold and central banking is more than a historical accident, but has a sound basis in economic theory. Commodity prices, in particular sensitive ones such as precious metals, react much more quickly than consumer prices. Thus they can be used as an advance indication of how central bank policy is affecting the economy. Economists over the years, notably Irving Fisher, have theorized about using "baskets" of sensitive commodities prices as a guide for monetary policy. As Bob Mundell said at Michael 1, it doesn't *have* to be gold.

Gold was often misunderstood even when it was widely used. The mercantilist economists against whom Adam Smith inveighed thought of gold accumulations as national wealth. In fact, no huge gold hoard was necessary to use a gold-price target for monetary policy. David Ricardo, that epitome of classical economics, had worked out wider "bond points" and narrower "gold points." If you bought and sold bonds you would expand or contract the money supply, without ever reaching the point to buy or sell gold.

This scheme too is not without its difficulties, historical prejudice aside. Gold is not immutably linked to the general price level; historically big discoveries of gold and silver have caused inflation in monetary systems based on them. Especially now that all currencies are divorced from gold, it's not easy to know the appropriate price. Picking too low a price will cause monetary contraction, picking too high a price will cause inflation.

To complete the intellectual possibilities, a central bank can simply target an exchange rate. The Austrian central bank, for example, could simply target the German mark, accepting German monetary policy as its own. Or all nations in a currency bloc could target the nth nation, which then would set monetary policy for all, either as a matter of discretion or by targeting one anchor or another. For example, all nations could fix their currency to the dollar, and the Federal Reserve could target gold at, say, $35 an ounce. This is how, intellectually at least, Bretton Woods was supposed to work.

• • •

What Volcker conceded after Belgrade was that Fed Funds targeting did not work in the superheated 1970s. Using the overnight rate to control inflation depends on predicting the rate at which reserves will be injected or drained, and the Fed couldn't keep up with inflationary expectations. It would set a Fed Funds target expecting to drain bank reserves and slow inflation, but the market would push rates up even faster, and to hit the target band the Fed would find itself injecting reserves. Interest rate targeting had become an engine of inflation.

So after Belgrade the Fed chose to target a path for the reserves in the banking system, trying to achieve a given growth of the monetary aggregates. In the first week of the experiment, Fed Funds were allowed to trade as high as 14¾ percent and as low as 7 percent. Soon everyone in the financial markets was watching the weekly release of the M-1 aggregate as the cue to Fed actions.

Given the intellectual constellations of the time, this choice was for practical purposes inevitable. Milton Friedman's brilliance had not only reestablished classical economics in the face of the Keynesian consensus, but had stamped "the money supply" on the foreheads of a generation of disciples. If the Fed was to abandon its traditional procedures, his monetarist alternative was the obvious one.

It was not the alternative, though, anyone at Michael 1 would have chosen. They would have advised a "price rule"—that the Fed should target a sensitive price, usually but not necessarily gold, determined in the marketplace and thus reflecting both the *supply* of money and the *demand* for money.

The "money supply," as commonly understood, is more properly called a "monetary aggregate," that is to say, a compilation of various financial statistics. An aggregate measures the *quantity* of money, produced by an interaction between the supply of money and the demand for money. While a central bank determines the supply, the marketplace determines the demand. Reserves injected into the banks by the Fed grow into demand deposits when the banks make loans. So if M-1 grows, we do not know for sure whether it's because the Fed injected more reserves, or because the banks' customers sought more loans. Does the statistic move because the Fed supplied more money, or the market demanded more money?

In technical jargon, is "velocity" stable or easily predictable? Velocity, the rate at which the money supply is turned into GNP, is a reflection of the demand for money. So is the "multiplier," the rate at which bank reserves, called "high-powered money," are turned into demand deposits and counted in M-1. In the monetarist framework, these factors are assumed to be constant or easily predictable. Yet not entirely predictable, even monetarists concede, which is why they urge the Fed to eschew fine-tuning and simply expand a chosen aggregate at a constant rate, say 3 percent a year.

The diners at Michael 1 doubted that money demand was stable in the world they saw around them. Perhaps it is stable in stable times, especially when currency is also linked to gold, as it was under Bretton Woods prior to 1973 and also in the bulk of the period studied by Friedman's epic with Anna J. Schwartz, *A Monetary History of the United States, 1867–1960*.[1] But nothing looked very stable in the inflationary, fiat-currency 1970s.

With big inflation, for example, consumers would not want to hold currency. They would shift to high-interest deposits not counted in narrow aggregates, or to real assets like real estate or gold, not counted at all. This would mean that demand for money would fall, pulling down the statistical aggregate. When the aggregate fell, the Fed would inject more bank reserves, fueling the inflation. Yet if the real economy swung into boom, say because taxes were cut, the demand for money would grow, pushing up the aggregates. Watching the aggregates grow because of higher money demand, the Fed would worry about inflation, choke off bank reserves, curtail the availability of credit, push up interest rates and stop the recovery. In the post-1979 experiment, both happened.

• • •

The 1979 change to money-supply targets did start to break the inflation. Inflation peaked in January 1980, with the consumer price index jumping 1.4 percent in a single month, and price of gold peaking at incredible heights, $850 an ounce at the London fixing and trading at $875 on the Comex in New York. This was 25 times the official price when President Nixon closed the gold window less than nine years earlier.

Among the effects of this incredible run-up, above all in 1979, was a revival of interest in gold as a measure of monetary policy and a predictor of inflation. We argued in the *Journal:*

> An ounce of gold has undergone no permutations this summer. But the dollar that was worth 1/300th of an ounce of gold six weeks ago is worth only 1/380th of an ounce today. With the dollar declining that spectacularly in its ability to purchase one thing, can a further decline in its ability to purchase other things be far behind?
>
> Nor has the supply of gold in the world changed much since mid-August. The supply of dollars, however, has continued to surge. Naturally, each dollar is worth less gold. Even more importantly, this surge has led people to expect still further dollar creation in the future, diminishing their willingness to hold dollars or dollar assets. In short, the demand for dollars has fallen, and the other side of that is an increase in the demand for gold.[2]

This drew on discussions not only at Michael 1, but even more intensively at the Lehrman Institute. Lewis Lehrman was a disciple of the late French economist Jacques Rueff, the architect of General de Gaulle's economic policies. Rueff had suggested salvaging Bretton Woods by raising the $35 gold price, an idea that drew derision from sophisticates in the United States. Their thinking stopped with the observation that such a change would only help the French, who illogically held large gold reserves, and the two big producers, the South Africans and Russians. In fact, Rueff's suggestion would in all likelihood have saved the world untold misery.

As the gold price soared from $380 to $875 in 1979 and 1980, we discovered Professor Roy W. Jastram of the University of California at Berkeley, who went on to publish "The Golden Constant."[3] In September 1979 he published "The Cautionary Demand for Gold," which noted that when one nation shows economic and political turbulence, its currency will decline as holders seek safe havens in other currencies. "But what happens when danger is sensed in every direction? There is one 'currency' with no indigenous difficulties—gold. The cautionary demand for it is really a short position against all national currencies."[4]

In 1980, Sen. Jesse Helms and Rep. Ron Paul managed to attach to a passing bill an amendment directing the secretary of the treasury to set up and chair a commission to "conduct a study to assess and make recommendations with regard to the policy of the United States Government concerning the role of gold in domestic and international monetary systems."

With a little lobbying by David Stockman and others, the 1980 Republican platform read: "The severing of the dollar's link with real commodities in the 1960s and 1970s, in order to preserve economic goals other than dollar stability, has unleashed hyperinflationary forces at home and monetary disorder abroad, without bringing any of the desired economic benefits. One of the most urgent tasks in the period ahead will be the restoration of a dependable monetary standard—that is, an end to inflation." As Ronald Reagan put it on the campaign trail, "No nation in history has ever survived fiat money, money that did not have precious metal backing."[5]

• • •

No one in the Carter administration had studied economics at Eureka College, however, and an air of economic crisis surrounded the 1980 presidential campaign. In particular, with the shift to monetary aggregate targets interest rates had suddenly come unhinged. When inflation started to fall after the January peak, Irving Fisher and all previous experience taught that interest rates should also decline. But under money-quantity targets prices started to fall but interest rates surged. The Fed Funds rate rose to 17.19 percent in March from 11.43 percent in September of 1979. The average prime rate reached 19.77 percent in April, up from September's 12.90 percent. And Treasury bonds, long rates, rose to 11.87 percent in March from 8.68 percent the previous September.

Casting about for an anti-inflation program, the Carter administration discovered that in abolishing price control authority, Congress had overlooked the Credit Control Act of 1969. After all, the act had never before been used. Arguably it was never intended to be used, having been passed primarily to embarrass President Nixon into imposing controls. It modestly provided that the president could direct the Federal Reserve to "regulate or control any or all extensions of credit."

In March of 1980, President Carter announced he was invoking the act so that monetary restraint "can be achieved in ways that spread the burden reasonably and fairly." The notion was that the Fed would stop the extension of credit for purposes deemed bad, leaving more money and lower interest rates for purposes deemed good.

The Fed knew better; indeed in announcing the credit controls Chairman Volcker proclaimed himself against credit controls. But it felt it had to go along, in part because it too was rattled by the curious path of interest rates. What emerged was a series of complicated regulations requiring banks to post new reserves at the Fed—in effect a tax since banks don't receive interest on Fed reserves. The new reserves were due if banks made frowned-upon loans such as increases in outstanding credits on credit cards, bank overdrafts and money market funds. Nicer loans, for mortgages, autos and furniture, needed no special reserves. But banks were expected to hold the growth of all loans during the year to 6 percent to 9 percent.

Chairman Volcker explained there would be "a consultative process." Which is to say, details would be made up as you went along. After mobilizing a staff of paper shufflers and parceling out different sectors of the economy to various members of its Board, the Fed found itself facing the same kind of questions the Nixon price controllers faced in 1971. For example:

Q: Regulation Z, various state laws (and possibly other federal regulations) require a creditor to give a consumer advance notice (the Board's Division of Consumer Affairs has estimated this may range from 15 to 105 days notice) of adverse changes in the terms of consumer credit agreement. Many creditors believe that in order to minimize the amount of the special deposit required by the Board's Credit Restraint regulation they will have to modify the terms of existing credit accounts. Will the Board amend Regulation Z and preempt federal and state law in order to accelerate the effective days of modified account terms?
A: The matter will be presented to the Board in the near future for its consideration.

Q: Many creditors believe that in order to minimize the amount of the special deposit they will have to modify the terms of existing credit accounts. Across-the-board modifications of account terms may have a disparate effect on certain protected classes of borrowers. Will the Board amend or interpret Regulation B to protect a creditor that makes such modifications against the allegations of Regulation B violations?
A: This matter is currently under consideration.[6]

In his announcement of controls, Chairman Volcker also said, "I'm sure we can expect the cooperation of the banks." This proved to be an understatement; the controls spooked the bankers. Confused by the regulations, they stopped making loans at all. The economy plunged. Officially the 1980 recession started in January 1980; that is, January was the peak of the previous expansion. Some slackness seemed apparent in February, and industrial production was clearly falling as the controls were implemented in March, also the month in which Congress passed the "windfall profits tax" on domestic oil production. But in April, unemployment soared by 800,000 workers. The economy seemed in a free-fall.

In May the Fed eased the credit controls, citing success in "moderating credit demands." Chairman Volcker sounded plaintive: "In particular, the program isn't designed to exert restraint on the agricultural, small business, home construction and improvement (including energy conservation), home mortgage and auto-related credit." Businesses "enlarging production capacity in response to urgent needs, such as energy, may warrant accommodations," he added.[7]

On July 6, the Fed abolished the credit controls, noting "in recent months, there has been apparent contraction in consumer borrowing. Indications are that anticipatory and speculative demands for credit have subsided and funds have been in more ample supply." President Carter put out a statement that the controls could now be removed "precisely because those controls have accomplished their purpose."[8]

The economy promptly recovered. The trough of the 1980 recession is dated to July—a six-month recession, the shortest on record.

By December the Congress had repealed the Credit Control Act, effective in 1982. The fiasco was the last gasp of the notion of running the U.S. economy through price controls. But another lesson of the episode was not learned; the remarkable credit control recession provided a foretaste of the economic dynamic that a decade later brought the Seven Fat Years to their end. In the credit crunch of 1990 we revisited the unlearned lesson of 1980. To wit, nothing causes a recession as quickly as spooking the bankers.

• • •

The credit controls and the 1980 recession left a more immediate legacy, throwing the burden of anti-inflationary adjustment forward into the Reagan administration. For the obvious shifts in the demand for money led to a burst of money creation that set back Chairman Volcker's efforts to wrench down the escalation of prices.

With spooked bankers collapsing the economy, the demand for money plunged and slowed the growth of the monetary aggregates. To meet its aggregate targets, the Fed pumped up bank reserves, trying to boost the supply of money to overcome a fall in demand. Its Open Market Committee voted to ease on April 22, May 6, May 20 and July 9. The artificial credit controls were removed in July, and money demands naturally increased. In August M-1 soared at an annual rate of 20 percent.

So a year after Belgrade, the consumer price index was still rising at 12 percent a year. And the presidential election loomed in November.

Volcker and Company hit the brakes, starting even before the election. On September 25, the Fed raised its discount rate by 0.5 percent to 11 percent. Immediately after the election the Fed, faced with a lame duck on one side and a president-elect on the other, boosted the discount rate by another percent, and to 13 percent by year-end. The prime rate soared to a record 21.5 percent on December 21, 1980. This was the monetary climate when Ronald Reagan took office in January of 1981, when Kemp and Stockman penned their "Dunkirk" memo, when John Rutledge's forecasts were sacrificed at the last supper.

As 1981 developed, inflation headed down but interest rates still refused to follow. The Fed Funds rate ranged from 14 percent to more than 19 percent. The prime got back to 20.5 percent. On the long end, Treasury bond yields actually rose to 14.14 percent in September from 11.65 percent in January. Correspondingly, of course, bond prices plunged. All this was before any tax cut had even passed, let alone taken effect. Instead of soaring in expectation of a future bonanza, bond prices collapsed.

The falling bond prices would normally be a signals of expected future inflation, but as we observed in the *Journal*, this signal was confounded by signs of continued disinflation in other markets. The gold price remained reasonably steady below $500, other commodity prices were actually falling, and the dollar was strong in the foreign exchange markets.[9]

Something curious was afoot. In his *Newsweek* column, Milton Friedman ruled out the obvious answers. Interest rates were not high because of tight money, he said, because new types of accounts made narrow aggregates misleading, and M-2 expanded 9.1 percent in the 12 months ended in July. High current budget deficits were not the answer, he said, because the current deficit was less than 3 percent of GNP, well within a historical range when interest rates had been lower. Nor was the prospect of future deficits the cause, because short-term interest rates were higher than long-term rates, which would be even more affected by future deficits and future inflation. Perhaps the bubble would burst, he said. "If it does not—back to the computer."[10]

The Michael 1 supply-siders had a diagnosis—that the problem was targeting the monetary aggregates as demand for money changed. When the credit controls killed demand in 1980, the Fed inflated the supply to meet its money quantity targets. When the economy started to pick up with the Reagan election and the prospect of better policies, rising demand for money pushed up the aggregates. Then to constrain the "money supply," the Fed would choke off credit, crippling the economy and the bond markets.

In "The Quality of Money," the May 1981 investment letter for A. B. Laffer Associates, Chuck Kadlec wrote, "Finally, the absence of the 'demand for money' in monetary policy considerations in conjunction with an overriding commitment to restrain money growth has created a policy trap for the Administration and Federal Reserve." To wit, "any increase in the demand for dollars and incipient fall in velocity can be expected to meet with stiff resistance by both the Administration and the Federal Reserve." Crimping the money supply to offset an increase in the demand for money only hampered the recovery, but by thus reducing the supply of goods for money to chase, actually was an impediment in fighting inflation. Policy should attend not the quantity of money, but the "quality of money."[11]

No one much understood this argument, let alone accepted it. Only the tiny band from Michael 1 even made it. Only a few Keynesian holdovers at the Fed questioned the emphasis on the monetary aggregates, preferring to target interest rates or the real economy. The Fed, smarting from the inflation of the 1970s, was prepared to err on the side of caution, and the administration was a force for the monetarist creed.

In April 1981, with the tax bill still in the Ways and Means Committee, the monetary aggregates started to mount. M-1 surged at an annual rate of 14 percent, and the broader aggregates were also above the Fed targets. In retrospect, we do not know the cause of this surge; was something wrong with the supply of money, or was monetary demand pushing up the quantity of money? Perhaps this was the start of the big expectational effect, but if so, it was not allowed to happen.

For the Fed was alarmed by the increase in the aggregates. Its response was characterized by Neikirk as "one of the roughest the Fed had taken during the entire three-year experiment with trying to control the monetary aggregates."[12] In its May 18 policy directive, the policy-making Federal Open Market Committee called for a "substantial deceleration" of its principal monetary aggregate, and allowed a "shortfall in growth" would be acceptable. This policy was adopted by unanimous vote; two months later the economy was in recession.

Greider remarks that the call for deceleration was "strong language compared with the bland phrases usually contained in the FOMC's policy decisions. As Volcker saw it: M-1 was rising again. He decided to step on it."[13] The money supply actually started to dive; this was when the Fed Funds rate went to 19 percent, and the bond markets soured.

The tax bill passed in August, effective in October, and stretched out into 1983; the recession was fully apparent by fall. But suddenly, in December and January, the monetary aggregates started to surge again. The administration economists, who had supported the May tightening, grew alarmed.

So did the Fed. On February 1, the Fed tightened again in the face of recession. The FOMC directive said "the committee seeks no further growth in M-1 for the January-to-March period." It added that "some decline" would be acceptable. By then the economy had already been in recession for six months.

At a press conference later that month, Ronald Reagan said,

I want to make clear today that neither this administration nor the Federal Reserve will allow a return to the fiscal and monetary policies of the past that have created the current conditions. I have met with Chairman Volcker several times during the past year. We met again earlier this week. I have confidence in the announced policies of the Federal Reserve Board. The Administration and the Federal Reserve can help bring inflation and interest rates down faster by working together than by working at cross-purposes. This administration will always support the political independence of the Federal Reserve Board.[14]

This statement stands in decided contrast to the rhetoric of most presidents and treasury secretaries, which usually want to blame the Fed for whatever goes wrong. The Reagan statement—then coming in the depths of a recession, with the prime rate over 16 percent and with a growing threat to the Reagan economic program and the Reagan presidency, reflected the monetarist advice he received from his advisers, and no doubt some personal admiration for Volcker. But most of all, it reflected what the president learned at Eureka College.

The president, it seems, believed that beating inflation was the first priority, and that a recession might be the price. Volcker would surely agree, and clearly wanted to err on the side of tightness. In the fraternity of central bankers, indeed, there is a strong strain of thought that the way to cure inflation is to provoke a recession, that the way to break inflationary expectations is to hold the economy down as long as it can take it. Not even the participants probably know how much their decisions were shaped by these attitudes, and how much by confusion over M-whatever. But it's indisputable that the May 1981 tightening came just before the peak of the expansion, and the February 1982 tightening came with recession already weighing down the economy.

That is to say, it's hard to sustain an argument that the recession was caused by tax policies not even passed when it started, or with deficits real or expected. Whether it represented confusion over monetary targets, or simple bloody-mindedness, or the inevitable price of curbing the inflation, the 1981–82 recession was preeminently a monetary event.

The lesson the nation was to carry away, of course, was entirely the opposite.

8

The Panic of '82

The mental image American society drew from the 1982 recession, and still carries around in its collective head, had nothing to do with monetary policy, or even with the end of the 1970s stagflation. Instead, the conventional wisdom is that a small band of ideologues took over the U.S. government and left future generations with a mountain of debt. For irresponsible tax cuts created a horrendous deficit, forced up interest rates, provoked the recession and upset the halcyon economy of the Carter years.

One root of this notion is simple political partisanship, which is why it's surprising to recall the contributions to the 1981 tax cut by the likes of Lloyd Bentsen and Dan Rostenkowski. But the conventional wisdom is certainly bipartisan, for it also draws on primordial Republican instincts, the ones that led Herbert Hoover to fight the depression by increasing taxes in 1932, taking the top rate to 63 percent in an effort to trim the deficit. This is not to say that adherents of the conventional wisdom are not sincere; their impression was forged in the crucible of experience, in the interplay of ideas and events in and around the recession that immediately preceded the Seven Fat Years.

It's possible to identify the precise day, indeed, that the writ was issued; it was Tuesday, December 8, 1981. The context was a gathering recession and mounting deficit predictions; the numbers ranged as high as $162 billion for fiscal 1984, compared to the fiscal 1976 record high of $66 billion (in nominal dollars). On that Tuesday an extraordinary meeting at the American Enterprise Institute featured the whole Reagan Council of Economic Advisers and a clutch of former Nixon advisers led by the ubiquitous Herb Stein, present here as he was at Camp David in August 1971. William Niskanen of the Reagan CEA, an economist courageous enough to have resigned as director of economics for Ford Motor Company over its turn toward protectionism, tried to play Galileo, with much the same immediate result.

Niskanen reported that, in simple statistical tests, there is no correlation between high deficits and high interest rates. So, too, high deficits do not seem to correlate with high inflation. Indeed, he said, "The simple relationship between deficit and inflation is as close to being empty as can be perceived." And in this, he reported, his own work was consistent with the academic literature; the finding, he said, "has surprised us and others."[1]

He received some support from the other two members of the Reagan CEA. Jerry Jordan forecast, correctly as it turned out, that despite mounting deficits and deficit forecasts, interest rates would continue their recently begun decline. And chief economic adviser Murray Weidenbaum said that while government borrowing represents a claim on private saving, the crowding out of private borrowing was not a first-order concern during a recession, when capacity was ample and private borrowing declining. He stressed that the administration still predicted *spending* would fall as a percent of GNP—that is, that ultimate government demands on the economy would decline.

Niskanen mused as to why deficits did not correlate with interest rates or inflation. For one thing, he said, there is "no necessary relationship" between deficits and monetary expansion. (As Mundell would say, fiscal and monetary policy are two separate levers). For another, inflation erodes the value of federal debt already outstanding, so part of the deficit is an inflation illusion. Also, part of the deficit may actually be healthy if it is used for government investment. But mostly, Niskanen thought the effect was international. In a world of capital mobility, you can't isolate the effect of any one economy's deficit; any crowding-out would have to be global and couldn't be detected by simple correlations within any one national economy.

These are essentially modest points, and they are pretty well supported by the academic research at the time and even more so subsequently. They are also pretty much what John Rutledge said before the last supper. With a recession, Niskanen said, "It is now recognized that some of the expected effects of the Reagan program are inconsistent and something has to give." He said he did not believe that deficits were harmless, and that he thought it would be beneficial to reduce them if other things were equal. But "the question is the balancing of other measures, and my judgment is that it is preferable to tolerate deficits in those magnitudes than to either reinflate or to add substantially to tax rates or the tax base."

Some of the ensuing discussion was academic. William Fellner of AEI engaged Niskanen, questioning "the emphasis on the world relationships," because "the $160 billion is a very large amount to be taken care of by international capital movements." (That is, the Saudis wouldn't finance it.) Also, Fellner observed, capital flows on this scale would imply a huge U.S. trade deficit.

Herb Stein's style was different. "Thank you very much for that reassuring explanation of the $160 billion deficit," he snorted at one point in the proceedings. "Somebody ought to say something on the part of Mr. Reagan, who seems to be the only member of his administration who believes deficits are inflationary."

A better measure of President Reagan's attitudes might be his remark to a group of Republican congressmen a few weeks later that he'd never been able to see why deficits "crowd out" but taxes don't. And in the event, of course, deficits were allowed to rise, inflation was curbed more quickly than most believed possible, and foreign capital inflows into the United States reached some $144 billion by 1986. But predictably, in December 1981 Herb Stein carried the day.

"Reagan Aides Abandon GOP Stance on Deficits; Economic Adviser to President Presents New Stance on Deficits," read the headline in the next day's *Washington Post*. "Budget Deficits Won't Damage Economy, Council of Economic Advisers Contends," read *The Wall Street Journal. The New York Times'* version read, "Reagan Aides Defend Deficits." All stressed the departure from traditional Republican dogma.

The next day David Broder reported, "The Reagan administration spent much of yesterday trying to quash suggestions by some of its own leading economic spokesmen that the president has gone soft on budget deficits." At the White House, spokesman Larry Speaks said the reported Niskanen statements "did not reflect the president's opinion or administration policy." At breakfast, Treasury Secretary Donald Regan had already said that the prospects of enduring deficits had "horrified" the financial markets. Vice President George Bush told an AEI luncheon that the president is "terribly concerned about the deficit."[2]

Niskanen recalls in his book that three "conservative Senators called for my immediate resignation." He reflected, "After I made peace with the White House and the senators and refused calls from the press, the controversy died away quickly. My first exposure to Washington controversy, however, led me to be extraordinarily careful with the press and to recognize that for the White House, loyalty was a one-way street."

And of course, other potential Galileos kept their peace, even until now.

• • •

Even more important in cementing the conventional wisdom was David Stockman. Indeed, the stage for Niskanen's chastening was set by Stockman's famous trip to the woodshed a month earlier. Bright and engaging, the young congressman had quickly found his way to the heart of the supply-side movement. In our circles he made his debut in 1975, with his article "The Social Pork Barrel" in Irving Kristol's *The Public Interest*.[3] By 1980 he was a mainstay, for example coauthoring the Dunkirk memo with Jack Kemp. He was also the principal force behind the 1980 Republican platform plan complaining about the "severing of the dollar's link with real commodities."

When the Reagan cabinet was announced, I was invited to appear on a television show assessing it, and the host seemed surprised that my favorite choice was Stockman. A few nights later I was approached at my tennis club by an old-line insurance executive, who asked how I could be so enthusiastic about someone "who only a few years ago had been a member of the Students for Democrat Society," the radical anti-Vietnam War student group. I replied that well, he certainly seemed all right today. My interlocutor shrugged and turned away as if I'd missed the point. I had: It was not hidden radicalism, but intellectual instability.

I knew something was amiss after "John Maynard Domenici." One of my stylistic innovations at the *Journal* was the two-name editorial, starting in 1977 with "Jimmy McGovern," saying of the Carter cabinet appointments, "if he intended to follow the foreign and defense policies so roundly rejected by the voters four years ago, it would have been nice if he had told us so during the campaign."[4] Stockman called to incite me to take on Budget Committee Chairman Pete Domenici, who was insisting on budget projections showing the Reagan program would fail. In an editorial entitled "John Maynard Domenici," we suggested, "First, if you think any of these estimates can tell you what the deficit will be in 1984, lie down until you get over it." And that if you use out-year deficit estimates to stop tax cuts, "We will be back in the same old rut of trying to balance the budget three years hence by allowing inflation to raise taxes."[5]

The editorial's impact was helped by catching Senator Domenici on recess in New Mexico, and I believe helped keep the Reagan tax bill on track. Craig Roberts wrote that Senator Domenici blamed him, calling Treasury Secretary Regan to complain. But this one was Stockman's doing.

So far fine; I do take suggestions, especially from my intellectual allies, though sometimes I reject them too. In the two decades and more that I've done this, the Domenici editorial was totally unique. For almost overnight I received and quickly published a letter defending Domenici. "The President's goal, supported overwhelmingly last Nov. 4 by the people, and shared completely by Chairman Domenici, is federal budget reduction and tax reduction. Nobody has contributed more to this cause, or worked harder to carry out this mandate, than Sen. Domenici." Signed, David Stockman, director of the Office of Management and Budget, and James A. Baker, III, chief of staff and assistant to the president.[6]

When Stockman vented his frustration in the interviews William Greider published in *The Atlantic* as "The Education of David Stockman," I concluded that Stockman's apostasy had three roots. One was simply congenital restlessness. But another was his belief in the extreme expectational argument, à la Feldstein.

"The whole thing is premised on faith," he told Greider. "The inflation premium melts away like the morning mist" once financial markets are convinced the program will in fact be implemented. "It would be cut in half in a very short period of time if the policy is credible. That sets off adjustments and changes in perception that cascade through the economy. You have a bull market in '81, after April, of historic proportions."[7] When the bond markets instead collapsed in April, he threw the baby out with the bathwater, swinging to the opposite camp, the deficit is everything.

Last, as chief budget-cutter, Stockman found deficit-mania an effective tool. Especially so since his main preoccupation was curbing the welfare state—ending "the social pork barrel," in the title of his *Public Interest* piece, or the "coast-to-coast soup line," in the phrase from the Dunkirk memo. The job of budget director is extraordinarily frustrating, dealing day after day with congressmen intent only on preserving their pet boondoggle; in recent years most budget directors have ended up seeing no alternative to higher taxes.

The Greider article was quickly read into the *Congressional Record* by gleeful Democrats. Laced with convenient tag lines like "trickle down" and "Trojan Horse," it provided as proof that the Reagan policies were an intellectual fraud, and that the tax cuts had caused the recession even before they became effective.

Even so, our assessment at the *Journal* was generally supportive of Stockman; the article was "a story about an idealist frustrated in confrontation with reality." Stockman's critics included Sen. Don Riegle, a potential adversary in Michigan politics; "Senator Mark Andrews, recently engaged in hot battle with the budget director over his pet federal program, rural electrification"; Sen. Larry Pressler and his gasohol still; Amtrak; sugar subsidies; and the Clinch River Breeder Reactor. Stockman, we said, "got far more in expenditure restraint than most budget directors or budget committee chairmen have before turning, as all of them invariably have, to leading the drive for higher taxes."[8]

Stockman's first half-year as budget director, indeed, was about the only time the machinery of the 1974 budget act actually worked. The administration was able to use its "reconciliation" process to force up-or-down votes on whole packages of budget cuts; congressmen who opposed one or another narrow-interest cut felt they had to go along with a comprehensive package aimed at budget control. Billing the measure a vote on the entire Reagan economic program, the administration was able to win on the Gramm-Latta bill in May by a margin of 60 votes.

As he made clear in his book, though, Stockman belonged to the school of thought that felt the administration didn't ask for enough, that in the first flush of electoral victory it should have sought more painful cuts. Peter Peterson's 1987 *Atlantic* article outlined such a program, arguing for a big boost in the gasoline tax, lower taxes on investment, a cut in social security benefits, a lid on the consumption of health care, and lamenting the lack of vision among our politicians. In particular, the thinking goes, the president should have used his victory to press for control of "entitlements," the vast sums of spending that Congress sets in motion when it sets up social security or medical benefits, but never reviews on a yearly basis.

Perhaps, but that wasn't the strategy of the president Stockman served; as far back as Policy Memorandum No. 1, Reagan had committed to gradual rather than drastic budget restraint. And Reagan's political judgment seems vindicated by the failure of Stockman's "September offensive." In particular, his second round of budget cuts sought to tackle social security with immediate deep reductions in the benefit levels for retirement between ages 62 and 65. This gave up-front budget cuts, but did not dent the true problem of the accumulating long-term deficit. The cuts were politically inept, immediately wrecking the plans of people about to retire, and were quickly rejected. The result was to make sensible long-term reform of social security more difficult than ever.[9]

Yet the Greider article was published at precisely the opportune moment, just as tight money and the delay of an effective tax cut were putting recession into place. Stockman's background as a supply-sider made him an effective spokesman for the opposite point of view. The Lou Cannon Reagan biography, which records everything and understands nothing, puts the conventional wisdom explicitly: with the publication of Greider's Stockman interviews "the shaky underpinnings of Reagan's economic assumptions were disclosed."[10]

Stockman was never able to repeat the budget-cutting prodigies of early 1981. Later that year the government ground to a halt in a budget dispute. With not a single appropriations bill even sent to the president seven weeks after the fiscal year began, American Enterprise Institute scholar Norman Ornstein wrote that the 1974 budget act "looks like a lemon in 1981."[11] Stockman left government in 1985 to join Salomon Brothers; shortly after the departure of his Salomon mentor Henry Kaufman, he joined Peterson's investment banking firm. As a spokesman for the dangers of a deficit-financed welfare state, he finally seems to have found a comfortable spiritual home.

Stockman's odyssey, though, contributed mightily to the legacy of misunderstanding. From it the nation learned that the deficit caused the recession of 1982 and would abort any recovery in 1983. And would collapse the expansion, as the conventional wisdom held in 1984, 1985, 1986, 1987, 1988 and 1989. From David Stockman and the events around him, we learned that the Seven Fat Years could never happen.

• • •

The conventional wisdom had a pillar not only in Washington but on Wall Street. Henry Kaufman put a stamp on the thinking of our time by popularizing the "flow of funds," that is, trying to predict interest rates by tabulating the supply of and demand for funds in the bond markets. By 1982, his repeated predictions of higher interest rates had earned him the moniker "Dr. Doom" and made him the rage of Wall Street. "How Henry Kaufman Gets it Right" was the title of a *Fortune* profile in May 1981, for example.[12]

For a time, Kaufman's predictions would have an immediate impact on the bond markets; when he predicted higher interest rates, bonds immediately fell. When such a fashion grips the market world, it's not really clear whether this is because anyone believes the forecast—after all, the traders haven't had time to read it. It's good enough for them if they believe everyone else will believe it. For a time Joe Granville, much less an establishment figure than the scholarly Dr. Kaufman, had a similar effect on the equity markets.

In person Henry Kaufman is anything but frightening; strong in opinions but meek in demeanor. I have trouble thinking of him as Dr. Doom, and think of him instead as Mr. Flow-of-Funds. He produces yearly masterpieces trying to figure out where every scrap of borrowing will come from and where it will go.

Salomon Brothers' "1981 Prospects for Financial Markets," for example, had 20 pages of tables on the "Supply and Demand for Credit." Demand includes items such as privately held mortgages, or short-term business borrowing and, of course, government debt. Supply includes thrift institutions, pensions, banks, state and local governments. Various subtables give you, for example, the increase in one-to-four family residential mortgage loans to be provided by, among others, state and local housing agencies. The idea is that if you can predict all the little numbers, you can predict the big one.[13]

Now, someone has to collect these numbers, though on its face the exercise seems faintly preposterous. Some lines are little booby traps; "foreign," for example, or lines predicting the change in the portfolio of the Federal Reserve system. There is also a big theoretical catch: Irving Fisher's distinction between real and nominal rates. When lender and borrower agree on a loan, both are including an implicit forecast of the inflation rate over its term; this expectation can change even if the supply and demand for credit does not. And in inflationary times like the late 1970s, this may have a bigger impact on interest rates than anything in the real economy.

Still, totting up the supply and demand for funds, like totting up the supply and demand for oil, is likely to give you a forecast of higher prices. And in inflationary times, interest rates—the price of credit—will rise. So Dr. Doom's forecasts were repeatedly proved right.

Until, that is, interest rates broke in 1982. As late as May, he predicted that bond rates "will return to the highs of last year." But *Barron's* reported that "By late July, when Kaufman announced he was bullish for the short term, the bond market already had been rallying for three weeks." Even then, he added the prediction of "further easing in money rates over the very near term, but a subsequent reverse and sharp rise within a few months."[14] No doubt the traders on Salomon's bond desk, who follow the seat of their pants rather than their economist, caught the trend earlier.

Henry Kaufman, who left Salomon in 1988 to form his own firm, is still a highly respected figure on Wall Street, though no longer a mythic one. But his influence lives on in public policy; indeed, William Simon, the treasury secretary who once sold me on "crowding out," was a Salomon Brothers alumni. In the whole flow-of-funds analysis, the one line public policy can directly change is government debt. It follows that if you want to lower interest rates, you reduce government borrowing. And never in those 20 pages of statistics, nor in the conventional wisdom that unwittingly relies on them, do tax rates appear.

• • •

If Dr. Doom was late on the 1982 break in interest rates, John Rutledge was not. "Why Interest Rates Will Fall in 1982" was the title of his *Journal* article on December 14, 1981. It was our version of his remarkable exposition on interest rates, so far as I know breaking new methodological ground. Interest rates are not determined by the *flow* of funds, he argued, but by the market for the *stock* of assets.

Economists are always careful to distinguish between flows, like income, and stocks, like wealth. James Tobin had just won a Nobel Prize for his work on portfolio balance, which said, to quote Rutledge, "[P]rices (interest rates) of financial assets will go to whatever level will make investors just content to hold the available stock of those assets." Rutledge applied the same idea to the balance between financial assets such as stocks and bonds and tangible assets such as real estate, gold and art.

The inflationary climate of the 1970s favored tangible assets, he argued, but as Volcker squeezed away inflation, financial assets became more attractive. So households would try to shift from tangible assets to financial assets, bidding down the price of the former and bidding up the price of the latter—that is, since bond prices are the reverse of yields, bidding down interest rates. The stock of assets is so huge that a small change in the desired holdings would dwarf any likely change in the flows, including new federal borrowing.[15]

Rutledge put the implications of his assets market approach even more clearly in a 1983 article, "The 'Structural-Deficit' Myth":

> Clearly, higher government deficits mean higher interest rates in this framework as well. But in the asset-market view, the relevant question is not "What increase in interest rates is necessary to attract sufficient savings to finance a $300 billion deficit?" Instead, the relevant question is "What must happen to the structure of prices—and therefore yields—on more than $20 trillion in private assets in order to make people willingly own an additional $300 billion in Treasury securities?" Thus, the relevant question is a comparison of the proposed security issue with the size of the asset market, not with savings flows. Clearly, one could imagine a government debt issue accepted by the market even if there were no savings at all.
>
> Once we have posed the question in this way, the answer seems obvious. It would be surprising if $100 billion in government borrowing had a big impact on interest rates because $100 billion just isn't very much money when standing next to $20 trillion. . . .
>
> The evidence suggests that each $100 billion of government borrowing, in and of itself, raises the level of interest rates by about sixty basis points, or six-tenths of one percentage point. This suggests that $300 billion deficits, if they were to occur, might raise the level of interest rates by as much as two percentage points. At 5% inflation in 1988—higher than our forecast—this would put Treasury bill rates at 7% to 8%, hardly a catastrophe by current standards.[16]

The conventional wisdom preferred Henry Kaufman, but Rutledge's treatise on interest rates attracted the interest of business managements operating in a more serious world, forming the cornerstone of his practice as a business consultant.

• • •

In 1982 our solons carried the conventional wisdom to its Hoover-esque conclusion, increasing taxes explicitly to fight recession. The Tax Equity and Fiscal Responsibility Act of 1982 was a Republican measure, spearheaded by Senator Robert Dole. After defeating a Democratic proposal to delay the 1981 tax cuts for the "wealthy" until the federal budget was balanced, the Republican-controlled Senate passed TEFRA without a single Democratic vote. In the House it faced a rebellion led by Jack Kemp, but was passed with the help of Democrats after President Reagan promised to send each member a personal letter thanking them for their vote, thus immunizing them against the issue in the fall election.

For President Reagan, it was a curious period of hibernation. He would publicly pledge adherence to his tax policies, but his aides would contradict him. On December 17, 1981, the President declared in a nationally televised press conference that "I have no plans for increasing taxes in any way." A few minutes later press spokesman Larry Speaks said he didn't mean it. But in the end the tax revolt was quashed; old-time Reaganite Lyn Nofziger, who had initially opposed tax increases, came out of a White House meeting saying he now supported it. "They done explained it to me."

The notion, of course, was that the not-yet-implemented tax cut had caused the deficit, which had caused the higher interest rates, which had caused the recession. So the obvious answer was to reverse the whole process, restoring tax revenues, curbing the deficit, paring interest rates and causing recovery. Some of us kept looking for the economics textbook where this prescription was written.

"Where Did All the Keynesians Go?" Craig Roberts wondered in a *Journal* article in December of 1982.[17] A recession was clearly the time for "pump priming"; where were all the Keynesians to tell us that the deficits were a good thing? Instead, they were mostly critical of the president. Only the Congressional Budget Office, under Craig's old foe Alice Rivlin, had stuck by its Keynesian principles. It reported that under the Keynesian precept of a high-employment budget, which estimated the tax revenues that would be produced if the economy were at full employment, the 1981 deficit of $58 billion was equivalent to a high-employment surplus of $7 billion. The CBO also gave estimates of subsequent deficits that did not seem outside of historical experience as a percent of GNP.

TEFRA mercifully left the individual tax rates mostly untouched, tinkering with the alternative minimum tax and passing a requirement for withholding on interest payments. The following year the latter was hooted back out of Congress, over the objections of the administration and congressional leadership, when bank lobbying managed to stir a popular reaction against the paperwork involved. TEFRA concentrated its revenue measures on business. Only half of business entertainment expense would be deductible—the 1.5 martini tax. Various pro-business provisions, accelerated depreciation and "safe-harbor leasing," were repealed. Some of the changes may have been individually defensible, but others were pure Mickey Mouse. The point was revenues.

The emphasis on business taxes, though, made the underlying premise of the act even more clearly ludicrous. Its proponents wanted tax revenues to reduce the deficit to lower interest rates so businesses could borrow more. So they were taking money from businesses in taxes so that businesses could borrow it back in the bond markets. The president ultimately defended his support of the bill with assertion that for every dollar of tax increase he got three dollars of spending reduction; everyone else recognized this as laughable. One would like to think he did as well, but his memoirs quote diary entries taking it seriously.

• • •

The likes of Laffer, Wanniski and Kemp spent most of late 1981 and 1982 talking about the price rule. Conventional wisdom types scoffed at them for trying to change the subject now that their tax cuts had proved so disastrous. But of course, since Michael 1 there had always been two sides to the policy mix. And as Fed tightenings in May of 1981 and February of 1982 indicate, the problem *was* getting monetary policy right.

Lehrman declared himself publicly. The version in our pages was called simply "The Case for the Gold Standard." Laffer and Mundell also came out of the closet.[18] Another sympathetic economist was Alan Greenspan, back at his consulting firm after having been chairman of the Council of Economic Advisers; he suggested experimenting by starting with an issue of five-year Treasury notes payable in grams or ounces of gold.[19]

Alan Reynolds discovered a 1933 pamphlet entitled "The Means to Prosperity" by John Maynard Keynes. It suggested new international notes, much like later IMF Special Drawing Rights, but having some defined relationship to gold. He remarked, "It may seem odd that I, who have lately described gold as a 'barbarous relic,' should be discovered as an advocate of such a policy . . . It may be that, never having loved gold, I am not so subject to disillusion. But mainly, it is because I believe that gold has received such a gruelling that conditions might now be laid down for its future management."[20]

In the same pamphlet, Keynes also said that "taxation may be so high as to defeat its object, and that, given sufficient time to gather

the fruits, a reduction of taxation will run a better chance, than an
increase, of balancing the budget."

Then there was of course Eureka College economist Ronald Reagan, who said at a briefing in the second month of his presidency:

> One economist pointed out . . . when we started buying the oil over
> there [in] the OPEC nations, 109 barrels of oil were sold for the price
> of an ounce of gold. And the price was pegged to the American dollar.
> And we were about the only country left that still [was] on a gold
> standard. And then a few years went by and we left the gold standard.
> And as this man suggested, if you look at the recurrent price rise, were
> the OPEC nations rising the price of oil or were they simply following
> the same pattern of an ounce of gold? That as gold in this inflationary
> age kept going up, they weren't going to follow our paper money
> downhill. They stayed with the gold price. Of course, now, if we
> followed that, why they could be coming down."[21]

The oil price broke within weeks of this prediction.

In June 1981, the Gold Commission was appointed. Its members
included a diverse lot: Lehrman and Congressman Ron Paul supporting gold, Milton Friedman's great collaborator Anna Schwartz leading
a monetarist bloc as staff director, Federal Reserve governors to
champion discretion, and two conventionally liberal congressmen
who ridiculed the whole discussion. Also, the minutes of the first
meeting disclosed that the commission was confronted by Edward
Durell, who was preoccupied with whether all the gold really was in
Fort Knox, and Robert Ellison, of the Gold Bond Holders Protective
Council, who held gold-backed bond issued before ownership of gold
was outlawed in 1933.

I had requested the minutes under the Freedom of Information
Act after the Treasury at first tried to hold private meetings. Subsequent meetings were open, as the Federal Advisory Committee Act
required, and in the end the commission produced a long and scholarly tract reaching the conclusion:

> The majority of us at this time favor essentially no change in the
> present role of gold. Yet, we are not prepared to rule out that an
> enlarged role for gold may emerge at some future date. If reasonable
> price stability and confidence in our currency are not restored in the
> years ahead, we believe that those who advocate an immediate return
> to gold will grow in numbers and political influence. If there is success
> in restoring price stability and confidence in our currency, tighter

linkage of our monetary system to gold may well become supereroga-
tory.[22]

After looking into the matter, in other words, nearly all of the
commission could agree that while the nation was not yet ready for
gold, the idea wasn't buggy after all. Since 1981, the price of gold has
stayed between $300 and $500. Between 1988 and 1991, it has not
strayed much above $400 or below $350. Wayne Angell, a Federal
Reserve governor appointed in 1986, has supervised the construction
of a commodity-price basket, and follows it in his decisions on the
Open Market Committee. His independent course has made him an
increasingly influential figure on the board.

While it didn't have to be gold, the Michael 1 crowd saw some kind
of price rule as the immediate solution to the problems of 1981.
"Optimism in the current outlook requires a belief that the President
or Fed Chairman Volcker will initiate a new monetary policy capable
of restoring low and stable interest rates," Kadlec and Laffer wrote in
their June investment letter.[23] The same month, we editorialized
"Bring Back Bretton Woods," saying that Bretton Woods was a price-
rule system, and that "the first step is a serious look at putting the
Fed back on some form of price rule."[24]

Jack Kemp had, unwisely I thought, gone so far as to call for
Volcker's resignation and cast his lot with liberal congressmen trying
to curb the Fed's independence. He urged a program including a new
international conference on exchange rates and redefining the dollars
in terms of gold, with an interim target of "some proxy for the price
level. The all-commodity index or strong-currency price change rates
would be second best, but the best would be the dollar price of gold."

• • •

In passing TEFRA, Congress was expressing yet another view of
monetary policy. It was supposed to raise $100 billion in revenues
over three years, but the Republicans in Congress and the White
House had in mind something more than the mechanical effects on
the credit markets. They viewed the tax boost, coming not only in a
recession but in a congressional election year, as their sacrifice to the
great god Volcker. If propitiated, they hoped, he would ease.

Around the world and throughout history, the notion of an independent central bank runs like this: It is impolite for finance ministers
or even elected heads of government to talk about monetary policy.

And except among themselves, central bankers don't talk about monetary policy either. In public, instead, they offer a lot of advice on fiscal policy. And since, like Henry Kaufman, they spend their lives reading reams of statistics in which deficits appear but taxes do not, their advice invariably is to cut spending but failing that raise taxes.

And in fact, after TEFRA passed in mid-August, the Fed eased, and the politicians patted themselves on the back (and the connection is still stored in their memories). But as Greider found, "In fact there was no real connection between the two events. Volcker did not wait for the tax legislation to pass before taking action. The Fed had decided to ease interest rates a full month before final passage of the bill was a certainty."[25]

What caused Volcker to ease—or perhaps more to the point, stop targeting M-1—was the impending threat of financial collapse. Throughout the world, loans had been made on the implicit forecast of further inflation. When the inflation ended, the loans could no longer be serviced, especially if interest rates stayed high. And if too many loans went into default, banks would be threatened. You could imagine a spiral of bank failures and runs by depositors feeding on each other and producing a general collapse of economic confidence, as was thought to have happened at the onset of the Great Depression. The issue was how much disinflation the economy could take without collapse.

Foreigners who borrowed in dollars were doubly exposed, not only from a general business downturn but from the exchange rate risk, since their own currencies would fall in value against a non-inflationary dollar. Their incomes were in local currencies and their debts in dollars; the exchange rate would determine whether the debts could be repaid. And of course, the debts were held by U.S. banks; if foreign debts couldn't be repaid the banks were in jeopardy. The inflation of the 1970s and its end in 1979–82, in short, created the Third World debt problem.

In the 1970s, Mexico discovered it had huge oil reserves, somehow overlooked after the 1936 nationalization of the American oil companies. In the midst of the energy crisis, it set out to become a rich nation; its president, José Lopez Portillo, set out to become a rich man. Its northern states, with their proximity to the United States, had developed truly first-rate modern businesses, led by Grupo Industrial Alfa of Monterrey. Impressed U.S. bankers showered the government and the businesses with loans.

But the oil price broke in 1981, shortly after President Reagan ruminated about the relative price of oil and gold. With this, the Mexican peso came under pressure. As 1982 dawned, Lopez Portillo vowed to defend the peso "like a dog." In February, facing capital outflows of $100 million a day, he devalued. In floating markets, the peso fell from 27 to the dollar to 37-to-41. (Citizens of Mexico City have since slapped the nickname "dog hill" on Lopez Portillo's compound of expansive personal residences.) As the year wore on, he confiscated the dollar deposits held in Mexican banks and finally nationalized the banks entirely, without telling presidential candidate Miguel de la Madrid, who eventually started Mexico on its recovery.

The Mexican devaluation was also the beginning of the end of aggregate targets in U.S. monetary policy. In April, Alfa defaulted. It owed some $2.3 billion to domestic and foreign banks. Since much of this debt was denominated in dollars, the devaluation increased the peso cost of its debt service, by one estimate in an amount equivalent to $140 million. Citibank and Continental Illinois, each holding more than $100 million of Alfa debt, transmitted the pressure to the U.S. banking system. At the end of the month, the Fed was forced to loan the Mexican central bank $600 million in stopgap funds, and the problem threatened to get worse, imperiling all the big banks with big Mexican loans.

The Mexican threat was quickly followed by the collapse of Drysdale Government Securities, a small government securities dealer with a big loan from Chase Manhattan Bank. This sent tremors through the financial world and required a Fed rescue operation. Then came the collapse of Penn Square Bank in Oklahoma, which like Mexico had bet big on continuing escalation of the oil price. All the while, M-1 was soaring; it said the Fed should tighten to squeeze money out of the system.

The FOMC convened on July 1, just as the Penn Square episode broke; the bank was officially closed July 5. Despite the strength in M-1, the committee voted to ease, and said that it would permit the money supply to rise above its targeted ranges if this was needed to solve financial problems. The bond markets started to rally; yields, which had held at almost 16 percent for nearly a year, fell from 15.75 percent in July to 14.64 percent in August to 12.15 percent in December.

Volcker reaffirmed the money targets in congressional testimony, but in October he spoke to the Business Council meeting in Hot Springs, Virginia. He claimed that a discount rate cut meant no basic change in policy. But he added, "We have to be alert to the possibility that relationships may be disturbed by technological or regulatory changes in banking, or more broadly by shifts in liquidity preferences and velocity." He talked of NOW accounts and the like, and added, "In these circumstances, I do not believe that, in actual implementation of monetary policy, we have any alternative but to attach much less than usual weight to movements in M-1, over the period immediately ahead."[26] The experiment with aggregate targeting that started October 6, 1979, was officially over.

How seriously Paul Volcker ever took the money targets is open to question. He is congenitally not in favor of rules but of discretion. Even at the height of the M-1 targets, for example in Congressional testimony in June of 1982, he would say things such as "The hard truth is that there inevitably is a critical need for judgment in the conduct of monetary policy." Unquestionably, as Greider stresses, the M-1 targets gave a political cover for the tight money policy Volcker in any event wanted to follow. He adopted the policies when his instinct said something new was needed to stem inflation, and abandoned them when his instinct said that despite their signal he had no choice but to ease money.

In abandoning the monetary targets, Volcker did not announce what would replace them. By the end of October, Laffer and Kadlec suggested that Volcker was secretly following some form of price rule. They pointed out that before the Fed's October meeting, M-1 had been rising but the Dow Jones spot commodity index had been falling. "The choice was clear," and instead of tightening as the aggregates indicated, the Fed did what commodity prices indicated, and lowered the Fed Funds rate. Whatever particular prices the Fed was following, they wrote, the commodity index produced "a fair summary of the effect of monetary policy during the past four months." They concluded, "A price rule for monetary policy—the financial precondition for the roaring '80s—is being put into place."[27]

And, of course, the phased-in tax cuts would finally arrive in 1983. Our first editorial of the year was entitled "At Last, a Tax Cut." We wrote, "Welcome to the new year. With any luck at all, it should be a better one. For one thing, this is the year in which we finally get a tax cut."[28]

As 1982 drew to a merciful close, both sides of the Michael 1 prescription were finally coming into place. The Seven Fat Years started in November.

9

Boom

As the Man from Mars discovered, the 92 months of expansion that started in November of 1982 added more than 30 percent—a West Germany, almost—to American output. They boosted per capita income by 20 percent. But this growth was not consumed in bigger and better tailfins or juicier steaks. The "decade of greed" was a time of almost instantaneous cultural change, of extraordinary creativity. The texture of daily life the Man from Mars saw in Kankakee is a product of the Seven Fat Years.

Above all, the 1980s witnessed a communications revolution. In 1980, you will not remember, only 1 percent of American households owned a video cassette recorder. By 1989, the figure was more than 58 percent. For all practical purposes, every video rental shop in the nation was started during the Seven Fat Years.

In 1980, cable television systems reached 15 percent of American households, mostly in remote areas with difficult reception. At the end of the decade, half of all homes were wired. MTV, for better or worse, beat its first drum on August 1, 1981.[1] Turner Broadcasting survived a near-bankruptcy, but its Cable News Network went on to victory in the Gulf War. After a generation of dominance, the network news divisions sputtered creatively and economically.

In 1980, of course, telephones had already reached 93 percent of occupied housing units, but consumers could choose basic black or a few other models. Today their choices seem endless. And we now have a plethora of long-distance services. In the immediate sense, of course, this was due to the AT&T antitrust settlement, but in a deeper sense it was due to underlying economics dictated by technological change. Cheap long-distance transmission undermined the rate structure on which the Bell system had been based.

And change here is only beginning. The future almost surely lies with fiberoptic cable; MCI Communications, one of AT&T's upstart competitors, built a nationwide network. Cellular phones suddenly blossomed. And by the end of the decade, the standard business communications was fax for letters and Federal Express for packages.

Standard, that is, meaning average or commonplace. The adept were into e-mail—as opposed, in their jargon, to snail-mail. Their conversations might go like this: "When you sign into the net, be sure to catch my new dot-sig file; I flamed that Smith guy who posts on talk-dot-politics-dot-misc." Or, "When I got back from vacation I had 51 messages in MCI mail." By 1990, a whole subculture was hooking itself together every night, posting messages, information, secrets and insults on tiny bulletin boards of silicon.

For most portentous of all, the Seven Fat Years witnessed the development of the personal computer. In 1981, when the Apple II was a hackers' toy, a little over two million personal computers were in use anywhere in the country. That year, IBM introduced its first PC, and Apple followed with the Macintosh in 1984. By 1988, the two million PCs had exploded to 45 million. Of this number, roundly half were in homes.[2]

This communications revolution changed American life not only directly but indirectly, for example by providing the infrastructure for almost instantaneous changes in fashion. Reebok sneakers, decorated with the Union Jack and selling for more than $60, were introduced in 1981. On October 15, 1984, Michael Jordan of the Chicago Bulls showed up on the court with the first pair of Air Jordans; with the help of publicity from the threat of a National Basketball Association ban, the shoes swept the nation. More than two and a half million pairs were sold in 1985.

Health clubs swept the nation, and while peaking, became a part of everyday life. Catalog merchandising proliferated, and urban department stores declined. The Universal Product Code sprouted little black bars everywhere; by the end of the decade supermarket checkout clerks were swiping prices into their cash registers. And of course, the automatic teller machine became a staple of American life; the federal government even experimented with using them to distribute certain types of welfare payments.

Frozen yogurt became a diet staple, with estimated sales increasing 300 percent between 1986 and 1990.[3] Whole ice cream chains were built on heavy formulas and Danish names; another was built by selling ice cream that was environmentally correct. In 1982, barely half of the top 50 food distributors even carried fresh produce; by 1990 nearly all did.[4] Per capita consumption of red meat fell to 144 pounds in 1987 from 156.9 pounds in 1980, while consumption of distilled spirits fell from 3.0 gallons per capita to 2.3. Cigarette consumption continued to slide, as it had since 1963.[5]

The renovation of the nation's culture meant something else to Americans: jobs. During the 1980s, the last of the baby-boom generation went to work, and workforce participation of women grew to 57 percent from 51 percent. The labor force swelled to nearly 125 million in 1990 from 106.9 million in 1980—more than 18 million new jobs, as the Man from Mars's Databoy showed.

A quarter of the new jobs were in business services and health services; the fastest-growing individual categories were computer and data-processing services and outpatient health care facilities. Essentially all of the job gain was in services, which now account for three-fourths of all employment.

The two-earner family became standard, 58 percent of all families. The work force grew more educated; by 1990 24 percent of men over 25 and 18 percent of women had four years or more of college, compared with 20 percent of men and 13 percent of women a decade earlier. The number of American households grew by 16 percent, while their average size shrank to 2.63 members from 2.76. The "traditional" family of mother, father and children shrank to 26 percent of all households in 1990 from 31 percent in 1980.[6] Not everything about these social trends was wholesome, of course, but in the main they represented the growing affluence of American society.

The communications revolution also represented a remarkable diffusion of economic and political power; almost surely it was a driving force in the political trends so evident with the fall of the Berlin Wall in 1989. By the end of the decade, a hacker could sit at his PC in Taipei, beating the pants off the Bundesbank in the foreign exchange markets. A visiting Russian scientist would be impressed by the computer equipment of his American counterpart, but moved almost to tears by the computer equipment of his counterpart's secretary.

• • •

The driving force in this remarkable reformation was technological, of course, but even microchips do not procreate by virgin birth. Someone has to invent the technology, recognize its possibilities and organize its production. Someone has to take the risk of raising funds, building facilities, making the product known to buyers, delivering goods and somehow seeing that the sales cover the costs of all this. In the Seven Fat Years, how were the technological possibilities harnessed?

The prototype for the decade's industrial development, Apple Computer, Inc., issued its first public stock in 1980. Steve Jobs and Stephen Wozniak invented the first personal computer in Jobs's garage in 1976. Their Apple I and Apple II machines beat IBM to the market, indeed created the market IBM started to tap in 1981. Apple consolidated its success with the introduction of the Macintosh in 1984. By the end of the decade, Apple was 95th on *Fortune's* list of 500 industrial companies. Jobs and Wozniak were gone from the company, but the two college dropouts had founded a new industry.[7]

Harvard dropout William Gates and a friend also started a small company in 1975, and in 1980 landed a contract to write the basic software for the IBM PC. They bought a computer operating system for $50,000, and turned it into MS-DOS, or Microsoft Disk Operating System. Microsoft Corporation issued public stock for the first time in 1986, raising more than $61 million from hopeful investors. By the end of the decade, Microsoft's success had thrown Apple and IBM into a defensive alliance and attracted an antitrust investigation by the Federal Trade Commission, which handles unserious antitrust work. Following its success with the Windows software, in 1991 Microsoft introduced DOS 5.0. It sold a million copies in 30 days. Of course, every personal computer already had an operating system; a million computer users had decided to upgrade immediately.

Mitch Kapor, a sometime disk jockey and transcendental meditation instructor, turned to computer programming. He founded a little company and shipped the first copy of Lotus 1-2-3 in January 1983. It sold $53 million in the first year, and went on to become the most popular single program for personal computers. Turning to a public stock offering for financing in its first year, Lotus Development Corporation grew from nothing in 1982 to sales of $684 million in 1990.

Philippe Kahn, an illegal immigrant, came to Silicon Valley looking for a job in 1983, but ended up forming a little company. He took out an ad in Byte Magazine, tricking the salesman into extending credit by hiring extras to make his office look busy and letting the salesman see a fake "media schedule" with Byte crossed out. The one ad sold $150,000 worth of software, and Borland International Inc. was off and running. In 1991, it acquired Ashton-Tate Corporation, and became the nation's third-largest supplier of personal computer software.

In 1982, three Texas Instrument managers resigned to form a new company. Their idea was to make the PC portable. They shipped their first computer by the end of 1982, and the next year sold $111 million worth. This performance allowed them to take the company public, and with this capital infusion Compaq Computer Corporation crossed the billion-dollar mark in 1987. It finished the decade as the 137th largest industrial corporation in America.

Also in 1982, four 27-year-olds founded a new company. One, an engineering graduate student at Stanford, had cobbled together some spare computer parts to work problems involved in designing integrated circuits. A Stanford MBA graduate, impressed by the machine, led the way in raising $4 million from four venture capital companies. Another Stanford MBA and a software wizard from Berkeley joined. Within six years, Sun Microsystems sold a billion dollars worth of computer workstations. In 1990, it ranked 181st on *Fortune*'s 500 list.

Explosive growth was not limited to the computer industry. At one point in the decade, the fastest-growing company in the United States was Reebok International Ltd., which grew from sales of $12.8 million in 1983 to $1.3 billion in 1987. Liz Claiborne, Inc., went public in 1981, when it had sales of $117 million; by the end of the decade its $1.7 billion in sales put it 237th on the *Fortune* 500. Ben Cohen and Jerry Greenfield opened an ice cream stand in Vermont in 1978, and a decade later sold $47 million worth of ice cream and environmental concern. Wal-Mart stores, already a billion dollar company in 1980, was a $25.8-billion company in 1990.

Genentech, the pioneer genetic engineering company, went public in 1980. With revenues of only $7 million, it raised more than $300 million in the capital markets. Two years later, its synthetic insulin was the first biologically engineered product approved by the FDA. In 1990, its sales reached $476 million.

Frederick Smith got a "C" on a Yale term paper suggesting a national overnight delivery service, but he founded Federal Express anyway. After a decade of struggling, it reached sales of $415 million in 1980. By 1990, its sales were $7 billion, and it had become an American institution.

The leader in the mushrooming cable TV industry, Tele-Communications Inc., had sales of $124 million in 1980 and $3.6 billion in 1990. Turner Broadcasting System grew from $54 million in

1980, when CNN was launched, to nearly $1.4 billion in 1990. Mc-Caw Cellular Communications offered its first public shares in 1986; its sales grew from $18 million that year to $1 billion in 1990.

This entrepreneurial efflorescence had as its counterpoint an equally remarkable leaning down of corporate America. In reporting on the largest 500 companies for 1990, *Fortune* noted that over the previous decade, the blue-chip companies had pared their payrolls by 3.5 million employees. Employment at General Electric had plunged to 280,000 in 1990 from 402,000 in 1980. Chairman John Welch, Jr., had vowed, *Fortune* reported, to cut another one-third of the company's management positions.[8]

The trend was toward flatter management structures, with fewer levels of reporting and smaller staff departments. It was also toward concentrating on fewer businesses. The diversified conglomerate of the 1960s was anything but fashionable; unrelated divisions were to be sold or spun off to shareholders. Harvard Business School professor Michael Jensen even speculated that the traditional corporation was obsolete; that the future belonged to small holding companies, Kravis Kohlberg Roberts being the prototype, whose basic contribution would be to structure incentives that tied the fortunes of operating companies and their CEOs.[9]

For companies that did not adapt to these trends, the discipline of the marketplace was harsh. *Fortune* reported that nearly half of the companies on its 1980 listed failed to appear in 1990, twice the turnover of the 1970–80 comparison. Most of the missing had been merged into other companies.

Earlier *Fortune* had reported on a poll of the CEOs of the top companies. "The CEOs reserve their most bitter bile for investment bankers," it reported. Some 68 percent of the respondents felt that takeovers and mergers driven by investment bankers hurt the nation's ability to compete in world markets and complained of too much emphasis on quarterly results instead of the "long term," and of emphasis on leveraged buyouts rather than "good, sound investments." *Fortune* also added, "A minority of the surveyed CEOs, 22%, follow a different line of reasoning, contending that the takeover wave is fundamentally good for the U.S. because it forces companies to cut fat, restructure, and become more efficient. Many economists endorse this view—but then they don't have jobs at stake when the raider comes knocking."[10]

Yet from the standpoint of efficiency, the leaning of payrolls was demonstrably good. Employment in manufacturing as a whole did not decline as dramatically as it did among the *Fortune* 500; essentially employment in the goods-producing sector was flat while employment in services grew. Thus factory jobs dropped to 18 percent of all employment from 23 percent. Manufacturing output, though, grew in line with total GNP, holding its share at 23 percent.

This is of course another way of saying that productivity surged. The Bureau of Labor Statistics index of manufacturing productivity reached 136.8 in 1990, compared with 96.6 in 1980. In other words, manufacturing output per employee hour was gaining at a rate of more than 3.5 percent a year.[11]

Traditionally productivity in the service industries is more sluggish than in manufacturing, at least to the extent we can measure it accurately. But productivity over the entire nonfarm business sector also gained in the 1980s, with the index rising to 110.8 in 1990 from 99.9 in 1980 (or 100 in 1982). This is a gain of barely over 1 percent a year, but of course, over the same time period the labor force incorporated 18 million new workers.

Productivity, like everything else, swings around the inflection years. In 1973, hourly output of all employees reached $18.101 in 1982 dollars. It crept up only slightly, to $18.774 in 1982, and then surged, to a record $21.306 in 1988.[12] Productivity hit a plateau after 1973, until the Seven Fat Years got it moving again. The key was fat-cutting at the top, and at the bottom, a burst of creativity from college dropouts, breakaway engineers and illegal immigrants.

• • •

If technology was the driving force, and if it was harnessed by entrepreneurs, there also had to be economic mechanisms and a political climate that allowed these upstarts to do their work. In particular, the entrepreneurs needed capital, the upfront investment money to build factories before products could be produced and sold. Here we arrive at the genius of American capitalism.

When Genentech raised $300 million from investors, it didn't even have a product, let alone an investment-grade bond rating. It had an idea and, to be strictly accurate, a patent. That proved to be enough to launch a multimillion dollar company. Actually, of course, the sale of shares, or IPO for initial public offering, is a latish stage in the capital investment process. Laying aside anything else, you need capital to pay the lawyers and investment bankers doing the IPO. The most crucial seed money comes earlier.

For this, U.S. capitalism has developed an industry too. It's called venture capital. Venture capital firms raise money on the bet that their management can pick out the most promising new firms, provide the initial funding and produce extraordinary returns. By the time of an IPO, the venture capitalists may even cash out, though a wise investor would not regard this as a good sign.

In the case of Genentech, the patent on techniques for gene splicing was held by Herbert Boyer, a molecular biologist. But he found backing from the venture capital industry. Indeed, Thomas J. Perkins, a leading venture capitalist, became its chairman. Robert Swanson, also from the venture capital industry, became Genentech's president and CEO. In 1980 the market valued this combination of science and management at $300 million. In 1991, Genentech sold a 60 percent interest to Roche Holdings of Switzerland for $2.1 billion; Roche also got an option to buy the remainder at a total price that if exercised would be 100 times Genentech's 1989 earnings.

Genetic engineering is of course precisely the kind of technology that various philosophers have in mind in advocating "industrial planning" by some omniscient bureaucracy in Washington and, they dream, Cambridge. So, a short quiz: Rank in order the most likely recipient of capital from an industrial planning bureaucracy:

(A) Steve Jobs's garage.

(B) IBM

(C) A company in the district of the most powerful congressman.

Welcome to the real world, and so much for that idea. In fact, college dropout Jobs got his stake with $57,600 from Arthur Rock, a famed venture capitalist. Rock also invested in Intel Corporation, the leading silicon chip maker, and a profusion of smaller ventures.

Perkins, similarly, sat as chairman not only of Genentech, but also of Tandem Computers Inc., and six smaller publicly held concerns. He was also an early investor in Compaq and Sun Microsystems. Indeed, Vinod Khosla, the 27-year-old MBA who put together the other Sun founders, went on to become a general partner of the Perkins' firm, Kleiner Perkins Caufield & Myers.

The Seven Fat Years were the great heyday of the venture capital industry. While pioneers like Rock and Perkins had started earlier, indeed, the venture capital industry as an institution was created by the Steiger capital gains cut of 1978. When the measure passed, *Business Week* predicted that the biggest gainers would be "venture capitalists, particularly those who back startup companies." It noted that "The venture capital industry—and in turn the flow of capital to new businesses—has been on the wane since 1969, when the capital gains tax started moving up from the old 25 percent level." It quoted Perkins, who said the cut in the rate "should make it far easier to raise funds, and it will bring entrepreneurs forward."[13]

So it proved to be. From a low of only $10 million net new capital in 1975 and a 1977 level of $39 million, the venture capital industry raised $600 million for investment in the year Steiger passed. With the passage of the Reagan tax bill in 1981, it raised $1.3 billion. With the true tax cuts in 1983, it raised $4.5 billion. It managed to raise $4.9 billion in 1987, after the 1986 increase in the capital gains tax to 33 percent from 20 percent. But the figures plunged to $2.1 billion in 1988 and $2.2 billion in 1989.[14]

So too with initial public offerings. After 1973, IPOs dried up, averaging only 28 a year from 1974 through 1978.[15] After Steiger, the number jumped to 103 in 1979, and except in the 1982 recession, generally upward to a record of 953 in 1986 when the capital gains tax was raised. Later dates show the number falling to 630 in 1987, 371 in 1988, 276 in 1989 and 186 in 1990.

Clark Judge, who called my attention to these figures in a *Journal* article, has updated the numbers and converted them into 1991 dollars. The effects of the marginal rate of capital gains taxation seem unmistakable; he titled his article, "The Tax That Ate the Economy."[16] In 1991 dollars, the venture capital industry raised around $300 million a year in the early 1970s, with only one year above $600 million. It grew steadily with the Steiger Amendment, the Brodhead Amendment and the Reagan tax cuts, reaching the $3 billion-a-year mark in 1983 through 1985, and $4 billion-a-year totals from 1986 to 1988. In 1990, it plunged to $2.1 billion.

So too with initial public offerings in 1991 dollars. They plunged in the early 1970s, from a high of $8.9 billion in 1972 to only $142 million in 1974. In 1980, they again broke $2 billion, and reached $24 billion in 1986. After the increase in capital gains rates in the 1986 tax bills, they sank to the $6–7 billion level in 1988–1990.

Judge also looked at Small Business Administration estimates of "angels," direct investors in local firms, and Federal Reserve estimates of non-corporate investment, or "mom and pop" capital. The 1991 dollar estimates for investment by angels fell to $20.8 million in 1990 from $39.6 million in 1987 and $40.9 billion in 1986, for example, while "mom and pop" investment fell to $62.4 million in 1990 from $87.0 million in 1987 and $110.9 million in 1986.

However, one source of funds has grown: foreign angels. "People involved in all parts of entrepreneurial finance report that Asians and Europeans have stepped forward, particularly for high-technology projects with international applications. Foreign investors are taxed at home, where capital gains taxes either don't exist or are lower than here."

During the Seven Fat Years, another source of capital for growth companies was the much maligned "junk bond" market. Whatever crimes he eventually confessed to, Michael Milken helped finance such companies as MCI, Tele-Communications, Turner Broadcasting, McCaw Cellular and a host of other smaller but growing concerns. Money raised in the high-yield bond markets rose from $5.4 billion in 1980 to a record of $46.0 billion in 1986, then running at around $35 billion a year through 1989. More than two-thirds of the money financed internal corporate growth rather than acquisitions of any kind.[17] In 1990, new issues of junk bonds almost vanished.

In 1991, these capital-raising vehicles showed some recovery from the 1990 "credit crunch." In particular, IPOs were strong, buoyed by a higher stock market despite the recession, and by the abatement of inflation, which provides some measure of relief on capital gains taxes. By some measures, IPOs recorded their second-best year ever. A few new issues of junk bonds also succeeded, but venture capital turned even drier. At an even earlier entrepreneurial stage, new business starts sank. These developments are discussed in Chapter 16, "Victorian Finance." Whatever the new decade ultimately holds, its opening financial developments make clearer than ever that the essence of the Seven Fat Years was a happy marriage between entrepreneurial vision and available capital.

• • •

If entrepreneurial vigor was the hallmark of the Seven Fat Years in our culture, in the economic statistics it was sheer staying power. Its duration of 92 months—seven years and eight months—was established by The National Bureau of Economic Research, the private academic group in charge of dating business cycles. This was more than twice the average of expansions since World War II. In the record books, it is exceeded only by the 106-month expansion from February 1961 to December 1969. Because of the impact of Vietnam, the NBER puts the 1960s in a subcategory of wartime expansions, considered somewhat artificial and of limited use in judging economic policy. The 92 months compares to the previous peacetime record of 58 months. When the Seven Fat Years began, the average duration of post-World War II peacetime expansions was two years and ten months.

This staying power is what allowed the economy to make its substantial gains, adding a third to the national economy and a fifth to the average living standard of Americans. Of the individual years, only 1984 was spectacular—its growth rate of 6.8 percent was higher than any other single peacetime year since before World War II. Only one other year was above 4 percent, a commonplace figure. But if you avoid recession, gains cumulate. You reap, as Joe DiMaggio explained in his TV ads for the Bowery Savings Bank, the power of compound interest.

The key to this sustained duration almost surely lies, ironically, in the 1980 banking legislation that did so much to create the savings and loan crisis, the most obvious blot on the Seven Fat Years. The Depository Institutions Deregulation and Monetary Control Act, DIDMCA, phased out price controls on what banks could pay for deposits. "Reg Q" is by now a forgotten regulation and its progeny, "disintermediation," a thankfully forgotten word. They were the keys to the periodic recessions known as "the business cycle."

It worked this way: Regulation Q required that banks pay no more than 5.25 percent on savings deposits (S&Ls got to pay 5.5 percent). A business expansion would start, but when the first signs of inflation appeared the Fed would tighten, raising short-term interest rates. When the rates hit the Reg Q ceilings, the economy hit a wall. Savers would start withdrawing their funds and looking for more profitable investments. This was called "disintermediation."

The deposit bases of banks and particularly savings and loans would shrink, and they would not have money to lend at any price. So even the best projects, especially in construction, could not be financed, and the real economy would stumble. Hence any attempt to curb inflation, a monetary phenomenon, was bound to crash the real economy. This gave us the business cycle, not to mention the Phillips curve.

In the 1970s, inflation left Reg Q ridiculous. With the prime rate soaring toward 20 percent, and money market funds sprouting to pay market rates of interest, banks and S&Ls had to be allowed to compete for funds or they would vanish. So the 1980 act, incidentally before Ronald Reagan's deregulators arrived on the scene, phased out Reg Q over a period of six years, later accelerated.

Without the interest rate ceilings to cause disintermediation, Fed policy had entirely different effects. An increase in interest rates would not slam the whole economy against a wall because funds simply were not available from traditional lenders. Instead the higher rates would gradually ration out the marginal projects across the whole economy. Inflation could be attacked as the monetary problem it is, indeed, without much impact on the real economy. As economist James L. Doti put it in a *Journal* article, "freer markets make it possible for the Fed to cure rather than kill the patient."[18]

This does not mean there will be no recessions. As the Council of Economic Advisers concluded in 1990, "Historical and international evidence shows that economic expansions do not die of old age. Expansions end because of particular external shocks to the economy, policy errors, or widespread imbalances, such as an overaccumulation of inventories, developing throughout the economy." In short, we are not helpless before some inexorable "cycle." Without such artificial impediments as wage–price controls or Reg Q, expansions can in theory go on indefinitely, even for more than seven years. An expansion will be ended by events—external shocks possibly, or more likely, mistaken policies.

• • •

One final aspect of the seven-year boom requires comment. It is what Keynes called "animal spirits." An economy is not an inanimate machine but a living organism. By 1980, the American nation had suffered through a long series of psychological traumas—the Kennedy assassination, Vietnam, Watergate, a raging inflation. By 1984, Ronald Reagan was running a "morning again" reelection campaign. Even those who thought him a dolt agreed that somehow he had revived a spirit of optimism. And if this uplift was later marred by the Iran-Contra episode, he was the first president since Eisenhower to serve two full terms.

The renewal of optimism and the renewal of economic growth feed on one another. The malaise of the 1970s had to do with a remembered series of traumas, but it had even more to do with inflation. Asked to name the most important problems facing the United States, respondents in 1977 ranked inflation first with 53 percent and unemployment or recession second with 39 percent. In 1981, inflation alone was mentioned by 70 percent. Poll-watcher Karlyn Keene says the impressive thing about polls on the economy over the 1980s was a decline in salience. By 1987, unemployment was mentioned by 13 percent, the deficit by 11 percent, the same as drug abuse. Moral decline rated 5 percent and AIDS 3 percent. Inflation was volunteered by 2 percent of the respondents.

10

Sincerest Flattery

Given the vigor of the Seven Fat Years, especially in contrast to what was thought possible in 1982, it's not surprising that others at home and abroad sought a piece of the action. The Reagan-Volcker policy mix not only spread around the world, it spread, if temporarily, to the opposition party in the U.S. Democrats were crucial to the 1986 decision to chop the top marginal tax rate to 28 percent.

In this the Democrats were led by Sen. Bill Bradley, and in his development of the issue Jude Wanniski played a crucial if oblique role, in the episode of his departure from *The Wall Street Journal*. I think Jude is the best journalist I ever worked with, in terms of finding *news*, which is to say something new instead of the same old stuff everyone else is reporting. This trait can be upsetting and annoying, especially to other journalists, a notoriously thin-skinned breed. One of the things that he found, of course, was supply-side economics.

To be sure, Jude's natural exuberance often needed a restraining hand. And it is perfectly true that in the fall of 1978 he crossed the line between journalism and politics, campaigning for fellow supply-sider Jeff Bell in the latter's seemingly hopeless effort to defeat incumbent Senator Clifford Case in New Jersey's Republican primary. Handing out campaign literature for Bell at the Morristown train station, Jude saw Ray Shaw, the president of Dow Jones, and went over to make sure he got his leaflet. Two days and one colorful conversation later, Jude had resigned.

This is my chance to tell the world what this was all about. Jude had already finished his book, with all modesty entitled *The Way the World Works*. He wanted to quit, but I kept talking him out

149

of it. This involved heated entreaties, invoking our common causes, his loyalty to the *Journal*, his loyalty to me and the security of his family. On that train platform in Morristown, Jude saw a way to get around me.

The bigger surprise was that Jeff Bell beat Senator Case. He would probably be a senator today except that in the general election he ran up against Bradley, basketball star and Rhodes scholar. That platform in Morristown was also the start of Senator Bradley's education in tax policy. The campaign debates with Bell were his Michael 1, and Bradley went on to establish a Democratic salient for the Mundell policy mix, chairing exchange rates forums with Jack Kemp and introducing the Bradley-Gephardt tax initiative. With a parallel Kemp-Kasten bill on the Republican side and a proposal from the Reagan Treasury initiative, a consensus formed behind the tax reform act of 1986, with its top-rate cut to 28 percent, the lowest since 1931.

• • •

If we now know this consensus was not an enduring one, neither was it an immediate one. In the 1984 presidential elections, the voters were offered a clear choice of economic policy. In accepting the nomination, former vice president Walter Mondale uttered the ringing declaration, "Let's tell the truth. Mr. Reagan will raise taxes, and so will I. He won't tell you. I just did."[1]

Fritz Mondale, whom I still see now and then as a Mayo trustee, is in my mind the last of a breed. The great mystery of the man is how and why he contrived to keep his personal wit and humor, readily apparent in even short private conversations as vice president, from showing on the campaign trail. He was surely a liberal, in the sense of using the powers of government to lift the poor and backward. But his was a liberalism both earnest and realistic, in the tradition of Harry Truman or Hubert Humphrey, Mondale's mentor, and in many ways Lyndon Baines Johnson.

This was pro-American liberalism, even Cold War liberalism. It was honed before the "peace marches" that sealed Vietnam's fate as a Gulag and cast boat people adrift on tropical seas. Nor was it the pocket-borough liberalism, merely a tool in the pursuit and maintenance of political power. Nor the combat-for-sport liberalism that savages distinguished judges and black conservatives. Later a different, cranky liberalism came to dominate the Democratic party primaries, with a result detrimental to the political process and fatal to the party's presidential prospects: Any candidate who could win the general election could not win the nomination, and vice versa.

Still, it is fascinating to browse through the Mondale acceptance speech, for its themes survived his crushing electoral defeat. His pledge to raise taxes was instantly applauded in the media. The *Washington Post* economic columnist Hobart Rowen declared, "Everybody in this town—Republican and Democrat—knows that taxes will have to be raised next year, and Mondale finally decided to say it."[2] The tax pledge was one of two convention events providing an excitement that would bring life to his campaign, the conventional wisdom went, the other being the vice presidential nomination of Geraldine Ferraro.

But Mondale also hoisted the flag of "fairness." For example, "Four years ago, many of you voted for Mr. Reagan because he promised you'd be better off. And today, the rich are better off. But working Americans are worse off, and the middle class is standing on a trap door." Or, "First, there was Mr. Reagan's tax program. What happened was, he gave each of his rich friends enough tax relief to buy a Rolls Royce—and he asked your family to pay for the hub caps." Or, "There's another difference. When he raises taxes, it won't be done fairly. He will sock it to average-income families again, and leave his rich friends alone. I won't."

And of course, the deficit: "Here is the truth about the future: We are living on borrowed money and borrowed time. These deficits hike interest rates, clobber exports, stunt investment, kill jobs, undermine growth, cheat our kids, and shrink our future. Whoever is inaugurated in January, the American people will have to pay Mr. Reagan's bills. The budget will be squeezed. Taxes will go up. And anyone who says they won't is not telling the truth. I mean business. By the end of my first term, I will cut the deficit by two-thirds."

And, more surprisingly for an internationalist liberal of Mondale's generation, overtones of protectionism: "Then they crimped our future. They let us be routed in international competition, and now the help-wanted ads are full of listings for executives, and for dishwashers—but not much in between. Then they socked it to workers. They encouraged executives to vote themselves huge bonuses—while using King Kong tactics to make workers take Hong Kong wages." And, "To big companies that send our best jobs overseas, my message is: We need those jobs here at home. Our country won't help your business—unless your business helps our country. To countries that close their markets to us, my message is: We will not be pushed around any more. We will have a president who stands up for American workers and American businesses and American farmers."

Reacting to these appeals, America's voters gave President Reagan 58.8 percent of their vote. Mondale carried his native Minnesota and the District of Columbia. The homefolks and the Beltway gave him 13 electoral votes. Reagan got 525, topping Franklin D. Roosevelt's record of 523.

• • •

The Democratic party at least momentarily got the message. The tax increase Mondale and others saw as inevitable did not happen in 1985; instead Congress was embarrassed into spending the year in one more attempt to face up to the 1974 budget act. It finally passed the Gramm-Rudman-Hollings Act, which Senator Rudman called "a bad idea whose time has come."[3] When he saw how it worked, Senator Hollings was to disassociate himself, leaving it the Gramm-Rudman Act.

The measure amended the 1974 act to provide a yearly deficit ceiling, declining to zero by 1991 (later pushed back to 1993). It set up a procedure for immaculate conception of a budget if Congress failed to produce one. The idea was that if spending threatened to exceed the deficit limit, there would be "automatic" cuts in a range of spending, with the exception of social security, interest on the debt and a range of veterans' and poverty programs. Authority to decide when the deficit was about to be broken, and how large a cut was required, rested with the General Accounting Office. The GAO is of course an arm of Congress; the congressmen were still trying to keep executive power out of the budget process.

Senator Mack Mattingly (R., Ga.) had proposed a legislated, two-year test of a presidential item veto, empowering the president to veto specific parts of spending bills, and Congress to override. He lined up 46 cosponsors in the Senate, but was stopped by Senator Mark Hatfield (R., Ore.), the appropriations committee chairman. He promised to "fight it on every issue, and bring any matter pending before the Senate to a halt to stop" what he called "this mad piece of legislation."[4] Senator Hatfield filibustered against the measure through three cloture votes. The 58–40 vote, two short of the super-majority needed to close debate under Senate rules, marked the high point of the attempt to restore the impoundment powers hamstrung by the 1974 budget act.

The following year, the Supreme Court held for executive power, ruling that the GAO could not be vested with the decision of when Gramm-Rudman had been violated.[5] A separate fallback provision in the legislation had provided for making the automatic cuts through expedited congressional action, an oxymoronic solution. In 1987, the Congress passed a new version yielding OMB the power to declare the "automatic" cuts, or order a Gramm-Rudman "sequester."

This was a limited power, providing the executive branch with an unpalatable alternative, especially since the new legislation was designed to bear especially hard on defense spending the president favored. Even so, it put the executive back in the budget game, and spending started to show some signs of restrained growth. After peaking at 24.3 percent of GNP in fiscal 1983, it drifted downward to 22.3 percent in fiscal 1989. Over the same years, the deficit fell from 6.3 percent of GNP to 3.0 percent of GNP. As the Seven Fat Years ended, both started to rise again.

Mondale's defeat also added momentum for further tax reform. President Reagan had declared it his top priority, and had ordered the Treasury to complete a new plan for release just after the election. The Bradley-Gephardt bill, based on the idea of slashing marginal rates but "closing loopholes," originally introduced in 1982, attracted new Democratic attention. Kemp-Kasten, introduced in 1984, was based on the same principle.

How these measures evolved into the 1986 tax bill is a dramatic story, done full justice by two members of *The Wall Street Journal* Washington bureau, Jeffrey H. Birnbaum and Alan Murray, in their *Showdown at Gucci Gulch*.[6] The Gucci-shod business lobbyists didn't want their loopholes closed; cutting the general corporate rate might more or less even things out for the businesses; but fewer loopholes would mean fewer fees for lobbyists.

Somehow this insurmountable obstacle was overcome, by an improbable coalition. House Ways and Means Chairman Danny Rostenkowski signed up with a bill. Richard Darman, point man for the James Baker Treasury, was a behind-the-scenes hero. At times it seemed the corporate interests were winning; the Senate Finance Committee adopted special break after special break. Stunned by how ridiculous the process was looking, Senator Bob Packwood sat down with an aide and some pitchers of beer, and decided to start over with a clean slate. The result was a relatively clean bill, with a top rate of 28 percent.

There is little point in rehearsing this drama, though it surely played a part in advancing the economic momentum of the Seven Fat Years. But a few points should be noted because they bear on subsequent events.

First, because of the pressure of the deficit, everyone agreed the 1986 tax bill should be "revenue neutral," that is, higher revenues from loophole closing should equal lower revenues from lower rates. These numbers are of course fictitious, estimates churned out by a computer fed some arbitrary and dubious assumptions. The assumption is "static analysis," that cutting a 50 percent tax rate to 40 percent will reduce the revenue take by 20 percent. But matters are surely not so simple; changing a tax rate is likely also to change the amount of income reported as subject to it. This is clearly true if the tax cut turns a laggard economy into a booming one, for example, and is even less disputable in the case of the capital gains tax, where the taxpayer controls when an asset is sold and the tax becomes due.

But myths do have power, and in 1986 the concept of "revenue neutrality" was surely a political key to a happy outcome. Without *some* element of discipline in the process, the Congress would have given everything to everybody. The myth lives on to haunt us, by now incorporated in laws and the thinking of tax writers in both the Congress and the executive branch. Lacking internal discipline, and still struggling with the budget act of 1974, the Congress feels it has to operate by squeezing judgment out of the equation, through arbitrary rules that kill the good along with the bad.

Second, the heirs of Michael 1 could by and large take "loophole closing" or leave it. They favored a tax code as neutral as possible between all types of economic activity, leaving to the market decisions about which ones are more appropriate. And surely the previous tax code had fostered a culture of loopholes. Many of these, for example tax incentives or investments in "alternative" energy sources, led to blatantly uneconomic activity, such as California mountain passes paved with windmills.

But the culture of loopholes was created by high marginal rates. A loophole that cuts your tax, say, from 70 percent to 40 percent doubles your return to 60 percent instead of 30 percent. So it's worthwhile to hire a lot of accountants, lawyers and lobbyists, and to do the dumb things they recommend. Figuring out some way to pare a 28 percent rate to 20 percent raises your return from 72 percent to 80 percent, which won't buy many lawyers. If you cut the rate to 28 percent, you don't have to launch a search-and-destroy mission for loopholes; they will dry up in any event.

Third, most of the furor at Gucci Gulch concerned corporate taxes, and in particular the arcane issue of depreciation. When corporations make investments, they do not charge the whole amount against current income. For both reporting and tax purposes, they "depreciate" or "write off" an investment over its assumed useful life. How fast equipment is depreciated makes a lot of difference in a corporation's tax liabilities.

In the inflationary 1970s, for example, there was a big issue about LIFO and FIFO, both conventionally acceptable ways of accounting for inventories. If you charge last-in-first out, you make money on your inventory during inflation, first-in-first-out loses money. There is no real economic change, of course, but *reported* profits change, and hence tax obligations. On such matters the corporate tax turns, as do the Guccis.

In tandem with the Guccied hordes, big-business populists like a tax code with a high rate but fast depreciation. That way politicians can posture at socking it to the filthy corporations, but corporations don't have to pay any taxes. Or at least, the heavy manufacturers who have big capital investments don't have to pay any, while potential competitors relying on brain instead of brawn get hit with the high rate. Other businesses with low capital investment, law and accounting firms for example, prefer a low rate.

Along with its cuts in the personal rates, the 1981 tax bill provided and maintained a Saturnalia of business tax cuts, a vastly accelerated depreciation schedule, an investment tax credit, "passive losses" in real estate investment trusts (in effect, a pass-through to individual returns of losses generated by generous depreciation). Congress started to take back these provisions in 1982, and with the 1986 bill they were pretty much eliminated. By then, Congress had harnessed itself to the fictitious figures of "revenue neutrality," and business tax increases were needed to pay for lower individual rates.

What to make of this is a bit of a mystery, since no one knows who actually pays the corporate tax. Corporations write the checks, of course, but all economists agree the expense is passed along to someone: shareholders in lower dividends, customers in higher prices, employees in lower wages. No one who understands the issue dares say which. The usually naive assumption is that shareholders pay, but in a perfect economy at equilibrium, it would probably be the customers. But such an equilibrium seldom obtains; the ability to pass the tax along in price may be capped, for example, by competition from imports from nations with different tax structures. It was during this debate that the Eureka College economist, Ronald Reagan, said he hoped someday we'd recognize that we can't tax corporations, only people.

This debate split even supply-siders. Art Laffer said, "I would not have gone for the accelerated depreciation for leaseholds and all that stuff. I would have reduced corporate tax rates, the way Kennedy did. That's the proper way to cut corporate taxes, not with gimmicks, tricks, write-offs, depreciation and all that nonsense."[7] But the Ture-Roberts-Entin contingent looked at the "cost of capital," and argued that the business tax increases would reduce investment and growth.

In 1985, as this debate started, we wrote in the *Journal*, "this constant churning of investment incentives is bound to produce economically costly frictions and uncertainties. But no matter, it is precisely the uncertainty that makes this kind of taxation politically irresistible. Now even the Reagan Treasury has joined the game; faced with a need to chalk up some new revenues so that static analysis will rule its bill revenue neutral, it cooks up some of the least generous depreciation schedules on record."[8]

This debate is relevant to some concerns of the 1990s, starting with the real-estate glut and its attendant banking problems. Real estate developers complain that they were yanked around when the 1981 act gave generous tax treatment and the 1986 act snatched it away. Projects and the loans supporting them went sour, they suggest, because of abrupt changes in the tax laws. A lot of loans to troubled projects were made after 1986, and the "snatching away" started in 1982. Still, there is no doubt some justice to the complaint.

The "cost of capital" debate, more importantly, bears on the issue of what happened to capital investment during the Seven Fat Years. Investment can look either robust or weak, depending on what figures you look at. And naturally people with different purposes point to different figures.

Gross investment looks historically strong. Except for a dip in the 1982 recession, business investment had been running around 12 percent of GNP since about 1978, up a percent from the 1960s and a couple of percent from the 1950s. But net investment—that is gross investment less the depreciation of old equipment—looks weak, generally on a declining trend since a peak in 1966. Changes in the tax law seem to have made only jiggles in either trend.

What has changed is depreciation, or in the National Income Accounts, capital consumption allowances. In calculating this figure, the Commerce Department tries to adjust depreciation reported for tax purposes into depreciation as an actual economic factor. That is, it tries to estimate how fast a building really wears out, and tries to fiddle with something called the "capital consumption adjustment" fast enough to sail a straight economic course as the winds of tax depreciation shift direction.

The capital consumption figures are, understandably, not something you would want to stake your life on. Probably gross investment is a more meaningful figure. Probably the U.S. tax code does raise the cost of capital, and perhaps in the 1990s we will want to redress this imbalance to help investment. It is certainly true that the United States taxes savings and returns from investment more heavily than Japan and Germany. They seem more intent on stimulating investment than in using their tax codes to redistribute income in the name of "fairness."

Still, given the uncertain incidence of the corporate tax, we can be more sure of what we're doing if we deal with individual returns. In particular, we should look askance at the argument, sure to be offered by big business, that to reduce the cost of capital we should cut taxes on corporations by boosting taxes on people. If people ultimately pay any tax, they also ultimately do all saving and investing. What counts is the tax rate on the ultimate provider of capital.

On one aspect of the 1986 tax act's treatment of capital, finally, supply-siders were united. All opposed the provision to raise the capital gains tax to the 28 percent rate, the same rate as "ordinary income." While this sounds neutral, it is not: The base for the gain is not indexed for inflation, so you could owe "tax" even if the asset you held fell in inflation-adjusted value. Also, since capital losses were not fully deductible from other income, they weren't being treated equally at all. While it's true that capital gains were not taxed at death, during life, when people actually make economic decisions, they were being taxed punitively. Again, this was driven by the fictitious figures of static revenue neutrality. It was assumed, contrary to experience, that a higher capital gains tax would produce higher revenues to "pay" for a lower personal rate.

What's more, capital gains were especially important to the young entrepreneurial company; this was the pot at the end of the rainbow that moves breakaway engineers to take out mortgages on their homes to start a business. These arguments were of course familiar from the Steiger amendment debate. From the same debate, we knew that the "Laffer curve" would be especially potent on the capital gains tax. We assumed that we could come back in a year or two and cut the capital gains tax again, with the argument that whatever static analysis said, it would provide more money for the Treasury.

As the 1986 bill passed, vistas seemed to open. Darman was a hero. Danny Rostenkowski was on board. Bill Bradley was ready to lead the Democrats into the fold. And in 1989, we almost got the capital gains cut we'd been looking for (see Chapter 17, "Turning Back"). But as it turned out, predictably I suppose, the bright political vista of 1986 proved too good to be true.

• • •

The Democrats at home were not the only ones jumping on the bandwagon, though. So was the rest of the world. The 1986 tax bill, with its eye-popping 28 percent marginal rate, stimulated lower taxes throughout the world. In a striking demonstration of global interdependence, other countries felt they had no choice but to follow U.S. leadership.

It did not come easily. I remember a conversation in the early 1980s with Sir Alan Walters, economic adviser to Prime Minister Margaret Thatcher. Sir Alan is a very distinguished economist, but of true-blue monetarist views. His adherence to an independent monetary policy led to his 1989 conflict with Chancellor of the Exchequer Nigel Lawson, who sought to link with the European monetary system. The conflict ultimately left both men out of their offices, and the Thatcher administration the poorer for it.

Sir Alan was intent on controlling the British money supply, and in the early 1980s Thatcher policy was intent on reducing the power of the labor unions—perhaps more appropriately than I allowed at the time. Neither priority left much room for tax cuts, but the Thatcher government had taken one whack at the notorious British tax rates, which reached a marginal rate of 98 percent on investment income and 83 percent on labor income. In Mrs. Thatcher's first year, her government had pared the "basic rate" from 83 percent to 60 percent. I wanted to know whether revenues in that range whet up or down. Sir Alan doubted that Her Majesty's Treasury would ever disclose such information.

Lo and behold, in May of 1986, Frank Field, a Labour MP, proposed a written question in the House of Commons. He wanted to know the percentage of all income receipts that had come from the top 5 percent of taxpayers in each year since the budget year 1978–79. Ferdinand Mount remarked in *The Spectator*, "The intention was

TABLE 10-1

British Revenues from the Rich

Earners	Percentage of Total Revenue	
	1978–79	1985–86
Top 1%	11.2	12.0
Top 2%	15.4	17.0
Top 3%	18.8	20.7
Top 4%	21.6	23.9
Top 5%	24.0	26.7
Top 10%	34.0	37.0

presumably to show how 'Thatcher's tax cuts for the rich,' had reduced the share of the national burden shouldered by her City friends."[9]

The Treasury delivered a table showing that at the lower rates, the rich paid more of the total burden. The Laffer curve was alive and well and living in Great Britain. *The Sunday Times* explained why:

> High earners who face penal marginal rates of income tax can do four things: escape into tax shelters; take any additional pay in the form of hard-to-tax perks; decide it is not worth doing any more work to increase their income if the taxman is going to confiscate most of it; or leave the country. All four steps reduce revenues to the Treasury.
>
> Slash their high marginal rates and they do the opposite: they stay in the country, they emerge from their tax shelters into the above-ground economy again; they want their pay rises in money rather than perks; and they rediscover the incentive to earn more. All of that increases the amount of income tax flowing into the Treasury's coffers.[10]

The specter of the brain drain was especially persuasive to foreign governments. One *Journal* story out of Canada reported, "There is a story circulating in the Toronto business district about a businessman who told his tax adviser, 'Forget the tax planning. Get me a green card.' " Canada, which only a year earlier proposed a surtax on high incomes, found it necessary to join the bandwagon. In a release to clients, economist David Hale explained the alternative:

> In recent decades, Canada has pursued a typically corporatist fiscal policy of taxing individuals heavily and business lightly. As with the

United Kingdom before Mrs. Thatcher, Canada's marginal tax rates on
personal income are far above tax rates in the U.S. but Canada's depreciation policies are among the most generous in the industrial
world. If Canada persists with such tax policies while maintaining a
relatively open trading relationship with the U.S., North America
could become an interesting laboratory for testing the impact of tax
incentives on resource allocation. The large differentials between U.S.
and Canadian taxation could encourage firms to locate their capital
intensive operations in a high depreciation corridor along the Ontario
border and their human intensive activities in a low personal tax corridor on the American side of the border. Under such circumstances,
Canada could develop an economy consisting of only three major
sectors—the government, traditional resource extraction industries
and a border corridor of robot operated manufacturing facilities managed by satellite remote control from the headquarters of expatriate
Canadian firms located in Buffalo, Detroit and Florida.[11]

Interest soon developed in supply-side policies throughout the
world. The German paper *Welt am Sonntag* published a chart of Die
Laffer-Curve, with shading over *Abnehmende*—"the prohibitive
range." The French developed a word for it, *"Theorie de L'Offre"* and
in 1987, French Finance Minister Edouard Balladur took time out
from the G-7 meetings in Washington to bestow Paul Craig Roberts
with the title, Chevalier of the Legion of Honor.

Internationally, even staid organizations took notice, the Organisation for Economic Co-operation and Development, for example. In
its December 1985 *Economic Outlook*, it described the evolution:

[G]overnments' use of the tax system to meet goals other than revenue
rising (such as income redistribution, energy conservation, investment
in regions with high unemployment) has greatly increased the disper-
sion of tax rates for different categories of income or expenditure. The
resulting narrower tax bases lead to high marginal rates, which signif-
icantly modify economic behavior. As only some of these changes in
behavior are intended by the government in pursuing these goals, the
growing interest in tax reform can be seen as reflecting concerns about
the appropriateness of using the tax system to pursue goals.

Personal income taxation is one of the most obvious cases. In particular, marginal personal tax rates, which are potentially the most
distorting, appear so high in some countries as to be significant impediments to personal initiative.[12]

At one international conference, I remember remarking that with
Sweden's tax rate of 87 percent on incomes over about $40,000, re-

warding an employee with a dollar raise costs the company seven dollars. The chairman of SAS got up to correct me. The company also has to pay a payroll tax, he noted, so to give a dollar raise cost $11.

By 1988, Sweden had pared its top rate to 75 percent, and Canada had dropped its top rate to 45 percent. Between 1984 and 1988, most European countries had started to pare rates, from 65 percent to 57 percent in France, from 73 percent to 68 percent in Denmark, from 65 percent to 60 percent in Italy.[13] Japan, which had maintained a high marginal rate at very high thresholds, above $300,000 in income, trimmed it from 73 percent to 68 percent. Germany was something of a holdout, but trimmed its rate to 53 percent in 1988.

In introducing his 1988 budget, Nigel Lawson said:

> It is now nine years since my predecessor, in his first Budget in 1979, reduced the top rate of tax from the absurd 83 percent that prevailed under Labor to 60 percent, where it has remained ever since. At that time, this was broadly in line with the European average for the top rate of tax. It is now one of the highest. And not only do the majority of European countries now have a top rate of tax below 60 percent, but in the English-speaking countries outside Europe—not only the United States and Canada, but Labor Australia and New Zealand, too—the top rate is now below 50 percent, sometimes well below.
>
> The reason for the worldwide trend towards lower top rates of tax is clear. Excessive rates of income tax destroy enterprise, encourage avoidance, and drive talent to more hospitable shores overseas.
>
> As a result, so far from raising additional revenue, over time they actually raise less. By contrast, a reduction in the top rates of income tax can, over time, result in a higher, not a lower, yield to the Exchequer. Despite the substantial reduction in the top rate of tax in 1979, and the subsequent abolition of the investment income surcharge in 1984, the top 5 percent of taxpayers today contribute a third as much again in real terms as they did in 1978–79, Labor's last year; while the remaining 95 percent of taxpayers pay about the same in real terms as they did in 1978–79.[14]

In the years before these rate cuts, there was a hybrid word—like stagflation or damnyankee—"Europessimism." Between 1980 and 1985, Europe had no net job creation. Unemployment hovered around 11 percent, and the best hope was that it might stabilize there.[15] By the late 1980s, European employment was growing at a rate of about 1.5% a year.[16] Most importantly, Europe had recovered its self-confidence and optimism, and was looking forward to unifying its markets in 1992, even before the Berlin Wall fell and Eastern Europe opened.

This did not, of course much reduce European complaints about the federal budget deficit, which when correctly accounted was never much larger than European ones (see Chapter 12, "The Dread Deficit"). Nor did it add much to the esteem of Ronald Reagan's economic policies either abroad or at home. But Anthony Harris, one of the *Financial Times'* leading columnists, did stop to ask, "If the policies were so wrong, why are they still being so widely imitated?"[17]

11

What You Learned if You Were Awake

To learn anything from the Seven Fat Years, we have to start by remembering what the economy was like before they came. Paul Volcker and Ronald Reagan inherited a nation and a world in the grips of an economic crisis. They led the way out of this wilderness and sparked an economic expansion of unprecedented duration. The economy they left to their successors of course has troubles, but they pale beside those of 1979. *Something* must have worked. To discern what, it will help to review the history related thus far.

Lest we forget, in 1979 the world stood on an economic precipice. Inflation ran 13.5 percent in 1980, real production dipped and the prime rate reached 21.5 percent. And economics as conventionally understood provided no intellectual tools for understanding this crisis, let alone curbing it. Worse, the affliction had struck the whole world, and threatened more damage to come.

The United States ran the world currency, with little understanding of the responsibilities and risks that carried. Mike Blumenthal came to understand the disaster scenario well enough to outline it to Jimmy Carter: the collapse of the dollar's store of value function throughout the world, a rush to liquidate the reserve currency stocks built up since World War II, soaring inflation and interest rates in the United States, an outbreak of protectionism, the strangling of world trade, the bankruptcy of the Third World countries who held dollar reserves, and a collapse of Western confidence in the face of a Soviet threat.

163

In the 1990s, this all seems remote. We have forgotten, willingly so, understandably so, blessedly so. We can remember to ridicule the Rosy Scenario, but the nightmare scenario we have repressed. We sensed at the end of the 1970s that we were flirting with some sort of economic breakup. Not many of us understood the precise mechanism of an international monetary collapse, but we could believe that the world was stumbling toward an economic catastrophe on the order of the 1930s. At Belgrade in October of 1979 it may have been only months away. At least, it could have been precipitated in months if the dollar's custodians had blundered.

Yet somehow the West found the moral and intellectual resources to grope back from the precipice—at times blinded and stumbling, but still, away from disaster rather than toward it. Somehow the impending worldwide collapse was averted. Somehow the inflation came down, much more rapidly than most would have dared hope. Somehow the abrupt end to inflation did not cause a depression. Somehow, indeed, vigorous growth reemerged in 1983. Somehow, no one any more talks of stagflation.

Somehow the crisis was over; somehow the system held. Somehow, indeed, a vigorous entrepreneurial expansion endured for more than seven years. This was a prodigious achievement.

Surely, then, there must be lessons to be learned. We have to start, it needs to be said, by remembering where we have been and recognizing where we have arrived. The conventional wisdom seems to be that the Reagan tax cuts started all our economic troubles; any memory of the 1970s shows this to be ludicrous. We started the 1980s with virulent stagflation then-conventional economics could not explain, let alone cure. Since then we have gone through an enormous economic adjustment.

Unless we recognize the enormous turn from stagflation to boom, we can't begin to draw the lessons of our experience. Nor, for that matter, can we understand the issues of the 1990s. The big savings and loan crisis, and the problems of the Third World, have their roots in the inflation of the 1970s, and in our efforts to cure it. But we are not likely to cope with the problems of the 1990s unless we understand the 1970s and 1980s. The stagflation crisis was cured; how?

The crisis was resolved, I argue, because the Mundell policy mix worked. This is not to say the diners at Michael 1 made it happen, or that anyone in power planned the policy mix or even understood it. But in its own mysterious, stumbling way, the system found it: Volcker's tight money killed the inflation; Reagan's tax cuts revived growth.

It took a time to find the right compass for monetary policy, and arguments about the deficit delayed the tax cuts. With this timing mismatch, we had a recession in 1982. But when fiscal and monetary policy finally both came into place in 1983, Bob Mundell's policy mix worked. This is the main lesson we need to remember in the 1990s.

It will be hard, no doubt, to persuade the doubters. But what other explanation is on the table? Something worked; we had Seven Fat Years. If not the mix of tax cuts and tight money, what did it? Is another hypothesis even offered?

The most plausible reply, I suppose, was that Volcker succeeded single-handedly—indeed, that Volcker succeeded in spite of Reagan and his reckless tax cuts. This assigns a rather larger role to monetary policy than Milton Friedman ever did: money matters, but fiscal policy doesn't. Alternatively, it is sometimes argued that Reagan succeeded despite Volcker, that his deficits produced a Keynesian boom. But how do deficits boost aggregate demand while tight money is constraining it? Anyway, if the Seven Fat Years were driven by the Phillips curve, what happened to the inflation?

Remember the sequence of monetary policy: Volcker started to tighten money in October 1979. He clamped down in earnest between the election and the inauguration. He clamped down even more in May 1981 and February 1982, when M-1 showed signs of "too much" growth. This checked the inflation, from 13.5 percent in 1980, to 10.3 percent in 1981, to 6.2 percent in 1982. The really good numbers, like 3.2 percent in 1983 and 1.9 percent in 1986, came when the economy started to revive. As Art Laffer said at Michael 1, you don't fight inflation by producing fewer goods.

However necessary, Volcker's monetary contraction was an enormous jolt to the real side of the economy, upsetting bets all over the world. Nearly everyone had bet on constantly increasing oil prices, for example. Hundreds of exploration firms in Texas had borrowed money at 15 percent or 20 percent interest, for example, with both they and their bankers expecting that it could be paid back out of the oil bonanza. But when money turned tight, the oil price couldn't go up and the loans couldn't be repaid. Penn Square Bank went down, and other banks started to shake.

It was not just the price of oil, of course, but the price of everything else. Farm land, for example, had also been purchased with borrowed money. So had real estate; the savings and loan problem we're grappling with in the 1990s had roots in the inflation of the 1970s. And if the borrowers all started to default at once, the banks would be endangered. If the banks couldn't make loans, even viable enterprises would be starved for credit, meaning more defaults, shakier banks, less credit, perhaps bank runs, and certainly a general loss of business and consumer confidence. With this adjustment, a spiraling implosion was not difficult to imagine.

Indeed, it was a near thing with Mexico. The whole country had bet on increasing oil prices. It was worse because both the Mexican government and Mexican business had borrowed in dollars, betting not only on the price of oil but the price of the peso. Mexico devalued, froze its domestic dollar deposits and then nationalized its banks. It was on the brink of collapse, and it threatened to take with it Citibank and the Bank of America, for starters.

Now, with these monetary conditions, integrate fiscal policy: Imagine that at this point you still had the 1980 Carter budget. It called, remember from Chapter 6, "Ronald Reagan," for taxes to increase by 3 percent of GNP between 1978 and 1984. It projected that the economy would grow by 68 percent, while tax revenues grew by 94 percent. The economy could not grow that vigorously with those taxes, let alone with Volcker's monetary policy. Loading this tax burden into 1982, with Mexico trembling, would have produced seven lean years, not seven fat ones.

In those circumstances, wouldn't anyone rather have the Steiger amendment, the first tentative steps of the Reagan tax cuts, the Brodhead amendment reducing the top rate on investment income to 50 percent from 70 percent, and the prospect of real tax cuts a few months down the road, on January 1, 1983? At the very least, the Reagan tax policies gave the economy breathing room while the Fed put its bear hug on inflation.

This is a most modest claim for the tax cuts. By contrast, Lawrence B. Lindsey, who became a Federal Reserve governor in 1991, has argued that inflation was licked on the fiscal side. Monetary policy, as measured by the aggregates, did not change enough to explain the collapse of inflation; but tax policy encouraged production and stimulated investors to move from real assets to financial assets.[1] While this analysis puts too much emphasis on the aggregates, it is a useful reminder that growth, not recession, is the best anti-inflation medicine.

Taking the period as a whole, you can see the policy mix at work. Inflation peaked when Volcker came back from Belgrade. The venture capital industry blossomed when the Steiger tax cut was passed.

Almost on the day that the first net tax cuts were effective, January 1, 1983, the Seven Fat Years started.

• • •

There was of course a recession in 1982, formally dated from a peak in July 1981 to the trough in November 1982. This is scarcely surprising, given the Federal Reserve policy described above. Probably the Fed overdid matters, especially in May, but tighten it had to, given the persistent inflation. In the view of most economists, recession would be a reasonable price to pay to end the inflation. In view of many central bankers, perhaps including Volcker, a recession was *the way* to end inflation.

Ronald Reagan was inaugurated in January. His tax bill went into effect in October, phased in over three years. In the face of bracket creep and previously legislated increases in the social security payroll tax, the first net tax cuts were to arrive in 1983. Yet conventional wisdom blames the deficits caused by the Reagan tax cuts for the recession that started before they were ever passed.

The 1982 recession was caused by monetary policy, for better or worse. Or, to view it more instructively, it was caused by a timing mismatch. The tight money part of the policy mix was put in place as early as October 1979, and especially in the fall of 1980. The tax cuts didn't start until October 1981, and were not effective on a net basis until January 1983. In between there was a recession.

The heirs of Michael 1 understood this perfectly well at the time. As early as November 1981, we wrote in the *Journal* that the premise of supply-side economics was "You fight inflation with a tight monetary policy. And you offset the possible recessionary impact of tight monetary policy with the incentive effects of reductions in marginal tax rates. Since we are now having a recession, you could claim the formula has failed, except for one detail: We've had tight money all right, but dear friends, we haven't had any tax cut."[2]

Or as Jack Kemp put it in a remarkable speech before a conference at the Federal Reserve Bank of Atlanta and Emory University in March 1982:

> [T]he idea of using fiscal incentives to cushion the immediate effects of disinflation was lost in the shuffle. President Reagan's original plan would have cut income tax rates 20 percent by January 1, 1982. Instead, the cut is only 5 percent. Because American families received

only a 1.25 percent tax credit last year, the Treasury estimates that taxes rose $15 billion in 1981—more than $150 for the average worker. American families bore the brunt of monetary policy without any of the planned incentives in place.

He noted, however, that tax cuts were coming, that "for the first time since 1948, there are tax incentives in place during a recession, in time to do any good."[3]

Or as Irving Kristol explained in November 1982,

Why did the economy collapse? The answer is obvious and has no connection with "Reaganomics." It was the collision between the swollen Carter budget for 1981 (which ended Sept. 30) and the tight money policy of the Fed, which combined to push interest rates sky-high and the economy into a decline.

It had nothing to do with Mr. Reagan's tax cuts, which are only now beginning to be phased in, and in a minimal way at that. It had nothing to do with Mr. Reagan's budget cuts, which are still largely on paper. And it certainly had nothing to do with an increase in defense expenditures, which are as yet a gleam in the Pentagon's eye. . . .

Meanwhile, we may as well clear our minds about the issue of "Reaganomics." One of the most distressing aspects of David Stockman's unfortunate interview is the distorted history of "Reaganomics" that it presents, one that is now being gleefully accepted and promulgated by Mr. Reagan's detractors. . . .

So there was no "Trojan Horse," no deception, no conspiracy. What is now called "Reaganomics"—the totality of those tax cuts—was a bipartisan creation. And in the long view, the totality of those cuts represents the most progressive piece of tax legislation in our history—"progressive" in the sense that it lays the groundwork for sustained and superior economic growth in the years ahead.[4]

Kristol suggested that the best policy would be to try to persuade Congress to advance the date of the tax cut, adding that cutting taxes in recession is also a good Keynesian prescription. Indeed, at one point this suggestion was floated by Treasury Secretary Regan, but given the prevailing deficit mania it inevitably proved a political nonstarter.

The alternative solution to the timing mismatch, of course, would be to delay the tight money until the tax cuts came into place. This, as Craig Roberts stresses, is precisely what Rosy Scenario was all about: The Fed should bring money growth down gradually, as tax incentives were put into place. Inflation would moderate more slowly, but without the price of a recession.

Logically, Rosy Scenario was a perfectly consistent policy, which is more than you can say of the various conventional wisdoms. But the issue is whether it would have worked in practice. Did the Fed have that much time, economically or politically? Did it have the knowledge and understanding sufficient to calibrate monetary tightness so precisely. (After all, the monetarist Treasury supported tightening in May 1981 and February 1982.) If we faced a dollar crisis, as I believe we surely did, Volcker's first task was to get the inflation stopped.

In retrospect, I would take the 1982 recession all over again, at least if I knew it would be followed by seven years of expansion. But if the tax policy had been bolder, if it hadn't been diluted by fear of the deficit, it's likely the recession could have been avoided. At least Mundell thinks so. "The monetary contraction was much in advance of the fiscal stimulus from the tax cuts," he has recently written. "Had the change in policy mix been executed correctly, the inflation could have been stopped without a major recession."[5]

• • •

Economically, the 1982 recession was costly; since peak unemployment hit 11 percent, it's usually been billed as the worst since the Great Depression. Politically, it threw the president on the defensive, and hurt the Republicans in the 1982 elections, in which they lost 27 House seats. In the public relations battles, it gave a black eye to supply-side economics. The term is not much to be regretted, since its adherents understood that new classical economics was a better one.

Intellectually, however, this public relations loss has obscured the nation's understanding of the lessons of the Seven Fat Years. For the "supply-side" movement is not remembered for its correct predictions about prosperity, but for the "Laffer curve," and its supposed prediction that the revenue effects of tax cuts would be large enough to shrink the deficit. The deficit, of course, expanded in the 1982 recession and has persisted since.

The prediction, however, is not one any of us really ever made. Perusing the documents of the 1978–81 period, of course, it's possible to find suggestions of an immediate boost in revenues from an across-the-board tax cut in a careless press release or political statement. In "The Kemp-Roth-Laffer Free Lunch," Walter Heller cited a 1978 issue of the "Kemp-Roth News," put out by congressional staff. And Ronald Reagan's invocation of Ibn Khaldūn can be read as not merely a dynasty-long outlook but a hope of an immediate payback from tax cuts, as had indeed happened with the Mellon and Kennedy tax cuts.

Still, as already mentioned in the context of the 1978 debate in Chapter 4, nothing in the Laffer curve predicts that all tax cuts will bring in new revenues. The curve demonstrates that a tax cut can raise revenues under certain circumstances. The circumstances, of course, are when the marginal rate is beyond the tip of the parabolic curve, when it's high enough to be in the "prohibitive range." Whether or not this circumstance prevails is an empirical matter, or given the lack of hard data, a matter of judgment.

The judgment at Michael 1 was that, with marginal rates reaching up to 70 percent, surely some parts of the U.S. tax code reached into the prohibitive range. Probably a lot. After all, cutting a 70 percent rate to 50 percent allows the taxpayer to keep 50 cents on the dollar instead of 30 cents, and a 67 percent increase in return can surely affect behavior.

My own guess has always been that the tip of the curve lies around a marginal rate of 35 percent, that making allowances for state and local income taxes the 28 percent top rate reached in 1986 was a pretty good approximation. High income taxpayers pay the highest marginal rates, so we would have expected increased revenues from this group. This is in fact what happened.

This increase in revenues from prosperous taxpayers would provide a "reflow" that would mean much less loss of revenue than predicted by the conventional "static analysis." In estimating the revenue effect of tax cuts, the Treasury and congressional tax committees would mechanically apply new tax rates to old tax bases, implicitly assuming that the tax rates will not change the behavior of taxpayers, either in work effort, in the timing of discretionary income or in the search for tax shelters. So they would underestimate revenues by missing the "Laffer curve" response of high-income taxpayers.

Supply-siders would predict something else: That in addition to stimulating some revenue reflows, there would be another response. If the tax incentives stimulated more production and a larger economy, there would also be a larger savings pool—to finance, among other things, government borrowing to fund the deficit. So between some direct revenue flow and an expanded savings pool, the tax cuts would be "self-financing," *in the sense that they would not exert any net upward pressure on interest rates.*

Saying this is quite different, obviously, from predicting the Kemp-Roth bill or the 1981 tax cut would actually produce more revenue for the Treasury in their first year. Many taxpayers pay less than the top rate, and everyone paid the bottom rate on some nonmarginal part of his income; no one expected that a tax cut for lower brackets would raise revenues. Rather it was a matter of fairness, especially since any wage-earner paid the rapidly increasing social security payroll tax; the 1981 tax bill removed millions of low income taxpayers from the income tax rolls altogether.

Craig Roberts reviewed supply-side predictions about the revenue reflows from the Laffer curve. Certainly the Reagan Treasury, of which he was part, made no prediction that the tax cuts would expand revenues. Its predictions are amply on record in the usual budget documents. Its February 1981 tables showed a net revenue loss of $718.2 billion over six years. In fact, Craig and Norman Ture at the Treasury were mostly annoyed by the Laffer curve, which they viewed as a distraction.

Similarly, the Reagan campaign's Chicago documents show revenue losses, estimating that only 17 percent of "static analysis" revenues would be recouped through faster growth. And Wanniski's article on "The Mundell-Laffer Hypothesis" modestly argued that "sufficient tax revenues will be recovered to pay the interest on the government bonds used to finance the deficit." No revenue-raising claim was made in Jack Kemp's book, *The American Renaissance*, which only asserted that the Laffer curve cast much doubt on the static revenue forecasts. Even the expansive George Gilder, in *Wealth and Poverty*, applies the Laffer curve only to high-income taxpayers.[6]

Finally, any fair reading of the record would also note that often advocates of tax cuts went to lengths to point out the caricature of their views. For example, in a letter-to-the editor of the *Journal*, Jack Kemp replied to an earlier article, "Some Supply-Side Propositions" by Herb Stein:

> Under some circumstances, cutting tax rates will increase revenue; under others, reduce it. Therefore we must be skeptical when Professor Stein's Proposition 9 ascribes to modern supply-siders the view that "A tax reduction, not accompanied by a reduction of government expenditures, will raise the total revenue, and will do so by operating on the supply side of the economy."
>
> After formulating this bald proposition (Any "tax reduction"? Always?), Professor Stein explains its arithmetical drawbacks.[7]

Or, take our own editorial, "The Economic Issue," a few days before the voters were to choose between President Carter and candidate Reagan:

> If marginal rates are prohibitively high, cutting the *rates* may actually increase tax *revenues* by expanding the production, realization or reporting of income subject to the tax. This "Laffer curve" has seemed to work with the Steiger capital gains tax cuts of 1978, and might work again with certain rifle-shot tax cuts, in particular dropping the 70% rate on investment income to the 50% maximum on labor income.
>
> The prohibitive range of the Laffer curve is an extreme case, and marginal tax rates for the ordinary workingman may not yet be this high (though they will rapidly increase in the absence of tax cuts to offset bracket creep). But even if a broad-based tax cut will not immediately pay for itself in increased revenue, the basic insights of supply-side economics remain. You increase incentives and encourage production if you cut marginal tax rates.[8]

How then did the world come to the understanding that the supply-siders said that the broad-based tax cuts would actually increase revenues. Because, with only a little help from the supply-siders themselves, their opponents succeeded in erecting this straw-man and demolishing it.

In "Revolution," Martin Anderson describes his quest for a citation, starting with a letter to Martin Feldstein, who left the Reagan White House and delivered a rather mean-spirited paper at the American Economics Association in 1985. He said that experience had not been kind to the "extreme supply-siders" who had predicted that an across-the-board tax reduction would, among other things, "increase tax revenue." Who said that? Anderson asked, never getting a satisfactory answer from Feldstein or several other prominent economists.[9]

In fact, the best citation I can think of was already cited in Chapter 6, "Ronald Reagan." It was Martin Feldstein who explicitly said, "[I]f it is done in the right way, a multi-year tax cut could bring immediate increases in investment, savings and individual effort without any increases in the government deficit now or in the future."[10] But of course, the big expectational effect didn't happen or wasn't allowed to happen.

If what didn't happen wasn't predicted, what was predicted certainly did. At marginal rates likely to be in the "prohibitive range," the Laffer curve worked. From taxpayers paying the highest marginal rates, revenues went up. These rates of course apply to our highest-income taxpayers, and by now it has been repeatedly demonstrated, even in figures compiled by a hostile Ways and Means Committee, that the rich did provide a higher percentage of the total income tax revenues than they did at the old rates.

By the 1990s, indeed, the argument has shifted away from this brute fact to more subtle objections. It is certainly true that for lower-income people, especially as they were relieved of income taxes, the burden of the social security payroll tax has loomed larger. But if the benefits this tax finances are also counted, the social security system as a whole redistributes income from top to bottom.

The more common objection was succinctly put in the Ways and Means Committee "Green Book" in discussing projections of the 1992 income distribution. To wit, "Because the incomes of the top 20 percent of families rose faster than average, they earned a higher share of overall family income in 1991 than in 1977. As a result, they paid a higher share of total Federal taxes, but they paid less of their income in taxes in 1992 than in 1977."[11] Laying aside the suspect nature of these statistics, to be discussed in Chapter 17, "Turning Back," what the committee is saying is that the Laffer curve works as advertised.

Larry Lindsey has done the most careful analysis of the revenue effects of the 1981 tax cut, The Economic Recovery Tax Act: "ERTA cost less than one-third as much as implied by the naively calculated direct estimate," he writes. "In 1982 this true revenue cost amounted to only $6.1 billion, compared to the $44 billion direct effect estimate." His work with the tax model at the National Bureau of Economic Research also led him to conclude, "By 1985, at a revenue cost in that year of $33 billion, economic output was between 2 and 3 percent higher than it would have been without the tax cut. That extra growth stands for millions of new jobs and a higher standard of living."[12]

• • •

The general optimism of the supply-siders contrasts, too, with the doom and gloom preached by, say, Henry Kaufman or the later David Stockman. The supply-side decreed: There is a way out. That was the message of Jude Wanniski's 1978 book *The Way the World Works.* Also of George Gilder's 1981 best-seller, *Wealth and Poverty.* It was the message Mundell offered in consulting with the Treasury as early as December 1974. It was the message Art Laffer pressed as a member of the President's Economic Policy Advisory Board, where he sat with such eminences as Arthur Burns, Milton Friedman, Alan Greenspan and Walter Wriston. [13]

Most especially, the heirs of Michael 1 thought that the delayed tax cut would hurt, but that recovery would start with 1983. In a December 1981 interview with *Barron's*, for example, Art Laffer had this to say: "1981, obviously, has been a bad year because they postponed the tax cuts, and 1982 doesn't look great." But, "Once we are in '83 and '84, we are going to be in a great economy." Are you sure, the interviewer asked, "Oh, yeah, there is no question in my mind. I couldn't be more certain of a proposition than I am of that, given the uncertainty of my profession." [14]

As 1983 dawned, most economists expected some recovery from the 1982 recession, but only a tepid one. The average of the economists polled by the blue-chip survey predicted real growth of 2.8 percent. An internal Federal Reserve study reportedly predicted only 2 percent. The stock and bond markets picked up when Volcker abandoned M-1; reflecting on this in October 1982, Paul Samuelson wrote, "President Reagan got his economics 180 degrees wrong when he claimed that the Wall Street rise was a recognition that his economic program was working. It was a recognition that his program was failing." [15]

"Be prepared for a major upturn in the economy," Kadlec and Laffer wrote in their investment letter in September 1982. They predicted an upturn starting in the first quarter of 1983, with growth above 3.5 percent and perhaps approaching 4.4 percent, and "even stronger expansion in 1984." [16] In October 1982, Alan Reynolds wrote of "a dazzling expansion." [17] And of course, in our "At Last, a Tax Cut," we contrasted the optimism of the supply-siders with the conventional wisdom that recovery would be aborted by high interest rates caused by the deficit.

In the event, the optimists were proved right. Real growth in 1983 hit 3.6 percent, while 1984 came in at 6.8 percent, the best peacetime year in modern history. *Something* must have worked.

• • •

More broadly, *everyone knew* that a policy mix of tax cuts and tight money would never work. Licking inflation, ratcheting down the Phillips curve, would be a long and tortuous process. And if you cut taxes, boosting demand, inflation control would become impossible. In 1980, this was both the conventional wisdom and the advice of our most distinguished economists. Take, for example, what some of the latter said in *The Wall Street Journal.*

Walter Heller of our Board of Contributors repeated his 1978 inflation prediction, "Kemp-Roth tax cuts, depreciation speedups and a Reagan defense buildup would inject between $150 billion and $200 billion of purchasing power annually into the economy by 1983. How can the economy absorb that big an expansionary punch without aggravating our already intolerable inflation?"[18]

Lester Thurow said that the combination of tax cuts and a defense buildup would "wreck the economy." And while some economists thought the 1980s would be healthy because of demographic trends, James Tobin faulted the Reagan policies for failure to break the wage–price spiral. In September 1981, he predicted that the most likely outcome of the Reagan policies would be "a continuation of stagflation, with little sustained progress against either unemployment or inflation."[19]

Perhaps the best collection of the conventional wisdom of the time was by Jack Kemp in his Atlanta speech, delivered in March 1982, in the depths of recession:

> Both before and since the 1980 elections, the biggest problem caused for us politicians by you economists has not involved your many disagreements, but rather a remarkable consensus among all of the various schools. On the left, Robert Lekachman warns us that "The era of growth is over and the era of limits is upon us. It means the whole politics of the country has changed." He goes on to urge redistribution of income as the answer to our problems. On the right, Friedrich von Hayek tells us that "we are much too afraid of another depression to really fight inflation." Hayek says "You cannot stop inflation without causing a depression."
>
> Barry Bosworth of the Brookings Institution says, "We could return to the low levels of inflation in the early sixties by a decade of major recessions." Kenneth Arrow, the Nobel Prize-winning Keynesian, confesses that "The position of the liberal activist has been greatly injured because we are unable to reconcile full employment and price stability."
>
> Herb Stein, who I guess qualifies as a conservative activist, outlined his plan for ending inflation as follows: "We can begin the process of gradual disinflation now—meaning monetary and fiscal measures to restrain the growth of demand, which would little by little reduce

inflation until some livable rate is reached. How long this would take, and how much unemployment would be entailed, are unknown although the period may be five years."

And even my good monetarist friend Beryl Sprinkel, before he joined the Treasury, said: "We're going to have to have restrained policies for several years with unemployment running in the 8% to 9% range." Such policies, he said, would reduce inflation from 9 percent to 10 percent annually to 6 percent to 7 percent.[20]

The prognosis of our best economists was most succinctly put by Professor Tobin in a letter to the *Journal* published on January 20, 1981:

> Re your January 8 editorial "Once More, With Feeling":
>
> If a west-bound locomotive is harnessed to one end of an Amtrak train in New Haven and an east-bound engine to the other end, will the train go simultaneously to New York and Boston? If a Volcker monetary locomotive pulls the economy one way while a Kemp-Stockman fiscal engine pulls it the other, will the train reach both destinations, disinflation and expansion?
>
> Your editorial attributes to Bob Mundell the old dictum that you need as many policy levers as goals but omits the crucial qualifications he knows, the words "at least." When the levers are connected to the goals by identical mechanisms, it does no good to have as many levers as goals, or even more. The dominant mechanisms relating fiscal and monetary levers to price and output goals are the same; both policies work via the pressure of demand on productive resources. The policy mix does matter, to be sure, for other objectives, e.g. the dollar exchange rate, capital formation.
>
> It's best to be realistic about stagflation. It can't be solved by assigning disinflation to the Fed while tax cuts and defense spending "get the economy moving again." The train may creep in one direction or the other, but the main result will be high interest rates, nominal and real.[21]

Well, there we stood during the Seven Fat Years, in New York and Boston too. Inflation was gone and prosperity reigned. The nominal interest rate broke the following year, and while inflation-adjusted interest rates remained high, something remarkable and instructive had happened. The outlook for the 1990s would be far more optimistic if anyone had been awake to notice.

INTO THE NINETIES

12

The Dread Deficit

Gazing over the magazine rack at the Kankakee mall, the Man from Mars shook his head. The headlines screamed crisis. The American economy was just as crisis-prone as Elizabeth Taylor, it seemed. One economic specter after another popped up in strange places, like Elvis. Maybe these Earthlings know something I don't, he thought. I can see they stumbled back out of the fix they stumbled into before 1983, but maybe I can't see the big problems ahead in the 1990s. What is it that's bothering them?

Let's see, he pondered, they talk about "the deficit." Actually, they're preoccupied with it. Then they worry about the twin deficits, about tight-fisted bankers turning careless, about greed, about fairness. Well at least on the deficit there ought to be some numbers, he thought, and pulled out his Databoy.

DEFICIT, he typed. The screen flashed back "Why do you want to know?"

JUST OFFICIAL NUMBERS, SMART ALEC, he typed. "OK," the screen flashed, "Exclude or include social security?"

WHAT? he typed. "Also," the screen flashed, "Exclude or include S&L bailout? Exclude or include government capital spending? Exclude payment of interest? Include contingent liabilities? Balance with government assets? Adjust outstanding government debt for inflation?"

Wait a minute, the Man from Mars thought, I don't want to get into economic concepts. How do we keep it simple?

CHART, he typed, FEDERAL RECEIPTS AND OUTLAYS. The Databoy found that easy:

Glancing at the chart, the Man from Mars saw that yes, outlays had

179

FIGURE 12–1

Federal Outlays and Receipts

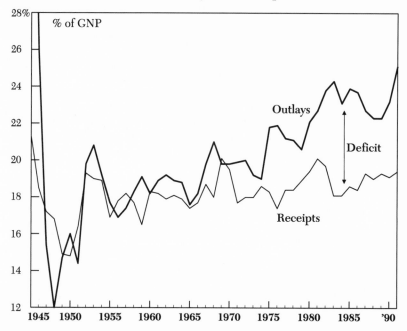

bulged over receipts. "Whatever happened in 1974?" he wondered. The receipts line looked essentially flat for 35 years. Maybe a little temporary drop with the famous Reagan tax cuts, or was it a little temporary bulge before them? But the outlays shot up sharply after 1974, and again in the early 1980s. The difference was "the deficit."

Or at least, that's how much the federal government had to borrow. Borrowing is some kind of a problem, he reasoned, but everyone borrows. Homeowners take out mortgages, for example, and corporations issue bonds. How much borrowing is too much, he wondered? Well, what have other governments been doing?

INTERNATIONAL COMPARISON, he typed. Well, he learned, most other nations don't have a "deficit"; they have a "public sector borrowing requirement," which has the ring of a more specific term, if a less cosmic one. And, he learned, most places don't have really independent state and local governments, and international comparisons include the whole public sector. On this basis, the U.S. deficit looks less frightening; most state and local governments have balanced-budget requirements and fund pension reserves. As net suppliers of funds in the credit market, they reduce government borrowing.

After explaining all the footnotes, the Databoy throws up an OECD table:

TABLE 12-1

General Government Financial Balances

	U.S.	G7	Japan	Germany
1971	-1.8	-0.8	1.2	-0.2
1972	-0.3	-0.8	-0.1	-0.5
1973	0.6	-0.2	0.5	1.2
1974	-0.3	-0.9	0.4	-1.3
1975	-4.1	-4.4	-2.8	-5.6
1976	-2.2	-3.2	-3.7	-3.4
1977	-1.0	-2.5	-3.8	-2.4
1978	0.0	-2.8	-5.5	-2.4
1979	0.5	-2.2	-4.7	-2.6
1980	-1.3	-2.7	-4.4	-2.9
1981	-1.0	-2.8	-3.8	-3.7
1982	-3.5	-4.0	-3.6	-3.3
1983	-3.8	-4.1	-3.7	-2.5
1984	-2.8	-3.4	-2.1	-1.9
1985	-3.3	-3.2	-0.8	-1.1
1986	-3.4	-3.2	-0.9	-1.3
1987	-2.4	-2.2	0.7	-1.9
1988	-2.0	-1.5	2.1	-2.1
1989	-1.7	-1.0	2.7	0.2
p-1990	-2.4	-1.5	3.1	-3.1
p-1991	-2.0	-1.5	3.3	-4.0
p-1992	-1.7	-1.2	3.4	-3.0

p–projected

Something going on in Japan in the late 1980s, the Man from Mars observed. Except for that, if the United States had a big deficit, so did everyone else. The United States was pretty much at the G-7 average, at least until 1988, when the Japanese and British started to run surpluses. Pondering what this may mean for the 1990s, the Man from Mars started to think about historical comparisons.

CHART, GOVERNMENT BORROWING, SOPHISTICATED VIEW, he typed. He learned that economists would be likely to judge debt load not by any one year's deficit, but by total debt outstanding as a percent of GNP. The Databoy threw up the historical chart:

FIGURE 12–2

The National Debt

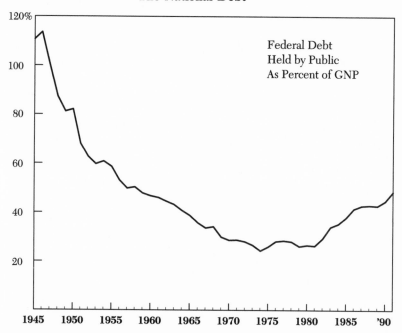

Yes, something's going on, the Man from Mars concluded. Debt as a percent of GNP had been falling since World War II, and started to rise in 1982. On the other hand, it didn't look like anything dramatic. By 1990, outstanding debt was back where it was in 1960, not such a bad time economically. It would be nice if it started coming back down, the Man from Mars thought, if they could reverse whatever happened in 1974. But in lifting the world out of stagflation, heading off the chance of a collapse and starting Seven Fat Years, it doesn't seem a terrible price to pay.

• • •

The deficit is not a meaningless figure, only a grossly overrated one. It measures something, but it does not measure the impulse of the economy—either pushing it up as the Keynesians believe or dragging it down as the flow-of-funds school holds. In particular, the deficit has no detectable effect on interest rates; if it tends to raise interest rates, its effect is swamped by other more important variables. And if it doesn't affect interest rates, it can scarcely affect the sectors of the economy thought to depend on interest rates, investment, for example. Nor is what we call "the deficit" an appropriate or particularly meaningful measure of the "burden we are leaving our grandchildren"; the federal government has many other ways of imposing future burdens, which may or may not move in tandem with its direct borrowing.

The fiscal health of the federal government certainly does matter, but the government's impact on the economy is far too large and diffuse to measure by any one number. A decent measure of the federal fisc would have to be something like the change in the net worth of the government; we have no such figure and, given its complications, are not likely to. But it will not help to pretend "the deficit" is some other figure we do not have, and then to invoke it in place of judgment. The deficit as we measure it is no sort of bottom line.

Yet we having increasingly made "the deficit" the centerpiece of economic policy, even writing it into law. Both the Gramm-Rudman Act and the 1990 budget deal pretend to control the deficit, or some convoluted version of it. Unable to do the right things on their own, our politicians have conjured the deficit into a bogeyman with which to scare themselves. In symbolizing the bankruptcy of our political process, the deficit has become a great national myth with enormous power. But behind this political symbol, we need to understand the economic reality, or lack of it. Otherwise the symbol may lead us to do dumb things, like trying to fight recessions by increasing taxes.

• • •

In the advanced economic literature, the big debate is over whether deficits matter *at all*. Professional economists have noticed that the much-publicized deficits of the 1980s somehow didn't spell the end of the world, or even the end of the economic boom. They understand that the prime rate was 20 to 21.5 percent in 1981, when the deficit ran 2.6 percent of GNP, and 7.25 to 8 percent in 1986, when the deficit was 5.3 percent of GNP. Unlike politicians or the articulate public, they have tried to adjust their thinking to this empirical reality.

Robert Eisner had the deficit particularly in mind when, as noted in Chapter 3, "Michael 1," he entitled his presidential address to the American Economic Association "Divergences of Measurement and Theory." He had many examples of how the statistics we were able to gather did not correspond to the statistical concepts we use in theory and that "as a consequence, popular discourse, policy-making, and

basic principles of economics have suffered inordinate confusion."
But his main dwelling-point was the deficit.[1]

There are of course still plenty of economists who were taught at
their major professor's knee that deficits are the center of the universe, as well as plenty of economists invoking the deficit to advance
this or that political agenda. The usual theory has been that deficits
add to the demand for funds and thus push up interest rates, but
falling interest rates with rising deficits leave much to explain. You
can of course adjust the interest rate for inflation, and argue that the
deficits pushed up the "real" rate of interest. But if you do this, how
can you ignore the fact that inflation also reduces the real value of all
debt outstanding? Are trained economists really going to argue seriously that a *nominal* increase in government debt causes a rise in the
real rate of interest?

This was Eisner's point precisely. You do not run a "real" deficit
unless you borrow enough to offset the effect of inflation on the outstanding debt. This is a large adjustment indeed. At the beginning of
fiscal 1979, for example, the public held just over $607 billion in
federal debt, and inflation was running at over 11 percent a year. So
just maintaining the real value of federal debt outstanding would
require a nominal increase of about $67 billion. In that year, the
official deficit was $40.2 billion, and debt held by the public increased
$32.7 billion.

Also, Eisner suggested a second large adjustment for the portion of
the deficit that went to capital spending by government; most economists would agree that it's entirely appropriate to borrow for capital
expenses and pay off the loan over the life of the asset. Eisner remarked, "These two adjustments, for capital expenditures and for
inflation, make such a huge difference in the Federal government
budget as to wipe out the much decried 'budget deficit.' " That is, the
two adjustments would move the 1988 federal deficit from its official
$155 billion to "virtual balance."

These words were uttered, remember, by the man the leading
association of academic economists had chosen as its president. Eisner's purpose was grander than defending the Reagan administration.
He had in mind nothing less than the resurrection of Keynes. In the
statistical confusion, he finds a Keynesian answer to the stagflation of
the 1970s; because of the high inflation, the apparent deficits were
illusory. The economy stagnated because, in "real" terms, the government was running surpluses.

In any meaningful economic theory, he argued, "the deficit" must mean an increase in the government's outstanding debt, since the deficit theoretically induces spending and growth by increasing private assets. He added, "To have this effect, as the neoclassical argument made clear, the increase in private assets must be real." In these terms, the Federal budget did not go into deficit until late in 1982. With a decline in inflation and a rise in deficits, the Reagan administration staged a Keynesian boom. Eisner remarked, "it should have been clear—dare I say 'perfectly clear'?—that it was the old-fashioned Keynesian stimulus of real budget deficits that has contributed mightily to cutting unemployment in half, from its recession high of almost 11%."

There is of course a second half to the stagflation puzzle: What caused the inflation? Eisner looked at the then six-year boom and asked, "Where, I might add, is that supposedly excess-demand 'accelerating inflation' we were taught to fear? Perhaps waiting to be confused again with the supply shocks of a new war or oil cartel in the Middle East!" The 1970s inflation, in other words, was caused by OPEC—an "exogenous shock," like an earthquake, that economic theory is not expected to explain. The inflation was exogenous, and restrictive fiscal policy, measured in "real" terms, caused the stagnation. Keynes lives.

The way a president of the American Economic Association looks on "the deficit" is, to underline the point, certainly different from the conventional wisdom we read every day in the headlines. Eisner is an intellectually consistent Keynesian, a refreshing contrast to the sort that in recent years has somehow wanted to increase taxes to fight recession. Yet the Keynes resurrection is likely to seem a bit arch to those of us who associate inflation with monetary policy.

Advanced economists are also debating a second cutting-edge economic theory attempt to deal with the 1980s reality of high deficits, prosperity, and falling interest rates. The theory of "Ricardian equivalence" has been extensively debated in the economic literature of recent years. Ricardian equivalence holds that deficits are simply irrelevant, or more precisely, in their economic effect indistinguishable from taxes. The theory is named after David Ricardo (1772–1823), the epitome of classical economists, though in fact Ricardo only toyed with these ideas. The modern theory is identified with Robert Barro of Harvard, one of the leading "new classical" economists, and also a contributing editor of *The Wall Street Journal*. Ricardian equivalence traces to his exquisitely timed 1974 article, entitled "Are Government Bonds Net Wealth?"[2]

The question seems an arcane curiosity, but is actually an Exocet aimed at the heart of the Keynesian universe. For if the government borrows now and promises to pay back later, a public sector with rational expectations would not feel itself wealthier. It would spend no more freely, and the deficit would have no effect.

Indeed, a perfectly rational public sector would recognize that in the future it would be taxed to repay the bonds it now receives, and would set aside some savings for that purpose. That is, government saving would decrease through the deficit, public savings would increase, total national savings would be unaffected; so nothing would change because the government chose to tax later instead of sooner.

Ricardian equivalence has been the subject of a wide-ranging debate on both theoretical and empirical grounds; in an 1989 reassessment, Barro cited more than 50 articles, nearly all directly on points he raised in 1974.[3] Details of the debate include intergenerational altruism, the smoothing of the income tax, glitches in the loan markets and other esoterica.

While the theory remains controversial, by 1989 Barro was able to assert, "[I]t is remarkable how respectable the Ricardian approach has become in the last decade. Most macroeconomists now feel obligated to state the Ricardian position, even if they then go on to argue that it is either theoretically or empirically in error. I predict this trend will continue and that the Ricardian approach will become the benchmark model for assessing fiscal policy." That is, "I would not predict that most analysts will embrace Ricardian equivalence in the sense of concluding that fiscal policy is irrelevant. But satisfactory analyses will feature explicit modeling of elements that lead to departures from Ricardian equivalence, and the predicted consequences of fiscal policies will flow directly from these elements."

Ricardian equivalence has also fared surprisingly well in studies trying to relate deficits and interest rates. As Barro put it, "Overall, the empirical results on interest rates support the Ricardian view. Given these findings it is remarkable that most macroeonomists remain confident that budget deficits raise interest rates."

At Eureka College in the 1930s they taught classical economics, and the Eureka College economist Ronald Reagan said things like he didn't understand why borrowing crowded out investment but taxes didn't. The heirs of Michael 1 would say that both taxing and borrowing take real resources from the private sector, and that any difference would depend on second-order effects (like which took resources at a lower marginal rate). On the whole, the schools of

thought represented by Eisner and Barro show that professional economists have been becoming increasingly ambivalent about the deficit.
At the same time, of course, politicians and public have been turning
it into an idol.

• • •

The lack of a correlation between deficits and interest rates is less
surprising if you understand that the deficit is a curious figure from
the standpoint of accounting. I remember sharing garden-party cock-
tails with Paul Volcker one summer night when he was approached by
the CEO of a highly successful regional retailer, demanding how the
government could go deeper and deeper into debt everywhere. He
was quite right in looking to Volcker for support of his view, but Paul
mischievously turned to me and said, "You answer that, Bob," then
grinned and ambled away leaving me with a worked-up CEO. Well,
I asked, doesn't your company add to its debt every year. I guess it
does, he responded, but that's different.

It sure is. Corporations have Generally Accepted Accounting Principles. The government has the National Income Accounts. If you are
going to speculate about the economic impact of "the deficit," you
have to have some sense of the differences among accrual accounting,
cash accounting and government accounting.

If a corporation borrows $200 million to build a shopping center,
this will be reflected in its balance sheet. It will have $200 million in
liabilities for the debt, and $200 million in assets for the shopping
center. But in its annual income accounts, it will not charge the entire
$200 million as an expense. Instead of "expensing" the sum in the first
year, it will "depreciate" it. That is, it will charge some portion of it
as an expense against income each year over the assumed useful life
of the shopping center.

Similarly, if a family takes out a $400,000 mortgage to buy a home,
it recognizes that it has gone $400,000 in debt. But in trying to match
income with outgo, it does not consider the $400,000 but the monthly
or yearly payment to amortize the mortgage. Both corporations and
households consider it entirely appropriate to borrow to buy capital
items, and pay off the loan as the asset is used. As former Citicorp
Chairman Walter Wriston put it, "The familiar refrain that every
family must balance its budget, so why can't the federal government,
has a nice ring to it, but no family I know of expenses its home." In
the federal budget, he added, "All in all, capital expenditures totaled

13.2% of total outlays, a not inconsiderable amount to expense, and if funded in a capital budget would produce near balance in the operating budget."[4]

So too with state and local governments. Typically they are required by law to "balance" their operating budgets, but this does not include bond issues for capital items, which usually must be approved by voters at referendum. Most foreign governments also have distinct capital budgets, if only for help in deciding how much yearly deficit may be sustainable. Not so the U.S. federal budget; indeed, Treasury Secretary Donald Regan was nearly laughed out of Washington for suggesting the government needs a capital budget.

So "the deficit" may be borrowing to pay welfare benefits or farm subsidies, or it may be borrowing to pay for a highway or an airplane. We have constructed our accounts to make it impossible to tell the difference. Partly this is because we don't trust our politicians to be honest in designating capital projects. Some state and local governments, New York City in particular, got into financial trouble by cheating on their capital budgets—by designating more and more operating expenses as capital expenses for which it was legitimate to borrow.

Even more importantly, the National Income Accounts reflect a Keynesian view of the world. Keynes felt that the depression was caused by a shortfall in aggregate demand because saving was too high and investment too low. The point of "investment" was to borrow the excess savings and spend them, thus boosting total demand. Whether the investments would pay for themselves economically made no difference whatever; indeed, worrying about waste could only be counterproductive.

In *The General Theory*, for example, Keynes suggests that the Treasury should stuff old bottles with banknotes and bury them in abandoned coal mines, then lease the rights to the mines, and "leave it to private enterprise on well tried principles of laissez faire to dig the notes up again." This would boost demand and eliminate unemployment. He added:

> The analogy between this expedient and the gold mines of the real world is complete. At periods when gold is available at suitable depths experience shows that the real wealth of the world increases rapidly; and when but little of it is available, our wealth suffers stagnation or decline. Thus gold mines are of the greatest value and importance to civilization. Just as wars have been the only form of large-scale loan

expenditure which statesmen have thought justifiable, so gold mining is the only pretext for digging holes in the ground which has recommended itself to bankers as sound finance; and each of these activities has played its part in progress—failing something better.[5]

Little wonder that accounts designed when such attitudes held sway would fail to distinguish between government consumption and government investment. If we pretend that accounts set up to answer some other question answer our questions today, we only confuse ourselves.

• • •

That the deficit does not account for capital spending is the good news, however. The bad news is that it also does not account for the government's future liabilities. One night in 1980, Congress increased federal deposit insurance to $100,000 an account from $40,000. This one act increased the liabilities of the U.S. government by some $150 billion, half the cost of bailing out the savings and loan accounts insured by the government. But it did not change the 1980 deficit a penny. The recorded 1980 deficit was $73.8 billion; the unrecorded liability of the deposit insurance boost amounted to twice the borrowing for all the government's on-the-book activities.

That's an example of why "the deficit" does not measure anything that could realistically be called "the burden we are leaving our grandchildren." What the federal debt represents is government bonds outstanding, or to put it plainly, that portion of future liabilities on which the government has chosen to pay interest.

The actual liabilities are far larger, so much so that changes in them can swamp changes in the official deficit; the deficit numbers can go up while the burden to our grandchildren goes down, or vice versa. In terms of the burden for our grandchildren, the elephant in the room is the social society system. At the end of fiscal 1981, in the midst of Ronald Reagan's first year in office, federal debt held by the public amounted to $785 billion. The unfunded liabilities of the social security system, however, came in at $5.9 *trillion*. The pension liabilities for federal personnel, at $842 billion, were themselves larger than the cumulative "deficits" over two centuries.

In the National Income Accounts these numbers do not count, of course; they are not relevant to the current year's aggregate demand. They are highly relevant, though, to the burden on our grandchildren. Is the government any more likely to default on a social security payment than it is on a Treasury bond? The danger to the latter is that its value will be inflated away, but under current law social security payments are indexed to inflation, while future benefits are linked to future wage levels, increasing with both inflation and real advances in the standard of living.

It is somehow not surprising that an administration that cuts taxes would also compile a better record on the government's off-budget liabilities. Also, slower inflation and more real growth make the fiscal climate easier, since figures like social security liabilities depend on estimates of future economic performance. The 1983 Greenspan Commission dealt with the social security deficit, in no small way by advancing previously scheduled increases in the payroll tax. With the economy performing better than expected during that reform, social security looks healthier, at least in the short term.

Thomas E. Daxon, a certified public accountant and former state auditor in Oklahoma, calculated the burden to future taxpayers in a 1989 article in *Policy Review*.[6] His calculation included interest-bearing debt, social security, personal pensions and a variety of other liabilities and offsetting assets. He concluded that the burden to future taxpayers was $7.185 trillion at the end of fiscal 1981, and $7.952 trillion at the end of fiscal 1987. As a percentage of GNP, it declined from 241 percent to 180 percent.

Such calculations need to be taken with a grain of salt, of course. We do not know which contingent liabilities may explode the way deposit insurance did with the S&Ls. Government has assumed much of the liability for medical care for the elderly, for example, and seems poised to assume more. The Greenspan Commission fix of social security really only pushed the problem into the future; if we want to reduce the burden on our grandchildren, the first thing we should do is reduce the incomes we expect to claim when we retire.

At the same time, government accounting takes no notice of the government's asset position. We know that federal debt held by the public is now some $2.7 trillion. But how does this liability compare with the asset of, say, federal land holdings—nearly all of Alaska and Nevada, for example, and much of California?

The deficit is not much of a measure of any of these issues. It seems likely that during the 1980s even as the deficit grew, other burdens on our grandchildren declined. Deposit insurance of course clouds the picture, and it's not easy to assess responsibility for these enormous costs (see Chapter 14, "The S&L Debacle"). Even so, it's possible that during the 1980s the net worth of the government, if we could measure it, may have gone up rather than down. This is perhaps a hidden secret of the Seven Fat Years.

• • •

Barro complains that Ricardian equivalence is sometimes taken to be that nothing matters, though it by no means denies that the government has a big impact on the economy through its demands on real resources. This we can measure; it's called government spending. In fact, as the Man from Mars' charts showed, the tax cuts have little to do with the rise in the deficit; what actually happened was that receipts stayed level while expenditures took off, starting in 1974.

Much of the debate over the deficit is a debate over how to get Congress to control spending. There are two schools of thought: One is that the deficit scares Congress into not spending more; or at least that making Congress borrow at the margin and pay interest curbs its appetite. The other view is that the balanced budget rule is, as Hayek said of gold, a device for scaring politicians, that breaking the myth will unleash a flood of spending. This was the issue when Bill Niskanen played Galileo in December 1981. At the American Enterprise Institute his colloquy with CEA Chairman Murray Weidenbaum and AEI scholars and former officials Herb Stein and Rudolph Penner went like this:

DR. WEIDENBAUM: I'd like to offer, hopefully, some insight into the continuing concern, at least in some quarters, about deficits. I think the underlying concern is a serious matter, and it is, and it's been alluded to earlier in these discussions, to control the growth of government.

And we measure that most conveniently by outlays. Surely the pressure for government spending growth is omnipresent. What is the counter pressure? In the legislative process, it certainly isn't something as esoteric as the percentage of GNP or even the aggregate growth rates of spending, nominal or real, but, and here we're led back to the concern over deficits.

And I think we need to keep in mind the underlying relationship between what seems the ephemeral concern over deficits and the underlying long-term concern about slowing down the growth rate of government, especially, federal government.

DR. STEIN: But aren't you worried that the whole trend of this discussion is reducing the inhibitions about running deficits, and therefore, weakening this restraining force against government spending.

DR. WEIDENBAUM: Maybe that's why I made my comment.

DR. STEIN: Well, that's a good reason to make the comment but something more needs to be said then. That is, you need to reestablish some defensible reason for not having deficits. If you've now told us that they don't cause inflation, they don't crowd out. You see, it is not sufficient, as we know, for a group of economists to sit around and say, "Well, a deficit of a hundred billion dollars doesn't have these adverse effects," because you're dealing with a bunch of Congressmen out these, and if we say 100 billion is OK, they will ask why not 200 or why not 300.

They have a certain feeling about zero. Zero is an intuitively appealing number. But we haven't found any other intuitively appealing rule, and that's what we've been missing.

• • •

DR. NISKANEN: Herb, I think there is a defensible approach which will be a little hard to explain because we have not kept a regular series on it, and that is to say we do not want to reduce the real net worth of the federal government.

And there is a specific deficit number that comes out of that—that is also a function of what the money is spent for, capital improvements or for transfers and current consumption.

If we do not reduce the real net worth of the federal government, we are not increasing the burden on future generations. . . . I think that a rule of no change or no reductions in the real net worth of the federal government would be a rule that we could stick with.

DR. PENNER: It's a nice sounding rule until you try to implement it, and until you try to decide what really belongs on the asset and liability statements. If you put Social Security, for example, on the liability statement, we are in very bad shape, indeed.[7]

The issue, in short, is whether Congress is more afraid of a deficit or of having to levy taxes; which will cause more restraint in congressional spending? This is of course not an economic question but a political and psychological one. For the record, as the Man from

Mars' charts showed, spending rose sharply in the early 1980s, pla-
teaued and started to decline as a percent of GNP after 1983, then
started to soar again in 1990. Of course, this measurement depends
not only on federal spending but on GNP, which grew nicely during
the Seven Fat Years.

Congress, it seems, is not much deterred by either fear of taxes or
fear of a deficit. Under the current institutional arrangements, an
administration does well merely to insure that federal spending grows
no more rapidly than GNP. This was accomplished in the 1983–90
period, in part because the Gramm-Rudman sequester gave the executive a bit more say in the process. It also no doubt helped that
James Miller, OMB chief during these years, never became a household word, unlike his predecessor or his successor. For some reason,
presidents seem to assign scatbacks to a post that requires an interior
lineman.

The broader issue, though, concerns the institutional arrangements
themselves. We know the answer to the Man from Mars' question
about what happened in 1974. The Budget Control and Impoundment Act of 1974, that's what. Congress won a fight with a Watergate-
weakened president over the previous practice of presidential
"impoundment" of congressionally appropriated funds. Henceforth
the president would be obligated to spend expeditiously whatever
Congress appropriated. And ever since 1974, Congress has been trying one expedient after another to try to prove it can behave itself in
spending money. The obvious truth is that establishing and enforcing
a budget requires someone to take responsibility, and Congress is a
committee of 535 members. Even with good will, not to be taken for
granted, it is not humanly possible.

Congress has further eroded executive powers by the practice of
wrapping all its spending into a last-minute "omnibus appropriation"
or "continuing resolution." A presidential veto, or even a Gramm-
Rudman sequester, would be a drastic act closing down the government. Nor does the president have time to deliberate, or even to
adequately read the legislation.

In his 1988 State of the Union Address, President Reagan dis-
played the continuing resolution passed the previous December,
some 1,194 pages and weighing nearly 30 pounds. As provisions of
this bill were digested, it was found to contain a stealth provision
increasing congressional staff salaries by 20 percent. The conference
report supposedly explaining the legislation had no mention of this
provision, and no one ever discovered where the law originated.

The same resolution also turned out to contain a provision putting Rupert Murdoch out of the newspaper business in Boston and New York. This time there was no mystery; Sen. Ted Kennedy inserted the provision to close down an unfriendly newspaper. Since the papers in question were financially strained, the Federal Communications Commission had exercised its discretion to give Murdoch waivers of the rule against owning papers and television stations in the same town; the continuing resolution provision said no funds should be expended to extend waivers "currently in effect." This applied only to Murdoch; the D.C. Court of Appeals struck down the provision as a violation of the constitutional provisions against bills of attainder, legislation intended to punish specific persons.

The obvious institutional change to correct such practices is of course the item veto, giving the president power to veto some items in a bill without vetoing the whole bill. In the states, 43 governors have item vetos, and it has been repeatedly called for by presidents of both parties. It is an injection of executive power and responsibility that would put some discipline in the budget process, which of course is why Congress has opposed it.

Before 1974 presidents asserted the impoundment power, if less sweepingly than President Nixon did. Whether through the loss of impoundment, the creation of the CBO, the institution of the "current services budget," some balance-wheel on spending went out of kilter in 1974 and needs to be set right if "the deficit" is ever to be brought under control.

Intriguingly, the 1975 Supreme Court decision on the Nixon water impoundments never reached constitutional issues. Stephen Glazier, a securities lawyer, started a constitutional debate by observing that the veto provision has two separate clauses. One requires that "every bill" be presented to the president for a veto, and the other requires the same for "every order, resolution, or vote" requiring action by both Houses. This means, he asserted, that the framers intended all along to give the president an item veto, a right exercised by impoundment until 1974 and overthrown by the Impoundment Act. Constitutional historian Forrest McDonald lent his support to this interpretation, but others disagreed.[8] There is also the issue of whether a thousand-page last-minute resolution is properly "presented" for the veto.

The control of spending, the government's unrecognized future liabilities, the capital investment in the nation's infrastructure—all these are serious issues. They have been obscured rather than clarified by preoccupation with a number called "the deficit."

By fiscal 1990 and 1991, for example, government spending was soaring to new heights. Some of this, of course, is for the Savings and Loan bailout, and there is a debate whether this spending "counts" as part of the deficit. Many economists view it as merely a shuffling of funds, without imposing new demands on the savings "pool." For that matter, some entirely respectable economists concentrate on the "primary deficit," excluding all interest payments as merely fund-shuffling with no effect in the real sector.

In terms of the government's net worth, some incalculable part of the S&L spending clearly should be netted out as acquisition of assets. The early years of the budget agreement do set high ceilings for program spending, and the apparent intention is to fund spending in later years by selling S&L assets. Good luck, but the immediate return on the 1990 budget agreement was that the deficit soared.

As a political matter, the most interesting observation is that just as the deficit soared in 1991, public rhetoric about it almost vanished. Partly this was recession and partly it was confusion over the increasingly convoluted numbers; economists disagreed on whether the S&L bailout numbers really counted. But mostly it was something else. Concern about the deficit vanished on June 26, 1990, when President Bush revoked his no-tax pledge.

The Congress and its boosters got what they wanted, and stopped stoking the fires of "the deficit." We are now back to the formula of spend, tax, and elect. To the extent conservative boosters of "the deficit" and "balancing the budget" hoped to restrain the government, their formula has proved a two-edged sword. The no-tax pledge was a crude instrument, but on the record reasonably effective in an unsatisfactory environment.

If we want a fiscal policy that speeds economic growth, we know what needs to be done with or without a deficit number: hold government spending to essentials, keep marginal tax rates as low as possible, keep the dollar sound, let the price mechanism work, avoid imposing unnecessary regulation and unnecessary costs. Preoccupation with "the deficit" was a hindrance the Reagan administration had to overcome in implementing the program that produced the Seven Fat Years, and in the 1990s the danger is that the same preoccupation will lead us away from these fundamentals.

Meanwhile, the deficit becomes less and less attached to reality. In

the 1990 budget agreement, the surpluses of the social security system have been taken out of the calculation, apparently to make the
deficit a bigger and better bogeyman. Looking at this, Robert Barro
sent me a note:

Dear Bob,
    You have bemoaned the government's plan to exclude social secu-
rity from its computations of budget deficits. Although this change will
raise the measured deficit, the idea also contains the potential for
eliminating the deficit entirely.
    We have merely to search for some other program that has desig-
nated expenditures that greatly exceed its designated tax receipts. I
suggest the defense tax. We can rename the federal excise tax on
telephone services as the "defense tax."
    With this definition, the defense budget's estimated deficit for fiscal
1990 is $293 billion; the $296 billion in defense spending less the $3
billion in defense taxes. Thus, instead of showing an estimated deficit
(from the budget presented last January) of $183 billion in fiscal 1990
(exclusive of social security), the newly defined budget would show a
surplus of $110 billion (exclusive of social security and defense).
    Presumably, if we followed this minor proposal then we could all
worry about something serious, like how much the government was
spending.[9]

13

The World

The Volcker-Reagan policy mix may have inspired derision from the president's foes and panic among his advisers, but it was a big hit with foreigners. There was a certain carping from abroad, of course, but it was overwhelmed by the sound of the world voting with its money. Investment inflows into the United States soared.

In 1979, foreigners invested $38.7 billion in the United States; in 1980 this number was $58.1 billion. But with tighter money and tax cuts coming into place, investment inflows jumped to $83.0 billion in 1981, $93.7 billion in 1982, $84.9 billion in 1983, $130 billion by 1985 and $229.8 billion by 1987.

American investments abroad, what in some contexts might be called flight capital, came to $64.3 billion in 1979, rose to $124 billion in 1982, then plunged to $56.1 billion in 1983 and as low as $27.7 billion in 1985. So in 1985, America attracted more than $100 billion of net capital; this is where the world's investors saw the most promising return.

And as the Seven Fat Years started, the American economy clearly pulled the rest of the world with it. In 1982, the whole world was in recession, with the United States declining, Europe barely growing, Japan slowing and the developing nations plunging into the debt crisis. But by 1983, the industrial world had stabilized, and the engine of growth was the United States.

The June 1985 *OECD Economic Outlook*, for example, cites "the more rapid growth of domestic demand in the United States than in the rest of the OECD—by nearly four percentage points in 1983 and over 6 percentage points in 1984." Europe, by contrast, was dependent on foreign markets. "Growth there is seen as continuing, but at a rate unlikely to prevent a further edging-up of unemployment. . . . The slow growth of European activity reflects relatively buoyant exports in combination with sluggish domestic demand. Last year, exports contributed half of the total increase of demand in Europe."[1]

All America gazed on these developments and decided the sky was falling. In sending their money here, those perfidious foreigners expected to get paid back. Indeed, the whole reason they were sending their money was that they expected a higher return here than they could get at home. Their eagerness to invest in America instead of at home was turning us into—shame!—a debtor nation.

And of course, the way the American economy lifted Europe out of despondency was by buying its goods. This resulted in—horrors!—a trade deficit. In all the pantheon of economic statistics, there is none so meaningless and misleading. The words "surplus" and "deficit" richly deserve the oblivion to which the 1976 advisory committee had tried to consign them, lest they be "used in lieu of analysis."

No subject so bedeviled the Seven Fat Years as the place of the United States in the world economy. They were years of great internationalization. The 24-hour trading markets were stitched together; dollars circled the world at electronic speed. Rock and roll subverted Prague and Moscow, and Japanese auto companies built plants in Tennessee (Nissan), Ohio (Honda) and Kentucky (Toyota). "Interdependence" became a byword.

And yet America has still not come to terms with its integration into the world economy. Somehow we have trouble remembering that commerce takes place between consenting adults, that the bargain makes both sides richer in one way or another. Instead, we tend to view trade as some kind of nationalistic competition. Winning, as best I can figure out, is selling more to the rest of the world than we buy from it. Laying aside the fact that this is ultimately impossible, why? If we could do it, what would we do with the proceeds, bury them in Fort Knox?

The notion of trade competition is in part an atavistic throwback to the mercantilism demolished by Adam Smith. Mercantilist kings really did think that burying gold in Fort Knox made their nations rich. In part, too, nationalism is fed by the very real competition between the transnational corporations headquartered in, say, Detroit, and the transnational corporations headquartered in Tokyo. If the losers in this competition are sometimes workers who have to find new jobs when their companies decline, the winners are consumers who get better and cheaper products.

In part, though, the confusions over the international economy are intellectual. The American elite has never bothered to understand that, as Bob Mundell put it, the only closed economy is the world economy. Clearly Richard Nixon had little idea of what he was doing in closing the gold window, and President Carter had little idea of what he was doing in appointing Paul Volcker to the Fed. Nor, for the most part, did the economists who advised them.

The international economy operated under floating exchange rates during the 1980s, and the value of the dollar against other currencies has been a recurring preoccupation. Chairman Volcker not only averted the freefall that seemed to impend at Belgrade, but as he tightened money the dollar came to be generally perceived as too strong. Later, especially around the time of the 1987 stock-market crash, it was perceived as too weak. The fluctuating dollar buffeted the economy in strange and little-understood ways, the heirs of Michael 1 believe, ever since President Nixon came back from Camp David on August 15, 1971. And resolving it is the one big unfinished task of the Seven Fat Years.

• • •

First, what are the international accounts? It cannot be emphasized too much that they are an accounting identity, that will balance tautologically, by definition. After all, for every buyer there has to be a seller. The various trade balances are only different stopping-places in a great circle of transactions. Except for zero, there is no bottom line.

Say an American spends a dollar on something from Hong Kong, perhaps a set of chopsticks. The dollar doesn't disappear; the chopstick maker only wanted it so he could buy something. Eventually the dollar will come back to the United States. Where it shows up in the international account—which "balance" it affects—depends upon what the chopstick maker decides to buy.

If he buys U.S. soybeans for tofu, his dollar shows up in the merchandise trade balance. It would also show up in merchandise trade if he used it to buy Oregon timber to chop into chopsticks or Alaskan oil to run the chopping machine, but he can't spend it on those commodities, since Congress interrupted its worries about the trade deficit to outlaw their export.

If the chopstick maker uses his dollar to buy a hotel room in San Francisco or a blueprint from Bechtel, it shows up in the current account, which includes not only goods but services. If he uses his dollar to buy a share of IBM or a Treasury bond, it doesn't show up in the trade balance at all, but in the investment accounts. So the chopstick maker's decision to buy IBM instead of soybeans swells the trade deficit.

The most constructive way to look at the international accounts is to divide them into three parts, which must by definition net out at zero. The two big halves are, first, trade in goods and services, and second, investment. These are essentially two sides of the same coin; normally a trade deficit is financed by an investment surplus, or inflow. And a trade surplus will accompany investment outflows. The third part of the international accounts is called "official financing"; if trade and investment don't offset each other, the central banks have to step in and act as balance wheel.

Given the investment–trade seesaw, a zero trade balance is not normal or even desirable. The United States ran a trade deficit for nearly all of its first 100 years, and generated trade surpluses under Smoot-Hawley in the midst of the Great Depression. Normally, a rapidly growing economy will demand more of the world's supply of real resources and run a trade deficit. It will also provide attractive investment opportunities and attract capital inflows. In a healthy world, the two will offset each other, for periods of perhaps a century.

The trouble comes when voluntary trade is not offset by voluntary investment flows, and central banks have to step in. They do this through buying and selling dollars in the foreign exchange markets. They "support" the dollar by purchasing dollars in their own currency; conversely, "supporting" another currency involves purchasing it, in this example with dollars. While a trade deficit means little, large support operations are reasons for a second look, and simultaneous outflows on trade and capital accounts, as in 1977 and 1978, are a symptom of dire health, as previously elaborated in Chapter 5, "Meanwhile, Money."

In 1984, the deficit in the balance on current account jumped to $99.0 billion. But foreigners made large purchases of dollar securities and U.S. banks stopped lending abroad, leading to net capital inflows of $98.9 billion. No official financing was needed; the $99 billion trade deficit was a nonproblem. Indeed, it was a benefit to the world, which needed economic stimulus somewhere.

The trade deficit, that is, was self-financing. Voluntary capital inflows turned up in the magnitudes that seemed so implausible to William Fellner when Bill Niskanen suggested the impending deficit could be financed without an increase in dollar interest rates. At the

TABLE 13-1

U.S. International Accounts

Year	Trade Account	Investment Account	Official Financing	
1960	2.8	-6.4	3.6	0.0
1961	3.8	-5.2	1.4	0.0
1962	3.4	-6.2	2.8	0.0
1963	4.4	-6.9	2.4	-0.1
1964	6.8	-8.7	1.9	0.0
1965	5.4	-6.8	1.3	-0.1
1966	3.0	-2.9	-0.1	0.0
1967	2.6	-6.1	3.5	0.0
1968	0.6	1.0	-1.7	-0.1
1969	0.4	2.1	-2.5	0.0
1970	2.3	-12.6	10.3	0.0
1971	-1.4	-28.5	29.9	0.0
1972	-5.8	-5.4	11.2	0.0
1973	7.1	-13.3	6.2	0.0
1974	2.0	-11.0	9.0	0.0
1975	18.1	-24.4	6.2	-0.1
1976	4.2	-19.4	15.1	-0.1
1977	-14.5	-21.9	36.4	0.0
1978	-15.4	-19.0	34.4	0.0
1979	-1.0	14.7	-13.7	0.0
1980	1.1	-9.7	8.6	0.0
1981	6.9	-7.7	0.8	0.0
1982	-5.9	7.2	-1.4	-0.1
1983	-40.1	35.5	4.6	0.0
1984	-99.0	98.9	0.0	-0.1
1985	-122.3	127.3	-5.0	0.0
1986	-145.4	109.5	35.9	0.0
1987	-160.2	105.7	54.4	-0.1
1988	-126.2	90.6	35.8	0.2
1989	-106.3	123.0	-16.7	0.0
1990	-92.1	61.9	30.2	0.0

Plus represent inflows and minuses outflows. For explanation of data presentation see notes for figures and tables.

time of the Fellner-Niskanen exchange, in December 1981, the prime rate was 15.75 percent, in 1984 it averaged 12.04 percent; in 1985 9.93 percent. As Bob Mundell predicted at Michael 1, the Saudis—that is, the rest of the world—financed a successful policy mix.

• • •

The failure to understand the basics of the international accounts is the source of a great deal of confusion around the world, and no little misery in developing nations. For in international markets Argentines and Mexicans usually have to borrow in dollars, assuming the risk of any devaluation in their own currencies. As the reserve currency country, the United States borrows its own currency. It makes no difference whether a Treasury bond is owned by an American citizen or a foreigner; in either case the interest is due in dollars. This means that there is no chance whatever that the foreign indebtedness of the United States could force it into the kind of crisis experienced by Mexico or Argentina.

It is especially important to remember that trade and investment accounts balance, there is no *a priori* way to tell which drives the other. The prevailing assumption is that Americans want to buy Toyotas, so they go out and borrow the money. But if the Japanese suddenly decided they wanted to invest in the U.S., the accounts would still have to balance. If Japanese funds came pouring in, the Americans would have to do something to get rid of the dollars, like buy Toyotas.

We do know one thing. In 1990, imports for the year came to $668 billion. That's less than two weeks' worth of dollar clearings in the world's financial markets. In terms of sheer volume, the financial sector, the net decisions of which become the investment account, overwhelms the real sector, which moves its product not down wires but in ships. In Angus Maddison's golden age, American investments fueled extraordinary growth in the developing world. Developing nations of course ran trade deficits.

Despite these realities, trade statistics have been a cause for alarm not only recently but historically. As worries over the U.S. trade deficit started to fester, Alan Reynolds documented the earlier hysteria over the big trade gaps of Japan and South Korea. In the late 1950s, reputable economists worried because Japan was importing twice as much as it was exporting. They also worried that its economy was overheating. Jerome Cohen had commented that its tax cuts were "foolhardy from an economic point of view." When Korea followed the urging of the International Monetary Fund to impose "fiscal discipline" by raising tax rates and tightening money in 1980, its otherwise surging GNP dropped 6.2 percent, with increases in both budget deficits and trade deficits.[1]

Both, we ought to be able to see by now, were classic cases of rapidly developing economies. Their surging and promising economies attracted investment inflows. In the international accounts this had to mean large trade deficits, and in any event, the rapidly growing economies needed more than their share of the world's goods, especially capital goods. Attempts to interfere with this natural process could only be destructive.

In the Seven Fat Years the U.S. imported capital, in large part because it was leading the world's growth. This was certainly salutary given the threat of worldwide collapse in 1982, but it would be more natural if the world's most developed economy were a capital exporter. Capital, and goods, ought to be flowing to development opportunities in the Third World, as they flowed to Japan in the 1960s and Korea in the 1980s.

There is, however, no significant way to shove capital into the Third World. It has to be pulled. The crucial variable is the economic policies of Third World nations. If their policies are destructive, they will suffer "capital flight," that is, their own citizens will make their investments abroad. But if their policies are correct, both their own citizens and foreigners will send money.

There is no better example of this than the remarkable recovery of Mexico from the depths it reached in 1982. Taking office at the end of that disastrous year, President Miguel de la Madrid Hurtado inherited a collapsed oil boom, recently nationalized banks, a bankrupt private sector and a huge foreign debt. As these problems were worked out over his six-year term, the standard of living of the Mexican people fell by 40 percent. Yet he left his successor an essentially promising legacy.

De la Madrid set the course of economic policy with a series of steps, for example fairly compensating the owners of the nationalized banks, changing regulations to allow private companies to become bank-like financial intermediaries, selling some 700 private companies, mostly small but including the state airline Aeromexico. With some help from the state, Alfa and other private companies snapped back smartly. In addition, de la Madrid made two seminal decisions.

The first was to join the General Agreement on Tariffs and Trade. Mexico had traditionally been an autarkical economy, with its policies and industries geared to import substitution. Foreign investment was discouraged; companies were required to have 51 percent Mexican ownership. The decision to join GATT, and to slash some tariffs from 100 percent to 20 percent, was a singular reversal of Mexican economic policy. Another tradition in Mexico was see saw politics, with one president moving right and the next moving left. De la Madrid's second seminal decision was to engineer the selection of a successor who would continue and extend his policies.

Carlos Salinas de Gortari took office in 1988 after a disputed election in which he officially won a bare majority of the vote, but rapidly seized the reins of power. He boldly arrested the head of the oil union and some prominent financiers on corruption charges, an act that sealed his popularity with the Mexican people. He quickly liberalized the foreign investment laws, and stepped up the pace of privatization. He denationalized the banks. He set out to sell the telephone company, Telefonos de Mexico, soon christened Telemex by eager buyers at home and on Wall Street.

President Salinas struck a deal with President Bush to negotiate a free trade accord, asking opponents in the United States whether they'd rather have Mexican goods or Mexican immigrants. Most startling of all in terms of Mexican history, by 1991 he was taking action to reform the *ejido*. This communal form of land ownership, with roots reaching back at least to the Aztec empire, has kept Mexican agriculture mired in the dark ages. Yet the last leader to try to reform it, Porfirio Diaz, was toppled in the Mexican revolution of 1910 to 1920. Zapata's great slogan, "Land and Liberty," was a call for the defense of the *ejido*.

On its present course, Mexico bids to become the next Korea. Provided of course that its internal politics remain supportive and that the United States and the world financial institutions don't do anything dumb. Rejection of the free trade agreement would pull the rug out from under Mexican modernization. And soon someone will be worrying about the Mexican trade deficit.

Late in 1991, Pedro Aspe, Salinas's finance minister, told me that in the first 10 months Mexico had capital inflows of $16 billion and that the pace had picked up after the *ejido* reforms were announced. I observed that they must have had a trade deficit of $16 billion. He replied, "By definition! Now Bob, would you please find somebody for me who can explain that to the IMF."

• • •

It needs to be explained as well to some of the most distinguished economists in the United States. For during the Seven Fat Years they repeatedly urged that national economic policy should be built around the objective of "curing" the trade deficit. They diagnosed our affliction as "twin deficits." The notion was that funding the fiscal deficit made it necessary to attract capital from abroad by keeping interest rates high, which depressed investment. And that this resulted in excessive consumption of Toyotas and other imports, creating the second deficit.

This thesis required that certain inconvenient facts be explained away. Instead of rising, for example, interest rates were falling. But since they weren't falling as fast as inflation the "real" interest rate was rising. (One would hope so, since in the Carter years it was negative.) And gross investment was strong, so you looked at net investment, after rapidly and somewhat mysteriously rising depreciation charges. And if the economy was generally in a boom, it couldn't last.

The diagnosis had a lot more credibility, though, than the prescription that often followed: We should devalue the dollar, and if that didn't cure the trade deficit, devalue it some more. The idea was that it would make Toyotas more expensive, of course, and U.S. exports cheaper abroad. This would cure the trade deficit, and maybe also its twin, which would make interest rates fall and investment boom.

It was not easy to discern when economists were advocating devaluation and when they were predicting it, but the "twin deficit" and lower dollar views were most vociferously popularized by Marty Feldstein, back at Harvard, and G. Fred Bergsten, a Washington consultant who'd been assistant secretary of the treasury for international affairs in the Carter administration. The general principle was that the dollar should/would decline to a level at which the trade deficit went away, or at least became "sustainable."

Devaluation to improve the trade balance has been tried over history hundreds of times by dozens of countries; to my knowledge no one has found an instance in which it ever worked. For one thing, the first effect of a devaluation is that you have to pay more for imports and get less for exports, so the same volume of trade gives you a higher trade deficit. The traditional way of overcoming this hurdle is to invoke a mythical creature called the J curve, which says yes, the deficit gets worse as prices change but will get better when volumes change. The up-side of the J comes when you capture the unicorn.

The reason is anything but mysterious to adherents of the law of one price. Art Laffer wrote in Michael 1 days, after all, about "The Bitter Fruits of Devaluation." Prices, which move up and down wires, can change a lot more quickly than volumes, which move in ships. And money is a veil, not affecting relative values of real goods. You can change the exchange rate between monies, but a bottle of wine is still worth the same loaves of bread. So by the time a devaluation might affect volumes, prices have already changed. In an extreme efficient-markets view, everything would instantly adjust and nothing would change except inflation. But things do not in fact work instantly, the higher initial prices at home, the lower prices abroad, the increased inflation, all are likely to come with a set of winners and losers. So you are likely to have both real sector disruptions and higher prices.

If the exchange rate can't determine trade flows, what can it do? What yardstick can you use to decide whether the dollar is "too high" or "too low?" Some will still say, of course, that there is no such thing, that whatever price the foreign exchange markets arrive at is the right one at the moment. Even so, there ought to be what economists call the equilibrium value of the dollar, a value that at least signals that things are healthy rather than sick. If we have an interdependent world economy, price signals ought to be accurately transmitted. Price changes affect the movement of goods and capital, and ought to reflect changes in supply and demand in the real sector. If they reflect changes in the financial sector, the result will be inefficiency and confusion.

Ideally, that is, the one closed economy ought to have one money, with one central bank, perhaps. A system of truly fixed exchange rates would stimulate a world money; so long as the exchange rate doesn't change, you would have a unitary money under different names in different nations. And under floating exchange rates, you would have the same efficiency if exchange rates settled at purchasing power parity, or PPP.

As the Man from Mars' Databoy taught, purchasing power parity means an exchange rate that leaves purchasing power unaffected when two currencies are exchanged. That is, a PPP rate will mean that you can exchange one currency into another, and buy the same basket of goods afterwards as before. The diners at Michael 1 thought of PPP as the equilibrium value of the dollar, but in recent years the best-known advocate of the idea has been Professor Ronald I. McKinnon at Stanford University.

Now, different experts have different estimates of PPP. Central bankers, ever suspicious of any rule that might limit their discretion, will be quick to suggest that this means you can forget the whole thing. But just because economists can't look up the exact rate scarcely means it doesn't exist. And over the past few years, it's clear, the dollar has been both far over and far under any reasonable estimate of PPP.

You can approach PPP empirically, actually constructing baskets of goods and measuring what they cost in New York, Tokyo, Paris and so on. The OECD actually does this, churning out PPP estimates from hundreds of calculations. Or you can approach it more theoretically, as McKinnon has, by picking the rates that actually prevailed when the world economy seemed generally in equilibrium.

McKinnon's choice is January 1986, when the dollar, mark and yen seemed at exchange-rate levels consistent with buying the same basket of wholesale commodities. In addition, the three economies seemed to be sustaining the same level of price inflation. Based on the rates at the time, McKinnon offered dollar exchange rates of 190 to 210 yen and 2.2 to 2.4 marks.

These rates have to be updated periodically if the three economies have different inflation rates, and in fact the dollar did inflate more rapidly. By 1989, the McKinnon PPP estimate was 155 to 175 yen and 1.9 to 2.1 marks.

The actual exchange rate of the dollar has swung widely around these values. In the middle of 1985, it was far above PPP, at about 240 yen and 3.0 marks. By the end of 1987, it had fallen by half, to about 120 yen and 1.5 marks, far below any reasonable estimates of PPP. In a single day, for that matter, the major exchange rates sometimes swing by more than 2 percent. On March 27, 1985, the dollar plunged 3.7 percent against the British pound, ending three weeks in which it lost 16.9 percent against the pound and 8.8 percent against the mark.[3]

Nothing in the economic fundamentals, the prospects of the U.S., Japanese and German economies, explains 100 percent fluctuations in 2½ years. Apparently what happens is that foreign exchange markets operate rather like futures markets, becoming hypersensitive to every tremor of monetary policy, and thus tend to "overshoot" when the indications point to tighter or easier money. These swings, indeed, swamp the profit margin calculations on which investment decisions are made. So the volatile exchange rates disrupt cross-border business decisions, and at least in the short run, may even open and close factories, destroy and create jobs. So they become matters of great political sensitivity.

One of the biggest barriers to understanding PPP is the notion that exchange rates *ought* to float so their value can be determined by "the free market." After one of our editorials suggested that exchange rates were "about right" at McKinnon's PPP values in January 1986, we received a rebuttal from Milton Friedman himself. "I await with interest the *Journal's* nomination of the price that is 'about right' for the stock market, or the bond market or an ice-cream cone or a restaurant meal."[4] Milton later expressed his delight at our treatment of him in reply:

> Being spanked by Milton Friedman is one of life's most humiliating experiences, so we feel compelled to fess up about when we'll proclaim the "right" price for ice-cream cones. We faithfully promise to do that on the day Milton Friedman proclaims the "right" percentage for annual growth in the ice-cream cone supply.
>
> The point is that money is a government monopoly, unlike ice-cream cones or stocks or bonds. The issue is what yardstick a central bank should follow in exercising this power, as Mr. Friedman's long-standing emphasis on money-supply targets implicitly recognizes. A monopolist's power consists of choosing his yardstick: He can stabilize the price of his product by adjusting the supply to meet demand, or conversely he can maintain a steady supply and allow the price to vary if demand changes. In terms of monetary policy, a central bank can follow a quantity rule, Mr. Friedman's choice, or a price rule, which we have come to favor in light of recent experience.
>
> What this choice has to do with fidelity to market principles is far from clear. There are still some who argue theoretically for private money, with freedom of entry for suppliers and other attributes of a free market. But short of that we are debating whether governments should exercise their monopoly power through variable x or variable y. This is an empirical matter; the only guide we have is what works in practice.
>
> In the ideal free-market world, of course, money would be a veil. What really matters is not the price of ice-cream cones in terms of dollars or yen, but the price of ice-cream cones in terms of loaves of bread and bottles of wine and haircuts and, yes, stocks and bonds. Money works its magic by simplifying these calculations, providing a timely and accurate reflection of the relative prices of various products. Given this information, markets can direct resources to their highest-value use, thus creating more wealth to share.

The system breaks down when the veil dominates the picture; when the value of money itself is so volatile the signal of other prices becomes meaningless. This, it seems to us, has been our experience with floating exchange rates. What the world economy needs is the monetary stability that allows free markets to work. Money matters, someone once taught us, in ways that make it more than just another commodity.[5]

• • •

During the 1980s, the leading finance ministers and central bankers seemed to be groping for purchasing power parity. On September 22, 1985, they reached the Plaza accord, under which the United States, abandoning the policy of "benign neglect," officially recognized that the strong dollar was a source of concern. At 225 yen and 2.7 marks, the dollar was too strong, agreed the G-5 group (the United States, Japan, Germany, France and Great Britain). Gold was $319 an ounce.

The dollar depreciated to McKinnon's PPP parities in early 1986. In February President Reagan included exchange-rate reform in his State of the Union address:

> The constant expansion of our economy and exports requires a sound and stable dollar at home and reliable exchange rates around the world. We must never again permit wild currency swings to cripple our farmers and other exporters. Farmers, in particular, have suffered from past unwise government policies. They must not be abandoned with problems they did not create and cannot control. We've begun coordinating our economic and monetary policy among our major trading partners. But there's more to do, and tonight I am directing Treasury Secretary Jim Baker to determine if the nations of the world should convene to discuss the role and relationship of our currencies.[6]

But the dollar kept falling. By early 1987, the G-7 nations agreed that the dollar was too weak. At the Louvre meeting on February 22, they agreed "to cooperate closely to foster stability of exchange rates around current levels." At that time the dollar was worth 153 yen and 1.83 marks. Gold was $403 an ounce.

The world, in other words, was groping its way back, if not to Bretton Woods, at least to some resemblance of exchange-rate stability. You can see here a fixed-exchange rate system, albeit with very wide bands: the dollar was low enough at 150 yen, but too high at 225; low enough at 1.8 marks but too high at 2.7. These bands also em-

FIGURE 13–1

The Dollar

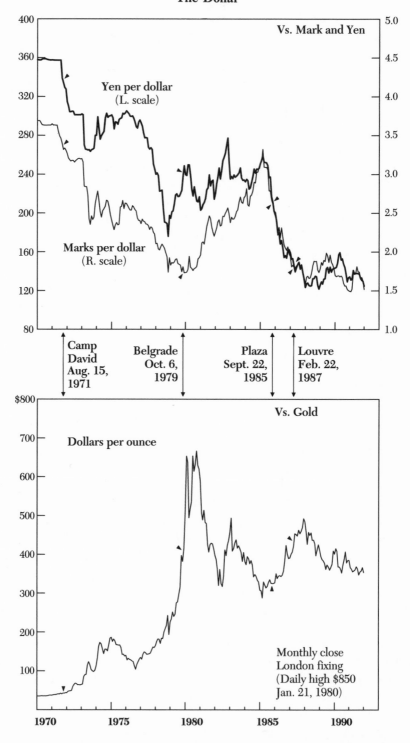

Vs. Mark and Yen

400

360

320

280

240

200

160

120

80

5.0

4.5

4.0

3.5

3.0

2.5

2.0

1.5

1.0

Yen per dollar
(L. scale)

Marks per dollar
(R. scale)

Camp
David
Aug. 15,
1971

Belgrade
Oct. 6,
1979

Plaza
Sept. 22,
1985

Louvre
Feb. 22,
1987

$800

700

600

500

400

300

200

100

Vs. Gold

Dollars per ounce

Monthly close
London fixing
(Daily high $850
Jan. 21, 1980)

1970   1975   1980   1985   1990

braced PPP—say 165 yen and 2.0 marks, to take the center of McKinnon's 1989 ranges.

To maintain any set of stable parities, of course, the respective central banks need to adjust their monetary policies. Either the weak-currency country needs to tighten money or the strong-currency country has to ease money, or both. Deciding which should do what requires some kind of outside reference point, some way of deciding whether the system as a whole needs more money creation or less. Or to say it another way, to avoid everyone merely inflating in tandem, the system needs an anchor.

Like gold, for example. Indeed, also implicit in the Plaza and Louvre decisions was a band for the gold price—$400 was high enough, but $320 was too low. In January 1986, McKinnon's reference point, gold was $352. Ten times 35 has always sounded reasonable to me.

On June 2, the White House announced Paul Volcker had declined to seek another term as Fed chairman. He did of course have family and financial reasons to leave, but it was also clear he no longer felt welcome. While the administration put out news leaks that he would be reappointed if he chose, it ignored his preferences to appoint other governors who did not share the old-time religion. In retrospect, it's clear that money was too easy in 1987, but Volcker felt unable to push the board to a test, though Greider reports that Wayne Angell was willing to tighten. If it had been up to me in 1987 I surely would have reappointed Volcker, but in terms of long-term confidence in monetary policy, there is much to be said for demonstrating that it does not depend on one individual.

Alan Greenspan, who took over the chairmanship in August, saw eye-to-eye with Volcker on most of the economic issues the Fed would face, but was decidedly a different personality. Where Volcker is saintly, Greenspan is worldly. Where Volcker is blunt, Greenspan has one of the most complex minds I've ever encountered. While seen as a compromise-prone Republican, he professes a philosophical debt to free-market firebrand Ayn Rand. He built his reputation and fortune on bringing some clarity to a bewildering profusion of economic statistics. When he was on Wall Street, we used to have long conversations on the economy; it was usually impossible to guess where his chain of thought was leading, but once he got there it made sense. My view is that the Republic was fortunate to have two people as qualified to lead its central bank. Greenspan's tenure has also been a notable success, and if he didn't have to deal with the

1979 stagflation, he quickly had to deal with the 1987 stock market collapse.

As the IMF convened in Washington in early October 1987, there was talk of further international cooperation. At that meeting, indeed, Treasury Secretary James Baker suggested that the G-7 nations partly base their coordination on "the relationship among our currencies and a basket of commodities, including gold." At the same Washington IMF meeting, British Chancellor of the Exchequer Nigel Lawson also urged that "special attention should also be given to the trend of world commodity prices," and contemplated "a more permanent regime of managed floating."[7]

By then it was perhaps too late. The dollar was at 147 yen compared to 153 at Louvre; against the mark it was at 1.84, actually a bit stronger than the Louvre parity. But gold had risen above $450 an ounce. While the Louvre had specified rates, it did not specify who should adjust to maintain them. Either the strong currency has to ease money, or the weak currency tighten money. Ideally, the choice should depend on the general impetus toward inflation—does the world as a whole need more liquidity or less?

And Secretary Baker and the Bundesbank quickly got into a spat over precisely this issue. The Americans wanted the Germans to hold the rate with easier money, but the Germans wanted to increase their interest rates. If they did, the United States could either follow or let the dollar decline. On Sunday the 18th, Secretary Baker went on "Meet the Press" to announce, "We will not sit back in this country and watch surplus countries jack up interest rates and squeeze growth worldwide on the expectation that the United States somehow will follow by raising its interest rates."[8]

The next morning the stock market dropped 508 points. The following day, as James Stewart and Daniel Hertzberg admirably recorded in their Pulitzer Prize-winning dispatch "Terrible Tuesday," the system tottered near collapse for the simple reason that traders did not know whose credit was good. The threat was a cascade of financial failures, like the Great Depression. Fed Chairman Greenspan issued a one-sentence statement affirming the Fed's "readiness to serve as a source of liquidity to support the economic and financial system."[9]

The crash was worldwide, and other central banks also rushed to supply liquidity. But the Louvre parities were out the window, and with them the momentum toward international monetary coordination. By the end of the year the dollar had tumbled to 122 yen and

1.58 marks, and gold climbed to $484. With the infusion of liquidity, dollar inflation rose from the 2 percent range in 1986 to the 5 percent range in 1989 and 1990.

Secretary Baker's television comment, of course, did not come as a bolt out of the blue. The crash had other causes as well. With values historically high, the market was perhaps ahead of itself. I doubt that portfolio insurance and computerized trading were as culpable as suggested by much of the commentary, including the official Brady report; but they did speed the correction.

More to the immediate point, on October 13, the House Ways and Means Committee adopted a harebrained scheme to stop corporate takeovers. A provision to disallow interest deductions for money borrowed for that purpose was attached to a pending bill with 15 minutes' discussion, and made retroactive to that date. Risk arbitrage stocks collapsed overnight, starting the full-scale plunge.[10]

Yet the Baker-Bundesbank controversy had already been feeding into the market, and his Sunday comments were attentively awaited. The international nature of the crash, in countries with and without widespread takeovers, with and without budget deficits, with and without program trading, suggests an international concern. I think that what the market was saying was that Secretary Baker was toying with the same dollar free-fall Secretary Blumenthal had outlined to President Carter nearly a decade before.

I find that at the time I wrote that Baker was right in his argument with the Bundesbank, that the market needed more liquidity. I can't imagine why, given the increase in the gold price. Somehow after the Louvre, in the transition from one excellent Fed chairman to another, we (given what I wrote) let money get away from us. It not only crashed the stock market, but lost the momentum toward what might have been achieved.

The case that concern over the dollar was at the heart of the market crash is bolstered by what happened later. Instead of plunging into another Great Depression, the stock market recovered and ultimately reached new records. More precisely, the tenor of all the financial markets stabilized and stocks started to recover on January 4, 1988. Trading for the year opened on that date, with the dollar hitting a post–World War II low of 120.25 yen in Tokyo. Then the world's central banks launched their most massive intervention in support of the dollar. The dollar started to rise, reaching 122.98 yen as the day's trading ended in New York. The Dow Jones Industrials soared 76 points and bond prices surged; the stock rally was repeated around

FIGURE 13–2

The Stock Market

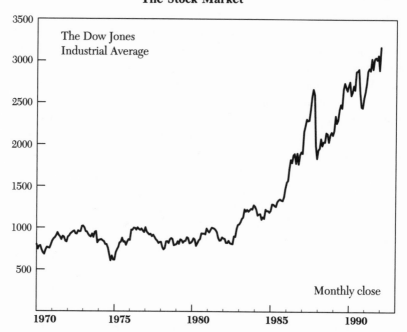

the world. The point was that with the restoration of central bank cooperation came the message that a calamitous collapse of the dollar would not be allowed.

Indeed, over time the dollar more or less recovered the Louvre parities. During April 1990, an exceptionally good month, it traded for an average of 158 yen, as against 153 at the Louvre. In August of 1991 it traded at 1.78 marks, compared with 1.83 at the Louvre. Gold, $403 at the Louvre and $484 later in 1987, traded below $345 in mid-1991. The Dow Jones Industrials—2722 at their 1987 high, 1738 at their post-crash low and 1938 at year-end—hit 3055 in mid-1991, and surged over the turn of the year, setting 10 new records in 15 sessions.

The involvement of the exchange rate with the huge stock-market plunge suggests the costs that volatile exchange rates impose. McKinnon has demonstrated that interest rates have been much more volatile under floating rates than they were under Bretton Woods. Just as Irving Fisher conceived an inflation premium as part of the interest rate, in today's world I suspect there is an exchange-rate premium as well, incorporating the risks of a floating dollar in an integrated world economy.

The biggest cost, though, is the rise of protectionism around the world. When exchange-rate swings can open and close factories, companies and their workers naturally look for ways to insulate themselves from these seemingly arbitrary shocks. Import protection, as well as "beggar-thy-neighbor" devaluations, were hallmarks of the Great Depression, also singularly an international event. World trade imploded, and prosperity with it.

Perhaps because of latent memories of that fate, so far the world has done reasonably well in containing the protectionist threat. Europe is stripping away internal barriers, and the United States has concluded a free-trade agreement with Canada and has agreed to negotiate another with Mexico. These regional arrangements actually worry some free-trade philosophers, since the multilateral Uruguay round seems to be foundering. But at the very least, it's instructive that regional free trade follows pools of exchange-rate stability, in a dollar area and within the European Monetary System.

The General Agreement on Tariffs and Trade held its 40th anniversary celebration in the wake of the stock market crash, on November 30, 1987. The meeting was addressed by Paul Volcker, who chose to reflect not only on trade but on exchange rates:

> At the time the regime of floating exchange rates was adopted in 1973, it was seen by most as, among other things, providing strong support for free trade. The point was that flexible changes in exchange rates in response to market forces would maintain a better equilibrium in national trade and current account positions, thereby removing one protectionist argument. A corollary was usually explicitly stated as well—real exchange rates, at least, ought to be pretty steady in practice, even if permitted to float in principle, since the underlying conditions affecting trade or the relative productivity of capital would change only gradually. If countries could manage to achieve a convergence of inflation rates at a low level, the argument ran, then nominal exchange rates would stabilize as well.
>
> Now, 15 years later, that kind of optimism looks pretty naive. Instead of exchange markets moving along a learning curve toward greater stability as time has passed, various measures of exchange-rate volatility—daily, monthly, and cyclically—have plainly increased. Clearly, there have been external shocks, but fewer in the 1980s than in the 1970s, so that can hardly explain the greater volatility. Moreover, the broadest indicators of economic performance among the leading industrialized countries have converged about as much as could realistically be expected; inflation rates generally are at the lowest levels in 20 years or more.

Economists debate the causes of the growing volatility of exchange rates and whether it has itself tended to restrain growth in trade and to distort and inhibit the investment necessary to support trade. Perhaps the rise in protectionism is explanation enough of the fact that international trade in the 1980s has no longer provided the leading edge to economic growth in the OECD countries. But it seems to me beyond doubt that the protectionist pressures in the United States, and probably elsewhere as well, have been fed by the well-founded impression that exchange rates have deviated widely from their equilibrium exchange levels. And at this point, it's difficult to maintain a sense of optimism that complementarity in national economic policies and convergence in actual economic performance—within realistic expectations—will by itself provide assurance of substantial stability in real or nominal exchange rates.

In their meetings at the Plaza in 1985 and at the Louvre early this year, the finance ministers and central bankers of the major industrial countries explicitly recognized the importance of appropriate exchange rates not only in contributing to better economic balance but also in restraining protectionist pressures. However vaguely their exchange-rate objectives were stated, the official agnosticism and passivity toward the appropriate level of the main dollar exchange rates characteristic of most of the 1970s and the first half of the 1980s was abandoned. The ministers and governors also clearly recognized that exchange-rate objectives could be reached only in the context of a mutually appropriate pattern of economic policy adjustments.

The understandings reached at the Louvre about the effort to stabilize exchange rates have recently been criticized as at least premature and at worst entirely wrongheaded. The argument of some seems to be that the agreement sacrificed appropriate internal economic management to the requirements of a stable exchange rate. That seems to be a misreading of both the nature of the understanding and, more broadly, the need to accord the requirements of exchange rate stability more prominence in economic policy making.

The 40th anniversary of the GATT is not the appropriate place to debate either the details of exchange-rate policy in 1987 or the nature of needed long-term reforms of the international monetary system—although I might happily overlook that nicety had I a blueprint to unveil. What I will assert is that the health and vitality of an open international trading order will be importantly dependent over time upon the willingness of governments of large trading countries to reach some realistic collective judgments about the broadly appropriate level of exchange rates. Those judgments will, in turn, need to influence the design and implementation of domestic policies if they are to be meaningful and durable.

I know something of how difficult it is to achieve recognition of the international consequences of domestic policy actions in the United States as elsewhere. I also know something of the political constraints on economic policy making, even without taking account of the need to find an appropriate blend of policies internationally. But I also insist that we cannot count on floating exchange rates to smooth over all the difficulties—not if we are interested in turning back protectionism and achieving more open trade.[11]

14

The S&L Debacle

If international monetary cooperation was the big missed opportunity of the Seven Fat Years, the big debacle was the savings and loan crackup. Like most debacles, this one was a long time in the making. It all started with the Pecora hearings.

In January 1933, a subcommittee of the Senate Banking and Currency Committee appointed a new counsel, Ferdinand Pecora, a native of Sicily who'd become a Teddy Roosevelt–Woodrow Wilson reformer, and who'd rung up an 80 percent conviction rate as an assistant district attorney in New York. The subcommittee had been conducting an inconclusive investigation of Wall Street, partly sparked by President Hoover's notion that his problems were caused by short-sellers in the stock market, not by his own tariff or tax increase. Special prosecutor Pecora changed the course of history, down to this day. The following account of his hearings draws on Ron Chernow's *The House of Morgan*, which describes his effect:

> Smoking a blunt cigar, his shirtsleeves rolled up, the hard-bitten Pecora captured the public's attention. For six months, the hearings had been stalled. Republicans and Democrats, with fine impartiality, had feared fat cats of both parties might be named and united in a conspiracy of silence. With Pecora as counsel, the hearings acquired a new, irresistible momentum. They would afford a secret history of the crash, a sobering postmortem of the twenties that would blacken the name of bankers for a generation. From now on, they would be called banksters.[1]

Beyond doubt, Pecora exposed much skullduggery. In the market excitement of 1929, Albert H. Wiggin, the head of the Chase Bank,

219

borrowed $8 million from his bank to finance a short position in its own stock, clearing several million for his own account. After the crash, the top 100 officers of the National City Bank took and never repaid interest-free loans totalling $2.4 million. And National City's retail brokerage arm had pushed Latin American bonds on the public while the bank suppressed its own reports presaging the LDC debt crisis of that day.

The hearings, though, had targets beyond obvious miscreants like Wiggin. The strategic objective was the pinnacle of American finance, the Morgan empire, an international collection of partnerships centered on J. P. Morgan and Company at 23 Wall Street. Morgan had no stock to diddle, and would not stoop to retail brokerage. While not immune to human nature, as later events were to show, its partners by and large seemed too priggish to be likely suspects of gross dishonesty.

Morgan did, however, handle hot new issues in the go-go market of 1929. Indeed, many of its issues traded on a "when-issued" basis, fetching sharp premiums even before they were released to the market. This means hefty profits for the underwriter, who pays the issuing price to the client and sells at the market price to the public. Rather than keep all these gains for itself, Morgan shared the wealth, spreading it where it would do the most good.

Recipients of Morgan issues at the inside price included former President Calvin Coolidge and Charles O. Hilles, chairman of the Republican National Committee. But also John J. Raskob, chairman of the Democratic National Committee, William H. Woodin, FDR's treasury secretary, and Sen. William G. McAdoo, who sat on the Pecora Committee. The balance of the list comprised the nation's business and financial elite.

These revelations surely showed that Morgan was an immensely powerful backroom presence and revived the strain of anti-finance populism that reaches back to the nation's origins. Jefferson, for example, suspected that the first Bank of the United States was Hamilton's plot to restore the monarchy. And the second Bank of the United States was destroyed when Nicholas Biddle lost his power struggle with Andrew Jackson.

A host of other social and cultural ingredients inevitably plunged into the heady brew. In one letter J. P. Morgan, Jr., referred to Pecora as a "dirty little wop," and the ethnic antagonism was no doubt reciprocated. As Biddle's New York banking competitors chortled at Jackson slaying "The Monster of Chestnut Street," so Chase and

National City were found supporting the legislation to dismember the House of Morgan.

Most of all, though, the ultimate issue was: Who's to blame for the depression? After his bank holiday, Roosevelt proclaimed, "The money changers have fled from their high seats in the temple of our civilization. We may now restore that temple to the ancient truths." Yet however sordid Wiggin's short sales, they were not, pick your cause, the mismanagement of the money supply, the Smoot-Hawley tariff, the 1932 tax increase, the mismanagement of war debts and reparations, or the undervaluation of gold and a shortage of international liquidity.

"I wish we could get from the bankers themselves that in the 1927 to 1929 period there were grave abuses and that the bankers themselves now support whole-heartedly methods to prevent recurrence thereof. Can't bankers see their own advantage in such a course?" FDR wrote to Russell Leffingwell, a supporter at Morgan. Leffingwell replied, "The bankers were not in fact responsible for 1927–1929 and the politicians were. Why then should the bankers make a false confession?"[2]

In this cauldron, the structure of today's finance industry was concocted. The deepest roots of the S&L debacle lie in structure forged from Pecora's revelations and diagnosis. Chernow, for example, writes that in severing commercial and investment banking and dismembering the House of Morgan, the Glass-Steagall Act "was as much an attempt to punish the banking industry as it was a measure to reform it."[3]

While at it, Congress structured the savings and loan industry that collapsed into crisis during the Seven Fat Years. Legislation to restructure the financial industry included the Federal Home Loan Bank Act of 1932, the Home Owners' Loan Act of 1933 and the National Housing Act of 1934. There had earlier been state-chartered thrift institutions, naturally in great difficulties during the depression, and the new structure was in part intended to rationalize their regulation. It was also intended to subsidize housing, since commerical banks at the time concentrated on business loans and neglected mortgages. But this structure also fit the purpose of splintering the financial industry to reduce its power.

This is a purpose, I should make clear, with which I have considerable personal sympathy, not being an admirer of the highly centralized financial systems of Germany or Japan. The tight linkage of finance with existing business interests, I fear, stifles entrepreneurial creativity. On the basis of both personal taste and long-run economic performance, I must prefer a diverse system that opens the supply of capital to small, risk-taking new enterprises. So while the House of Morgan suffered rough justice, it certainly did not evolve into an American Duetsche Bank, as arguably it might have. So perhaps Ferdinand Pecora is due a moment of thanks from the college drop-outs, breakaway engineers and illegal immigrants who provided the impetus for the Seven Fat Years.

At the same time, though, the essence of financial safety is diversification. And a financial system that outlaws diversification—breaking finance into a succession of narrow splinters—is a series of disasters waiting to happen. For if a splinter of the economy gets into trouble it takes its financial institutions with it, deepening and prolonging the crisis. The interdependence of finance, too, may spread the trouble unnecessarily to other sectors.

The Farm Credit System, another depression-era creation intended to spur loans to farmers, had to be bailed out by the taxpayer in 1987 after the farm economy went sour. This too was a by-product of the inflation and weak dollar in the 1970s, which produced a surge of agricultural exports. This demand inflated land values and encouraged farmers to borrow against these values to buy more land. The high dollar of 1985 priced U.S. exports out of foreign markets, reversed the spiral, made a lot of farm loans unserviceable. And with a lot of its loans going into default all at once, the whole Farm Credit System was in jeopardy. Congress had to pony up $4 billion to right it in 1987, in a foretaste of the S&L disaster.

To top off the problem, the depression-era Congress decided that, to prevent bank runs, the taxpayer should insure bank deposits. The banking act of 1933 established the Federal Deposit Insurance Corporation insuring deposits up to $2,500. The 1934 National Housing Act established the Federal Savings and Loan Insurance Corporation, insuring S&L deposits up to $5,000, an amount quickly matched by FDIC coverage. And in extending deposit insurance, Congress ignored most of the devices commerical insurers use to limit risk: deductibles for example, and most important of all, matching premiums with risks. Premiums were based on the amount of deposits insured; as some critics saw in the 1930s, the effect of this arrangement would be to spread the problem of bad banks to the good banks.

Critics of deposit insurance in the 1930s included Franklin D. Roosevelt. At first he seemed ready to use his veto to stop the idea, but ultimately yielded to its growing popularity in the wake of widespread bank failures. No doubt he voiced his true feelings in his first press conference in office: "We do not wish to make the United States government liable for the mistakes and errors of individual banks, and put a premium on unsound banking in the future."[4]

· · ·

Collecting savings account deposits to invest in residential mortgages, the "thrift industry" was triply undiversified. Its loan were backed almost wholly by residential properties, usually concentrated in a narrow geographical region and, most dangerous of all, uniformly carried long terms at fixed rates. This profile of interest-earning assets was backed by liabilities to savings account customers, who had the option of withdrawing their accounts. The thrifts were borrowing short to lend long. In stable times, this yields an easy profit, and S&Ls were a sleepy business memorialized in, every account of the crisis seems obligated to say, Jimmy Stewart's 1946 film, *It's a Wonderful Life*.

The Achilles heel of this scheme is inflation, as Irving Fisher might have explained. The appearance of inflation drives up all interest rates, as both lender and borrower contemplate repayment in cheaper dollars. Thrifts could raise their interest rates only slowly as old mortgages expired and new ones were made; the terms prevented them from increasing rates on existing mortgages.

Depositors, however, could withdraw their money and walk out the door, and were bound to do so if dramatically better rates were available elsewhere. Spurts of such withdrawals went by the unlovely name of disintermediation. At a minimum, the decline in deposits would mean S&Ls would have no new money to lend. Money would still come in through payments on existing mortgages, of course, probably providing a positive cash flow when set against withdrawals. But if a thrift started to show accounting losses its capital cushion would start to decline, and when it reached a certain minimum regulators might close it down. If capital—the bank's own money instead of depositors'—sank to, say, 3 percent of assets, it would be ruled "safe and unsound."

As inflation picked up in the 1960s, the threat of disintermediation rose and Band-Aids were applied. In 1966, Congress sought to limit competition among thrifts by making it illegal for them to offer more than a set interest rate, and to enhance their competition with banks by allowing them to pay a bit more than banks could. This was the famous Regulation Q differential; in 1966 thrifts could pay 4.75 percent while banks could pay 4.0 percent; as inflation mounted these figures were raised but the differential remained.

Trying to lasso the markets seldom works for long, of course, and only so long as the restraint makes relatively little difference. As inflation started to accelerate, big investors who had alternatives started to shun thrifts and banks, so by 1970 Reg Q had to be lifted for certificates of deposit of more than $100,000. The following year saw the first money market fund, which collected deposits from small savers to invest in CDs. That still more inflation could cause a thrift crisis was completely predictable.

Indeed, it was predicted. A perusal of my files turns up a clients' letter from Townsend-Greenspan & Company dated April 17, 1974. Alan Greenspan probably did not foresee himself dealing with the aftermath when he wrote, "The necessity of bringing inflation under control is becoming urgent largely because of the growing threat to the financial viability of our thrift institutions." Because old mortgages did not pay current rates "it is virtually impossible for these institutions to pay current money market rates for their short-term liabilities," hence their support for Reg Q.

However, he continued, there were by now a number of money market funds offering small savers rates of around 10 percent rather than the Reg Q's 5.25 percent. So far, "the diversion of funds from thrift institutions has not been significant." But "should we run into an acceleration of the inflation rate in the years, say, 1977–1978, short-term interest rates could easily move into the 12 percent to 15 percent range." With this differential, Reg Q would not hold and "this could lead to a degree of financial disintermediation so vast that the federal government would probably intervene to bail out the thrift institutions."[5] This would involve, Greenspan added, an increase in money creation and further inflation.

Inflation and interest rates peaked as Greenspan departed Wall Street to be chairman of the Council of Economic Advisers. Rates reached double digits again toward the end of 1978, bringing the thrift crisis he'd predicted. In 1978, money market fund assets tripled, from $3.3 billion to $9.5 billion. In 1979 they leapt to $42.9 billion and by 1982 had reached $236.3 billion. These deposits, by the way, carried private insurance, no federal guarantee. The thrifts hemmorrhaged, and turned to Washington for salvation.

In the early hours of the morning on March 5, 1980, Rep. Fernand St Germain staged a coup in a House-Senate Conference Committee. The committee was reconciling House and Senate versions of DID-

MCA, the Depository Institutions Deregulation and Monetary Control Act of 1980. One difference was that the House bill left the maximum for deposit insurance untouched at $40,000 an account, up from $25,000 four years earlier. The Senate bill raised the maximum to $50,000. St Germain arranged at a compromise increasing the amount to $100,000, as we saw in Chapter 12, more than doubling taxpayer liability for sick thrifts.

St Germain was later voted out of his previously safe Rhode Island district after exposure of his relations with the thrift lobby. St Germain had become a millionaire on a congressman's salary, with the help of generous loans from the banks under his committee's jurisdiction. In 1987 House Ethics Committee found "no evidence suggesting improper influence," and dismissed reporting violations as "a good-faith mistake." After a grand jury investigated allegations that he had received tens of thousands of dollars in free meals, drinks and entertainment from a thrift lobbyist, the Justice Department declined to indict but referred the matter to the ethics committee. In the final days of the 1988 campaign, court documents were released showing that Justice had alleged "substantial evidence of serious and sustained misconduct."[6]

Helping in the increase of deposit insurance to $100,000 was Sen. Alan Cranston, according to Martin Mayer, who says he carried the ball for large California thrifts. Cranston was of course later to become one of the "Keating Five," senators who intervened directly with regulators on behalf of Charles Keating's Lincoln Savings and Loan.

And again, the premiums for the $100,000 in insurance were entirely unrelated to the risk of default. A *Journal* editorial from 1982 explained the problem.

[A] bank with dubious loans and a thin capital cushion could pay the same premium as a bank with blue-chip loans and a plump capital cushion, even though the first is clearly more risky. But since the strategy of the first bank can also be more profitable and since fixed-rate premiums mean there is no penalty for following a high risk strategy, banks have an incentive to behave like high rollers. In short, the current insurance system encourages banks to pursue high-return strategies at the expense of sound ones.[7]

The increase in deposit insurance would not in itself solve the thrift's problems, of course, so DIDMCA offered another formula: The thrifts were to be allowed to bid more aggressively for deposits;

Regulation Q ceilings would be phased out over five years. And in order to earn the money to pay the higher interest rates, thrifts would be given investment powers reaching beyond home mortgages. DID-MCA allowed them to invest 20 percent of their assets in consumer loans, commercial paper or corporate debt. They could also offer credit card services and hold money market funds and issue NOW accounts, which were interest-bearing checking accounts.

March 1980, when DIDMCA passed, was six months after Paul Volcker had returned from Belgrade. The Carter administration credit controls were announced between the conference report and signing of the act. The prime rate was going up through 18 percent, inflation over six months was running at annualized rate of 14 percent. Money market funds would reach $76.8 billion in assets during 1980, compared with $42.9 billion the year before. In January 1981, Ferdinand Pecora, Fernand St Germain and Jimmy Carter turned this mess over to Ronald Reagan.

• • •

As Ronald Reagan came into office, of course, Volcker tightened money again. By July 1981, the prime rate was, after a slight dip, again at 20 percent. Richard T. Pratt, the new chairman of the Federal Home Loan Bank Board, testified that month that 80 percent of the nation's 4,600 savings and loans were suffering operating losses, that a third of them were not "viable under today's conditions." The "most troubled" category comprised 263 thrifts, he added, facing total losses of $60 billion, of which perhaps $15 billion would be recouped from the sale of assets. July also marked the onset of the economic contraction that was not to end until November of 1982.

At its best, which is seldom, the notion that the S&L crisis was caused by Ronald Reagan's "deregulation" has primarily to do with what Pratt did then when faced with this unappetizing dilemma. Martin Mayer describes Pratt as "withal a nice fellow and (unfortunately) by far the most intelligent man ever to hold that job." He adds, in a view that seems to me to assume that history started in 1982 and ended about 1985, that "if you had to pick one individual to blame for what happened to the S&Ls and to some hundreds of billions of dollars of taxpayer money, Dick would get the honor without even campaigning."[8]

For Pratt was ingenious in designing ways to relax accounting standards to keep the thrifts afloat through the recession. Financial intermediaries intermediate between saver and borrower. Depositors give a bank (or S&L) their money, and the bank lends it to others. If nothing ever intruded on the pure mathematics, this could go on forever. In theory, a bank with no capital of its own can continue to operate; it doesn't vanish in a puff of smoke when it reaches zero net worth. Unless depositors start to run, regulators have to close it.

In making this decision, regulators look at the institution's capital or net worth. That is, the percentage of assets accounted for by the bank's own money rather than depositors'. But Moses' tablets did not include a number at which an institution has to be closed. This is an arbitrary decision. What's more, at different times and in different nations different things count toward "capital." That is, capital is what the regulators say it is.

In his attempt to keep the thrift industry from collapsing in 1982, for example, Pratt greatly expanded "supervisory goodwill." That is, thrift A could buy thrift B, and include some of its own purchase price as capital, to be written off over 40 years. Pratt got into an argument with the Financial Accounting Standards Board, with him saying that applying strict accounting rules would sink every thrift in the country, and the FASB countering that he should use normal accounting and merely set capital requirements at zero or even less.

The Garn-St Germain bill did vastly deregulate the thrifts, carrying the formula of DIDMCA to its logical conclusion; allowing both banks and thrifts to pay unlimited interest rates in competition with money market funds, and allowing them a broader range of investments. After the two bills, thrifts could hold 40 percent of their assets in commercial real estate, for example.

Garn-St Germain also sanctioned direct regulatory infusions into bank capital, through an exchange of notes with the federal insurers. Such assistance could cover 70 percent of losses for thrifts with net worth below 1 percent, for example, and 60 percent for thrifts with net worth between 1 percent and 2 percent. St Germain backed a more generous infusion, 100 percent of losses at a net worth below 2 percent. His bill passed his committee on a party-line vote; on the floor he argued it had "no cost, not one red penny."

The deregulation of interest rates and lending authority would have been costless to the taxpayer, indeed, except for deposit insurance and especially the spectacular increase in it St Germain had helped engineer two years earlier. Thrifts could borrow at maximum interest rates and lend, for example, to speculative shopping centers. Soon "brokered deposits" arose to make government-insured

$100,000 deposits in whatever thrifts offered the highest rates—that is, the riskiest ones.

In defense of Pratt's decisions, you have to remember 1982. Mexico devalued the peso in February; Grupo Alfa defaulted in April, threatening to take U.S. banks with it. The banks' Third World debt turned sour around the globe. If the economy started to recover, the money supply would grow and the Fed would tighten to cut it off. A default by Drysdale Government Securities, previously almost unknown, shook the whole financial system. Energy loans were also going under water, and Penn Square Bank went down. Mexico nationalized its banks on September 1.

Despite Mayer's contrary example of the Mutual Savings Banks, Pratt was entitled to a view that the last thing the nation needed was a string of collapsing S&Ls. Perhaps his accounting tricks confused subsequent regulators, but he was perfectly straightforward about what he was doing and why. And he was perfectly clear about the risks; in December 1982, he warned that the insurance fund "will be exposed to operating risks such as have never occurred in the past." In April 1983, the most intelligent thrift regulator ever left to run the brokered deposit business for Merrill Lynch. By then everyone understood the thrifts were in deep trouble; the time to straighten them out was after recovery started.

It didn't happen. Ed Gray, who took over from Pratt, can tell you why. It's not that he and his subordinates didn't try.

As highflying thrifts go, a record of sort was set by Vernon Savings and Loan; when finally seized by regulators, some 96 percent of its loans were in default. Its head, real estate developer Don Dixon, was in the end sentenced to five years in jail for misappropriating some $600,000 of the thrift's funds, a tiny fraction of its $1.2 billion loss. The rest went in bad but legal loans.

While vacationing at home in California around Christmas 1986, Gray got a call concerning Vernon from incoming Speaker of the House Jim Wright. The speaker said that he understood that the bank board was going to close Vernon either that day or the next. When Gray replied it wasn't being "closed down," the speaker asked him to investigate and report back. Richard J. Phelan, whose work as special outside counsel to the House Ethics Committee precipitated Speaker Wright's resignation, concluded that "in and of itself," this exchange was not a violation of House rules.

It came, though, in the context of numerous previous interventions on behalf of Texas S&Ls. At a September 1986 meeting, Wright complained of "heavy-handed" or "Gestapo-like" tactics by the regulators in Dallas. Wright would not identify the institutions subjected to such treatment, but prior to the meeting a House aide had suggested that Gray should do "only one thing. Just find out who Tom Gaubert is."[9]

Thomas M. Gaubert was head of Independent American Savings Association. He was also treasurer of the Democratic Congressional Campaign Committee, a fund-raising operation headed by Tony Coelho, who shortly became House majority whip. In early November 1986 Wright phoned Gray specifically about Gaubert. Independent American was grossly insolvent, according to the Phelan report. Despite rules against the chairman meeting directly with heads of thrifts under his adjudication, Wright urged Gray to meet directly with Gaubert.

This, Mr. Phelan found, was an ethical violation, as was a later Wright request that Gray "get rid of" Joe Selby, head of regulatory affairs in Dallas. Even more pertinently, all this took place while the thrift insurance fund was nearly insolvent; since closing insolvent thrifts typically requires a federal payout, this hamstrung its efforts. A recapitalization bill that would have allowed it to close money-losing thrifts stalled on Capitol Hill.

The Phelan report summarizes the impressions of Gray and his subordinates. "The Bank Board officials adamantly believe that Wright coerced them—or attempted to coerce them—into changing regulatory responses with regard to three of the four individuals. They believe that Wright sought specific regulatory results. Moreover, they believe that Wright had placed a 'hold' on the FSLIC recapitalization bill until the Bank Board complied with his demands."[10]

By 1986, the economic expansion was well established and sick thrifts could have been closed without serious financial repercussions. But they couldn't be closed, Phelan's evidence suggests, because the Speaker of the House of Representatives wanted regulators to go easy on Texas thrifts. And he was willing to end the clean-up effort until he got his way; the cost of the bailout soared. Those the speaker protected included one of the most egregious thrifts on record.

The House Ethics Committee decided the speaker's intervention with the regulators was perfectly okay, with the scope of "the technique and personality of the legislator." Ed Gray remarked, "The message the committee is sending is that members won't be punished for subverting the regulatory process. It's open season for lobbyists to ask congressmen to lean on the SEC, the EPA, etc." But the committee criticized Wright on some other charges, and he felt he had to resign. Everyone understood he had to go because of the thrift crisis.

Wright's resignation was shortly followed by that of Tony Coelho. His problem concerned belated payments for fundraising use of "High Spirits," a yacht the Vernon, Texas, savings and loan kept on the Potomac. So the two top members of the House of Representatives left essentially because of actions that blocked the thrift cleanup. While Reagan's penchant for deregulation is blamed for the crisis, the man trying to regulate was Ed Gray, one of Reagan's California appointees.

In the other wing of the Capitol Building, meanwhile, senators were gathering to protect another thrift record-holder, Charles H. Keating, Jr., and his Lincoln Savings and Loan. Lincoln was the only thrift to go beyond its insured deposits, raising money by marketing uninsured subordinated debentures in its parent company, American Continental Corporation. William Davis, chief deputy commissioner of the California Department of Savings and Loan, said, "This is the only subordinated debt I know of that was marketed not through brokerage houses, but directly to the consumer."[11] Late in 1991, Keating was convicted of securities fraud in the sale of the debentures.

No doubt many of the most elderly purchasers failed to distinguish between the debentures and insured deposits. One Lincoln branch selling the debentures was next to the Leisure World retirement community. When California ruled that Lincoln employees could not sell the debentures, the company set up desks manned by others in its offices; when that was banned, it rented space upstairs. By the time ACC went into bankruptcy, some 22,000 investors owned more than $200 million in uninsured debt.

Meanwhile, Lincoln was investing heavily in Arizona land and real estate development. In fact, Federal Judge Stanley Sporkin found in dismissing a Lincoln suit against regulators, it created "sham" transactions in land sales in order to book profits. It then would remit "tax sharing" payments to ACC although "Lincoln on a stand-alone basis essentially owed no taxes." In reviewing the record, Judge Sporkin used the word "skullduggery."[12]

The full extent of what was happening at Lincoln was not immediately apparent. Indeed, Federal Reserve Chairman Alan Greenspan, then a private consultant, wrote a testimonial letter to regulators on Lincoln's behalf in early 1985. Eying the speculative investments of the thrifts, Ed Gray had promulgated a regulation saying they could put no more than 10 percent of their assets into direct investments. Lincoln, building the 600-room Phoenician Hotel near Phoenix, lobbied for an exemption allowing direct investment of 40 percent.

The senators who intervened on Lincoln's behalf are now immortalized as the "Keating Five." All had received campaign contributions from Mr. Keating, the minimum being $34,000. They were led by Dennis DeConcini (D., Ariz.). The leading contribution recipient was Alan Cranston (D., Calif.), who solicited $850,000 for his "voter registration" groups. The others included Banking Committee Chairman Don Riegle (D., Mich.), who received contributions from 57 executives of Keating companies the month prior to his intervention. And also John McCain (R., Ariz.) and John Glenn (D., Ohio); after his investigation, Senate Ethics Committee counsel Robert Bennett recommended senators McCain and Glenn be cleared, largely because they ceased their efforts on behalf of Lincoln when they learned it was being referred for possible criminal proceedings.

The five senators intervened with Ed Gray to relax his rule on direct investments. Gray arranged for them to meet with San Francisco regulators directly responsible for Lincoln: James Cirona, Michael Patriarca, William Black and Richard Sanchez. Black kept extensive notes of the meeting, providing a vignette of life in the World's Greatest Deliberative Body. Some excerpts:

DECONCINI: We wanted to meet with you because we have determined that potential actions of yours could injure a constituent. This is a particular concern to us because Lincoln is willing to take substantial actions to deal with what we understand to be your concerns. . . .

Lincoln is a viable organization. It made $49 million last year, even more the year before. They fear falling below 3 percent and becoming subject to your regulatory control of the operations of their association.

They have two major disagreements with you. First, with regard to direct investment. Second, on your reappraisal. They're suing against your direct investment regulation. I can't make a judgment on the grandfathering issue. We suggest that the lawsuit be accelerated and that you grant them forbearance while the suit is pending. I know something about the appraisal values of the Federal Home Loan Bank Board. They appear to be grossly unfair. I know the particular property here. My family is in real estate. Lincoln is prepared to reach a compromise value with you.

CRANSTON: I'm sorry I can't join you, but I have to be on the floor to deal with the bill. I just want to say that I share the concerns of the other senators on this subject. . . .

GLENN: Well, in any event, ACC is an Ohio chartered corporation. I've known them for a long time, but it wouldn't matter if I didn't.

Ordinary exams take up to 6 months. Even the accounting firm says that you've taken an unusually adversary view toward Lincoln. To be blunt, you should charge them or get off their backs. If things are bad there, get to them. Their view is that they took a failing business and put it back on its feet. It's now viable and profitable. They took it off the endangered species list. Why has the exam dragged on and on and on? . . .

CIRONA: This meeting is very unusual, to discuss a particular company.

DeCONCINI: It's very unusual for us to have a company that could be put out of business by its regulators. . . .

RIEGLE: Where's the smoking gun? Where are the losses?

DeCONCINI: What's wrong with this if they're willing to clean up their act?

CIRONA: This is a ticking time bomb.

SANCHEZ: I had another case which reported strong earnings in 1984. It was insolvent by 1985.

RIEGLE: These people saved a failing thrift. ACC is reputed to be highly competent.

BLACK: Lincoln was not a failing thrift before ACC acquired it. It met its net worth requirement . . .

PATRIARCA: I'm relatively new to the savings and loan industry, but I've never seen any bank or S&L that's anything like this. This isn't even close. You can ask any banker you know about these practices. They violate the law and regulations and common sense.

GLENN: What violates the law?

PATRIARCA: Their direct investments violate the regulation. Then there's the file stuffing. They took undated documents purporting to show underwriting efforts and put them in to the files sometimes more than a year after they made the investment.

GLENN: Have you done anything about these violations of law?

PATRIARCA: We're sending a criminal referral to the Department of Justice. Not maybe, we're sending one. This is an extraordinarily serious matter. It involves a whole range of imprudent actions. I can't tell you strongly enough how serious this is. . . .
DECONCINI: I'd question these reappraisals. If you want to bend over backwards to be fair I'd arbitrate the differences. The criminality surprises me. We're not interested in discussing those issues. Our premise was that we had a viable institution concerned that it was being overregulated.[13]

Ed Gray's term as head of the Federal Home Loan Bank Board expired a few weeks later. He was replaced by M. Danny Wall, who once described himself as a "child of the senate," though he says this did not affect his regulatory actions. The San Francisco examiners sent a 285-page document recommending that the board seize Lincoln. Lincoln threatened lawsuits; Washington regulators disagreed, and one who recommended seizure was replaced. Wall met with Keating; no examiners visited Lincoln for 10 months. In early 1988, the bank board took jurisdiction away from the San Francisco examiners and transferred it to Washington. Lawrence J. White, a respected academic economist, dissented in the 2–1 vote.

When Congress created the Office of Thrift Supervision in 1989, it included a provision that "notwithstanding" the usual process for confirming the head of a government agency, the head of the new agency should be "the chairman of the Federal Home Loan Bank Board," to wit, M. Danny Wall. In 1990, a federal court granted a restraining order against the agency on the grounds that Mr. Wall had not been properly confirmed, jeopardizing all of the OTS regulatory actions. By the time of the ruling Wall had resigned. The apparent purpose of Congress' extraordinary legislation was to get Wall in the job and at the same time avoid confirmation hearings, which inevitably would have dealt with the Lincoln case.

Lincoln was ultimately closed in April 1989. Two days before the seizure, Senator Cranston called board member Roger Martin at home at 10 P.M. urging the board to allow a last-minute sale of Lincoln instead; at 6:30 A.M. the following day, Martin received a similar call from Senator DeConcini.

Holders of the subordinated debentures are out their $200 million. A spokesman, Dr. Don Mikami, a dentist in Fountain Valley, California, has said, "I am almost 100 percent certain that if the Senators and Danny Wall hadn't acted that Lincoln would have been seized two years ago, and most of these worthless bonds would never have been peddled."[14] Taxpayers, of course, will have to clean up after the deposits covered by federal insurance. That will come to an estimated $2.5 billion.

These costs arose because senators intervened to stop Ronald Reagan's regulators from seizing Lincoln, no doubt chilling other regulatory action as well. Jim Wright intervened to keep Ronald Reagan's regulators from refinancing in time to seize thrifts. Ferdinand Pecora shouldered the bankers with blame for the depression, leaving a banking system prone to disaster. Richard Nixon and Jimmy Carter created and fostered the inflation that kicked the thrifts into crisis. Fernand St Germain kicked deposit insurance through the roof.

The Reagan/Volcker policy mix licked the inflation and, while it was a dicey thing in 1982, started the Seven Fat Years. Yes, Dick Pratt decided not to overturn the applecart in 1982. Ideally, the thrift mess should have been cleaned up as prosperity dawned, but Jim Wright and the Keating Five kept Ed Gray from doing that. Yet the myth persists that the S&L debacle was solely and purely the fault of Ronald Reagan's deregulatory excesses.

At the *Journal* in 1991 we wrote an editorial defending the anti-paperwork efforts of the Office of Management and Budget, which some in Congress were trying to curb. We got a letter to the editor starting,

> "Deregulation was a pillar of Reaganomics," according to your June 17 editorial "The Reregulation President." Yes, and the American people will be paying for that over the next 50 years. With banks failing, thrift bailout costs rising and insurance companies shaking, now is no time to wax nostalgic about deregulation.[15]

It was signed by Senator John Glenn.

15

Greed and Envy

In 1933 Matthew Josephson published a book and enriched American idiom. His title *The Robber Barons* will forever evoke the names of titans—Rockefeller, Carnegie, Morgan, Mellon, Vanderbilt—who built industrial empires in the years between the Civil War and the turn of the century. These men, Josephson conceded, "more or less knowingly played the leading roles in an age of industrial revolution." They introduced large-scale production and efficiency. For all their faults, "many of them showed volcanic energy and qualities of courage which, under another economic clime, might have fitted them for immensely useful social constructions, and rendered them glorious rather than hateful to their people."

Josephson discerned a flaw in their efforts. "But all this revolutionizing effort is branded with the motive of private gain on the part of the new captains of industry. To organize and exploit the resources of a nation upon a gigantic scale, to regiment its farmers and workers into harmonious corps of producers, and to do this only in the name of an uncontrolled appetite for private profit—here surely is the great inherent contradiction whence so much disaster, outrage and misery has flowed."[1]

Josephson, it should be readily enough apparent, operated from a political viewpoint. A banker's son who spent the 1920s with the surrealists in Paris, he had returned as the depression descended to join *The New Republic*. During the 1932 election campaign, he helped draft a manifesto for a group of intellectuals that backed the Communist candidate for president, William Z. Foster. Unlike Sidney Hook and James Burnham, however, he never joined the party. He explained, "I know I'm not virtuous enough."[2]

235

The Robber Barons dwells entertainingly on the foibles of its subjects, their intrigues, their ruthlessness, their lavish parties. And of all the Robber Barons the most scandalous was Jay Gould, the entry rating more lines than any other in Josephson's index, beating Rockefeller, Carnegie and (by a nose) J. P. Morgan. To Josephson, as indeed to others, Gould was "The Mephistopheles of Wall Street."

For even in his own time, Gould had become the most hated man in America, or at least the most hated man in the New York newspapers. As *The New York Times* recorded his death, it contrasted him with Astor or Vanderbilt. "In serving their own ends they were serving public ends, while Gould was a negative quantity in the development of the country where he was not an absolutely retarding and destructive quantity." The *New York Herald* said, "His financial success, judged by the means by which it was attained, is not to be envied." The *World,* which he had once owned, was even harsher. "The bane of the social, intellectual and spiritual life of America today is the idolatrous homage of the golden calf," it said, "Nothing else has contributed so much to promote this evil condition as the apparent worldly success of Jay Gould."

Maury Klein, an academic historian who collected these eulogies in his 1986 biography, *The Life and Legend of Jay Gould,*[3] concluded that Gould was a misunderstood man. The legend that he was a stock manipulator grew from the "Erie War" and the "Gold Corner"— "watering" the stock of the Erie with excessive issues, and his gold purchases and sales leading to the collapse of the market on Black Friday, September 24, 1869.

In the Erie, Klein concluded, Gould was not manipulating the stock for paper profit, but battling Vanderbilt in trying to forge a bona fide and useful railroad. In his gold operations, veterans of Michael 1 will recognize, the real issue was exchange-rate policy. It was the midst of the Greenback era, when U.S. currency was not linked to gold. Grain growers in the heartland were paid in Greenbacks, but the London grain markets were based on gold-backed sterling. So a high enough price of gold would open the export market for grain and fill Gould's boxcars.

Gould sold out when he learned the government would intervene, selling gold and depressing the dollar. His sometime partner "Diamond Jim" Fisk plunged ahead, until the market collapsed on the government announcement.

By the end of his life Gould had assembled his railroad, the Union

Pacific, and linked it with communications, Western Union. He was not a speculator but a builder. "Looked at with a sense of detachment, Gould's business ethics were probably no worse and in some respects better than those of most men. What separated him from others was not the dishonesty but his talent, his daring, his sense of vision," Klein concluded. He added that "no study of the past is more urgently in need of revision than *The Robber Barons*," although "its influence persists, partly because it is an appealing, even beguiling work, and partly because it says what many readers want to hear."[4]

"In an age of tumultuous change, however, rules have a way of getting bent," Klein continues, "The shock waves of change unleashed by industrialization affected every aspect of American life, leaving in their wake confusion and a sense that everything had been pulled to polar extremes. Progress spawned great wealth and immense poverty, success and scandal, materialism and misery. Growth seemed to pull society apart at the seams, embroiling it in ugly and often violent clashes. Prosperity brought with it problems on a scale never before imagined. Amid this upheaval the old verities no longer seemed sure guides to behavior; often they seemed irrelevant or inapplicable to the new realities."[5]

Such ages, Klein suggests, not only spawn ambitious visionaries like Jay Gould. They also spawn legends like Jay Gould.

• • •

"The Ishmaels and the Insulls, whose hand is against every man's," intoned Franklin Delano Roosevelt. In these more enlightened times, it would be considered indelicate for FDR to pick on poor Ishmael, son of Abraham, half-brother of Isaac and grandfather of Islam. But of course, presidential candidate Roosevelt's real target was Samuel Insull, the disgraced Chicago utilities magnate, by then stripped of his empire, already abroad and soon to be indicted for embezzlement and to flee to Greece, which had no extradition treaty with the United States.

The majesty of the U.S. government finally did bring Insull to justice. President Hoover asked Premier Mussolini to seize him as he passed through Italy, but he had already left. The Senate hastily ratified a long-pending extradition treaty, but Greek judges refused the first extradition request for want of evidence, and a second because mail fraud was not a crime in Greece. The directors of Insull's former companies cut off his pensions, and with his fortune destroyed he had to be sustained by friends.

After Greek judges dismissed a third extradition request, the U.S. State Department approached the Greek-American Merchants Association, with the threat that the government would cut off transfers of funds to Greece. The Greek government ordered him to leave, and with money borrowed from friends in London, he chartered a Greek vessel and cruised for two weeks in the Mediterranean. The U.S. Congress rushed through a bill authorizing the U.S. government to seize Insull in any nation in which by treaty it had extraterritorial rights. When his ship tied up in Istanbul, the State Department demanded that the Turks arrest Insull despite lack of any treaty rights, and the Turks seized him and handed him over to the Americans.

When he arrived in Chicago, his attorneys had negotiated and raised $100,000 bail, but upon booking were confronted with bail twice that. Insull was thrown in a common cell with vagrants, being transferred the next day to a hospital cell. The trial, on accusation of defrauding investors to "buy the worthless stock of this corporation at highly inflated and fictitious prices," spent seven weeks arguing over accounting practices and the like. The jury reached a verdict in five minutes, but for the sake of propriety spent two hours cooling its heels before coming back to report, not guilty.

Forrest McDonald's *Insull,* from which this account is drawn, says that early on a former sheriff on the jury remarked that the prosecution was building its case on the companies' books, but that the only crooks he knew about kept no records, falsified them or destroyed them. McDonald also reports that during Insull's testimony his son had a men's room conversation with the prosecutor, who asked quizzically, "Say, you fellows were legitimate businessmen."? Insull was quickly acquitted in three other trials.

What Insull didn't understand, McDonald concludes, is that big profit in utilities does not lie in operating them but in financing them. He may have gone too far in pyramiding his utilities out of fear of a takeover, but his empire was brought down through a bear raid by New York interests seeking the bond business that had been going to Halsey, Stuart and Company in Chicago. At the heart of the New York bond ring was the House of Morgan, with a wide circle of allies including Chase and National City Banks. Of this group, McDonald remarks:

The group was rarely creative. It did not support the new, the radical, the different. Quite the opposite: It sought stability, order, rationalization—and financing by New York—in every major field of economic endeavor and opposed innovation as it opposed such other disorderly activities as embezzlement and competition. Because it regularly brought order out of chaos, its benefactions were large; but because in doing so it stifled creative nonconformity, the social cost of its benefactions was sometimes immeasurable.[6]

In assessing Insull, McDonald notes that his companies and his securities in fact weathered the depression better than most, and that a generation after his death his companies still produced an eighth of the electric power and gas consumed in the nation. Insull died of a heart attack in the Paris subway, his body lay unidentified for several hours for want of papers and police reported he had eight francs in his pocket. The theme of news reports was of a fallen titan dying in anonymous poverty. Pointing out that what clearly happened was someone took his wallet from his corpse, McDonald concludes in his book, "And so in his death, as in his life, Samuel Insull was robbed, and nobody got the story straight."[7]

• • •

These anecdotes should scarcely suggest the ages of Gould or Insull were ages of consummate honesty. The center of the most sensational financial and political scandal of the 19th century, for example, was the Union Pacific railroad that Gould later was to acquire, lose and reacquire. As the route was being slashed across the continent, no one quite knew what freight railroads were supposed to carry over this vast wilderness. Its promoters saw the money in the construction contracts. At the Union Pacific, they formed the Credit Mobilier of America to receive the contracts and collect the profits.

And they spread Credit Mobilier stock widely in the Congress that had authorized a construction subsidy of $60 million, or nearly $1 billion in 1990 dollars, plus the grant of 20 million acres of land. This revelation led to a series of comic opera congressional investigations of itself reminiscent of the House and Senate Ethics Committees' behaviors in the savings and loan scandals. But the Republicans, the party of power, lost 96 of their 203 House seats in the 1874 midterm elections.

"Building railroads from nowhere to nowhere at public expense is not a legitimate business," snorted Cornelius Vanderbilt. Yet in 1867 an Illinois entrepreneur named Joseph G. McCoy bought up a load of lumber and shipped it out to the end of the tracks of the Kansas Pacific. In Abilene he built some pens and loading chutes and founded an industry. Soon cowboys drove cattle from Texas to Abilene, shipping them on by rail to the Chicago stockyards. The western railroads had found the first cargo with which they were to forge a continental nation and, within a generation, to close the frontier.[8]

The froth of Insull's times, similarly, hoisted not only visionaries but charlatans. By far the most spectacular of the latter was Richard Whitney, president of the New York Stock Exchange, who was sent to Sing Sing for embezzlement. Brother of leading Morgan partner George Whitney, Richard was also the hero of Black Thursday, when his bidding as agent for the bankers' pool had stabilized the market for the afternoon. His bid of $205 for U.S. Steel remains a Wall Street legend. He was also, as Thomas W. Lamont of Morgan later called him, "a thoroughgoing crook."

Richard Whitney had run up huge debts in trying to support various speculations, and when credit ran short helped himself to some extra loan collateral, securities owned by the New York Yacht Club and the stock exchange's gratuity fund, which provided death benefits to members' families. It's probable, John Brooks speculates, that "Whitney did not think of himself as a thief. Rather, he thought of himself as one who would not be a thief no matter what he did; that is, as a moral superman."[9] But at the end he made his famous confession at the Links Club on March 5, 1938. Morgan partner Frank Bartlow said, "This is serious," and Whitney replied, "This is criminal."

Richard had been propped up by loans from his brother and from Morgan. Ultimately, out of family honor George Whitney made good on all of Richard's loans and embezzlements, which totaled $27 million in 1938. Three months before his confession, Richard had approached his brother for a loan, telling him of the misappropriation of exchange securities. George Whitney in turn told Lamont, who wrote out a personal check for $1 million. Because they did not report Richard's crime to the authorities or the exchange, the Morgan partners were guilty of a misprision of a felony. New York County District Attorney Thomas A. Dewey exercised his discretion not to prosecute, much to the disgust of Securities and Exchange Commission Chairman William O. Douglas.

• • •

Given the history of the Gilded Age and the Roaring Twenties, it can scarcely be surprising that the Seven Fat Years should throw up a swirl of scandals, real and imagined, serious and overblown. At this short remove it's hard to tell which is which, of course, but history suggests a pattern. Some arch-villain will be selected, and used to tar the whole commercial class, the "robber barons" Josephson pilloried or the "moneychangers" FDR promised to drive from the national temple. The arch-villain need not be a thoroughgoing crook like Richard Whitney, whose crimes are merely written up to ordinary human foibles. Good arch-villains must pose sins that are more complicated and less easily understood. Likely, indeed, their sins will be sharp tactics in crossing swords with the financial establishment of their day, as Sam Insull slighted the Morgan circle and Jay Gould battled Vanderbilt.

The accusation levied against such upstarts, by the Morgans and the Vanderbilts and their allies conscious and unwitting, will of course be consummate greed. For capitalism runs on the acquisitive instinct; indeed, this has been the historical critique of capitalism itself. The Morgans and the Vanderbilts have seldom understood with whom they were making common cause, that they too would go down as robber barons and moneychangers.

The historical debate goes back at least to Adam Smith, who so clearly stated the premise of the system. "It is not from the benevolence of the butcher, the brewer, or the baker, that we expect our dinner, but from their regard to their own interest. We address ourselves not to their humanity but their self-love, and never talk to them of our own necessities but of their advantages."[10] Yet each individual is "led by an invisible hand to promote an end which was no part of his intention. Nor is it always worse for the society that it was no part of it. By pursuing his own interest he frequently promotes that of the society more effectually than when he really intends to promote it. I have never known much good done by those who affected to trade for the public good."[11]

The invisible hand has by now been more concretely explained as the efficiency of the market mechanism. At the abstract extreme of the financial markets, we have the "efficient markets" hypothesis; with enough bidders in the marketplace the vagaries of human judgment will wash out and the facts will prevail. In general, "the market" is smarter than the smartest of its individual participants.

Even in less sophisticated arenas, the decentralized decisions of profit-motivated actors will outperform the most intelligent central planner. Iowa was drenched with rain in early 1991, keeping tractors out of the fields during the normal planting season; when I visited in May the entire seed corn industry was busily shipping its inventory 100 miles south, putting the early-maturing varieties where farmers would now want them. No collectivized Agriculture Department could conceivably have accomplished that. And in this remarkable efficiency, the motive force was profit, if you must, "greed."

This is not a defense of greed properly defined. Greed, or more properly covetousness, is one of the seven deadly sins, along with pride, lust, anger, gluttony, sloth and—not so incidentally—envy. As the list shows, sin is an inordinate excess of ordinary and even healthy human emotions. Greed is an excess in the normal pursuit of self-interest, or as Adam Smith called it, self-love. The issue is: What constitutes excess? The problem for capitalism and capitalists is that the better the system works, the more evidence there is to suggest excess. Depressions do not bring accusations of greed; booms do.

Not all of these accusations come from Mother Teresa or the Dalai Lama. More prominently we are treated to the jeremiads against affluence written by John Kenneth Galbraith in his den at Gstaad. Or to denunciations of excessive wealth by scholars on grants from the Ford and MacArthur foundations. Or to scapegoating by politicians seeking to shift blame and garner votes. Or to utopias constructed by philosophers who would build for us a more just economic order.

Capitalism seeks freedom, socialism seeks equality and traditional societies seek order, Michael Novak has written.[12] In 1933, it made some sense for Matthew Josephson to write that the admitted accomplishments of the robber barons were sullied because they were done "only in the name of an uncontrolled appetite for private profit." But this historic debate was settled in Berlin in 1989. The world now understands that as an organizing principle, the alternative to self-interest is terror. The era in which terror was finally vanquished is called, predictably, "a decade of greed."

• • •

The "greed" accusation, equally predictably, goes rather lightly on the truly ruinous scandal of the Seven Fat Years, the S&L debacle. Donald Dixon and Charles Keating have been convicted. The palm-greased senators have so far escaped—even Alan Cranston, the club's designated fall-guy, suffered only the mildest wrist-slap. Of course, we may yet see more in terms of political repercussions; the

S&Ls look a bit like Credit Mobilier. Then too, the 1990s may see some lightning from the Bank of Credit & Commerce International; the BCCI storm was only gathering as the decade opened. Never mind, "the greed decade" was about the "insider-trading" scandals.

Even the label is not helpful. The prosecutions of Wall Street figures should be called "the takeover-war scandals." While there were a few peripheral cases, this was the essence of the matter. The driving force in the scandals was big, quick profits to be gained in corporate takeovers. And the scandals were shaped by the peculiar way the United States regulates attempts to buy a controlling interest in public corporations. It should be said at the outset, of course, that even peculiar laws should be obeyed.

Still, one of the perennial issues of modern capitalism has been to whom corporate management is responsible. A chief executive reports to his board, nominally elected by shareholders but in fact typically recruited by the chief executive himself. It is a tribute to the professionalism of corporate management that this system of self-selection works as well as it does. But management has huge powers, and it's hard to displace a chief executive who digs in; Saul Avery of Montgomery Ward was carried out in his chair.

The stock market provides a discipline; when a company's shares sell at too low a price, another management that thinks it has better ideas can start to buy the stock, and eventually assume control. This upsets management, but the great burden of academic research shows it a good thing, providing a way to displace poor management and a discipline on all managers. This was recorded, for example, in a chapter on "The Market for Corporate Control" in the 1985 Economic Report of the President, prepared under the direction of William Niskanen, the Galileo of the deficit.

The rules for the takeovers are determined in a running battle between the "entrenched managers" and "hostile raiders." The British have evolved a civilized system, with regulation directed at protecting the interests of shareholders rather than managements. The rules facilitate takeovers but protect minority shareholders who might otherwise be forced to accept less than those who sell first. In the United States, by contrast, the rules take the form of a series of hurdles an acquirer must leap.

The basic regulation is the Williams Act, which requires that anyone who acquires 5 percent of a company's stock must pause and give notice. This alerts the management, and also increases the price for the acquirer. The increase in price creates gains for someone, however, and has created a whole new financial occupation of "risk arbitrageur." Risk arbitrageurs speculate in possible takeover stocks, trying to discern which of them might come under scrutiny of a possible acquirer. And when an acquisition attempt is announced, the "arbs" speculate on how likely it is to succeed; if it collapses, those who bought at the higher price can lose big. Given the Williams Act, the "arbs" serve the useful function of allowing long-time holders to cash out at a good price, while assuming the risk of failure. The attitudes of the relatively small community of arbs can make or break a takeover, and of course, their stock in trade is gossip.

This, it scarcely need be said, is scandal waiting to happen. The arbs can make huge overnight profits on skimpy information. The raiders and entrenched managements have incentives to stroke the arbs one way or another. Everyone, while on good days not lying outright, tries to manipulate everyone else.

In the United States, we have tried to police this by outlawing "insider trading," though the statutes have never deigned to explain what this is. The general notion is that top executives and their outside advisers are not to use confidential information to trade for their own accounts. If the information makes the shares go up, the idea is, morality requires that the gains be distributed by lottery. Extreme free market types oppose the laws, saying that shareholders ought to have the option of compensating executives by allowing them to reap these gains but paying lower salaries.

In the real world, corporate "insiders" probably need to be controlled somehow. Certainly it is a conflict of interest, for example, for the head of a corporation to short his own company's stock, like Chase's Wiggin during the crash. The laws are also supposed to make small investors feel better while swimming with the sharks, and thus help keep the markets liquid. In themselves, the laws would be unimportant, but get to be a serious issue when whiffs of information are worth fortunes to the arbs.

To complete the legal context, a final law needs to be mentioned, the Racketeer Influenced and Corrupt Organizations Act. As its name suggests, RICO was passed in 1970 primarily to combat the shadowy network of organized crime. It provides that if a person or business commits two or more felonies as part of a "pattern," it can be branded a racketeering enterprise. This carries jail terms up to 20 years, and provides for the confiscation of all property and earnings from the enterprise, even if not related to proven wrongdoings. The property subject to possible confiscation can be impounded pending trial.

Preconviction confiscation obviously would ruin a financial firm overnight. So far as I know the first RICO charge against a market trader was brought by Rudolph Giuliani, U.S. attorney for the southern district of New York, in his 1983 indictment of Marc Rich, the world's biggest commodity trader. Rich, charged with RICO over trades that allegedly converted "old oil" into "new oil" under the nonsensical energy-crisis price controls, fled like Insull before him. His firms were so important the government felt it had to settle with them while he was still a fugitive. Living in exile in Switzerland and Spain, he remains one of the world's biggest businessmen, so far as I know in no difficulty with law enforcement officials outside the United States.

The insider-trading powder keg was ignited in May 1985, with an anonymous letter to Merrill Lynch postmarked Caracas, Venezuela. It asserted that two brokers in its local office were trading U.S. stocks on inside information. Large brokerage firms maintain "compliance" departments to investigate such matters; when Merrill unleashed its computers it not only confirmed the Venezuelan trades just prior to takeover news but spotted the same trades by others, including Bank Leu International in the Bahamas. Merrill gave this information to the Securities and Exchange Commission, which followed its suspicions to one Dennis Levine, a mergers and acquisitions hotshot who'd worked at four brokerage houses.

In May 1986, a year after the anonymous letter was received, the SEC landed on Levine with charges of illegally trading in 54 different companies over 5½ years. SEC enforcement director Gary Lynch described it as "the largest insider trading case we've ever brought."[13] Levine quickly struck a plea bargain, cooperating with the government by fingering the biggest arb on the street, Ivan Boesky.

Boesky struck his own bargain, and was soon wearing hidden microphones during conversations. He implicated Boyd Jefferies, head of an important West Coast trading firm, and Martin Siegel, a young investment banking star who Boesky had provided with suitcases full of cash. In turn, Jefferies implicated a client, James Sherwin of GAF. And Siegel struck his bargain by implicating figures in the arbitrage department of three major brokerage firms. And word quickly spread that Boesky had also implicated the only bigger fish in the pond, "junk bond" inventor Michael Milken of Drexel Burnham Lambert.

The cooperators did well, even after confessing trading information for suitcases of cash, surely an indication of *mens rea,* or criminal intent, a historical test of a felony that might be missing in a normally innocent act like buying or selling stock. Levine was sentenced to two years in prison, and by 1991 was selling a book on his experiences. Boesky got permission to unwind his market position without revealing the inside information that he was headed for three years in jail. Jefferies, who pled to "parking" stock—carrying it in his own books while pledging the gain or loss to someone else, previously a violation but not a prison offense—was sentenced to community service, which turned out to be running a golf program for kids in Aspen. Siegel, who had received $700,000 in suitcases, cooperated so well he was sentenced to two months.

Something, though, went wrong.

The information Siegel offered so impressed Giuliani that even before officially booking his immediate suspect, he moved to arrest the three arbs Siegel had implicated: Federal marshals nabbed Timothy Tabor at his apartment in the evening, jailing him overnight when he couldn't make bail. The next morning they arrested Robert Freeman, head of arbitrage at Goldman, Sachs. And they threw Richard Wigton of Kidder, Peabody up against the wall in front of his colleagues, leading him away in handcuffs and tears.

"The government has concluded that the indictment must be dismissed," the prosecutor in charge of the case said four months later and just before a scheduled trial date. Assistant U.S. Attorney Neil Cartusciello, however, rebuffed arguments that the cases against Wigton, Tabor and Freeman should be dismissed with prejudice. The government was readying a new and broader indictment, he said, the dismissed one was "merely the tip of an iceberg."[14]

The next time the government spoke was two years later. The prosecution announced that the investigation against Wigton and Tabor had been concluded, and no charges would be filed. The deadlock was broken not so much by the departure of Giuliani to run for mayor of New York, but by the agreement of Freeman to plead guilty to one charge. Big accusations concerning Unocal and Storer vanished, but Freeman pled guilty to hearing the words, "Your bunny has a good nose."

This sentence was uttered by Siegel in a conversation with Freeman after the latter said Bernard "Bunny" Lasker, a floor trader, told him there were problems with the proposed acquisition of Beatrice Companies by Siegel's client, Kohlberg Kravis Roberts. The allusion can be seen as an illicit "inside" confirmation of rumor. But it probably didn't change Freeman's trading, since he had already started selling after talking to Henry Kravis. Kravis was a principal rather than an agent, so any information he releases is by definition authorized. Judge Pierre Leval sentenced Freeman to a year in prison with the last eight months suspended, still twice the jail sentence Siegel received. Indeed, Siegel's two-month sentence came after the Freeman verdict made clear the true value of his cooperation.

Jefferies' cooperation lead to the GAF trials. A judge threw out the first trial because a prosecutor withheld a document from the defense. In the second trial, the jury hopelessly deadlocked after 93 hours of deliberations. In the third, the government got a conviction, only to have it busted by the Second Circuit. One judge noted that the prosecution had failed to investigate telephone records that impunged one of its witnesses. Before any fourth trial, he wrote, the government is "inescapably obliged to investigate fully."[15]

The whole GAF case seemed to revolve around jiggling the price of Union Carbide stock by ⅛th point. The defendants did agree to settle civil charges with the SEC by paying 25 cents for each Carbide share the GAF sold or $1.25 million. The trials cost more than $10 million.

The first criminal nabbed on Boesky's information was Lisa Ann Jones, a 26-year-old trading assistant at Drexel. A teenage runaway who got a start with a bank teller's job and a high-school equivalency degree, she didn't cooperate with the government's efforts to implicate her superior. Convicted of perjury for failing to remember certain transactions that may or may not have been illegal, she was sentenced to 18 months, nine Siegels or half a Boesky, though this was reduced to 10 months after intervention by the Second Circuit.

Trying to forge a connection between Milken and Freeman, a force of 50 federal marshals, armed and wearing bulletproof vests, suddenly descended in December 1987 on the pastoral offices of Princeton/Newport Limited Partners, previously a scarcely known but highly successful hedging operation designed by math wizard Edward O. Thorp and run by James Sutton Regan, who had the misfortune of being a friend and college classmate of Freeman and having done some business with Milken. Sweeping through desks and filing cabinets, the marshals carried out nearly 300 boxes of documents. While their search warrant concerned tax charges, news reports at the time said they were seeking a Freeman-Milken connection.[16]

Guiliani slapped Princeton/Newport with RICO. Defense lawyers repeatedly charged, and the prosecutors denied, that the government said it would forgo RICO if Princeton/Newport officials helped in other investigations. The RICO requirements forced defendants to post a bond of $14 million, though the allegedly illegal profits amounted to only $446,000. The unindicted partners, fearing the firm would suffer penalties or legal costs, withdrew their capital. Before it ever had a day in court, Princeton/Newport collapsed.

At trial, Regan and his partners were convicted on 63 of 64 felony counts; this outcome for his friend was reported to have been a big influence on Freeman's decision to plead guilty to the "bunny" charge. There had been some incriminating-sounding phone recordings, but the defendant's tax authorities were not allowed to testify the trades were legal all along. The judge gave only three-to-six month sentences, and rebuked the application of RICO to the case, refusing to go beyond a normal tax fraud case. In 1991, the Second Circuit threw out most of the convictions, saying the defendants should have been allowed to present the tax expert testimony, and would prevail if their reading of the tax law had been made "in good faith." The appeals court added, "Before this lengthy case is retried, the government may decide to withdraw the RICO count in view of the Department of Justice's July 1989 guidelines, which substantially curtail the use of tax frauds as direct or indirect RICO offenses."[17] Heeding this advice, the government dropped its case.

By 1991, indeed, the Second Circuit was throwing out every insider-trading case it could get its hands on. It started with the conviction of Robert Chestman, who'd traded on family news that had ultimately come from an insider. The reversal freed Chestman from federal prison in Allentown, Pennsylvania, where he had already been serving time. A full panel of the Second Circuit later validated his prison time by reinstating part of his conviction, while reviving an SEC rule the original appellate panel had destroyed but erecting barriers to prosecutions on such remote information.[18]

The GAF and Princeton/Newport reversals were also stunning defeats for the U.S. attorney's office. The Second Circuit also reversed the RICO conviction of Ed Meese intimate Robert Wallach, warning that prosecutors ought to have known their lead witness perjured himself.[19] Whatever their standing in the press, the prosecutors seemed to lose credibility with the appellate judges.

In July 1991, the Second Circuit reversed the insider-trading conviction of John Mulheren, Jr., the only case in which Boesky ever testified. Reviewing the supposed instructions from Boesky to Mulheren to push stock up to a certain price, the court concluded, "We are convinced that no rational trier of fact could have found the elements of the crimes charged here beyond a reasonable doubt."[20]

• • •

These rulings came as a scant comfort to Drexel Burnham Lambert, by then in the hands of a bankruptcy court, or Michael Milken, who had already started his ten-year term at an 85-inmate minimum-security prison at Pleasanton, California, 40 miles east of San Francisco. Threatened with RICO, Drexel had agreed to admit felonies in a plea bargain two weeks after the liquidation of Princeton/Newport. Indicted on 98 counts, including RICO, Milken had copped his plea a month before the Second Circuit Court threw out the Chestman conviction. Drexel and Milken were the most celebrated of the "insider-trading" cases, of course, because they were the biggest Wall Street figures of the Seven Fat Years.

The fortunes of both were built on Milken's invention of the "junk bond." A bond, of course, is a financial instrument signifying a loan, paying interest and promising to redeem the principal. In the event of bankruptcy, bondholders are due their money first, before holders of stock. In the event of lush profits, shareholders get the bounty, while bondholders get only the agreed interest. The price of bonds in the marketplace does go up and down, however, depending on the general level of interest rates and also the prospect that the bond might not be repaid.

Traditionally bond finance had been the province of companies "rated" by agencies as "investment grade." But only some 800 U.S. corporations have issued bonds of investment-grade ratings, and there are some 23,000 companies in the United States with revenues of more than $35 million a year. If the other 22,000 issue bonds, they are "junk." Traditionally the "junk" market consisted of "fallen angels," that is, companies that had once been "investment grade" but had stumbled nonetheless. Michael Milken's original insight was that the yields on noninvestment grade bonds *more* than compensated for the defaults actually experienced.

On this insight, he and Drexel set out to build a market for high-yield issues, reaping above-average returns for his investors and opening a vast new source of capital for noninvestment grade companies. In recounting this history Glenn Yago concludes, "In essence, junk bonds gave many smaller businesses the access to capital, and hence to many of the privileges, once exclusively enjoyed by our nation's largest corporations. Junk bonds became an important agent of social and economic change."[21]

Naturally, the issuers of junk bonds were not the rating agency 800, the *Fortune* 500 or the Business Roundtable 200. Instead, they were fresh entrepreneurial upstarts. The scions of the American business world and of Wall Street might be expected to look down their noses at this new source of competition, the risky new way it was being financed and the roguish investment house behind them. Worse, in 1984 and 1985, junk bonds started to be used to finance corporate takeovers.

In 1985, Drexel raised $3 billion in financing commitments for Mesa Petroleum's takeover of Unocal. Mesa's T. Boone Pickens, Jr., and Unocal's Fred Hartley were adversaries who deserved each other. Mr. Hartley said when he learned of the attempt he went home to his wife. "I told her that I was born in World War I, survived World War II and now my management and I were going to gird for World War III."[22]

Mr. Hartley won, thanks to an unconscionable ruling by the Delaware Supreme Court that Unocal could offer above-market prices for some of its shares while refusing to make the same offer for Mesa's shares. [23] Mr. Hartley leveraged up his company to buy in shares, and Mr. Pickens stood down. But big business understands the ability to raise $3 billion; that meant even the biggest corporation was threatened by a takeover.

So big business and much of Wall Street cheered as Boesky's plea bargain offered up Milken, and Giuliani moved on Drexel. Drexel's plea was motivated by its natural desire to maintain an ongoing firm; it had 10,000 employees. It agreed to plead to felonies, pay a fine of $650 million and cooperate against Milken. It completed its then-pending financing of the biggest buyout in history, KKR's $25 billion buyout of RJR Nabisco. But its fortunes started to decline with the fine, the defection of Milken loyalists and some heavy weather in the junk-bond market. In the second month of the 1990s, the stellar brokerage firm of the 1980s filed for protection under Chapter 11 of the bankruptcy act.

Two months later, under threat of a still larger indictment, Milken himself agreed to a plea, confessing six felonies. Four were Boesky-related offenses: entering a conspiracy of secret recordkeeping on securities held by Boesky to conceal true ownership, helping Boesky evade net-capital rules by parking stock, having Boesky take a secret position in Fischback Stock to aid the takeover by Victor Posner and fraudulently concealing the fact that Golden Nugget had sold its stake in MCA. The other two crimes concerned David Solomon, head of a junk-bond mutual fund. They involved false reporting of bond sales within the public bid-asked spread, with Milken's junk-bond department keeping the proceeds, and aiding a tax evasion by Solomon.

These were not merely technical violations, but showed advance scheming—for better or worse scheming of a rather careless sort. However, none was insider trading. After an inquiry to determine the damage to the marketplace from the crimes, Judge Kimba Wood came up with the figure of $318,000, representing the commissions Drexel collected from Solomon's fund under an arrangement that would have been legal if disclosed to shareholders. The RICO counts were dropped. So were all charges against Milken's brother Lowell, who had maintained throughout he had nothing to do with any of the transactions in the allegations.

The penalties, however, were substantial. The government collected $600 million in fines, less whatever private investors can claim. Judge Wood sentenced Milken to a jail term of 10 years, compared with the 3 years for Boesky, 11 years for Al Capone and 5 to 15 years for Robert Chambers, convicted of New York's notorious "preppie murder." Milken's sentence was subject to parole, and the parole board eventually indicated he would serve from 39 to 44 months.

Judge Wood's sentence also provided for reduction if Milken cooperated with the government in further investigations. Hearings on this issue gave her the opportunity to explain the rationale behind the 10-year sentence:

> [T]he court believed that a period of 36 to 40 months incarceration fit the crimes and the offender, based on the evidence before the court, and was in proportion to the sentence given to defendant's co-conspirator Ivan Boesky by Judge Lasker, when you take into account that had Ivan Boesky not been credited by Judge Lasker as being the most useful cooperator in the history of the securities laws, Boesky would likely have actually served somewhere between five and seven years, that is, a little more than two or three times the period he actually served. When I say "in proportion," I mean taking into account the relative harm to confidence in the integrity of the securities markets caused by each man's actions, his involvement of others in the schemes, efforts to cover up the wrongdoing (which can evidence both a conscious commitment to wrongdoing over time, and a failure to acknowl-

edge and accept responsibility for wrongdoing) and finally, each man's character, as revealed, for example, in service to the community.[24]

Boesky was a bigger crook, in short, but a better cooperator. In Milken's case, the government recommended against a reduction in sentence. "While Mr. Milken has devoted substantial time and energy to the process and certain of his disclosures have resulted in the commencement of criminal and SEC investigations as set forth below, his cooperation has not resulted in any indictments or convictions," read the filing of prosecutor John K. Carroll. "Finally, based upon other available evidence, the Government expected Mr. Milken's cooperation to be more extensive than it has been, and, therefore, we do not believe that Mr. Milken has completely disclosed all of the wrongdoing of which he is aware."[25]

These words have to be read against the series of Second Circuit reversals, which cast a pall over the whole issue of cooperation. Boesky, the greatest cooperator in the history of the securities laws, took the stand only in the Mulheren case, the one in which the appellate judges decided "no rational trier of the facts" could sustain a conviction. In the Wallach case, the government overlooked its cooperator's perjury. The reversals carry the plain inference that the appellate judges do not trust the products of cooperation recently coming out of the U.S. Attorney's office.

Giuliani almost won his race for mayor. In the Republican primary, he bested millionaire Ronald Lauder. While running as a Republican in New York City is usually a forlorn task, Giuliani lost to Democrat David Dinkins by only 47,000 votes out of nearly 1.9 million cast. Lauder, whose candidacy was supported by Senator Alphonse D'Amato, ran in the general election on the Conservative Party line, spending an ultimate total of $14 million, most of it in negative advertising against Giuliani.

The Republican split developed after D'Amato felt Giuliani had tried to usurp Senatorial prerogatives by attempting to choose his own successor as U.S. Attorney. Giuliani's former assistant Benito Romano took over on an acting basis and, for example, negotiated the Milken plea. But D'Amato finally prevailed with the appointment of Otto Obermaier to the permanent post. As he took office Obermaier said, "I have absolutely no ambition to be Mayor of New York."[26]

The controversy over Milken will no doubt go on for generations, as it has over Jay Gould. My colleague James Stewart made the case against Milken, as well as Freeman and Princeton/Newport, in his best-selling *Den of Thieves*, which bids to become *The Robber Barons* of our era. Among his revelations is that Milken's cooperation "provided incriminating information about James Dahl, Terren Peizer, and David Solomon—all of whom testified against him and have immunity."[27]

Stewart is a thorough reporter, and I'm confident his account is as factual as any that could be compiled without the tools of subpoena and cross-examination. Milken perhaps made a mistake in refusing to be interviewed; in the sidebar to the extract in the *Journal*, Stewart explains that when differences arose he chose to believe Boesky.[28] But while demonizing Milken and others as Josephson demonized the Robber Barons, Stewart does not share the urge to make a case against "the system." Indeed, he seems to take for granted that it's a sad day when a well-known corporation is taken over against the wishes of its CEO.

In his epilogue, in particular, Stewart's reportorial honesty waxes full. He quotes the Second Circuit on the Mulheren case. He says the prosecutions "call into question the wholesale criminalization of the securities laws," and calls for a statutory definition of the crime of "insider trading." And in many ways most interesting of all, he predicts that the junk-bond market will "take its place among other useful but stodgy capital-raising alternatives."[29]

For this was the essence of what Milken's harshest critics insinuated—that the whole junk-bond market was a scam, based on his bribing fiduciaries—the managers of mutual funds, insurance companies and S&Ls—to invest their institutions' funds in otherwise worthless securities.

Evidence introduced at the pre-sentence *Fatico* hearings did show that in at least one instance some fund managers received warrants— that is the right to buy stock at prices above the current market— when their institutions bought bonds in the same company. Though the warrants would not pay out if the bonds failed, this practice is surely suspect. Judge Wood held it was criminal, indeed, but dismissed it because prosecutors had not linked it directly to Milken. It would be interesting to know more, but prosecutors did not press the issue.

Apparently they did not feel they could make this case, even with the power of subpoena, the cooperation of Drexel, immunity for some of Milken's closest associates and microphones on Boesky. To judge by the plea they accepted, for that matter, they were not confident of proving "insider trading" beyond a reasonable doubt. Of course, there may be trials yet to come. While the plea bargain was presumably intended to end prosecution, the government offensive lives on in civil suits by the Resolution Trust Corp. over junk-bond losses by savings and loans, taken on a contingency-fee basis by the powerhouse Wall Street law firm Cravath, Swaine & Moore.

Still, the notion that the junk bond market was a scam is hard to sustain in the face of that market's spectacular recovery in 1991. The Salomon Brothers long-term high-yield index, just below 350 in July of 1989, plunged to 280 late in 1990 after the Drexel bankruptcy, the Milken plea and the FIERRA requirement forcing savings and loan institutions to dump their holdings. Recovering from these blows, the index reached 390 by the middle of 1991, without the benefit of any fixing by Milken or Drexel. The taxpayer might have saved Cravath's fees, indeed, if thrifts seized by the RTC had simply been allowed to hold their junk portfolios.

Which perhaps explains why Milken has his loyalists despite his admissions. In June of 1991, with Milken cleaning toilets at Pleasantown, one of his closest associates, Lorraine Spurge, held a party in his memory. Or more specifically, a party for an eight-pound picture book, *Portraits of the American Dream*, featuring 146 corporations that Drexel had helped finance in the Milken years—nearly all of them below investment grade. Safeway chairman Peter Magowan gave a speech, saying, "Michael Milken is here in our hearts." There was some snickering, but so far as I know, no one was foolish enough to dispute Ms. Spurge's assertion that companies like those in her book "accounted for nearly all the job growth in the decade of the 1980s."[30]

My own view is that the spectacle of arbs elbowing each other in the marketplace could be ended with the British takeover rule, and that in any event it's less a menace to society than the litigious mania that has seized our age. Also less costly to the economy than entrenched managements, as Judge Wood's finding on the financial impact of Milken's crimes suggests.

As for Michael Milken, I'm sure he was guilty of hubris, and perhaps for a time had more power than society can tolerate in any one man. I think of him as "The Master of the Universe" in Tom Wolfe's *Bonfire of the Vanities*, a financial mastermind so powerful he persuades himself a few cut corners could not matter.[31] He had no need to truck with the likes of Boesky, and Michael Milken must accept a responsibility for the large costs his follies imposed on himself, his firm and the economy broadly. It is also true, however, that Milken was ensnared by far larger social forces and resentments, like Gould and Insull before him.

In Wolfe's novel, the Master of the Universe went on to become "the Great White Defendant." The original "bonfire of the vanities" was a ritual conducted by Savonarola; the 15th-century Florentine moralist urged his followers to purify themselves by burning their worldly affectations. Perhaps this is the higher morality, but it does not promote an atmosphere for entrepreneurial creativity and economic growth.

16

Victorian Finance

In 1990, three Americans shared the Nobel Prize for Economics. Merton Miller, William Sharpe and Harry Markowitz were financial economists, pioneers in modern portfolio theory. That is, they were the academic forefathers of the "rocket scientists" at places like Salomon Brothers, Drexel Burnham and Goldman, Sachs.

Miller, the eldest of the three, lent the first initial of his name to the famous M&M propositions, the other "M" coming from Franco Modigliani, already a Nobel laureate in 1985. What the M&M proposition holds, basically, is that leverage does not matter. That is, it makes no difference how much of a firm's capital it raises from debt and how much it raises in equity. The division will shift some of the risk back and forth between holders of bonds and holders of stock, but the total risk to the firm—and to society—will not depend on leverage but on real-sector factors like price, quality and management.

It happened that 1990 was also the year of the Drexel bankruptcy and Michael Milken's plea bargain; the kings of leverage, at least in the popular mind, were toppled. It was also the year that Congress passed a savings and loan bailout requiring thrifts to divest their junk bonds. A number of firms financed with the bonds were collapsing in bankruptcy. Not to mention that 1990 was the year President Bush revoked his no-new-tax pledge and struck a budget deal with Congress to boost spending and taxes; it was also when bank examiners moved into New England banks and cast beady eyes on real estate loans, sending tremors of a regulatory credit crunch vibrating through the economy.

That is, 1990 was the year when the Congress, regulators, the administration, Wall Street and the public shifted their eyes from

257

opportunity to danger. After endless warnings over the dread deficit, after the 1987 stock market crash, after the S&L debacle, after the "greed" of the insider-trading scandals, they decided to purge the economy of risk. They suddenly became preoccupied with leverage.

This irony was not lost on the new Nobel laureates, least of all on Miller. "I hope I will be pardoned for dwelling in what follows almost exclusively on U.S. examples," he told the Stockholm audience for his Nobel Memorial Prize Lecture on December 7. "It's just that a particularly virulent strain of the anti-leverage hysteria seems to have struck us first. Perhaps others can learn from our mistakes."[1]

• • •

The mood to which Professor Miller alluded had a great deal to do with bringing the Seven Fat Years to a close, at least momentarily checking the economic expansion they embodied. It casts a spell, too, over the 1990s. We hear on every hand about the "excesses of the 1980s," meaning too much debt, too much risk, too much leverage. We see in real life the S&L debacle, and we see that junk bonds were peddled by crooks; hang Nobel professors of finance, what do they know, only theories.

The most tangible manifestation of this mood was FIRREA, the Financial Institutions Reform, Recovery and Enforcement Act, signed by President Bush on August 9, 1989. The ostensible purpose of the act was to "clean up" the savings and loan mess, providing $50 billion over three years to sell off or close down insolvent thrifts. This might have been enough when Jim Wright blocked essentially the same recapitalization three years earlier, but in the event it now proved far short.

Lawrence J. White, the academic economist who served on the Federal Home Loan Bank Board, offers an assessment of the act, recalling Chernow's view that Pecora-era banking legislation was as much an attempt to punish as to reform. "In an important sense, the FIRREA was an Act of anger," White wrote in his book.[2] The same Congress that had doubled deposit insurance in 1980 now thought that making good on its reckless promise was "bailing out" the thrifts. Congress was angry not only at the poor thrifts, but also the good ones.

It set out to "solve" the crisis of unprofitable thrifts by shrinking thrift profits, through higher insurance premiums, more indirect taxes, higher capital requirements, other increased regulation and a reduction in diversification authority. White wrote that this legislation "had a rebound effect that has increased *the public's costs* of cleaning up the insolvents."[3] Indeed, I am coming to suspect that the original S&L debacle has a rival in the S&L cleanup debacle, and that FIRREA will prove to be the most destructive piece of legislation since the Smoot-Hawley Tariff.

The first thing to note is that FIRREA did nothing to curb deposit insurance, neither risk-rating the premiums as White recommended, nor reversing Fernand St Germain's boost in the coverage. Richard Breeden, who before moving to the SEC designed the White House proposal that became FIRREA, says he didn't want to tackle deposit insurance because he feared a nationwide run on the S&Ls, and needed to act quickly. I suspect what he means is that little banks see deposit insurance as their way of competing with big banks and, like the local S&Ls, are a potent lobby.

Instead, deposit insurance was to remain untouched, but regulators were to stop thrifts from doing all those *risky things*. Regulators were to seize miscreants forthwith, closing them down and selling their mortgages, the real estate collateral on bad loans and any other assets they could find. And regulators were to look over everybody's shoulder to make sure all the loans were safe. Thrifts were to use their federally insured deposits only to make loans that carry no undue risks.

In particular, Congress sent the clear message that weak thrifts should be closed forthwith. No doubt regulators had been too slow to close bad thrifts; Lincoln should have been closed when the Keating Five stopped the San Francisco examiners from doing so, for example, and Vernon closed when Jim Wright intervened. But the costs of the bailout can also be increased by swinging too far in the opposite direction. As William Seidman observed when he was chairman of both the FDIC and the Resolution Trust Corporation, when regulators seize an institution it loses its franchise value, and faces the loss of employees and customers, so its value plunges 10 percent to 15 percent overnight.

The issue is whether regulators can tell which thrifts really need to be seized, and which have the prospect of a cheaper resolution if allowed to operate. The later option used to be called "forbearance." But forbearance has been tarnished by the Lincolns and Vernons, so the current wisdom is that there is never ever a case in which it would be appropriate. Even the word is unmentionable. The capital-adequacy rules are to be applied mechanically, without judgment, as if accounting rules were brought down from Mount Sinai on stone tablets. Trouble is, accounting is not a stone tablet or even a science; it's an art.

So it's not surprising that the Office of Thrift Supervision quickly became embroiled with the courts. When it seized the Kansas-based hedging operation Franklin Savings and Loan the case came before Federal District Judge Dale Saffels, himself a former thrift regulator. While the circuit court overturned Saffels's rulings, arguing that the judge should not consider the merits but only the regulators' powers, his decision still rings caustic.

"There has been no allegation or even hint of illegal or unethical conduct by Franklin's management or directors. Essentially this case boils down to a dispute over accounting practices," he wrote. The examiners in charge, he added, were smarting from earlier laxity with the Silverado and CenTrust thrifts, and "appeared to lack adequate training and understanding to evaluate the nature of Franklin's operation."[4]

Judge Owen Panner also enjoined the seizure of Far West Federal of Portland, Oregon. In late 1988, Danny Wall, lacking financial resources to close ailing thrifts, made a series of generous deals with acquirers. Far West's owners put in $27 million of their own capital and were given a big government loan and a promise that the deal would hold "notwithstanding any subsequent changes in the definition of regulatory capital." When Congress voted stricter standards for regulatory capital, regulators moved to seize Far West. Judge Panner held that a contract was a contract, but regulators ignored his injunction and seized it anyway.

In the Franklin case, the circuit court, while complaining that the thrift's owners paid themselves dividends, essentially seemed to be ruling that thrift regulators have no obligation to be reasonable. Even if this becomes law it's still possible, and indeed is being tested in the Far West case, that the government may have to pay compensation for taking property, further widening taxpayer liability. Perhaps even more significant is Judge Panner's remark that Far West's buyers had put up their $27 million in good faith and "To abrogate such an agreement would practically guarantee that potential investors will look elsewhere."[5]

For the thrift regulators' biggest problem may be disposing of the assets they seize. By mid-1991 the RTC held more than $150 billion in assets, including $18 billion in real estate. At least at one point it also held the nation's biggest junk-bond portfolio. Experience shows that under government management the value of these properties will decline—except perhaps, Martin Mayer notes, for raw land.[6] While it has unloaded securities, its efforts to sell properties have been hampered by the fear that the buyer may make a profit and that Congress may criticize the sale price as too low.

Thus the sale of property is encumbered with rules. There are rules against "conflicts of interest" by potential bidders, for example. An "ethics" rule prohibited bids from anyone who'd cost the deposit insurance system more than $50,000, which eliminated most potential bidders in Texas. Under original rules, the RTC couldn't lower its asking price until the property had been on the market six months, and then only by 15 percent; this was later relaxed to 20 percent immediately and 40 percent after six months. A poll of 2,000 real estate brokers in January 1991 found that no one was satisfied after dealing with the RTC, and that 65 percent said they'd never deal with the agency again. They said RTC stood for Red Tape Central.[7]

In mid-1991, Seidman was experimenting with sales of packages of property, mixed between profitable and unprofitable buildings, backed by heavy government financing, but with the government to get 25 or 30 percent of capital appreciation on the property after 12 years. As he prepared to turn the agency over to former American Airlines chairman Albert Casey, this approach was starting to show some promise.[8] This would surely be constructive if it actually got the properties off the government books, which is not all that clear given the lingering involvement. Any progress was an achievement for Seidman, given the regulatory structure Congress designed with FIRREA, depicted in a maze-like organization chart the agency stopped circulating when it became subject to ridicule.

The "seller financing" being adopted in 1991 was one of the ideas proposed more than a year earlier by Daniel Kearney, who resigned in frustration after four months as president of the RTC oversight board. A mortgage expert and veteran of both Washington and Wall Street, Kearney seemed ideal to run the bailout; after resigning he became chief financial officer of Aetna Life & Casualty. His deputy, Fred Alt, resigned with him. "What's been done here is, everyone's been given an excuse," he explained. "It isn't set up to succeed. It's set up to have no one make a move without five people asking him why."[9]

This complaint was forcefully echoed by Arizona Banking Superintendent William H. Revoir, III, before a regional RTC advisory board in June 1991. "The RTC's basic design, and virtually all of the

policies and procedures that have emanated from it during its relatively short life, have only one true underlying purpose—to shift
blame," he testified. "There is a policy or a procedure at every step
in the process that requires either a mechanical application of a formula or the shifting of the decision to someone outside the RTC. The
result has been indecision on so massive a scale that words are inadequate to describe it."

He added, "Instead of concentrating on how to obtain the highest
net recovery on a particular asset, local RTC personnel are convinced
that they have some sort of divine patriotic duty to reek moral retri-
bution on everyone who was ever associated with a savings and loan,
even an innocent borrower. The head of the Phoenix office and his
subordinates told me this directly. They believe they must enforce
moral obligations (as they see fit to define these obligations) even
where there exists absolutely no legal obligation."[10]

Now of course, the RTC will learn over time; it's a fledgling bureaucracy still low on the learning curve. In branding FIRREA an act
of anger, White remarks, "With respect to the bank board, the punishment was straightforward, abolish the agency and distribute its
powers to other agencies."[11] The necessity of creating a new bureaucracy in the midst of crisis has already vastly increased the costs of the
bailout, and the economy faces further costs as well. So long as real
estate remains in government hands, for example, it will be an "overhang" that depresses other property values because it could suddenly
be dumped on the market. Of course, the more the costs of a bungled
bailout rise, the more they will be blamed not on present policies, but
on the "excesses" of the Seven Fat Years.

• • •

For good measure, Congress stuck another provision in FIRREA
prohibiting the thrifts from owning "junk bonds." *Everyone knew* that
junk bonds were a risky investment. Hadn't Drexel confessed and
wasn't Milken a crook? So Congress had another target for anger:
Milken and Drexel and "junk bonds" in general.

Never mind that only four months earlier the General Accounting
Office, Congress' financial watchdog, had reported on precisely the
issue of junk and the thrifts. It concluded, "So far, high yield bonds
have been attractive for thrifts compared to many alternative investments, and high yield bond investments have not contributed to the

thrift industry's current problems." Indeed, junk bonds were second only to credit cards as a thrift profit center.[12]

The GAO warned that the bonds had not been tested by a recession, which would be expected to increase the default rate. But it also noted that the FHLBB had just, in January 1989, taken steps to establish new standards for thrift investment in bonds. It concluded, "If properly understood and enforced, these standards should help assure that thrifts invest in high yield bonds without incurring unnecessary or unreasonable risk."

It reported that only five percent of the 3,025 federally insured thrifts owned any junk bonds. And ten institutions owned 76 percent of all the junk bonds owned by thrifts. Junk bonds had played a role in only one failing thrift, and "in that case, mismanagement of the institution's high yield bond portfolio was only one part of a broader pattern of unsafe lending and investment practices leading to the institution's collapse."

Nonetheless, insured deposits shall not be used to buy junk bonds, Congress decided. Thrifts could no longer buy the bonds. Those that already held them were given five years to divest. This was supposed to make the process gradual, but Congress didn't understand the arbitrary intricacies of regulatory accounting practices. In calculating the "capital position" of a financial institution, a bond it intends to hold to maturity is counted as an asset at face value. But one it expects to sell before maturity must be "marked to market."

At the time of FIRREA, the junk market was already entering a correction, and as prices fell FIRREA forced thrifts holding junk bonds to write down their capital. Overnight, they were "insolvent." Their economic position had not changed overnight, of course. Most of the bonds were paying the same high interest rates they had been paying, so the thrifts' cash flows remained healthy. But since the accounting for their assets had changed, they were no longer ahead of their liabilities. Their "capital" had vanished, and they were now bait for a regulatory takeover.

The need to bolster "capital" put extraordinary pressure on the thrifts to dump their junk bonds, not over five years but today. Naturally, this drove the junk market down further, and the fall in the market further depressed thrift capital, etc., etc. Whereas only a few months before the GAO found that junk bonds produced high yields for the thrifts, Congress' edict that they were "unsafe" produced a self-realizing spiral. John Shad, the former SEC chairman who took over as chairman of Drexel as it went under, has said nothing surprised him more than how much the forced divestiture of the bonds had to do with the bankruptcy.

Of course, the initial market correction was no doubt appropriate. No type of investment produces above-average yields forever; it keeps getting more and more popular until yields sink to average. And as FIRREA passed, Drexel, the market-maker in many of the bonds, had been crippled by a $650 million fine and the loss of Milken and some of his loyalists. The highly publicized default of Integrated Resources, a Drexel client, had just taken place. And the problems of the Campeau issue, not by Drexel, were in the news.

The market on its own, in short, was correcting "overleveraging." As Miller said in his Nobel lecture, "Something very much like this endogenous slowing of leveraging could be discerned in early 1989 even before a sequence of government initiatives (including the criminal indictments of the leading investment bankers and market makers in junk bonds, the forced dropping of junk bond inventories by beleaguered S&L's and the stricter regulations on leveraged lending by commercial banks) combined to undermine the liquidity of the high-yield bond market."[13]

Similar assessments were offered by Miller's co-laureates. In his Nobel lecture, William Sharpe said, "Given the bewildering pace of such innovation, it is not surprising that some individuals and organizations have at times found it difficult to fully understand the proper uses of some of the new instruments and procedures. Evidence abounds that those who fail to learn the principles of financial economics in more formal ways will do so through experience. Markets are effective although sometimes cruel teachers. In general, financial systems are self-correcting. Given time, participants learn to use new instruments and procedures to improve overall welfare, not just to reallocate wealth from one set of hands to another. It is usually best to wait until the forces of competition are able to regulate a market rather than to impose regulations prematurely."[14]

The third laureate, Harry M. Markowitz, waited a few months before delivering an extraordinary lecture, "Markets and Morality, or Arbitrageurs Get No Respect." He was critical of Milken, and indeed found some excessive leverage in the 1980s, due to the pools of the S&L money that could be put in risky investments while enjoying a deposit-insurance guarantee. But the thrust of his lecture was elsewhere:

The invisible hand is clumsy, heartless and unfair, but it is ever so much more deft and impartial than a central planning committee. Consequently, I am troubled by the indiscriminate way many Americans use "greed" as an explanation of economic events.

The blanket condemnation of the "greedies" of the 1980s fails to distinguish between the complaint that too many people sought to maximize their own well being, as Adam Smith would have us all do, legally, and the complaint that too much leverage was used in the 1980s. . . .

The blanket condemnation of the greedies of the 1980s blurs other important distinctions. It lumps together people who were remarkably stingy with those who were remarkably generous, either with public donations to good causes or with quiet private help to others in need. It lumps together those whose sole interest in life was the winning of the finance game, as measured by their accumulating wealth, and those who played the game well, accumulated fortunes, but found time for other interests. It lumps together those who committed well-defined crimes and deserved the punishment they got, and perhaps more, with those who were arrested conspicuously, left waiting for the next round of charges, then had their cases dropped as a big mistake; and those whose crimes had been civil offenses before, but now were elevated to criminal offenses.[15]

In general, though, society was impatient with such caveats and distinctions, even from Nobel economists. The Congress, the regulators, the press and the public remained preoccupied with risk and leverage.

· · ·

This preoccupation pumped new life into the bond rating houses, Moody's and Standard & Poor's. They provide ratings that claim to predict the likelihood of default by having analysts pour over the finances of the issuers of various bonds. But then, thousands of analysts in hundreds of brokerage houses do the same thing every day. No one at Michael 1 would believe that an individual bond rater could outguess the collective decisions of the market; if he could, he'd be rich and not have to work in such a stodgy place. The only sensible thing for raters is watch the yield of the bond and adjust their ratings accordingly. If the bond raters had done that, they wouldn't have been tardy in spotting spectacular defaults like New York City and Washington Public Power Supply System, or WHOOPS. Nonetheless, various laws, regulations and trust provisions prohibit some investors from buying bonds that aren't certified as "investment grade" by the rating houses.

The leverage preoccupation has not, however, led to any serious attempts to level the playing field between how equity is taxed and how debt is taxed. Bonds, whether junk or investment grade, have an important advantage over stocks. Under the U.S. tax code, corporations can deduct interest paid to bondholders before calculating the corporate tax, but dividends paid to shareholders are not deductible. In either case, the recipient is taxed on the income. This "double taxation of dividends" makes no particular economic sense, but something has to count as "profit" for the corporate income tax to tax. (Peter Drucker has written that profit is that portion of a corporation's tax flow the government has decided to tax.) It does mean that debt is a cheaper source of capital than equity, a point to be pondered every time you hear talk about "excessive debt."

This tax problem is also a big reason why junk bonds were structured as bonds. In paying high yields on untested companies, they actually had more of a cast of equity. It was expected that some of them would default, and the junk issues were usually subordinated to more senior debt like bank loans—that is, in bankruptcy the bankers got paid first, leaving junkholders with risks approaching those of shareholders. Indeed, some of the bonds held covenants on how to handle default; the idea was to avoid the bankruptcy courts and the dead-loss cost of lawyers. Junk bonds could just as well have been called preferred stock, except that then payments to holders would be called "dividends" instead of "interest," and wouldn't be deductible from corporate income tax.

Much of the concern over leverage, finally, is connected to the takeover wars, to the battle between those trying to protect old capital and those trying to build new capital. A monopoly on bond finance is of course very comfortable for the 800 rated companies.

A lot of the talk about "too much leverage," indeed, arose directly out of the takeover wars. Takeovers typically did involve building the corporation's debt, so CEOs worried about leverage. They often were willing, however, to take on more debt in defending against takeovers. They were also the source of concern about the "long-term view," meaning the CEOs don't want to have to worry about their share prices. Somehow "international competitiveness" got mixed in the brew, though Japanese firms are more highly leveraged than American ones. In 1988, according to the IMF, the ratio of debt to total assets in production industries came to 45.3 percent in the U.S., 55.7 percent in Germany, and 69.6 percent in Japan.[16]

Aside from complaining about leverage and short-term views, the Business Roundtable and many individual corporations lobbied vigorously for protections from raiders. Back when they supported Jimmy Carter's price controls, they'd opposed restrictions on mergers; before junk they were the only ones that could finance them. If a company felt it had a special reason it needed unusual protection from takeovers, nothing prevented it from asking shareholders to change the bylaws. Dow Jones & Company did this in enacting a plan with two classes of stock, common in the newspaper industry. But few CEOs were willing to put their various plans to shareholders; courts, legislatures and regulatory bodies seemed more promising venues.

In any event, in the 1990s the corporate CEOs will have plenty of protection from buyouts. The Delaware Courts have now expanded the "business judgment" rule to say that directors can accept one bid for a company without letting shareholders vote on a higher one.[17] After the court let Time Inc. become Time Warner Inc. despite Paramount's $200-a-share bid, the shares sunk below $100.[18] At this point Time Warner wanted to tap shareholders for yet more money in a coercive "rights offering," but backed down to protests from shareholders, including large pension funds. The Business Roundtable is now at work trying to curb the pension funds. My own sense is that the issue of corporate governance is not settled, as the growing controversy over executive compensation attests.

Merton Miller cited the academic studies on the leveraged buyouts in Stockholm. "Mikhail Gorbachev, the 1990 Peace Prize Winner, may have popularized the term *perestroika*, but the LBO entrepreneurs of the 1980s actually did it, and on a scale not seen since the early years of this century when so much of what we think of as big business was being put together by the entrepreneurs of consolidation like J.P. Morgan and John D. Rockefeller."[19]

• • •

More worrisome to the outlook for the 1990s is the spread of the regulatory narrow-mindedness to financial institutions such as banks and insurance companies. Shortly after Congress passed FIRREA, for example, bank regulators promulgated new guidelines for "highly leveraged transactions," the apparent purpose being to curtail loans for corporate takeovers and restructuring. The Comptroller of the

Currency, the Federal Deposit Insurance Corporation and the Federal Reserve Board issued a letter saying that loans would be classified as HLTs if they were made to a company where debt exceeded 75 percent of assets, or if there was a doubling of debt to a level above 50 percent of assets. Rather than limit deposit insurance, the Fed and other regulators would have their army of examiners police the banks for risky investments.

To begin with, there is no such thing as a riskless investment. I remember a conversation with a wealthy friend during the 1970s; an intermediary had come to him asking for charity for a friend's widow. Her husband had left a comfortable inheritance, but her banker had conservatively invested it in the traditional safe haven of municipal bonds. Such bonds of course pay paid fixed interest on the face amount, and inflation and the run-up in market interest rates had eroded their principal value. And while they still paid the same dollars in interest, the dollars were worth far less. Because of her "safe" investments, the widow couldn't meet her inflation-driven expenses. What regulator would have nudged banks out of municipals in 1972? For that matter, residential mortgages are much like municipal bonds, which is how thrifts got in trouble in the first place.

There is also the issue of whether the examiners are better at making credit judgments than the bankers are. In mid-1991, the Comptroller of the Currency's office had 2,376 examiners to regulate 3,950 banks. The average examiner was 35 years old, with eight years' experience, and made $47,000 a year. Without in the least denigrating the overworked examiners, you can only expect so much. And even examiners like the comptroller's, not involved in the thrift debacle, certainly did not want to get caught with the next Lincoln Savings.

There is also the issue, why now? American banks have hosts of problems, the main one being that their role as an intermediary is being eroded as more of their traditional loan customers develop direct access to the credit markets through commercial paper and the like. But by the traditional measures the banks' capital positions did not deteriorate during the 1980s but improved. By 1989 capital at the nine largest banks reached 9.3 percent of assets, compared with 4.5 percent in 1980.[20]

So the HLT rules faced the bankers with new regulations being interpreted on the run. Are public utilities, which often have less than 25 percent equity because of steady cash flows, really risky? What about debtor-in-possession loans, made after a company entered bankruptcy and thus number-one in the credit line? Once listed as a HLT, how do you get delisted?

Faced with confusion and with a sharp change in regulatory mood, bankers reacted much as they had to Jimmy Carter's 1980 credit controls. They stopped lending, especially in suspect areas like take-overs and real estate. Commercial bank lending was negative in 1990; more loans were closed or withdrawn than opened. Business loans from other lenders and mortgages also turned negative, while com-mercial paper issued by big companies fell.[21] Also, of course, the flow of investment funds from the junk bond markets dried up. After its bankruptcy, Drexel Burnham stopped issuing the data cited in Chap-ter 9, but there is a slightly different series complied by the *Invest-ment Dealer's Digest*. It showed proceeds from high yield securities dropping from $25.2 billion in 1989 to $1.3 billion in 1990 and, as prices of bonds recovered, $3.4 billion in the first three quarters of 1991.[22]

In 1991, John Heimann, the highly regarded former Comptroller of the Currency now at Merrill Lynch, wrote "Bank Examiners, Trust Your Judgment," an open letter to his former colleagues and employ-ees. "No examiner has ever been criticized for being too tough. So, some examiners have discarded balanced judgment for the most con-servative application of the rule books. Then bank officials, to reduce assets classified as problems, stop making loans, refuse to renew loans in fields subject to intense regulatory scrutiny, such as real estate, and call loans at the slightest pretext." He concluded with the hope, "While the politicians, rating agencies and others who should know better are covering their past mistakes, only the bank examiners can be a voice for reason and balance."[23]

In early 1991, bank regulators issued clarifications relaxing the HLT rules, and lending started to improve, though scarcely bounding back the way it did when credit controls were lifted in 1980. Later the same year, Congress passed a banking bill doing little about deposit insurance but squeezing discretion out of bank regulation. Clearly, regulatory and public attitudes toward credit will overhang the 1990s. The issue is whether any balance will be struck; we don't want the Congress leaning on regulators to go easy on hustlers, but neither do we want the economy asphyxiated for want of credit.

As Merton Miller put it in his Nobel lecture, "Drawing the wrong moral from the S&L affair can have consequences that extend far beyond the boundaries of this ill-fated industry. The American hu-morist, Mark Twain, once remarked that a cat, having jumped on a hot stove, will never jump on a stove again, even a cold one. Our commercial bank examiners seem to be following precisely this pattern."[24]

• • •

The leverage preoccupation leaves a dubious legacy for the 1990s. Even if the *Fortune* 500 is protected from domestic raiders, it faces the lash of foreign competition. It will have no choice but to become more and more efficient, which is to say, to lay off more and more employees. If prosperity is to reign, somehow the economy will have to find rising entrepreneurs to create jobs, as they did so robustly during the Seven Fat Years.

This means that somewhere the entrepreneurs must find capital. For companies well enough established to issue public stock and join the over-the-counter markets, IPOs turned healthy in the strong stock market of 1991. But the pipeline has to be kept filled. Venture capital and junk bonds remained paltry. And banks, the traditional sustenance of small business, were under regulatory pressure to shrink; they withdrew more funds from the market than they added.

The Commerce Department compiles an index of new business incorporations, which during 1988 and 1989 had been running about 125 (against a base of 1967 = 100). The index hit a recent peak of 125.9 in January 1990. By June it had slumped to 121.1, and by September of 1991 it had touched 113.3, its lowest point since the depths of 1982. Such an index would be expected to fall in any recession, of course, but in the context of the early 1990s recession it seems far more central than is usual. For the savings and loan debacle and the takeover wars gave birth to a leverage preoccupation that brought the Seven Fat Years to an end.

The issue for the 1990s will be whether entrepreneurs will find the capital they need to grow and recreate the jobs the established CEOs must slash. Or will regulators and public opinion rule that you can't raise capital unless you already have it? The Victorians were people who, discovering sex, thought the human race was about to vanish. In 1990, the Americans discovered credit.

17

Turning Back?

The mood-shift that threatens the 1990s is measured not only by Merton Miller's "anti-leverage hysteria," but by a second ominous development, the reemergence of "the fairness issue." This is the same issue that the Carter administration vainly invoked against the Steiger amendment, of course, and the same issue that won Walter Mondale Minnesota and the District of Columbia. As it magically vanished in 1978, it magically reappeared in 1989.

The crushing Mondale defeat, indeed, led to an explicit reconsideration of the "fairness" issue. The Democratic Party launched a $200,000 study of voter attitudes, and in 43 focus groups found fairness was a dud. "When party leaders talk fairness, middle class voters see it as a code word for giveaway," one party official said.[1] Through the ensuring debate, however, there remained one true believer, Senator George Mitchell of Maine; in 1987 he solicited a Congressional Budget Office study to show that the poor suffer most from taxes; the CBO carefully cited "methodological judgments and compromises that bear critically on the results obtained."[2] In 1988 the Democratic party chose George Mitchell as Senate majority leader.

In 1989 he used his statistics, and his powers as Senate leader, to stop a proposed cut in the capital gains tax. The measure was sponsored by the administration and had already passed the House, with nearly a quarter of the Democratic members deserting their leadership to side with the president. The majority leader first objected to its inclusion in the deficit-reduction bill required by the Gramm-Rudman law, arguing that the administration insistence on the cut was blocking the bill. He won Republican assent to remove it the day before the sequester deadline. He then threatened to raise proce-

271

dural roadblocks if the measure were attached to bills necessary to raise the federal debt limit. These efforts culminated in an agreement to let the bill come to the Senate floor, on the understanding that Senator Mitchell would lead a filibuster, requiring 60 votes to close debate. The cloture motion drew 51 senators; a majority of both houses favored the capital gains cut. But Senator Mitchell had won, in the process of reestablishing the fairness issue and, perhaps, setting the mood of the new decade.

• • •

The *sine qua non* of the fairness issue is not one statistical abstraction, but a whole blizzard of them. In the pantheon of empty statistics, "the deficit" is not quite holy, still having some attachment to the real world. At the top of Olympus, right up there with the trade deficit, is the distribution of incomes. Readers not anxious to enter this statistical maze need know only one thing: If the congressional leaders change their view of their political interest in tax policy, the Tax Committee and Congressional Budget Office staffs will take another look at their statistical models. On the other hand, whole best-sellers have been crafted around these numbers, so it will pay to understand their limitations.

By now most alert Americans are familiar with the ubiquitous reports on the *income* of the bottom quintile, or lowest 20 percent of income-earners. However, Bureau of Labor Statistics surveys also produce less-noticed statistics on the *consumption* of various income quintiles. In publication USDL 90-616, "Consumer Expenditures in 1989,"[3] these intriguing lines appear:

TABLE 17-1

Income and Expenditure by Quintile

	Income before taxes	Average annual expenditure
Lowest 20%	$ 5,720	$12,119
Second 20%	13,894	17,616
Third 20%	23,856	24,476
Fourth 20%	37,524	34,231
Highest 20%	75,406	53,093

Yes, the *consumption* of the lowest quintile is more than twice the *income* of the lowest quintile. This is not a fluke, but what the BLS surveys find every year. Somehow the bottom fifth of the income distribution finds twice as much money to spend as it receives within the definitions of income that have preoccupied the debate over Senator Mitchell's numbers. Yet in any real concern over the welfare of the bottom fifth, or at least its standard of living, the income figures would seem less relevant than the consumption ones.

The BLS studies further divide the data by types of expenditure, and the editors of *American Demographics* have combed this data to compare consumption patterns of high-income and low-income groups. Being careful demographers, they started with the observation that the average high-income household has 3.2 people, compared with 2.0 people in the average low-income household. Accordingly, they kept the classification by income group, but converted the per-household spending into per-capita figures.

Doing this with the 1987 consumer expenditure survey, they found that low-income households spent $7,200 per capita; in high-income households, spending was twice that, $14,400. The low-income households per capita expenditure for food came to 81 percent of the high-income households. Low-income households spent more per person on cigarettes and other smoking supplies. For clothing the figure was 42 percent, for transportation 26 percent. On medical care, expenditure was nearly identical—$445 per person in low-income families and $470 per person in high-income families. The big bulge in high-income spending, on a per capita basis nine times that of low-income households, was for insurance and pensions.[4]

How can this be? Where does the money come from in low-income houses. Partly it's explained by underreporting of income; the separate census figures show slightly higher incomes in all quintiles—$6,994 for the bottom 20 percent in 1989 versus the BLS's $5,720. While low-income families receive substantial in-kind income support, public housing for example, this would not appear to explain cash expenditure, but would be in addition to it.

The biggest explanation lies in the composition of the bottom 20 percent of "households," which include both families and single people. The bottom fifth of households includes a disproportionate number of the elderly—retired people who may own their own homes and have capital to draw on. It also includes a disproportionate number of young people—for example students receiving financial support from their families.

Yet in our mind we identify the bottom quintile with the chronically poor, only a subset. And we measure their standard of living by income rather than the actual resources they command. The income-distribution figures, that is, are a classic case of what Robert Eisner described in his presidential address to the American Economic Association: "To put matters bluntly, many of us have literally not known what we are talking about."

Actually, the economists, or at least the demographers, understand the limitations of these statistics. For one thing, an "income distribution" is a snapshot in time. In terms of social justice, what really counts would be equity over a lifetime, but we have no measure of this. The banker's graduate student son, destined to work on Wall Street, may show up in the bottom quintile. Even movements in and out of the poverty population are far more dynamic than usually supposed.[5]

Similarly and perhaps most important, the income distribution figures are highly sensitive to broad social trends. Indeed, understanding these trends is their most important serious use. Historically and across cultures, the amazing thing has been the stability of the distribution, and since sometime in the middle or late 1970s, something has been going on in American society. By the usual measures such as the "Gini index," the distribution has been growing more unequal. In recent reports, Census Bureau demographers have speculated as to why:

> While there seems little doubt that the income distribution has become somewhat less equal over the past 20 years, the reasons for this trend are not as clear. Certainly, part of the growing inequality of the income distribution can be attributed to the changing composition of families and households. One of the compositional changes is the growth in the elderly population. In March of 1990, 21.6 percent of all households had a householder 65 years old or older. The comparable figure for 1970 was 19.3 percent. Since elderly households have considerably lower incomes than nonelderly households (in 1989 the ratio of elderly to nonelderly median household income was .48), this compositional change would tend to increase income inequality.
>
> Another compositional change is the growing number of persons living in nonfamily situations (those who live either alone or with nonrelatives). In 1970, 18.7 percent of households had a householder

either living alone or with nonrelatives. By 1990, that figure grew to 29.2 percent. Since these households have a much lower median income than family households ($17,120 versus $34,630 in 1989), their increase would certainly have an effect on the inequality of the household income distribution.

A trend that is associated with the increasing inequality of the family income distribution is the growing percentage of families with a female householder, no husband present. Between 1970 and 1990, families with a female householder, no husband present grew from 10.8 percent of all families to 16.5 percent. Data from the CPS show that about one-half of all families with a female householder, no husband present were in the lowest income quintile. The increase in this type of family would cause an increase in measured income inequality.

Other factors may be associated with the growing inequality of the income distribution, including aging of the "babyboom" generation, the growth in the labor force participation of women, and the changing occupational structure. Understanding the reasons behind the growth in income inequality would require estimating the separate effects of each of the factors noted above (and perhaps others) on this phenomenon.[6]

All of this refers to pretax income, of course. In a separate report, the Census Bureau has studied the effect on the income distribution of taxes and government benefits. It is studded with interesting data. For example, "The inclusion of net imputed return on home equity did not have an effect on the Gini index, a reflection that homeowners are spread throughout the income distribution." Or on the issue of Medicare and Medicaid: "The market value of these benefits was frequently very high, compared with the poverty thresholds, and sometimes exceeded them."

The census study follows an elaborate path of excluding government cash transfers from reported money income, considering nonreported private income such as capital gains, fringe benefits and imputed home equity; taxes including social security, income taxes and state taxes; the value of various government cash payments and noncash benefits such as medical care and school lunches. The greatest inequality was recorded for pretax money income as usually reported, less government cash transfers plus capital gains. The result after all considerations showed that taxes and transfers tripled the income share of the lowest quintile while reducing the share of the top quintile by 6.8 percentage points.

TABLE 17-2

Income Share by Quintile

Quintile	Money income (usual form)	Less transfers, plus capital gains	Income after tax, transfers
lowest	3.9%	1.5%	5.1%
second	9.6	7.8	10.8
third	15.9	15.3	16.4
fourth	24.0	24.2	23.5
highest	46.7	51.1	44.3

The Census report reaches two conclusions:

> The use of a fully adjusted income definition, that is, one that includes the effect of taxes, cash and noncash benefits, capital gains, employee health benefits, and net return on home equity results in a more equal distribution of income than under the official money income definition.
>
> It has long been known that both taxes and transfers have an equalizing effect on the distribution of income. One of the important findings of the Bureau's tax and benefit research is that the effect of government transfers is much more significant than taxes in redistributing income.[7]

A substantial redistribution does take place. There are few guidelines for saying how much is enough. The census study covered only one year, so we have no earlier comparable figures. We do not know anything conclusive about movements over time of the income distribution after tax and transfers.

What conclusions lurk in this statistical morass? Perhaps most generally, income quintiles are far too gross a measure to capture our real problems, such as the shortfall of educational performance or the scar of the "homeless." In particular, what the statistics show above all is smaller families. In one sense, this is a sign of affluence; as a society we can now afford to live in smaller households. In another, it's a symptom of pathology; too much family splitting is bad for us, especially for children.

Possibly, too, something in the statistics measures an aspect of our Second Industrial Revolution. Even if the consumption figures suggest the *welfare* of the bottom quintile is underestimated, the income distribution figures measure the *earning power* of the bottom quintile, plausibly an independent source of concern. Of course, the quickest way to change the numbers would be to provide incentives for the elderly to stay in the labor force.

Yet it is also true that while an information-based society will offer huge opportunities for the educated, the uneducated may be left behind. International competition has not been good for the wages of unionized auto workers, and deregulation has not been good for the wages of unionized airline pilots—though both have been good for the welfare of consumers. One wage series, the BLS constant-dollar data on production and non-supervisory workers, has actually been falling, though the real earnings of all workers have not. Economists interpret this as a rising return to investment in education.

The moral ambiguities of redistribution, too, have to be kept in mind. We have here the debate between John Rawls and Robert Nozick. Does morality lie with a community deciding how to distribute its goods, à la Rawls? Or does it lie with the individual, who has a right to the fruit of his efforts, à la Nozick? For that matter, before Rawls and Nozick, the issues were extensively examined by Walter J. Blum and Harry Kalven, Jr., in a book entitled *The Uneasy Case for Progressive Taxation.*"[8] Of course, a modest tax rate and income inequality can be justified even by the Rawls criteria, if they improve the absolute situation of the poorest. That is, if low taxes increase incentives and lead to more production, and if the wealth is shared in a way that increases the standard of living of the poor.

Nozick's point about an individual's right to his or her own income seems especially pertinent if you recognize that in 1989 the top quintile of households started at an income of $53,711, and the top 5% at $91,751. Much of the increase in income of the top fifth arises because this dividing-line moves upward as more and more families reach incomes that used to be the top fifth. The typical way to achieve the top fifth is for a wife to work. To what extent is it just for the state to tax the income she produces to redistribute to others, including elderly social security recipients who already own the home she is trying to buy?

Those with truly large incomes are few, and also capable of arranging their affairs to avoid taxes. When you talk about taxing "the rich," you are talking about taxing a two-earner family making $90,000 a year. And we know that a substantial redistribution already takes place, not through tax policy but through expenditures. And we know that in the consumption statistics, the bottom fifth spends half as much per capita as the top fifth.

• • •

These are the statistics as the demographers know them, intriguing, sometimes revealing and often ambiguous. Yet after Senator Mitchell's capital gains victory they once again became intensely politicized. For the next February, House Ways and Means Chairman Danny Rostenkowski joined the fray. He had helped frame the 1986 tax cut and supported the Brodhead amendment in 1981, and in 1990 he wanted to raise the top marginal rate to 33 percent from 28 percent, scarcely the stuff of wholesale redistribution. But he had his staff churn out a Mitchellesque report on taxes and quintiles.

The report showed that the share of taxes paid by the top 20 percent of households had increased; in 1989 they accounted for 46.8 percent of reported income, and paid something on the order of 58 percent of all taxes. Top earners were paying a larger share of the income tax than before, also of social security taxes, the corporate income tax and excise taxes. But the top quintile was paying more because its income was rising rapidly (as probably happens in most economic booms and as the Laffer curve would predict). So, while the "rich" were paying more as a percentage of tax collections, as a percentage of their incomes they were paying less than they had been. Thus the tax system, it was argued, had become less "fair."[9]

A CBO study showed that the top fifth of families pays about 26 percent of all its income in federal taxes, compared with 9.5 percent for the lowest fifth. There is no objective measure of what disparity is "fair." The operational definition of "fairness" seems to lie in the *change* in the average tax rate per quintile; a tax proposal is "fair" if it increases the disparity, and unfair if it does not.[10]

If the income distribution statistics are a statistical morass, of course, the taxes-by-quintile statistics are a minefield. The Ways and Means tables chose a 1980 base year, as if anyone could seriously want to go back to the economic conditions prevailing then. Republicans Pete Domenici and Phil Gramm went back to the CBO statistics and started with a different base year. Between 1983 and 1989, the real income of the bottom quintile rose 11.8 percent, while the real income of the top quintile rose by 12.2 percent. By contrast, between 1979 and 1983, the real income of the bottom quintile fell 17.4 percent, while the real income of the top quintile rose 4.8 percent. Once the tide actually started to rise, in other words, it did lift all boats.[11]

A White House refutation of the Ways and Means numbers also noted the tendentious detail of the committee's statistics. The "effective excise tax rate" for the top 5 percent of the population was reported at 0.4 percent in both 1990 and 1980, but was said to have dropped 11.7 percent—perhaps, that is, from 0.43 to 0.38. By the same reasoning, the income tax in the lowest quintile dropped 275 percent, but Ways and Means did not mention this.[12]

Even in the more evenhanded reports of the Congressional Budget Office you will find a curious statement: "In this table and all subsequent tables, the tenth of the population with the lowest incomes excludes families without positive incomes, although these families are included in the totals."[13] You see, those who report zero or negative incomes—not a trivial number—are presumed to be wealthy individuals arranging their tax affairs; but if they had arranged to report income of, say, plus $100, they would be members of the bottom quintile.

Since incomes are based on tax returns, similarly, they do not necessarily reflect economic income, especially for those near the bottom receiving noncash transfer payments, or those near the top, who are likely to have nontaxable income—interest on municipal bonds, for example. In particular, owners of small businesses have considerable discretion over how they compensate themselves. So when we see the "incomes" of the top quintile rising, we have no ideal whether their economic incomes are actually going up, or whether they are simply choosing to expose more of their income to taxation. Gary and Aldona Robbins have elaborated this point.[14]

Finally, the Ways and Means/CBO results depend chiefly on one egregious bit of statistical sleight of hand. The 1991 *Green Book* shows that the income of the top 1 percent of families increased to $198,542 in 1990, compared to a 1977 income, in 1990 dollars, of $95,553. This 107 percent increase was led by a 171 percent increase in income from capital gains. But it turns out that everything has been restated in 1990 dollars with one exception: The original purchase price of the assets being sold to produce the capital gains remains in nominal dollars. Treating nominal capital gains as real vastly inflates the income and deflates the tax burden of "the rich," particularly the top 1 percent.

Congressman Richard Armey got CBO director Robert Reischauer to admit that if the effect of inflation on capital gains could be removed "the distribution of the tax burden would then be seen to fall more heavily on upper-income groups than is depicted by the currently available analysis." This gaping flaw in the data was missed by most who write about the income data, with the exceptions of the late columnist Warren Brookes and Ed Rubenstein of the *National Review*.[15] It means the Ways and Means data is worthless, or more bluntly, a lie.

Yet Senator Mitchell and Congressman Rostenkowski were able to make these numbers the *very first* test of any tax policy. They sent any tax proposal off to some computers at the Treasury and CBO to be "scored" on "fairness." All the "scoring" numbers are fictitious, of course—what a computer spews out when fed certain assumptions. The distributional effect of government spending is not considered. Neither is any likely change in the behavior of taxpayers; the new rates are simply rubber stamped onto conditions assumed for the coming year or years. And once the fictitious numbers are in hand, the test of fairness is not whether the top fifth of taxpayers pay more tax, but whether they pay a larger percentage of their income.

Consider the 1990 budget negotiations; a *Journal* story by Alan Murray and Jackie Calmes described the scene at Andrews Air Force base:

> Nothing at Andrews proved more divisive than the battle of the distribution tables.
>
> They were mere spreadsheets, computations by the congressional Joint Tax Committee showing how each proposal shifted relative tax burdens among various income groups. Senate Majority Leader George Mitchell, in particular, had insisted from the beginning that the wealthiest taxpayers pick up more of the tab. Now, the nearly instant availability of the distribution tables cast every offer and counteroffer in terms of fairness between rich and poor. And every plan involving a cut in the capital gains tax invariably showed a windfall for the rich. Messrs. Darman and Sununu angrily attacked the charts. "This methodology could not withstand serious academic scrutiny," Mr. Darman charged. The Democrats leaked a copy of the distribution tables to the news media, making the fairness issue public and intensifying the battle inside the bargaining room. After a meeting on Sept. 16, Mr. Gephardt turned to Mr. Sununu, incredulous at his unyielding defense of the capital gains cut.
>
> "Why would you want to help people making over $1 million?"
>
> "It's the American dream," Mr. Sununu snapped.[16]

These negotiations, in turn, reversed the course of tax policy. On June 24 President Bush put out a statement annulling his "read my lips" tax pledge. His approval ratings started to fall. On August 1, Iraq invaded Kuwait, riveting the president's attention and the world's. As the president tried to rally the world to resist, the budget negotiations went forward. The final result, again under the gun of a budget sequester closing much of the government, was a deal on September 30, which included no capital gains cut but tax increases that raised the 28% top marginal rate to 31%, plus a series of gimmicks that raised it further to more than 34%. The direction established in 1978 was at least momentarily reversed in 1990. Tax policy was now focused on "fairness," not on economic growth. With this series of events, the economy sank into recession.

In the larger scheme of things, I find it difficult to fault President Bush for his 1990 budget decisions, except in sticking to them too long. For economic decisions must have been shaped by the impending war in the Persian Gulf. When Saddam Hussein struck, the White House had seemed on the verge of recognizing the revocation of the tax pledge as a mistake. By the final hours of the budget negotiation, the president was necessarily preoccupied with support for the war. While I have been unable to find any evidence this explicitly weighed on his decision, by any logic it had to, at least in the president's own mind. He did not need a Gramm-Rudman sequester and a mammoth fight with the Congress while trying, ultimately with narrow success, to win a vote on his war policy.

The administration can be faulted, though, for failing to confront the congressional Democrats, who again in 1991 used procedural dodges to avoid a vote on the president's capital gains proposals. In particular, the administration was gun-shy about "fairness," spooked by an issue that had been buried in three successive presidential landslides and 43 Democratic focus groups. To understand this, you have to understand Republican bloodlines.

George Bush, to begin with, is the son of the head of a major Wall Street firm who became a U.S. senator. The eventual U.S. president was president of the senior class at Phillips Academy in Andover, Massachusetts, and a member of Skull and Bones at Yale. His business adventures in the Texas oil fields did give him a touch of capitalist vigor, but in staffing his administration he turned to respectability.

Treasury Secretary Nicholas Brady grew up on an estate in Far Hills, New Jersey, next door to that of Clarence Dillon of the Wall Street firm Brady later headed. He attended St. Mark's School in Southboro, Massachusetts, Yale and Harvard Business School. When

Mr. Brady headed it, Dillon Read was an investment banker for Unocal in fending off Boone Pickens. Unocal chief Fred Hartley explained that he insisted on investment bankers "spiritually committed to what I consider to be the American economic way."[17]

Robert Mosbacher, President Bush's commerce secretary and manager for his re-election campaign, was the son of a stock trader who made a fortune on the Curb Exchange and cashed in before the crash. He attended Choate School in Wallingford, Connecticut, and Washington and Lee University. Richard Darman, budget director and critic of "now-nowism," was the son of a textile mill owner, captain of the lacrosse team at the Rivers Country Day School in Weston, Massachusetts, and attended Harvard and Harvard Business School. Secretary of State James Baker, son of the founder of Houston's biggest law firm, attended the Hill School in Pottstown, Pennsylvania, Princeton and law school at the University of Texas.

John Sununu, chief of staff when the budget deal was struck, was the top-ranking cadet at LaSalle Military Academy on Long Island, which he attended on scholarship after parochial elementary school in Queens. Public high schools are represented in the Bush brain trust by Chief Economic Adviser Michael Boskin, the son of a construction contractor, and Vice President Dan Quayle, who was graduated from the local high school in Huntington, Indiana, and despite his image of wealth waited tables at a college sorority.

Men from privileged backgrounds are not likely to be comfortable arguing that "fairness" is bunk. For that you need someone like Ronald Reagan, the son of a shoe salesman with alcohol problems and a graduate of Eureka College. Or perhaps a disruptive buccaneer cut from the mold of William Simon or Donald Regan. A former professional quarterback might do, but in the Bush cabinet Jack Kemp was regulated to the Department of Housing and Urban Development.

Yet so long as the statistical blizzard blinds tax policy, clear growth initiatives will be impossible. If we want more investment to boost productivity, for example, the obvious solution is to charge lower taxes on investment and the savings that finance it. But "fairness" will preclude any such initiative, since those who save and invest are likely to be "rich" in the tables compiled by Ways and Means and the Joint Tax Committee. Somehow those who talk most loudly of "international competitiveness" seldom note that most other industrial nations tax capital far more lightly than the U.S. does.

Capital gains is a leading example. In the European tradition, capital gains have not usually been considered income at all. Only one other nation, Australia, taxes capital gains as an ordinary income, and the only other steep tax on gains was Great Britain's 40%. But both indexed the base of the gain, and the British simply exempted all gains prior to the imposition of the tax in 1982. Germany has no tax whatever on gains on securities held more than a year, and Belgium exempts both long-term and short-term gains. Japan instituted a maximum of 5% on securities transactions only in 1990. France taxes both long-term and short-term gains at 16%. Even Social Democratic Sweden has an 18% rate on securities held for two years.[18] Thanks to the preoccupation with "fairness," in short, the United States has the world's harshest treatment of capital gains.

This is particularly relevant given the key role that real estate values played in the 1990 recession. Commercial property was clearly overbuilt, but the regulatory credit crunch depressed residential property as well. The value of the nation's owner-occupied housing declined by $141 billion in 1990, the first drop since 1946. Correspondingly, the net worth of American households declined for the first time in two generations, naturally leading to consumer edginess.

The change was invisible to the Keynesian National Income Accounts, of course, since it did not affect the flow of incomes. The wealth effects are recorded instead in the Federal Reserve's data on household balance sheets, consulted among others by John Rutledge, ever sensitive to stocks rather than flows.[19] I balk at Rutledge's prescription of using monetary policy to stabilize property prices; but a cut in the world's steepest capital gains tax would have an immediate effect on property values, as would a rapid disposal of the RTC inventory overhanging the real estate market.

The social background of the Bush decision-makers is a handicap in dealing with another change in the early 1990s, the decline of the entrepreneur. For a sociological chasm rends the Republican party, and conservative or "pro-business" circles generally. Those sensitive to the preservation of capital, respectable and prudent, are quite distinct from the forces for creation of capital, self-made men and admirers of risk-takers. As one can see in the history of Jay Gould or Sam Insull, or the Business Roundtable support of price controls and maneuvers against takeovers, these two groups are seldom allies for long. Thus from the start the Bush administration has watered down its capital gains proposals with incentives to hold gains, that is, preserve capital.

Yet the challenge of the 1990s will be to make entrepreneurs flourish again, to encourage not the CEOs with the "long view," but the college dropouts, breakaway engineers and illegal immigrants. As already outlined in Chapter 16, "Victorian Finance," the *Fortune* 500 will continue to shed employees for the sake of efficiency, and new businesses must rise to replace the jobs. The entrepreneur especially needs capital, and during the Seven Fat Years could find it. Perhaps too much of it in the case of the S&L property developments, and perhaps with the Master of the Universe cutting some corners. Yet the new companies did develop, growth and productivity returned and 18 million jobs were created.

In an age of Victorian finance, Drexel is bankrupt. Banks are frightened, closing loans as rapidly as opening them. Venture capital funds have been shrinking. Junk bond prices have recovered, but new issues remain stunted. Commercial paper has been sluggish. The Delaware courts have protected the Unocals and Time-Warners. Congress has not started on banking reform, let alone broached the true issue of deposit insurance. As an election campaign dawns, Democrats seem to have abandoned "fairness" for the poor in favor of breaks for "the middle class," a label even less susceptible to statistical rigor. The Republican administration apes this concern and makes bows to anti-Japanese sentiments.

Left to its own devices, the economy may yet sweep all of this aside. The surge in the stock market as 1991 closed was surely impressive, not only for the steepness of the gain but for the context. It was clearly sparked by the Federal Reserve's dramatic one-point cut in the discount rate, but the truly impressive thing was the Fed's ability to make this cut without immediately disturbing long interest rates or the price of gold or other commodities, and with only minor and temporary reaction in the foreign exchange markets.

To the extent that this happy conjunction persists, it suggests that the Greenspan Fed is achieving not only its tactical goal of low inflation—the 3.1 percent rise in consumer prices in 1991 was the lowest since 1986—but also its strategic goal of anti-inflation credibility over the long term. Despite the worries and entreaties of the White House and Treasury, the Fed has somehow followed a policy that seems to have stabilized the price of gold at, no surprise to the heirs of Michael 1, just over $350.

While marginal tax rates have ascended, they too remain low by historical standards. Jack Kemp has predicted the nation will never return to truly destructive marginal tax rates. Intriguingly, at the moment of their victory in overturning the Bush tax pledge, Democrats capped the rate on capital gains at 28 percent as the ordinary income rate went to 31 percent and higher with gimmicks. They accepted at least a token of the principle of a "capital gains differential." Why? Because above this rate even a CBO study suggests the capital gains tax would start to lose revenue.[20] In other words, the CBO and congressional Democrats adopted the Laffer Curve. Perhaps some lessons have been learned after all.

SEC Chairman Richard Breeden, too, says one of his highest priorities is designing ways for smaller companies to tap the capital markets.[21] It is of course ironic to have the junk bond reinvented by the agency that did so much to fell Drexel, but at least Breeden understands the problem. He thinks, indeed, about securitizing small business loans, allowing banks to market certificates backed by packages of loans, as they already do for mortgages and credit card receipts. This is surely a good idea, a method of relieving banks' capital pressures and providing readier credit for new businesses.

Then too, the underlying fundamentals are so positive. The Second Industrial Revolution proceeds, and the necessity to prepare for large wars recedes. An integrated world economy can build wealth for all. It is even conceivable that the 1990 recession could prove to be a slow-motion version of the 1980 recession, coming with credit controls and going away when they're lifted. This time there is no credit control legislation, of course; the crunch is merely a matter of mood.

Still, the mood is also the worrisome thing. The Seven Fat Years are somehow considered a failure rather than a success. No one remembers that the malaise and stagflation of the 1970s were overcome. The effort is not to divine the formula that worked, but to blame the 1980s for our present discontents. From our intellectual leaders, we still hear cries to raise taxes to close the federal deficit, proposals to cheapen the dollar to balance the trade deficit and incantations of shopworn Keynesian formulas. Our relationship with Japan is increasingly seen not as an arrangement for mutual benefit but as an excuse to fight. A series of credit-killing regulatory missteps has received general applause, from nearly everyone except a few Nobel laureates who understood what was going on.

The risk for the 1990s is that all this expresses a fundamental change in the national mood, the end of an era of optimism and progress. It may be that George Mitchell's capital gains triumph in 1989, to pick a precise date, was not a single-handed affair after all, any more than Bill Steiger's was in 1978. Perhaps it somehow registered a tipping-point in the national mood, perhaps we are entering another new era of repeated tax increases, of preoccupation with income redistribution instead of incentives, of chasing Joe Barr's 21 millionaires. Perhaps the era of self-realizing pessimism has arrived, perhaps we have left a decade of greed for a decade of envy.

Perhaps, that is, American society has learned nothing from its Seven Fat Years. During those years, the pot was fuller for all; as the Man from Mars found, between 1982 and 1990 real disposable income per capita grew by 18 percent; an entrepreneurial boom created 18 million new jobs. And the U.S. was able to lead the world toward free markets and free elections. To return now to the policies of the 1970s would be ludicrous, indeed neurotic. Worst of all, it would sacrifice the unmatched opportunity of the 1990s.

18

Another *Belle Époque?*

The consciousness of everyone alive today was forged in an abnormal era, a century of world war, revolution and totalitarianism that started with the assassination of Archduke Francis Ferdinand in Sarajevo on June 28, 1914. The brightest hope for mankind today is the possibility that this beastly era ended on November 9, 1989, with the breaching of the Berlin Wall. After all the necessary caveats, the opening of the wall and the failed coup in Moscow in 1991 pose more than a chance that totalitarianism is finished, and with it global confrontation.

It is a time for large thoughts and large ambitions. The tide in the affairs of men is running, and we must take the current when it serves.

For while mankind has always suffered wars and other miseries, our century ranks with the most wretched in history. Technology turned battle from a contest of knights into an assault on whole civilian populations. A Great Depression sunk the world economy. With the rise of Hitler and Stalin, the human soul was under siege. World War II dissolved into a worldwide confrontation between the West and Communism, in which sage philosophers talked of "mutual assured destruction," deterring war by targeting women and children with nuclear missiles.

At issue was the nature of man, a cog in the great dialectical machine of history, or an autonomous individual capable of free will and self government? If reform succeeds in Russia, or even survives, all this will be history. We will have a new era to define.

The skyline of Paris is dominated by the great monument to an earlier and less gruesome era. The Eiffel Tower was erected for the

287

Paris Exposition of 1889 to celebrate the scientific and engineering prowess of the *Belle Époque*. *La Belle Époque* of course, is typically associated with *fin de siècle* Paris, the Paris of Toulouse-Lautrec. It was an age of an extraordinary flowering of the arts, when Manet, Degas and Monet fought the battles leading to the *Salon des Refusés*. It was also an age of extraordinary science, represented by the likes of Louis Pasteur and Madame Curie. Most of all, it was an age of faith in human progress. Even the dour Émile Zola invoked "a century of science and democracy."

Against the temptation to fantasize the past, this exciting age did not bring happiness to everyone. Its denizens too suffered pain from too much change, too much progress. In his *France, Fin de Siècle*, Eugen Weber explains, "This is what caught my eye about the circumstances: the discrepancy between material progress and spiritual dejection reminded me of our own times. So much was going right, even in France, as the nineteenth century ended; so much was being said to make one think that all was going wrong."[1]

Still, World War I changed mankind's life and outlook, in ways by no means confined to France but throughout a common trans-Atlantic civilization and beyond. By now we have forgotten the spirit that was swept away in 1914, and also the extraordinary economic underpinnings of this efflorescence of science and culture. These were once described from the perspective of London by an old friend, John Maynard Keynes:

> What an extraordinary episode in the economic progress of man that age which came to an end in August 1914! The greater part of the population, it is true, worked hard and lived at a low standard of comfort, yet were, to all appearances, reasonably contented with this lot. But escape was possible, for any man of capacity or character at all exceeding the average, into the middle and upper classes, for whom life offered, at a low cost and with the least trouble, conveniences, comforts and amenities beyond the compass of the richest and most powerful monarchs of other ages. The inhabitant of London could order by telephone, sipping his morning tea in bed, the various products of the whole earth, in such quantity as he might see fit, and reasonably expect their early delivery upon his doorstep; he could at the same moment and by the same means adventure his wealth in the natural resources and new enterprises of any quarter of the world, and share, without exertion or even trouble, in their prospective fruits and advantages; or he could decide to couple the security of his fortunes with the good faith of the townspeople of any substantial municipality

in any continent that fancy or information might recommend. He could secure forthwith, if he wished it, cheap and comfortable means of transit to any country or climate without passport or other formality, could depatch his servant into the neighbouring office of a bank for such supply of precious metals as might seem convenient, and could then proceed abroad to foreign quarters, without knowledge of their religion, language, or customs, bearing coined wealth upon his person, and would consider himself greatly aggrieved and much surprised at the least interference. But, most important of all, he regarded this state of affairs as normal, certain, and permanent, except in the direction of further improvement, and any deviation from it as aberrant, scandalous, and avoidable.[2]

The hub of this civilization was Great Britain. With the repeal of the Corn Laws it practiced free trade *unilaterally,* to the benefit of its own consumers and the advancement of underdeveloped nations. With the Royal Navy it protected freedom of the seas (and suppressed the slave trade). With the pound sterling, it was the anchor of an extraordinarily efficient international monetary mechanism known as the gold standard. Goods, labor and capital moved freely to their most productive uses throughout an integrated economy spanning two continents and more.

The biggest beneficiary of this system was the United States of America. Open immigration peopled its lands. Open markets in Europe took its grain, at the expense of agricultural interests in Europe and especially England. Despite these sales, its hunger for capital goods was such that it ran trade deficits year after year, but this mattered little because of consistent investment inflows. For most important of all, the London financial markets mobilized the capital of the civilization as a whole for the prodigious and exciting task of developing the North American continent.

London's capital allowed the labor of American pioneers and workers and the organizational talents of its Robber Barons to tame the continent. By 1890, the census numbers suggested that the frontier had closed. By 1895, the United States was producing more steel than Great Britain. Above all, between the end of the Civil War and the turn of the century, the United States punched five great railroads through the Rockies, expanding its rail network five times to a total higher than all of Europe's. Yet today our history books sweep over this great period, leaping from the Civil War to the Age of Reform in a sentence or two. We have forgotten the history that may be most relevant to the era now dawning.

For the *Belle Époque* was punctured at Sarajevo. Those of us living in the 1990s have been taught from the cradle not to believe in dreams. We are cynical about politicians, and they live up to our expectations. Instead of a century of science and democracy we have Andy Warhol proclaiming that everyone will be famous for 15 minutes. Instead of Toulouse-Lautrec we have Mapplethorpe. Instead of Seven Fat Years we see a nation in decline.

Science, happily, has continued to advance. And in the evolution of technology there is a promise to be exploited. The Eiffel Tower was the product of a master engineer, in its way a monument to central planning. The smelting of steel and building of railroads are enterprises that demand central planning and the mobilization of massive capital. Napoleon had demonstrated how to conscript whole societies for war, and in the ensuing century the experience of mankind taught it efficient logistics and bureaucratic order. The very advance of science taught philosophers like Marx to think of "laws of history." In 1914 this technology, combined of course with the recurrent follies of mankind, marched the world into war.

Ever since, we have been struggling with taming the impact of technology and the mindset it engenders. As the assembly line turned men into interchangeable cogs, the centralized, bureaucratic state became a breeding ground of totalitarianism. Orwell feared that by 1984 it would give tyrants total control. His nightmare was wrong, and here lies our hope for the 1990s and beyond.

The microchip is a liberating invention; its effect is to put power in the hands of individuals at the expense of central authorities, whether public or private. Already it is making itself powerfully felt in world affairs, indeed in the two breathtaking events at the advent of the 1990s. The precision weapons demonstrated with such effect in the Gulf War, an aspect of information technology, promise to make combat once again the province of professional warrior against professional warrior, and once we fully understand this it will redound to the benefit of civilians everywhere.

The events in Eastern Europe and Russia, too, are a testimony to the power of communication. The totalitarians could not control a people in touch with the outside world. In Albert Wohlstetter's phrase, *the fax shall make you free.* So there is a hope here built on something more than momentary events. The events are an expression of a dawning underlying reality, a technological reality far more hopeful than the one that dominated the age in which today's generation was reared.

So opportunity lies before us if we can recognize it. Limited by our experience, we may not realize we are afloat on a full sea. But if we can overcome the cramped and pessimistic outlook in which we've been nurtured, those of us living in the 1990s have a chance to try to put the dream together again. We should dare to think that we can create a new *Belle Époque* of peace, prosperity and progress.

• • •

As we move into the 1990s a vast panoply stretches before mankind—and most of all before the United States, the scientific, economic, political and creative leader in the world. One option, though, America does not have. There is no way it can stop the world and get off. America has no choice but to lead. It weighs so large in the world economy, and so dominates the world's creative processes, that it inherits responsibilities whether it wants them or not. If America now shirks its responsibilities, retreats into isolationism and protectionism, the world will be poorer, and America most of all.

The first task of leadership is understanding. In the 1970s, the United States led the world to the brink of economic crisis without ever knowing it. It simply didn't understand what it was doing. Its elites had not thought seriously enough to understand the system in place, or even to understand that they were in charge. In the 1980s, the United States evolved a policy mix that curbed inflation and sparked renewed growth around the world. This too was a kind of an accident, or at best a response to inchoate instincts of a healthy body politic. A few of us at Michael 1 understood what was happening, I think, but scarcely anyone else.

And even today, American society misunderstands its own experience. It has obliterated all memory of the economic crisis of 1979. It somehow believes that a record peacetime prosperity was a failure. It believes its problems are measured by "the deficit" and proceeds to enact policies that produce a larger deficit.

Much of this is the result of faulty economics, with most of the American elite carrying in its head a version of the Keynesian model that has been abandoned not only by the heirs of Michael 1, but the rising generation of academic economists. Even the good academic economists still tend to think of international economics, the crucial economic arena of an interdependent world, as a kind of plumbing system connecting different national economies. The world economy—in

Bob Mundell's phrase the only closed economy—is instead a living, breathing, interacting whole.

Much of the misunderstanding, too, is fueled by threatened self-interest, real and imagined. Ronald Reagan was a threat to the self-esteem of a whole intellectual and quasi-intellectual class that considered itself enlightened. Michael Milken admitted crimes, but his biggest mistake was to threaten entrenched financial interests, above all the jobs of corporate chieftains. Large slices of our various elites are not yet willing to consider that anything in the 1980s either did go right or could possibly have been right.

Then too, much of the misunderstanding is a failure of spirit. We are pounded by constant change; we are confused by the swirl of events. We cannot conceive that in the midst of this maelstrom we are somehow winning, or at least advancing. Yet it clearly must be true. In 1980 the world economy was in chaos, and Communism still seemed the winning side. A decade later the Western world had grown enormously in wealth, and Communism was passing into historical memory.

Surely we need to understand this momentous experience. To put it as modestly as possible, surely something went right during the 1980s. Not everyone will understand this experience as I do, but at least they should make an effort. Surely there is something to be learned from the Seven Fat Years. Surely there is an understanding of our economy and our society that can help guide us during the 1990s.

• • •

How then would the lessons of the 1980s apply to the 1990s? Let us try a set of hypotheses from the perspective of Michael 1. What are the attitudes and policies that could help us create, if not a new *Belle Époque*, at least another Seven Fat Years?

First, the attitudes. It's a global world; we need to work toward institutions that reflect this tautology. We are in this together; if Eastern Europe falters the world is poorer. If Africa can develop the world is richer. The United States shares in whatever happens, and by default if nothing else the United States must lead.

Leadership does not mean a Marshall Plan for Russia; if anything it means pointing the Russians toward the human, legal, financial and moral infrastructure that let the Marshall Plan succeed. It does not mean a vast outpouring of foreign aid to the governments of Africa, though it might mean using the United Nations to embarrass Africa's nations to go beyond the principle that every man has a right to be ruled by a thug of his own race. Leadership does not mean vast military garrisons around the world, though the suppression of piracy was the Royal Navy's boon to the *Belle Époque,* and Norman Schwarz-kopf's role in Iraq. The new era will require missile defenses and stealth aircraft.

Leadership does mean working for open trade around the world, in particular resisting the temptation to close the U.S. market. Advancement for underdeveloped nations is the world's big opportunity, and this depends primarily on access to markets. The most promising development opportunity lies at America's doorstep: Mexico has rejuvenated itself and bids to join the world. United States–Mexican free trade arrangements will enrich the people on both sides of the Rio Grande. The next biggest opportunity is Eastern Europe, and we should entreat the Europeans to take advantage of it rather than to close their market to its first potential, agriculture.

Leadership also means working toward financial stability. Calling a new Bretton Woods conference tomorrow probably would not work. But we need stable exchange rates to optimize the world's use of resources, reduce the likelihood of financial jolts like the 1987 stock market crash, and avoid unnecessary political pressures for protectionism. The form these arrangements take will depend on the context of the times, but we should seize the time when it arrives.

With respect to the domestic economy, we have to stop substituting numbers for understanding. The economy is too complicated to encapsule in any one number, let alone one as theoretically problematical as "the deficit." This does not mean that the federal fisc doesn't matter, but if we need a single number, federal expenditure as a percent of GNP will do much better as a measure of government, and GNP per capita as a measure of prosperity.

In paving the way for more rapid growth, the first imperative is to keep the system open to entrepreneurs, the college dropouts, breakaway engineers and illegal immigrants. In an age demanding creativity, such talent is the wellspring of creative vitality. In the 1990s, we have developed a climate far less hospitable to the entrepreneur. Capital gains are now taxed punitively, and regulators and rating agencies are choking off finance for all but the established and stodgy.

The opening for entrepreneurship is, in particular, vastly more important than the consumption–savings ratio. We do need capital formation, and it is true that the U.S. tax code penalizes savings. We very well may need to address this as the supply of Japanese savings inevitably diminishes, and of course the "fairness" issue will be an obstacle to any conceivable reform, for encouraging savings means rewarding those who can afford to save.

We of course want the established businesses to buy new equipment that will allow them to maintain production with fewer workers. But as they reduce their workforce, we need rising businesses to put the people back to work. This comes from the entrepreneurs. We will not gain much from a system that encourages U.S. citizens to save mightily and funnels the resulting investment into more of the same old things, disgorging labor in the process.

Since the latter is of course precisely what established and powerful capital wants, it is never easy helping the entrepreneur who mounts a challenge. This was the particular genius of the Seven Fat Years, and the first thing to go with a new, more establishmentarian Republican administration.

We need to remember that capitalism, as Joseph Schumpeter said, is a process of creative destruction. I remember Lord Peter Bauer telling me, "It's not the quantity of investment, it's the quality of investment."

• • •

From these perspectives, then, a few more specific policy prescriptions. In considering them, I recommend a dash of suspended disbelief. That is, lay aside for the moment the question of whether proposals are "politically feasible." I do not think any of the following suggestions are beyond the existing consensus. I am not about to suggest abolishing the income tax in the United States or repealing Lloyd George's social reforms in the United Kingdom, though both came at the end of the age of rapid industrial development. But the political side of these proposals can be discussed later. Anyway, I can remember being told repeatedly in the 1970s that tax cuts were not "politically realistic."

First, the policy mix. The Federal Reserve monetary policy should be focused on containing inflation. That is, we should not look to monetary policy to "stimulate" the real economy. Though of course we do not want a deflationary price structure anymore than an inflationary one, politicians should stop blaming the Fed's anti-inflation policies for the lack of growth caused by what the politicians do with fiscal policy. We should pass a law directing the Fed to stabilize the price level, period. Perhaps surprisingly, this has never been done.

The real economy is the province of fiscal policy. This does not mean "fine-tuning" the federal deficit. It means using tax policy to structure and maintain a proper set of incentives. It particularly means resisting tax increases as much as possible, and especially boosts in taxes on "the rich" that reimpose the self-defeating high marginal rates of the 1930s and 1970s.

Of course, most of the super-high rates were removed in the 1980s, and can't be removed again. You are not going to get much "Laffer curve" effect cutting marginal rates below the 28 percent of 1986. One major opportunity does remain, which is the capital gains tax. It also is especially helpful in entrepreneurial calculations, as well as in real estate, a particular problem as we move into the 1990s.

Beyond that, however, lower taxes will require more restrained government spending. Our biggest problem, expressed in a soaring deficit with level revenues, is that the federal budget is beyond control. The problem is the Budget and Impoundment Control Act of 1974, in which the Congress volunteered to take control of spending (though it has never volunteered to stop blaming the president for the deficit).

Congress is a committee of 535 strong-willed people, especially with "reforms" that destroyed any vestige of internal discipline, each one a law unto himself. There is no way any such body can make the decisions necessary to take responsibility and accountability for the overall level of expenditure; there is no way to keep a majority focused on the task of saying no. Especially so since Congress is designed and elected to represent narrow interests. This is perfectly legitimate; such interests deserve to be represented. But inevitably the narrow interests push for more spending than serves the general interest.

The only way to control this is a stronger hand for the executive department, which is more unified and disciplined, and also elected by and responsive to a national constituency. As we have seen, the 1974 act pushed spending out of control precisely by reducing the president's de facto authority; the budget can be controlled only by restoring presidential authority in one way or another.

In other governments around the world, a legislature would never think of rejecting the executive's budget (or Supreme Court nominee). This would immediately topple the government and precipitate an election. We do not have a parliamentary system in the United

States, of course, but one of checks and balances. Without suggesting we totally remake our remarkably durable institutions, state governments based on our constitutional principles have found that budget-making requires an item veto. This is not a panacea, of course, but it hardly seems a revolutionary change when federal budget-making is so clearly out of control. The words "item veto" are not magic, nor does the form much matter. But the restoration of de facto authority—and responsibility—does.

We can improve our economic performance, too, by structural policies going even beyond the Carter-Reagan emphasis on deregulation. Through Vice President Dan Quayle, the Bush administration has already tabled proposals to reform the legal system, cutting the enormous parasitic costs that make us the laughing stock of the international business community.[3] The Quayle proposals to have the losing side in civil suits pay the legal costs of the winner and to limit punitive damages would curb nuisance and speculative suits. They would even remove an incentive for the tort-liability bar to finance and nurture the safety mania that seems confined only to the United States, just as the legal contingency fee is.

Similarly, we need to improve our educational system. The educational level, skills and self-discipline of the workforce will bear enormously on economic performance in the economic universe dominated by knowledge industries. Nothing could bear more on our future international competitiveness, if you choose to use that concept. I would prefer to say on our future contribution to the world's economic welfare. The current system, by universal consensus, is woefully inadequate.

We are not likely to succeed, though, by pouring more resources into the same system. The ideal of school choice, of vouchers for students to spend at a school of their choice, is a promising alternative for introducing competition and improving performance. But it may not be the only way. Universal public schools worked once.

The nub of our educational problem is over the last generation or so we as a society have not taken education seriously. Teaching students to read and write has been low among the priorities of what society has expected of schools. The first priority, for example, has been to make every conceivable effort to insure that a black pupil sits next to a white one. Another overriding priority became to protect children from the dangers of asbestos, if any, at huge expense. Then too, society expects schools to inculcate children with a proper attitude toward whales. Somewhere down the list comes education.

This is the attitude that has to be changed. The Bush administration's plans for national student testing are a groping start toward this goal. Other specific initiatives, movement toward a standardized national curriculum, may also help. But the important change is attitudinal. In the schools, we need to put education first.

We need, similarly, a hardheaded approach to the problem of what we call "the homeless." This problem was created by two "reforms," the deinstitutionalization of the mentally ill and the legal neutering of vagrancy laws.[4] While not all street people are former mental patients or druggies or alcoholics, that is where the fashion started. In the notorious Billie Boggs case, the New York American Civil Liberties Union arranged representation for a bag lady picked up by New York police; they cleaned her up and won her case. Shortly after lecturing at Harvard and appearing on "Donahue," she was back panhandling, increasingly sinking back to her former condition. But the New York effort to take custody of the deranged homeless was stopped.

Similarly, Federal District Judge H. Lee Sarokin ruled against the efforts of the public library in Morristown, N.J., to expel one Richard Kreimer on sanitary grounds. On the urging of the American Civil Liberties Union, he ruled that the rules of the library applied to the homeless man were unconstitutionally "vague." Mr. Kreimer went on to file a series of suits against the town of Morristown, which he agreed to drop when the town paid $150,000.

I relate these anecdotes because I find that the "homeless" are the last-resort argument that tax policy has oppressed the poor. I do not know whether Mr. Kreimer paid taxes on his $150,000, but I'm sure most of the homeless do not. It's hard to see how the maladies of the homeless can be addressed through leveling taxation. I am prepared to believe that many of these unfortunates are happier on the streets than they would be in mental institutions, but I would like to see something like the ACLU defend the right of ordinary people not to be assaulted with squalor.

We can further improve our economic performance, however, by starting to cut back on some of the promises we make to ourselves. I recognize that social security is taken as politically untouchable, but with rising payroll taxes this position may be starting to wane. In 1990, Sen. Daniel Patrick Moynihan proposed to cut the social security tax now, letting it rise to even more formidable heights later as the proportion of retirees increases. He was supported by many tax-cutting conservatives.

While a lower social security tax is desirable, it would ultimately be helpful only if it is coupled with, or leads to, a reduction in the promised benefits. The system's burden on the economy can be greatly eased without reducing benefits of current retirees, and without forcing future retirees to accept less than current ones. For as the system works, the future beneficiaries are promised higher benefits than current ones—the starting retirement benefit goes up with the general rise in wage levels.

So if future retirees would agree to accept the same standard of living as current retirees, we could reduce the tax and still keep the system in actuarial balance. In return, we would greatly expand the amount of money retirees are allowed to earn without sacrificing benefits. The current limitation, indeed, amounts to a huge marginal tax rate, and may be another instance in which the "Laffer curve" would greatly reduce and perhaps overcome the estimates of static revenue loss.

Finally, it is absolutely true that in the long run we will be unable to control government expenditure if the government keeps assuming new responsibilities. In particular, it seems clear that in the early to mid 1990s we will hold a great national debate on the financing of health care. With medical expense constantly increasing as a percentage of GNP, and with many health care institutions coming under increasing pressure, this surely is a perplexing topic. Surveys find millions of Americans, especially employees of small businesses, without health insurance.

Americans seem unable to believe, however, that for all its fault their medical care system vies with the best in the world. The often vaunted Canadian system relies on postponing care for many sick people, and probably only holds up because the United States offers a safety valve. Part of the U.S. problem, too, arises because elderly patients are essentially prohibited from spending their own money on medical care. Doctors cannot bill more than the price that Medicare pays. This wage-price control shifts more and more of the cost of medical institutions onto the nonelderly population.

When medical insurance coverage is mandated, experience shows, there is enormous pressure for it to cover more and more services, mostly from providers of the services not yet covered. If the government is going to assume or mandate universal health care, we will have to draw a line somewhere, at some basic level beyond which care is the patient's financial responsibility. Of course, patients must be allowed to pay for such services. If we cannot do this, medical care will grow into a limitless entitlement, defeating any attempt to hold the line on spending and taxes.

In saying that government spending counts, I do not propose any drastic slash in current expenditures; it does not take that much. In its spending game, Congress assumes a "current services budget," with automatic increases in future years, then says a "cut" is any increase less than projected. Wonders could be done by merely freezing the budget, or even containing its increase, a common budgeting practice of all other sectors of American life. Government spending grew by 21 percent in real dollars between 1985 and 1989, but as a percentage of GNP dropped to 22.3 percent from 23.9 percent. This kind of "restraint," if sustained, would do nicely.

Provided, that is, that GNP can be kept growing. The moral of the Seven Fat Years is that economic growth counts. If we get a good growth, we can afford better health care and a host of other good things. If we do not achieve growth, we cannot afford these things, either from our own pockets or through the government.

The keys to growth are evident. Keep taxes low, especially the marginal rate of taxation. Keep spending under *some* control. Keep the currency stable. Keep markets open. Do not censor price movements, a form of communication. Seek free exchange over the broadest section of the world. Let entrepreneurs compete. We always knew these answers; somehow during the Seven Fat Years we managed to practice them better than we usually do.

• • •

Which raises the final question. Lift the suspension of disbelief. How do we discipline our politicians to make them do all these wondrous things? Our political system seems frozen in stasis. Incumbents can be removed only through scandal, if then. Republicans cannot win the Congress; their presidential candidates, even while confronting the establishment à la Reagan, act as if they don't care. Recent experience suggests that, except perhaps for an unknown like Georgia Governor Jimmy Carter, a Democrat who might win the presidency cannot win the nomination. Democrats in Congress increasingly try to run the nation from their citadel, as if they never expect to hold the White House. And of course the same personalities occupy the same committee posts, making the same decisions they have always made. From such a political structure, how can we expect a coherent policy, let alone one that takes bold departures from the past?

Perhaps, one strain of thought runs, the American public prefers this stasis, with a permanent party of the presidency and a permanent party of Congress. Surely polls show that the typical voter approves of his individual congressman while disapproving of Congress. Fewer and fewer congressmen are even opposed, and voter participation keeps sinking to new lows.

For all that, public discontent with the political system seems to be scaling new heights. The resignation of the speaker of the House and his majority whip, the Keating Five scandal, the inability of the congressional ethics committees to call their own to account, have all taken their toll in public esteem. The Senate proceedings over the Clarence Thomas nomination to the Supreme Court glued the entire nation to television screens, in itself an extraordinary event.

Meanwhile, of course, government has continued to grow, bringing riches from over the land. The Washington metropolitan area is a company town, devoted to one industry. Yet so prosperous an industry that five of the six highest-income counties in the nation are centered there.

As it happens, another branch of modern economics has something to say on the subject. In 1986, James Buchanan won the Nobel Prize for economics for founding the "public choice" branch of the discipline. This holds that economic policy cannot be understood apart from the politicians who enact it, and of course the politicians are trying to maximize their own interests, just like any other economic actor.

"We do not expect businessmen to devote a great deal of time and attention to maximizing the public interest. We assume that, although they will of course make some sacrifices to help the poor and advance the public welfare, basically they are concerned with benefiting themselves. Traditionally economists did not take the same attitude toward government officials, but public choice theory does," writes Gordon Tullock, Buchanan's top collaborator, in *Palgrave's*. Public choice theorists keep trying to find ways to make legislators more responsive to voters, and bureaucracies more responsive to their political directions. Everyone in the system has a bias of self-interest, it finds, except the individual voter.[5]

One of our stylistic accomplishments at *The Wall Street Journal* was to establish "The Beltway" as an American idiom. All America understands the phrase and sympathizes with its anti-Washington overtones. More recently we have touched a similar groundswell by promoting term limits for Congress. This squares with the public's anger at the Congress while approving of individual congressmen. Every few years give us a new gladhander to push our interests; maybe the constant churning will make the system work better. For many years, after all, most members of Congress practiced voluntary term limitation, and men such as Henry Clay still ran up distinguished careers by switching around among positions.

Yet it can be a mistake to trust too much in institutional changes, whether term limits, an item veto or even requiring a 60 percent majority for appropriations. Often changes in public attitudes and perceptions permeate any institutional arrangement. Perhaps the largest importance of the thrust for term limits lies in the tenor that the ruling class has become increasingly isolated from the public, that some check must be placed on politicians becoming a class unto themselves.

In this sentiment, we might conceive the tremors of a political earthquake, rearranging the tectonic plates of American politics. Even if that conception again proves itself a fantasy, for all their entrenchment politicians remain an insecure lot. Probably they find their calling out of a need for public approval. If in its mysterious heart the public wants reform, even if it wants a different demeanor from its governors, it probably can have it.

• • •

In a sense, the Seven Fat Years show this. The miracle was less that the economic policy mix was found than that the political stasis was broken. Broken, perhaps only momentarily, with a big enough crisis, with a powerful enough communicator as president, and with a degree of policy consensus evident as early as 1978. Somehow a widespread but inchoate desire by the larger society was felt and translated into policy. And the policy succeeded in ending an economic crisis and restoring stability.

If America really wants another Seven Fat Years, it will have them. The policies worked, as the Man from Mars saw, but so far have been judged a failure, particularly by the most articulate sectors of society. It is hard to know what, in the recesses of its soul, the nation wants. Will it choose to look away at the moment of its triumph, not even to reach for a *Belle Époque?* Does it really deplore a decade of greed, and seek atonement in a decade of envy? For the nation shall also have its way if seven lean years is what it truly wants.

Notes

In the following notes, these abbreviations are used:

WSJ   —*The Wall Street Journal*, news columns
WSJ R&O   —*The Wall Street Journal*, editorials, "Review and Outlook"
WSJ EDFE   —*The Wall Street Journal*, editorial page feature

The Wall Street Journal starting in 1984 is available in Dow Jones News Retrieval, data bases //text or //textm. Use search phrase "Review and Outlook" for editorials.

Various short quotations, such as Mundell or Laffer aphorisms, are from memory. I have tried to indicate such instances in the text.

PREFACE

1. Martin Anderson, *Revolution: The Reagan Legacy* (Stanford, Ca.: Hoover Institution Press, 1990), p. 151.
2. Rudiger Dornbusch and Stanley Fischer, *Macroeconomics*, 5th ed. (New York: McGraw-Hill, 1990), p. 4.
3. Victor A. Canto, Douglas H. Joines and Arthur B. Laffer, *Foundations of Supply-Side Economics: Theory and Evidence* (New York: Academic Press/Harcourt, 1983), p. xv.
4. N. Gregory Mankiw, *A Quick Refresher Course in Macroeconomics* (Cambridge, Mass.: National Bureau of Economic Research, NBER reprint No. 1528). Reprinted from *Journal of Economic Literature*, Vol. XXVII, No. 4 (December 1990). Quotes from pp. 1646, 1645.
5. *Ibid.*, p. 1645.
6. Angus Maddison, *The World Economy in the 20th Century* (Paris: The Organisation for Economic Co-operation and Development, 1989), p. 34.

CHAPTER 1

1. These numbers come from Alan Reynolds of the Hudson Institute, "Reagan's Awesome Economic Boom," *WSJ* EDFE, May 7, 1991.

2. Richard B. McKenzie, "Decade of Greed? Far From It," *WSJ* EDFE, July 24, 1991.

3. These and the following figures are from *The Economist Book of Vital World Statistics*, American ed. (New York: The Economist Books/Times Books/Random House, 1990).

4. See Kenichi Ohmae, *The Borderless World: Power and Strategy in the Interlinked Economy* (New York: Harper Business/HarperCollins, 1990), and Richard B. McKenzie and Dwight R. Lee, *Quicksilver Capital: How the Rapid Movement of Wealth Has Changed the World* (New York: The Free Press, 1991).

5. Jean-François Revel, *How Democracies Perish*, trans. by William Bryon (Garden City, N.Y.: Doubleday, 1984), *The Totalitarian Temptation*, trans. by David Hapgood (Garden City, N.Y.: Doubleday, 1977), and *Without Marx or Jesus*, trans. by J.F. Bernard (Garden City, N.Y.: Doubleday, 1971).

6. Paul Kennedy, *The Rise and Fall of the Great Powers* (New York: Random House, 1987), p. 526.

7. The text of the Lloyd Bentsen acceptance speech was widely reprinted, for example, by the *Washington Post*, July 22, 1988, p. 31.

8. Paul Kennedy, "A Declining Empire Goes to War," *WSJ* EDFE Jan. 24, 1991.

9. I am indebted to Karlyn Keene of the American Enterprise Institute for surveying poll results on these and other issues.

10. Peter G. Peterson, "The Morning After," *The Atlantic*, October 1987.

11. Charles Wolf, "America's 'Decline': Illusion or Reality?" *WSJ* EDFE, May 12, 1988.

12. Francis Bator, "Must We Retrench?" *Foreign Affairs*, Vol. 68 (Spring 1989), p. 93.

13. Samuel T. Huntington, "The U.S.—Decline or Renewal?" *Foreign Affairs*, Vol. 67 (Winter 1988/1989).

14. Joseph P. Nye, *Bound to Lead: The Changing Nature of American Power* (New York: Basic Books, 1990).

15. Karen Elliot House, "World Leadership," a page-one *WSJ* series, part of the *Journal's* centennial coverage "The Second Century," published on Jan. 23 and 30, Feb. 6, 13 and 21, 1989.

16. Kevin Phillips, *The Politics of Rich and Poor* (New York: HarperCollins, 1990).

17. Richard Darman, "National Press Club Luncheon Speaker, Richard Darman, Director, White House Office of Management and Budget, July 29, 1989," Federal News Service.

18. Joseph A. Schumpeter, *History of Economic Analysis*, edited from manuscript by Elizabeth Boody Schumpeter. (New York: Oxford University Press, 1954.) The discussion of Malthus on population, "The Principle of Population," is on pages 250–58. Quotes are from pages 251 and 252.

19. "Treasury Chief Warns of Taxpayer Revolt, Cites $50 billion a Year in Preferences," *WSJ*, Jan. 20, 1969.

20. Genesis 41:49 (Revised Standard Version).

21. Genesis 47:13–26.

22. Exodus 1:8.

CHAPTER 2

1. Maddison, *op cit.*, pp. 85–90.

2. McCracken and Volcker quotes are from Richard F. Janssen, "Nixon's Economic Credibility Gap," *WSJ* EDFE, Sept. 21, 1971.

3. Alfred L. Malabre, Jr., "Economic Laws Still Work, if Applied," *WSJ* EDFE, Aug. 23, 1971.

4. "Remembering the Basics," *WSJ* R&O, Aug. 18, 1971.

5. "Mr. Meany's Dissent," *WSJ* R&O, Aug. 18, 1971.

6. James P. Gannon, "Business' Strange New Silence," *WSJ* EDFE, Dec. 8, 1971.

7. "More Official Replies to Freeze Questions," *WSJ*, Sept. 2, 1971, and "More Answers on the Wage-Price Policy, *WSJ*, Sept. 3, 1971.

8. Richard F. Janssen, "A Heavy Freeze: The Wage-Price Thaw Might Be Years Away, Some Officials Hint," *WSJ* p. one, Sept. 2, 1971.

9. "Weimar, U.S.A.?" *WSJ* R&O, Dec. 20, 1971.

10. Address to the Nation About Vietnam and Domestic Problems, March 29, 1973. 1973 Pub. Papers 234.

11. The text of the OPEC resolution is available from the Organization of Petroleum Exporting Countries, Obere Donaustrasse 93, 1020 Vienna, Austria.

12. "Oil Industry, Consumers Face More Woes As Export Bloc Formally Posts Demands," *WSJ*, Oct. 6, 1971.

13. John Brooks, "Mr. Nixon's Paper Standard," *The New York Times*, Aug. 24, 1971.

14. Forrest McDonald, "The Framers' Conception of the Veto Power," *Pork Barrels and Principles* (Washington: National Legal Center for the Public Interest, 1988).

15. See *Congress and the Nation*, Vol. IV, 1973–76. (Washington: Congressional Quarterly, Inc., 1977) p. 60.

16. *Train, Administrator, Environmental Protection Agency v. City of New York et al.* 420 U.S. 35.

17. "Clouds at the Summit," *WSJ* R&O, Sept. 27, 1974.

18. William Simon, "The Energy Policy Calamity," *WSJ* EDFE, June 10, 1977.

19. Walter Heller, "Economic Recovery is Still Flabby" *WSJ* EDFE, Jan. 7, 1977.

20. "The System Works," *WSJ* R&O, Mar. 30, 1977.

21. James Schlesinger commencement address to University of Virginia, May 22, 1977. Extracted, "Administration Position" in "Selected Readings on Energy," *WSJ* EDFE, May 27, 1977.

22. W. Philip Gramm, "The Energy Crisis in Perspective," *WSJ* EDFE, Nov. 30, 1973.

23. "1001 Years of Natural Gas," *WSJ* R&O, Apr. 27, 1977. See also "Jimmy Carter on the Run," *WSJ* R&O, June 14, 1977; "Good Bye, Dr. Mc-Kelvey," *WSJ* R&O, Sept. 16, 1977; and "The Memory Hole," *WSJ* R&O, Apr. 4, 1978.

24. Jessica Mathews, "A Wager on the State of the World," *Washington Post*, Dec. 14, 1990, p. A27.

25. "Down With Big Business," *WSJ* R&O, Apr. 18, 1979.

26. T. A. Murphy, "Letters to the Editor: A Reply from General Motors," and R. G. Ullman, "Remembering GM," *WSJ* EDFE, April 23, 1979.

27. "Energy and National Goals, Address to the Nation, July 15, 1979," 1979 Pub. Papers 1235.

CHAPTER 3

1. Daniel Seligman, "Keeping Up," *Fortune*, Dec. 1976, p. 69.

2. Alan Reynolds, "Supply-Side Tax Policy: Some International Comparisons," *Cato Journal*, Vol. 5, No. 2 (Fall 1985).

3. James Callaghan quoted in "Keynes is Dead," *WSJ* R&O, Jan. 31, 1977.

4. F. A. Hayek, "The Austrian critique" in "The Keynes Centenary," *The Economist*, June 11, 1983 p. 45; U.S. edition, p. 39.

5. Arthur B. Laffer, "The Bitter Fruits of Devaluation," *WSJ* EDFE, Jan. 10, 1974.

6. Marina v.N. Whitman, "Global Monetarism and the Monetary Approach to the Balance of Payments," *Brookings Papers on Economic Activity*, Vol. 3 (1975), p. 491–555.

7. See Thomas Sowell, *Say's Law: an Historical Analysis.* (Princeton: Princeton University Press, 1972).

8. Robert A. Mundell, "The Global Adjustment System," *Rivista di Politica Economica* (Rome: SIPI, December 1989). The discussion of the depression is on pages 366–72.

9. See "Paul the Navigator," *WSJ* R&O, Feb. 2, 1982.

10. Robert Eisner, "Divergences of Measurement and Theory and Some Implications for Policy," Presidential address to the American Economic

Association, delivered Dec. 29, 1988. *The American Economic Review*, Vol. 79, No. 1 (March 1989), p. 2.

11. "Report of the Advisory Committee on the Presentation of Balance of Payment Statistics," *Survey of Current Business*, Vol 56, No. 6 (June 1976), pp. 18–27.

12. Norman Ture, " 'Supply-Side' Analysis and Public Policy," The Lehrman Institute, Economic Policy Round Table, Nov. 12, 1980. mimeo.

CHAPTER 4

1. "President's Tax Measures May Die Soon At Hands of Democrats on House Panel," *WSJ*, Apr. 20, 1978.

2. Jude Wanniski, "It's Time to Cut Taxes," *WSJ* EDFE, Dec. 11, 1974.

3. Jude Wanniski, "The Mundell-Laffer Hypothesis—A New View of the World Economy," *The Public Interest*, No. 39, (Spring 1975), p. 31–52.

4. See "Toward the Next Economics," in *Toward the Next Economics and Other Essays* (New York: Harper & Row, 1981); originally published in "The Crisis in Economic Theory," *The Public Interest*, (Special Edition, 1980).

5. Paul Craig Roberts, "The Breakdown of the Keynesian Model," *The Public Interest*, No. 52 (Summer 1978), pp. 20–33.

6. Irving Kristol, "The Meaning of Proposition 13," *WSJ* EDFE, June 28, 1978.

7. *Congressional Quarterly Almanac 1978* (Washington: Congressional Quarterly, Inc., 1979), p. 226.

8. "Stupendous Steiger," *WSJ* R&O, April 26, 1878. See also "Footnotes to the Above," *WSJ* R&O, May 8, 1978.

9. "Tax Policy, Investment and Economic Growth," prepared by Securities Industry Association based on econometric studies by Data Resources, Inc., March 1978.

10. The Chase Econometrics estimates are elaborated in Michael K. Evans, *The Truth About Supply-Side Economics* (New York: Basic Books, 1983), pp. 163–85.

11. Joel Slemrod and Martin Feldstein, "The Lock-in Effect of the Capital Gains Tax: Some Time-Series Evidence," National Bureau of Economic Research, Working Paper No. 257, July 1978.

12. The materials on the capital gains proposal by Secretary Blumenthal were released as "Department of Treasury News, Secretary Blumenthal Opposes Ad Hoc Changes In Tax Rules for Capital Gains," May 15, 1978.

13. The three quotes are from *Congressional Quarterly Almanac 1978, op. cit.*, p. 219.

14. Walter Heller, "The Kemp-Roth-Laffer Free Lunch," *WSJ* EDFE, July 12, 1978, p. 19.

15. Paul Craig Roberts, "The Tax Brake," *WSJ* EDFE, Jan. 11, 1979.
16. Paul Craig Roberts, "The Economic Case for Kemp-Roth," *WSJ* EDFE, Aug. 1, 1978.
17. Walter Heller, "Letters to the Editor: A Reply From Walter Heller," *WSJ*, Aug. 7, 1978.

CHAPTER 5

1. President's News Conference, March 2, 1978. 1978 Pub. Papers 438.
2. J. [Jelle] Zijlstra, speech to 48th Annual General Meeting of the Bank for International Settlements, Basel, June 12, 1978. BIS Press communiqué of that date.
3. Quoted in " 'Malign Neglect,' " *WSJ* R&O, Dec. 9, 1977.
4. "Why No One Wants Dollars," editorial *The Times* (London), Jan. 4, 1978.
5. Martin Mayer, *The Fate of the Dollar* (New York: Times Books, 1980), p. 293.
6. William R. Neikirk, *Volcker: Portrait of the Money Man* (New York and Chicago: Congdon & Weed, 1987), p. 2.
7. Charles Kindleberger, *The World In Depression, 1929–1939.* (Berkeley: University of California Press, 1973), p. 53. Emil Moreau's memoirs have recently become available in English, *The Golden Franc* (Boulder, Colo.: Westview Press, 1991.)

CHAPTER 6

1. "Bentsen Warns: Neglect of supply side risks nation's economic future—announces JEC hearings," U.S. Congress, Joint Economic Committee Press Release, May 19, 1980. See also the Joint Economic Reports for 1979 (GPO, 96th Congress, 1st Session, Report No. 96–44) and 1980 (Senate Report 96–618).
2. Vice-presidential acceptance speech, *op. cit.*
3. JEC press release, *op. cit.*
4. Ronald Reagan, *An American Life* (New York: Simon & Schuster, 1990), p. 231.
5. "Transcript of President's News Conference on Foreign and Domestic Matters," *The New York Times*, Oct. 2, 1981, p. 26.
6. Martin Anderson, *Revolution, op. cit.* The text of Policy Memorandum No. 1 is on pp. 115–17.
7. Thomas Sargent and Neil Wallace, "Rational Expectations, the Optimal Monetary Instrument and the Optimal Money Supply Rule," *Journal of Political Economy* (April 1975).
8. Mark Willes, "The Rational Expectations Model," *WSJ* EDFE, Apr. 2, 1979.

9. Martin Feldstein, "Tax Incentives Without Deficits," *WSJ* EDFE, July 25, 1980.

10. Paul Craig Roberts, "Political Economy: Dawdling With Incentives," *WSJ* EDFE, Aug. 7, 1980.

11. "Avoiding a GOP Economic Dunkirk," *WSJ* EDFE, Dec. 12, 1980.

12. Paul Craig Roberts, *The Supply-Side Revolution*, (Cambridge, Mass.: Harvard University Press, 1984), p. 116. For a discussion of Rosy Scenario, pp. 110–18.

13. "Ways-Means Chief Seeks Tax-Cut Accord, Urges GOP to Drop Kemp-Roth Proposal," *WSJ*, Mar. 26, 1981.

14. Quoted in Robert W. Merry, "Rostenkowski and the Tax Bill," *WSJ* EDFE, Mar. 27, 1981.

15. A. B. Laffer Associates, "The 1981 Recession," September 21, 1981.

16. "Taxes and Recession," *WSJ* R&O, July 23, 1981.

CHAPTER 7

1. Milton Friedman and Anna J. Schwartz, *A Monetary History of the United States, 1867–1960* (Princeton: Princeton University Press for the National Bureau of Economic Research, 1963).

2. "Gold and Money," *WSJ* R&O, Sept. 26, 1979.

3. Roy W. Jastram, *The Golden Constant: The English and American Experience* (New York: John Wiley & Son, 1977).

4. Roy W. Jastram, "The Cautionary Demand for Gold," *WSJ* EDFE, Sept. 20, 1979.

5. Quoted in *The New York Times*, Mar. 14, 1980 p. D4.

6. Lindley H. Clark, Jr., "Speaking of Business: Credit Confusion," *WSJ* EDFE, Apr. 15, 1980.

7. "Fed Eases the Credit Restraints It Imposed in March," *WSJ*, May 23, 1980.

8. "Fed Ending Credit Curbs Pleases Bankers, Retailer and Fund Managers, but Immediate Impact Isn't Seen," *WSJ*, July 7, 1980.

9. "Reagan's Tet," *WSJ* R&O, May 19, 1981; "The Missing Keystone," *WSJ* R&O, Aug. 14, 1981.

10. "Milton Friedman," *Newsweek*, September 21, 1981, p. 39.

11. Charles Kadlec, "The Quality of Money," A. B. Laffer Associates, May 22, 1981.

12. Neikirk, *op. cit.*, p. 110.

13. William Greider, *Secrets of the Temple: How the Federal Reserve Runs the Country* (New York: Simon and Schuster, 1987), p. 387.

14. "President's News Conference on Foreign and Domestic Affairs," *The New York Times*, Feb. 19, 1982, p. 20.

CHAPTER 8

1. See William A. Niskanen, *Reaganomics: An Insider's Account of the Policies and the People* (New York: Oxford University Press, 1988) pp. 109–12. The quotes are also drawn from contemporary news accounts cited below and from a transcript of the question and answer session released at the time by the American Enterprise Institute.

2. *The Wall Street Journal, New York Times,* and *Washington Post* headlines appeared in the respective newspapers on Dec. 9, 1981. The David Broder report appeared in the *Washington Post,* Dec. 10, under the headline "President Is Not Soft on Deficits, Aides Say."

3. David Stockman, "The Social Pork Barrel," *The Public Interest,* No. 39 (Spring 1975).

4. "Jimmy McGovern," *WSJ* R&O, Feb. 8, 1977.

5. "John Maynard Domenici," *WSJ* R&O, Apr. 16, 1981.

6. "Letters to the editor: Sen. Domenici's Role in Shaping the Budget." *WSJ* EDFE, Apr. 22, 1981.

7. Greider, *Secrets of the Temple, op. cit.,* p. 369.

8. "Stockman's Future," *WSJ* R&O, Nov. 10, 1981.

9. See Niskanen, *op. cit.,* pp. 36–40.

10. Lou Cannon, *President Reagan: The Role of a Lifetime* (New York: Simon and Schuster, 1991), p. 232.

11. Norman Ornstein, "The Breakdown of the Budget Process," *WSJ* EDFE, Nov. 24, 1981.

12. Irwin Ross, "How Henry Kaufman Gets It Right," *Fortune,* May 18, 1982.

13. Henry Kaufman, James McKeon and David Foster, *1981 Prospects for Financial Markets* (New York: Salomon Brothers, 1980).

14. Matthew Winkler, "Has Henry Kaufman Peaked?" *Barron's,* August 9, 1982, p. 13.

15. John Rutledge, "Why Interest Rates Will Fall in 1982," *WSJ* EDFE, Dec. 14, 1981.

16. John Rutledge, "The 'Structural-Deficit' Myth," *WSJ* EDFE, Aug. 4, 1983.

17. Paul Craig Roberts, "Where Did All the Keynesians Go?" *WSJ* EDFE, Dec. 21, 1983.

18. Lewis Lehrman, "The Case for the Gold Standard," *WSJ* EDFE, July 30, 1981. Robert A. Mundell, "Gold Would Serve Into the 21st Century," *WSJ* EDFE, Sept. 30, 1981. Arthur B. Laffer and Charles W. Kadlec, "The Point of Linking the Dollar to Gold," *WSJ* EDFE, Oct. 13, 1981.

19. Alan Greenspan, "Can the U.S. Return to a Gold Standard" *WSJ* EDFE, Sept. 9, 1991.

20. John Maynard Keynes, *The Means to Prosperity* (London: Macmillan, 1933), an enlarged version of four articles printed in *The Times* in March 1933.
21. Breakfast for Newspaper and Television News Editors, Feb. 19, 1981. 1981 Pub. Papers 132.
22. Report to the Congress of the Commission on the Role of Gold in the Domestic and International Monetary Systems, Vol. 1 (March 1982), p. 21.
23. Charles W. Kadlec and Arthur B. Laffer, "The Mid-Year Outlook," A. B. Laffer Associates, June 28, 1982.
24. "Bring Back Bretton Woods," *WSJ* R&O, June 22, 1982.
25. Greider, *op. cit.* p. 515.
26. An excerpt of the Hot Springs speech ran as "Paul Volcker's Hot Springs Speech to the Business Council," *WSJ* EDFE, Oct. 12, 1982.
27. Arthur B. Laffer and Charles Kadlec, "Has the Fed Already Put Itself on a Price Rule?" *WSJ* EDFE, Oct. 28, 1982.
28. "At Last, a Tax Cut," *WSJ* EDFE R&O, Jan. 3, 1983.

CHAPTER 9

1. Figures on homes with cable television, telephones, VCRs are found in *Statistical Abstract of the United States 1990*, (U.S. Department of Commerce, Bureau of the Census), table 914.
2. Computer utilization is from *Statistical Abstract*, table 1340.
3. On frozen yogurt: Marty Friedman, "Healthier Eating Trends Spark Frozen Yogurt Sales, *Dairy Foods* (Gorman Publishing Co.), June 1, 1990.
4. On fresh produce: Dana Tanyeri, "Fresh Produce Takes Hold in the 80's," *Institutional Distribution* (Bill Communications), Sept. 15, 1990.
5. Food consumption figures are from *Statistical Abstract*, tables 202, 203 and 204.
6. Judith Waldrop and Thomas Exter, "Legacy of the 1980s," *American Demographics* (March 1991).
7. The corporate histories and sales figures in this section are drawn from various sources, principally: *Hoover's Handbook: Profiles of Over 500 Major Corporations*, edited by Gary Hoover, Alta Campbell and Patrick J. Spain (Austin, Tex.: The Reference Press, 1991), "The Fortune 500 Largest Industrial Companies," *Fortune*, Apr. 22, 1991, and the Dow Jones News Retrieval Service.
8. *Fortune*, Apr. 22, 1991.
9. Michael C. Jensen, "Eclipse of the Public Corporation," *Harvard Business Review* (September-October 1989), pp. 61–74.
10. "Who Business Bosses Hate Most," *Fortune*, Dec. 4, 1989, p. 107.
11. Lois M. Plunkert, "The 1990s: A Decade of Job Growth and Industry Shifts," *Monthly Labor Review*, Vol. 113, No. 9, p. 3.

12. Hourly output figures are from the *Economic Report of the President* (February 1991), table B-13.
13. "The Tax Cut Spurs Venture Capital," *Business Week*, Oct. 30, 1978.
14. These are the figures used in compiling the Clark Judge article cited below. Later series differ in detail, but show the same trend. They are compiled by *Venture Capital Journal*, published by Securities Data Co., New York.
15. The figures come from Rogert G. Ibbotson, Jody L. Sindelar, and Jay R. Ritter, "Initial Public Offerings," *Journal of Applied Corporate Finance* (Summer 1988). The figures exclude closed end-mutual funds and Regulation A offerings raising less than $1.5 million.
16. Clark Judge, "The Tax That Ate the Economy," *WSJ* EDFE, June 24, 1991.
17. Glenn Yago, *Junk Bonds: How High Yield Securities Restructured Corporate America* (New York: Oxford University Press, 1991). Table 4-1, p. 36; figures after 1986 supplied by Professor Yago.
18. James L. Doti, "Along the Learning Curve, Regulation Q," *WSJ* EDFE, June 29, 1989.

CHAPTER 10

1. The Mondale Presidential Nomination acceptance speech, quoted here and below, has been widely reprinted, for example in the *Washington Post*, July 20, 1984, p. 18.
2. Hobart Rowen, "Fritz Mondale Faces Reality," the *Washington Post*, July 21, 1984.
3. *Congressional Quarterly Almanac 1985*, (Washington: Congressional Quarterly, Inc., 1986) p. 459.
4. David Shribman, "Presidential Line Item Thwarted In Senate; Backers Vow Continued Fight," *WSJ*, July 25, 1985.
5. *Bowsher v Synar*, 478 U.S. 714 (1986).
6. Jeffery Birnbaum and Alan Murray, *Gucci Gulch: Lawmakers, Lobbyists and the Unlikely Triumph of Tax Reform* (New York: Random House, 1987).
7. "No Shrinking Supply-Sider," *Barron's*, Dec. 21, 1981.
8. "The Corporate Tax Conundrum," *WSJ* R&O, Apr. 8, 1985.
9. Ferdinand Mount, "How Mrs Thatcher Makes the Rich Pay More Taxes," *The Spectator*, Oct. 25, 1986, p. 6.
10. Editorial, "Who's Selling the Snake Oil?" *The Sunday Times* (London), Oct. 19, 1986.
11. David Hale, "Notable and Quotable," *WSJ* EDFE, Sept. 15, 1986.
12. *OECD Economic Outlook*, Vol. 38 (Dec. 1985), p. 6.
13. Alan Murray, "The Outlook: Lower U.S. Tax Rates Go International," *WSJ*, p. one, Apr. 4, 1988.

14. Nigel Lawson, quoted in "Supply-Side Britain," *WSJ* R&O, Mar. 17, 1988.

15. *OECD Economic Outlook*, Vol. 38, (Dec. 1985).

16. *OECD Economic Outlook*, Vol. 48, (Dec. 1990), p. 20.

17. Anthony Harris, "The Monday Page: Reaganomics, Judgment Reserved," *The Financial Times*, May 23, 1988.

CHAPTER 11

1. Lawrence B. Lindsey, *The Growth Experiment: How the New Tax Policy is Transforming the U.S. Economy* (New York: Basic Books, 1990) chap. 7.

2. "Recession Spectacle," *WSJ* R&O, Nov. 12, 1981.

3. Jack Kemp, "The Supply-Side Strategy for Lower Interest Rates," remarks before The Federal Reserve Bank of Atlanta and Emory University, Mar. 17, 1982.

4. Irving Kristol, "The Truth About 'Reaganomics,'" *WSJ* EDFE, Nov. 20, 1981.

5. Robert A. Mundell, "The Dollar and the Policy Mix," *Rivista di Politica Economica* (Dec. 1989), p. 68.

6. Paul Craig Roberts, "What Everyone 'Knows' About Reaganomics," *Commentary* (Feb. 1991), p. 25. He cites Jack Kemp, *The American Renaissance*, (New York: Harper & Row, 1979), and George Gilder, *Wealth and Poverty*, (New York: Basic Books, 1981).

7. "Letters to the Editor: Kemp on Stein: 'Are We All Supply-Siders Now?" *WSJ* EDFE, Apr. 4, 1980.

8. "The Economic Issue," *WSJ* R&O, Oct. 9, 1980.

9. Anderson, *op. cit.*

10. Martin Feldstein, "Tax Incentives Without Deficits," *op. cit.*

11. Committee on Ways and Means, U.S. House of Representatives, "Overview of Entitlement Programs: 1991 Green Book" (Washington: US-GPO, 1991), p. 1,257.

12. Lindsey, *op. cit.*

13. For a discussion of Reagan's Economic Policy Board, see Martin Anderson, *op. cit.*, pp. 264–71.

14. "No Shrinking Supply-Sider," *op. cit.*

15. Paul Samuelson, "Apolitical Science Supports the Fed," *The New York Times*, Oct. 24, 1982.

16. Charles W. Kadlec and Arthur B. Laffer, "Turning Points," A. B. Laffer Associates, Sept. 27, 1982.

17. Alan Reynolds, "The Path from Financial Recovery to Real Recovery," Polyconomics, Inc., Oct. 27, 1982.

18. Walter W. Heller "Can We Afford the Costs of Kemp-Roth?" *WSJ* EDFE, Feb. 10, 1981.

19. Thurow and Tobin quotations from Christopher Conte, "Looking Ahead: Analysts are Confident of Economic Health as the Decade Proceeds," *WSJ*, Sept. 14, 1981.
20. Kemp, "The Supply-Side Strategy," *op. cit.*
21. James Tobin, "Letters to the Editor: Slow Train," *WSJ* EDFE, Jan. 20, 1981.

CHAPTER 12

1. Eisner, *op. cit.*
2. Robert Barro, "Are Government Bonds Net Wealth?" *Journal of Political Economy*, Vol. 82 (November/December 1974), pp. 1095–1117.
3. Robert Barro, "The Ricardian Approach to Budget Deficits," *Journal of Economic Perspectives*, Vol. 3, No. 2 (Spring 1989).
4. Walter Wriston, "On Track With the Deficit," *WSJ* EDFE, Jan. 6, 1989.
5. John Maynard Keynes, *The General Theory of Employment Interest and Money*, 1st Harbinger ed. (New York: Harcourt, Brace, 1964) p. 130.
6. Thomas E. Daxon, "Shrinking Mortgage: Ronald Reagan Was a Friend to Future Taxpayers," *Policy Review* (Winter 1989), p. 68.
7. From transcript of American Enterprise Institute, "Public Policy Week," Dec. 8, 1981, mimeo.
8. See *Pork Barrels and Principles: The Politics of the Presidential Veto* (Washington: National Legal Center for the Public Interest, 1988).
9. Private correspondence with Robert Barro.

CHAPTER 13

1. *OECD Economic Outlook*, Vol. 37 (June 1985).
2. Alan Reynolds, "Growing Away From Large Deficits," *WSJ* EDFE, March 5, 1987.
3. Stephen Grover, "Dollar's Drop Among Largest For Single Day," *WSJ*, March 28, 1985.
4. Milton Friedman, "Letters to the Editor: Please Reread Your Adam Smith," *WSJ* EDFE, June 24, 1987.
5. "Money Matters," *WSJ* R&O, June 24, 1987.
6. 1986 Pub. Paper 137.
7. Walter S. Mossberg and Allan Murray, "Baker Suggests a Role for Gold in Setting World Economic Policy," *WSJ*, Oct. 1, 1987.
8. "NBC News Meet the Press," National Broadcasting Co., Oct. 18, 1987.
9. James Stewart and Daniel Hertzberg, "Terrible Tuesday," *WSJ*, p. one, Nov. 20, 1987.
10. Edward Yardeni, "That M&A Tax Scare Rattling the Markets," *WSJ* EDFE, Oct. 28, 1987.

11. Paul Volcker, "The GATT Under Stress—Is There Life after 40?" Geneva, Nov. 30, 1987.

CHAPTER 14

1. Ron Chernow, *The House of Morgan: An American Banking Dynasty and the Rise of Modern Finance* (New York: Atlantic Monthly Press, 1990), p. 355.
2. *Ibid.*, p. 355.
3. *Ibid.*, p. 375.
4. Quoted in James Ring Adams, *The Big Fix: Inside the S&L Scandal* (New York: Wiley, 1990), p. 12.
5. "Business Outlook: The Threat to Thrift Institutions," Townsend-Greenspan & Co. Inc., Apr. 17, 1974.
6. Brooks Jackson, "Court Papers on St Germain's S&L Ties Complicate His Re-Election Campaign," *WSJ*, Nov. 2, 1988; "U.S. Considered, Dropped Idea of Suing St Germain, *WSJ*, Nov. 11, 1988.
7. "Perfect Banking," *WSJ* R&O, Mar. 1, 1982.
8. Martin Mayer, *The Greatest-Ever Bank Robbery: The Collapse of the Savings and Loan Industry* (New York: Scribner, 1990), pp. 23, 61.
9. From the Phelan report. Excerpts ran as "Ethics Committee: No Problem Here," *WSJ* EDFE, Apr. 19, 1989.
10. *Ibid.*
11. Quoted in "Senatorial Shills," *WSJ* R&O, June 13, 1989.
12. *Lincoln Savings and Loan v. Office of Thrift Supervision.* An extract of Judge Sporkin's opinion was reprinted as "At Lincoln Savings: Skullduggery," *WSJ* EDFE, Sept. 19, 1990.
13. Extensive extracts from William Black's minutes of S&L Regulator's meeting with the "Keating Five" were published as " 'This is a Ticking Time Bomb,' " *WSJ* EDFE, June 13, 1989.
14. Quoted in "Senatorial Shills," *op. cit.*
15. Sen. John Glenn, "Letters to the Editor: Stop Daydreaming About Deregulation," *WSJ* EDFE, July 10, 1991.

CHAPTER 15

1. Matthew Josephson, *The Robber Barons: The Great American Capitalists, 1861–1901* (New York: Harcourt Brace, 1934), pp. vii, viii.
2. From Josephson's obituary, Alden Whitman, "Matthew Josephson, Biographer and Muckraker Dies," *The New York Times*, March 14, 1978.
3. Maury Klein, *The Life and Legend of Jay Gould* (Baltimore: The Johns Hopkins University Press, 1986), pp. 483–84.
4. *Ibid.*, p. 496.
5. *Ibid.*, p. 491.

6. Forrest McDonald, *Insull* (Chicago: The University of Chicago Press, 1962), p. 247.

7. *Ibid.*, p. 339.

8. See John Chamberlain, *The Enterprising Americans: A Business History of the United States*, updated ed. (New York: Harper & Row, 1974), pp. 133–39.

9. John Brooks, *Once in Golconda: A True Drama of Wall Street 1920–1938.* (New York: Harper & Row, 1969), p. 234.

10. Adam Smith, *The Wealth of Nations*, ed. with an introduction and marginal notes by Edwin Cannan (New York: The Modern Library, 1937), p. 14.

11. *Ibid.*, p. 423.

12. Michael Novak, *The Spirit of Democratic Capitalism* (New York: Simon & Schuster, 1982), pp. 92–95.

13. Scott McMurray and Daniel Hertzberg, "Drexel Official Accused by SEC of Inside Trades," *WSJ*, May 13, 1986.

14. James B. Stewart and Daniel Hertzberg, "Prosecutor Asks Judge to Dismiss Charges Against Three Arbitragers in Insider Case," *WSJ*, May 14, 1987.

15. *U.S. v GAF Corp.*, 928 F.2d 1253 (1991)

16. James B. Stewart and Daniel Hertzberg, "Insider Focus: Small Securities Firm Links Drexel's Milken, Goldman's Freeman." *WSJ*, Apr. 6, 1988.

17. *U.S. v Regan*, 937 F.2d 823 (1991) See also, L. Gordon Crovitz, "RICO Needs No Stinkin' Badges," *WSJ* EDFE, Oct. 4, 1989, and generally Crovitz's "Rule of Law" column on the insider-trading cases.

18. *U.S. v Chestman*, 1991 U.S. App. Lexis 23242 (1991); *U.S. v Chestman* 903 F.2d (1990)

19. *U.S. v Wallach*, 935 F.2d 445 (1991)

20. *U.S. v Mulheren*, 938 F.2d 364 (1991) See also, L. Gordon Crovitz, "Rule of Law: Witness for the Prosecution: Plea Bargains and Perjury," *WSJ* EDFE, July 18, 1990.

21. Yago, *op. cit.*, p. 10.

22. Frederick Rose, Laurie Cohen and James B. Stewart, "Battle of Titans: How T. Boone Pickens Finally Met His Match: Unocal's Fred Hartley," *WSJ* March 25, 1985.

23. Supreme Court of the State of Delaware, *UNOCAL Corp. v. Mesa Petroleum Co., et. al.* No. 152, 1985, June 10, 1985.

24. *U.S. v. Milken* S89 Cr. 41. Hearing before Hon. Kimba M. Wood, February 19, 1991, 10:30 a.m. Southern District Reporters, p. 6.

25. *Ibid.*, Redacted Affidavit, Government's response to motion of Michael R. Milken for a reduction of sentence pursuant to Rule 35, Oct. 16, 1991.

26. Stephen Labaton, "Business and the Law; Wall St. Ponders Prosecutor Shift," *New York Times*, Sept. 11, 1989, p. D-2.

27. James B. Stewart, *Den of Thieves* (New York: Simon and Schuster, 1991), p. 448.

28. James B. Stewart, "Irreconcilable Differences," *WSJ*, Oct. 2, 1991, p. B1.

29. Stewart, *Den of Thieves*, op. cit., p. 445–46.

30. *"Portraits of an American Dream* Debuts in Los Angeles," press release from Knowledge Exchange, Inc., and accompanying material.

31. Tom Wolfe, *The Bonfire of the Vanities* (New York: Farrar Straus Giroux, 1987).

CHAPTER 16

1. Merton H. Miller, "Leverage," Nobel Memorial Prize Lecture for presentation at the Royal Swedish Academy of Sciences in Stockholm, Dec. 7, 1990.

2. Lawrence J. White, *The S&L Debacle*, (New York: Oxford University Press, 1991), p. 180.

3. *Ibid.*, p. 182.

4. Extracts of Judge Saffels's opinion in the Franklin Savings case were published under the headline "At Franklin Savings: Capricious Regulation," *WSJ* EDFE, Sept. 19, 1990.

5. *Far West Federal Bank S.B., et. al, Plaintiffs v. Director, Office of Thrift Supervision, et. al.* 746 F. Supp. 1042. (1990); affirmed: U.S. Court of Appeals for the Federal Circuit (April 8, 1991); 1991 U.S. App. LEXIS 5570.

6. Martin Mayer, "The Insatiable Demands of the RTC," *WSJ* EDFE, Nov. 15, 1990.

7. Todd Mason, "No Sale: RTC's Many Miscues In Selling Off Property Rattle Local Markets," *WSJ*, Mar. 28, 1991, p. A1.

8. Paulette Thomas, "A Glimmer of Hope: Resolution Trust Corp. Makes Some Headway In Selling S&L Assets," *WSJ* p. one, Oct. 3, 1991.

9. Paul A. Gigot, "Potomac Watch: RTC's Kearney Got Stuck In S&L Muck," *WSJ* EDFE, Feb. 23, 1990.

10. "Statement of William H. Rivoir, III, Superintendent of Banks, State of Arizona before the Resolution Trust Corporation Regional Advisory Board Region 6, June 13, 1991," State Banking Department, Phoenix, Ariz.

11. White, *op. cit.*, p. 182.

12. General Accounting Office, General Government Division, "GAO/GGD 89-48 High Yield Bonds," Mar. 2, 1989.

13. Miller, *op. cit.*

14. William F. Sharpe, "Capital Asset Prices with and without Negative Holdings," Nobel lecture, Dec. 7, 1990.

15. Harry M. Marokowitz, "Markets and Morality, or Arbitrageurs Get No Respect," the 1991 Robert Weintraub Memorial Lecture at the Center for the Study of Business and Government, Baruch College. A long extract was reprinted under the same headline, *WSJ* EDFE, May 14, 1991.

16. IMF *World Economic Outlook* (May 1991), p. 110.

17. *Paramount Communications v Time Inc.* 371 A.2d 1140 (1990).

18. L. Gordon Crovitz, "Rule of Law: Can Takeover Targets Just Say No to Stockholders?," *WSJ* EDFE, Mar. 7, 1990.

19. Miller, *op. cit.*

20. International Monetary Fund, *World Economic Outlook* (May 1991), p. 113.

21. See Tim Ferguson, "U.S. Isn't Borrowing a Page From Its Last Recovery," *WSJ*, Aug. 20, 1991.

22. Data from Glenn Yago.

23. John Heimann, "Bank Examiners, Trust Your Judgment," *WSJ* EDFE, May 24, 1991.

24. Miller, *op. cit.*

CHAPTER 17

1. Paul Taylor, "Voters Wary of 'Fairness' Theme," *The Washington Post*, Nov. 23, 1985, p. 4. See also the editorial, "Democrats and Fairness,'" *The Washington Post*, Nov. 29, 1985, p. 22, and Paul Taylor, "Democrats Are Divided Over 'Fairness' Issue, *The Washington Post*, Dec. 14, 1985, p. 8.

2. "Thinking About Incomes," *WSJ* R&O, Nov. 3, 1988.

3. U.S. Department of Labor, Bureau of Labor Statistics, "Consumer Expenditures in 1989," USDL: 90-616, Nov. 30, 1990.

4. "The Numbers News," published by *American Demographics*, Vol. 10, No. 1 (January 1990).

5. See Greg J. Duncan, *Years of Poverty, Years of Plenty* (Ann Arbor, Mich.: Institute for Social Research, University of Michigan, 1984).

6. The Bureau of the Census, *Money Income and Poverty Status in the United States, 1989*, Current Population Reports, Series P-60, No. 168, Sept. 1990.

7. Current Population Reports, Series P–60, No. 169-RD, *Measuring the Effect of Benefits and Taxes on Income and Poverty: 1989*, Sept. 1990.

8. Walter J. Blum and Harry Kalven, Jr. *The Uneasy Case for Progressive Taxation* (Chicago: University of Chicago Press, 1953).

9. "Committee on Ways and Means, Background Materials on Federal Budget and Tax Policy for Fiscal Year 1991 and Beyond," (February 1990). The material is also issued in the annual Ways and Means "Green

Book," for example, Committee on Ways and Means, Overview of Entitlement Programs, 1991 Green Book, Appendix I and Appendix J, pp. 1132–1299.

10. Congressional Budget Office, *The Changing Distribution of Federal Taxes, 1975–1990* (October 1987); *Trends in Family Income 1970–1986*, (February 1988); and Staff Working Paper, "The Changing Distribution of Federal Taxes: A Closer Look at 1980" (July 1988).

11. "Another Look at the 1980s: A Decade of Growth and Prosperity," prepared by Senator Pete V. Domenici and Senator Phil Gramm, Mar. 1991.

12. "Progressivity: An Analysis of the Ways and Means/Congressional Budget Office Study," prepared by the staffs of the Council of Economic Advisors and the Office of Management and Budget, Feb. 1990.

13. CBO (Oct. 1987) *op. cit.*, p. 35.

14. Gary Robbins and Aldona Robbins, *Tax Fairness: Myths and Reality*, National Center for Policy Analysis, Dallas, NCPA Policy Report No. 90 (March 1991).

15. Warren Brookes, "Green Book of White Lies," *Washington Times*, May 7, 1991, p. G1; Ed Rubenstein, "Right Data," *National Review*, May 13, 1991, p. 16.

16. "The Great Debate: How the Democrats, With Rare Cunning, Won the Budget War," *WSJ*, Nov. 5, 1990.

17. Frederick Rose, "Battle of Titans," *op. cit.*

18. Eytan Sheshinski, "Treatment of Capital Income in Recent Tax Reforms and the Cost of Capital in Industrialized Countries," in *Tax Policy and the Economy* 4 (Cambridge, Mass.: National Bureau of Economic Research/MIT Press, 1990). See also Lindley H. Clark, Jr., "Speaking of Business: Maybe the Bush Capital-Gains Plan Isn't Enough," *WSJ* EDFE, Feb. 16, 1990.

19. John Rutledge, "To Revive the Economy, Boost Land Prices," *WSJ* EDFE, Oct. 15, 1991.

20. Congressional Budget Office, *How Capital Gains Tax Rates Affect Revenues* (March 1988), p. 59-69. See also, CBO Papers, "Effect of Lower Capital Gains Taxes on Economic Growth," August 1990.

21. Kevin G. Salwen, "SEC Aims to Ease Way for Small Firms to Raise Capital," *WSJ*, Nov. 26, 1991, p. B2.

CHAPTER 18

1. Eugen Weber, *France, Fin de Siècle* (Cambridge: Belknap Press of the Harvard University Press, 1986), p. 2.

2. John Maynard Keynes, *The Economic Consequences of the Peace* (London: Macmillan, 1920).

3. See Peter W. Huber, *Liability: The Legal Revolution and its Consequences* (New York: Basic Books, 1988) and *Galileo's Revenge: Junk*

Science in the Courtroom (New York: Basic Books, 1991); Walter K. Olson, *The Litigation Explosion: What Happened When America Unleashed the Lawsuit* (New York: Truman Talley Books/Dutton, 1991).

4. See Rael Jean Isaac and Virginia C. Armat, *Madness in the Streets: How Psychiatry and the Law Abandoned the Mentally Ill* (New York: The Free Press, 1990).

5. Gordon Tullock, "Public choice," *The New Palgrave: A Dictionary of Economics*, eds. John Eatwell, Murray Milgate, and Peter Newman (London: Macmillan, 1987), Vol. 3, pp. 1040, 1041.

NOTES FOR FIGURES AND TABLES

Figure 1–1. Misery Index. P. 5. The unemployment rate and the increase in the consumer price index by year, taken from *The Economic Report of the President*, 1991.

Figure 1–2. GNP Growth. P. 6. GNP growth in 1982 Dollars from *The Economic Report of the President*. Trend lines by calculation.

Figure 1–3. Marginal Tax Rate. P. 17. Top bracket marginal tax rate, federal income tax from House Ways and Means Committee Report "Overview of the Federal Tax System," 1991 edition (WMCP: 102–7), including data on tax and revenue measures within the committee's jurisdiction. Dated April 10, 1991. Available as Report No. 76, The Bureau of National Affairs, Washington, D.C., April 19, 1991.

The top bracket rate is in Table 1, History of the federal individual income tax exemptions and first and top bracket rate. The rate shown is the statutory rate, the highest effective marginal rate may be somewhat different depending on provisions of the law. The capital gains rate is reported separately in Table 9.

Figure 3–1. The Laffer Curve. P. 58. A pedagogical device, according to Arthur B. Laffer.

Table 4–1. Revenues on Capital Gains Tax on Individuals. P. 68. Treasury data reported by Oscar S. Pollock of Ingalls & Snyder. Published in "Footnotes to the Above," *WSJ* R&O, May 8, 1978.

Table 4–2. Tax Revenues from the Rich. P. 73. From Michael K. Evans, then President of Chase Econometric Associates, Inc., in "Taxes, Inflation and the Rich," *WSJ* EDFE, Aug. 7, 1978.

Table 6–1. Carter Administration 1980 Budget. P. 93. From budget documents, published in "The Planned Tax Increase," *WSJ* R&O, Jan. 30, 1979.

Table 10–1. British Revenues from the Rich. P. 159. From *The Sunday Times*, Oct. 19, 1986, p. 70.

Figure 12–1. Federal Outlays and Receipts. P. 180. Fiscal years. Data from *Budget of the U.S. Government*, Fiscal Year 1992, Historical tables, table 1.3.

Table 12–1. General Government Financial Balances. P. 181. From *OECD Economic Outlook 48*, December 1990, table R–14. General government balances, as opposed to central government balances, include the financial results of local authorities.

Figure 12–2. The National Debt. P. 182. End of fiscal year. Data from *Budget of the U.S. Government*, Fiscal Year 1992. Historical tables, table 7.1.

Table 13–1. U.S. International Accounts. P. 201. Standard data rearrayed. Trade account is balance on current account. Capital account is sum of changes in U.S. private assets abroad and foreign private assets in U.S., U.S. government non-reserve assets abroad and statistical discrepancy. Official financing is sum of change in U.S. official assets and changes in foreign official assets in U.S.

This data was from the *Survey of Current Business*, June 1991. Using line numbers from that presentation: Trade account = line 69. Capital account = line 43 + line 56 + line 39 + line 63. Official financing = line 34 + line 49.

Figure 13–1. The Dollar. P. 210. Prices are taken from *The Wall Street Journal.*

Figure 13–2. The Stock Market. P. 214. For background on the Dow Jones Industrial Averages, see Phyllis S. Pierce, ed., *The Dow Jones Averages, 1985–1990* (Homewood, Ill.: Business One Irwin, 1991).

Table 17–1. Income and Expenditure by Quintile. P. 272. Bureau of Labor Staistics, U.S. Department of Labor, "Consumer Expenditures in 1989," USDL: 90–616, Nov. 30, 1990.

Tabler 17–2. Income Share by Quintile. P. 276. Bureau of the Census, *Measuring the Effects of Benefits and Taxes on Income and Poverty in the United States, 1989*, Current Population Reports, Series P–60, No. 169–RD, Sept. 1990.

Bibliography

Adams, James Ring. *Secrets of the Tax Revolt*. New York: Harcourt Brace Jovanovich, 1984.
———. *The Big Fix: Inside the S&L Scandal*. New York: Wiley, 1990; Updated and expanded ed., 1991.
Anderson, Martin. *Revolution: The Reagan Legacy*. Stanford, Ca.: Hoover Institution Press, 1990.
Barro, Robert J. *Macroeconomics*. New York: Wiley, 1984.
Bartlett, Bruce. *"Reaganonics": $upply $ide Economics in Action*. Westport, Conn.: Arlington House Publishers, 1981.
Batra, Ravi. *The Great Depression of 1990*. New York: Simon & Schuster, 1987.
Bauer, P. T. *Reality and Rhetoric: Studies in the Economics of Development*. Cambridge, Mass.: Harvard University Press, 1984.
Blum, Walter J., and Harry Kalven, Jr. *The Uneasy Case for Progressive Taxation*. Chicago: University of Chicago Press, 1953.
Blumenthal, Sidney. *Our Long National Daydream: A Political Pageant of the Reagan Era*. New York: Harper & Row, 1989.
Boskin, Michael J., and Charles E. McLure, Jr., eds. *World Tax Reform: Case Studies of Developed and Developing Countries*. San Francisco: ICS Press, 1990.
Boskin, Michael J. *Reagan and the Economy: The Successes, Failures & Unfinished Agenda*. San Francisco: ICS Press, 1987.
———. *Too Many Promises: The Uncertain Future of Social Security*. Homewood, Ill.: Dow Jones-Irwin, 1986.
Brooks, John. *Once in Golconda: A True Drama of Wall Street 1920–1938*. New York: Harper & Row, 1969.
Bryan, Lowell. *Bankrupt: Restoring the Health and Profitability of Our Banking System*. New York: HarperCollins, 1991.

Bureau of Labor Statistics, U.S. Department of Labor. "Consumer Expenditures in 1989." USDL: 90–616, Nov. 30, 1990.

Bureau of the Census. *Measuring the Effect of Benefits and Taxes on Income and Poverty: 1989*. Current Population Reports, Series P-60, No. 169-RD, September 1990.

Bureau of the Census. *Money Income and Poverty Status in the United States, 1989*. Current Population Reports, Series P-60, No. 168, September 1990.

Bureau of the Census. *Statistical Abstract of the United States 1990*.

Cannon, Lou, *President Reagan: The Role of a Lifetime*. New York: Simon & Schuster, 1991.

Canto, Victor A., and Arthur B. Laffer, eds. *Monetary Policy, Taxation and International Investment Strategy*. New York: Quorum Books, 1990.

Canto, Victor A., Douglas H. Joines and Arthur B. Laffer. *Foundations of Supply-Side Economics: Theory and Evidence*. New York: Academic Press/Harcourt, 1983.

Central Intelligence Agency. *Handbook of Economic Statistics, 1990*. Washington: GPO, 1990.

Chamberlain, John. *The Enterprising Americans: A Business History of the United States*. New York: Harper & Row, 1961; New and Updated Ed., 1974.

———. *The Roots of Capitalism*. Indianapolis: Liberty Press, 1976.

Chernow, Ron. *The House of Morgan: An American Banking Dynasty and the Rise of Modern Finance*. New York: Atlantic Monthly Press, 1990.

Clay, Sir Henry. *Lord Norman*. London: Macmillan, 1957.

Committee on Ways and Means. *Overview of Entitlement Programs, 1991 Green Book*. Washington: GPO.

Congress and the Nation, Vol. IV, 1973–76. Washington: Congressional Quarterly, 1977, p. 60.

Congressional Budget Office. *The Changing Distribution of Federal Taxes, 1975–1990* (October 1987), *Trends in Family Income 1970–1986*, February 1988, and Staff Working Paper, "The Changing Distribution of Federal Taxes: A Closer Look at 1980" (July 1988).

Congressional Quarterly Almanac, various years. Washington: Congressional Quarterly, annual.

Cooper, Charles, *et al. Pork Barrels and Principles*. Washington: National Legal Center for the Public Interest, 1988.

Cootner, Paul H. *The Random Character of Stock Market Prices*. Cambridge, Mass: MIT Press, 1964.

Council of Economic Advisers. *Economic Report of the President*, various issues. Washington: GPO, annual.

Dornbusch, Rudiger, and Stanley Fischer. *Macroeconomics*, 5th ed. New York: McGraw-Hill, 1990.

Drucker, Peter F. *The Unseen Revolution: How Pension Fund Socialism Came to America.* New York: Harper & Row, 1976.

———. *Toward the Next Economics and Other Essays.* New York: Harper & Row. 1981.

Duncan, Greg J. *Years of Poverty, Years of Plenty.* Ann Arbor, Mich.: Institute for Social Research, University of Michigan, 1984.

Eatwell, John, Murray Milgate and Peter Newman, eds. *The New Palgrave: A Dictionary of Economics.* London: Macmillan, 1987.

Eisner, Robert. *How Real is the Federal Deficit.* New York: The Free Press, 1986.

Evans, Michael K. *The Truth About Supply-Side Economics.* New York: Basic Books, 1983.

Fellner, William, Kenneth W. Clarkson, and John H. Moore. *Correcting Taxes For Inflation.* Washington, D.C.: American Enterprise Institute for Public Policy Research, 1975.

Friedman, Milton, and Anna J. Schwartz. *A Monetary History of the United States, 1867–1960.* Princeton: Princeton University Press for the National Bureau of Economic Research, 1963.

Galbraith, John Kenneth, and Paul W. McCracken, *Reaganomics: Meaning, Means and Ends.* New York: The Free Press, 1983.

General Accounting Office, General Government Division. "GAO/GGD 89–48 High Yield Bonds," March 2, 1989.

Gilder, George. *Microcosm.* New York: Simon & Schuster, 1989.

———. *Wealth and Poverty.* New York: Basic Books, 1981.

Greider, William. *Secrets of the Temple: How the Federal Reserve Runs the Country.* New York: Simon & Schuster, 1987.

Hayek, Friedrich A. *The Road to Serfdom.* Chicago: University of Chicago Press, 1944.

Hazlitt, Henry, ed. *The Critics of Keynesian Economics.* New Rochelle, N.Y.: Arlington House, 1960.

Hector, Gary. *Breaking the Bank: The Decline of Bank America.* Boston: Little, Brown, 1988.

Hicks, Sir John, *The Crisis in Keynesian Economics.* New York: Basic Books, 1974.

———. *Critical Essays in Monetary Theory.* London: Oxford University Press, 1967,

Hoover, Gary, Alta Campbell, and Patrick J. Spain, eds. *Hoover's Handbook: Profiles of Over 500 Major Corporations.* Austin, Tex.: The Reference Press, 1991.

Huber, Peter W. *Liability: The Legal Revolution and its Consequences.* New York: Basic Books, 1988.

———. *Galileo's Revenge: Junk Science in the Courtroom.* New York: Basic Books, 1991.

International Monetary Fund. *World Economic Outlook,* various issues. Washington: IMF, annual.

Isaac, Rael Jean, and Virginia C. Armat. *Madness in the Streets: How Psychiatry and the Law Abandoned the Mentally Ill.* New York: The Free Press, 1990.

Jastram, Roy. *The Golden Constant: The English and American Experience.* New York: Wiley, 1977.

Johnson, Haynes. *Sleepwalking Through History.* New York: Norton, 1990.

Jones, Gordon S., and John A. Marinai, eds. *The Imperial Congress: Crisis in the Separation of Powers.* New York: Pharos Books for the Heritage Foundation and the Claremont Institute, 1988.

Joseph P. Nye. *Bound to Lead: The Changing Nature of American Power.* New York: Basic Books, 1990.

Josephson, Matthew. *The Robber Barons: The Great American Capitalists, 1861–1901.* New York: Harcourt Brace, 1934.

Kahn, Herman, *The Coming Boom.* New York: Simon & Schuster, 1982.

———. *The Next 200 Years: A Scenario for America and the World.* New York: Morrow, 1976.

Kaufman, Henry, James McKeon and David Foster. *1981 Prospects for Financial Markets.* New York: Salomon Brothers, 1980.

Kemp, Jack, and Robert Mundell, eds. *A Monetary Agenda for World Growth.* Boston: Quantum, 1983.

Kemp, Jack. *The American Renaissance.* New York: Harper & Row, 1979.

Kennedy, Paul. *The Rise and Fall of the Great Powers.* New York: Random House, 1987.

Kessel, John H. *Presidential Campaign Politics: Coalition Strategies and Citizen Response.* Chicago: The Dorsey Press, 1988.

Kettel, Brian. *Gold.* Cambridge, Mass.: Ballinger Publishing Company, Harper & Row, 1982.

Keynes, John Maynard. *The Economic Consequences of the Peace.* London: Macmillan, 1920.

———. *The General Theory of Employment, Interest, and Money,* First Harbinger edition. New York: Harcourt, Brace, 1964.

———. *The Means to Prosperity.* An enlarged version of four articles printed in *The Times* in March 1933. London: Macmillan and Co., 1933.

Kindelberger, Charles P. *Keynesian vs. Monetarism and Other Essays in Financial History.* London: George Allen & Unwin, 1985.

———. *The World in Depression, 1929–1939.* Berkeley, Ca.: University of California Press, 1973.

Klein, Maury. *The Life and Legend of Jay Gould.* Baltimore: The Johns Hopkins University Press, 1986.

Knight, Frank H. *Risk, Uncertainty and Profit,* with an introduction by George J. Stigler. Chicago: University of Chicago Press, 1971.

Kristol, Irving, and Nathan Glazer, eds., *The Crisis in Economic Theory. The Public Interest* (Special Issue, 1980).

Laffer, Arthur B., and Jan P. Seymour, eds. *The Economics of the Tax Revolt: a Reader.* New York: Harcourt Brace Jovanovich, 1979.

Laffer, Arthur B., and Marc A. Miles. *International Economics in an Integrated World.* Glenview, Ill.: Scott, Foresman and Company, 1982.

Lee, Susan. *Susan Lee's ABZs of Economics.* New York: Poseidon Press, 1987.

———. *Susan Lee's ABZs of Money and Finance.* New York: Poseidon Press/Simon & Schuster, 1988.

Leijonhufvud, Axel. *On Keynesian Economics and the Economics of Keynes: A Study in Monetary Theory.* New York: Oxford University Press, 1968.

Lindsey, Lawrence B. *The Growth Experiment: How the New Tax Policy Is Transforming the U.S. Economy.* New York: Basic Books, 1990.

Lorie, James, and Mary T. Hamilton. *The Stock Market: Theories and Evidence.* Homewood, Ill.: Richard D. Irwin, 1973.

Maddison, Angus. *The World Economy in the 20th Century.* Paris: The Organization for Economic Co-operation and Development, 1989.

Malabre, Alfred L., Jr. *Beyond Our Means: How America's Long Years of Debt, Deficits and Reckless Borrowing Threaten to Overwhelm Us.* New York: Random House, 1987.

———. *Within Our Means: The Struggle for Economic Recovery After a Reckless Decade.* New York: Random House, 1991.

Mankiw, N. Gregory. "A Quick Refresher Course in Macroeconomics." Cambridge, Mass.: National Bureau of Economic Research, NBER reprint No. 1528. Reprinted from *Journal of Economic Literature.* Vol. XXVII, No. 4 (December 1990), pp. 1645–1660.

Mayer, Martin, *The Fate of the Dollar.* New York: Times Books, 1980.

———. *The Greatest-Ever Bank Robbery: The Collapse of the Savings and Loan Industry.* New York, Charles Scribner's Sons, 1990.

McDonald, Forrest. *Insull.* Chicago: University of Chicago Press, 1962.

McKenzie, Richard B. and Dwight R. Lee. *Quicksilver Capital: How the Rapid Movement of Wealth Has Changed the World.* New York: The Free Press, 1991.

Meadows, Dennis, *et al. The Limits to Growth: A Report for the Club of Rome's Project on the Predicament of Mankind.* New York: Potomac Associations Books/Universe Books, 1972.

Melloan, George and Joan. *The Carter Economy.* New York, Wiley, 1978.

Moreau, Emil. *The Golden Franc.* Boulder, Colo.: Westview Press, 1991. Translation of *Souvenirs d'un Gouverneur de la Banque de France.*

Mundell, Robert A. "Debt and Deficits in Alternative Macroeconomic Models," *Rivista di Politica Economica.* (Rome: SIPI, July–August 1990).

———. "The Dollar and the Policy Mix," and "The Global Adjustment System," *Rivista di Politica Economica.* (Rome: SIPI, Dec. 1989).

———. *Man and Economics: the Science of Choice.* New York: McGraw-Hill, 1968.

Neikirk, William R. *Volcker: Portrait of The Money Man.* New York: Congdon & Weed, 1987.

Niehans, John. *International Monetary Economics.* Baltimore: The Johns Hopkins University Press, 1984.

Niskanen, William A. *Reagonomics: An Insider's Account of the Policies and the People.* New York: Oxford University Press, 1988.

Nixon, Richard. *In the Arena: A Memoir of Victory, Defeat and Renewal.* New York: Simon and Schuster, 1990.

Novak, Michael. *The Spirit of Democratic Capitalism.* New York: Simon & Schuster, 1982.

Nye, Joseph S., Jr. *Bound to Lead: The Changing Nature of American Power.* New York: Basic Books, 1990.

Ohmae, Kenichi, *The Borderless World: Power and Strategy in the Interlinked Economy.* New York: Harper Business/HarperCollins, 1990.

Olson, Walter K. *The Litigation Explosion: What Happened When America Unleashed the Lawsuit.* New York: Truman Talley Books/Dutton, 1991.

Organization of Economic Co-operation and Development. *OECD Economic Outlook,* various issues. Paris: OECD, semi-annual.

Ortner, Robert. *Voodoo Deficits.* Homewood, Ill.: Dow-Jones Irwin, 1990.

Paglin, Morton, *Poverty and Transfers In-kind.* Stanford, Ca.: Hoover Institution Press, 1980.

Paul, Ron, and Lewis Lehrman. *The Case for Gold: A Minority Report of the U.S. Gold Commission.* Washington: CATO Institute, 1982.

Phelps, Edmund S. *Seven Schools of Macroeconomic Thought.* Oxford: Clarendon Press, 1990.

Phillips, Kevin. *The Politics of Rich and Poor: Wealth and the American Electorate in the Reagan Aftermath.* New York: HarperCollins, 1990.

Reagan, Ronald, *An American Life.* New York: Simon & Schuster, 1990.

Reich, Robert B. *The Work of Nations: Preparing Ourselves for 21st-Century Capitalism.* New York: Alfred A. Knopf, 1991.

Revel, Jean François. *Without Marx or Jesus: The New American Revolution Has Begun,* trans. by J. F. Bernard. Garden City, N.Y.: Doubleday, 1971.

———. *How Democracies Perish,* trans. by William Bryon. Garden City, N.Y.: Doubleday, 1984.

———. *The Totalitarian Temptation,* trans. by David Hapgood. Garden City, N.Y.: Doubleday, 1977.

Robbins, Gary, and Aldona Robbins. *Tax Fairness: Myths and Realities.* National Center for Policy Analysis, Dallas, NCPA Policy Report No. 90, March 1991.

Roberts, Paul Craig. "The Breakdown of the Keynesian Model," *The Public Interest.* No. 52 (Summer 1978).

———. *The Supply-Side Revolution: An Insider's Account of Policymaking in Washington.* Cambridge, Mass.: Harvard University Press, 1984.

Rothchild, Michael. *Bionomics: The Inevitability of Capitalism.* New York: John Macrae/Henry Holt, 1990.

Rueff, Jacques. *The Age of Inflation,* trans. by A. H. Meeus and F. G. Clarke. Chicago: Regnery, 1964.

Rutledge, John, and Deborah Allen. *Rust to Riches: The Coming of the Second Industrial Revolution.* New York: Harper & Row, 1989.

Safire, William. *Before the Fall: An Inside View of the Pre-Watergate White House.* Garden City, N.Y.: Doubleday, 1975.

Schnitzer, Martin. *Income Distribution: A Comparative Study of the United States, Sweden, West Germany, East Germany, the United Kingdom and Japan.* New York: Praeger, 1974.

Schumpeter, Joseph A. *History of Economic Analysis.* Edited from manuscript by Elizabeth Boody Schumpeter. New York: Oxford University Press, 1954.

Schwartz, Anna, ed. *Report to the Congress of the Commission on the Role of Gold in the Domestic and International Monetary Systems,* March, 1982. Washington: U.S. Treasury.

Silver, Thomas B. *Coolidge and the Historians.* Durham, N.C.: Carolina Academic Press for the Claremont Institute, 1982.

Smith, Adam. *The Theory of Moral Sentiments,* with an introduction by E. G. West. Indianapolis: Liberty Classics, 1969.

––––––. *The Wealth of Nations,* ed. and with an introduction and marginal notes by Edwin Cannan. New York: The Modern Library, 1937.

Smith, Roy C. *The Money Wars: the Rise and Fall of the Great Buyout Boom of the 1980s.* New York: Truman Talley Books/Dutton, 1990.

Smith-Morris, Miles, ed. *The Economist Book of Vital World Statistics,* American Edition. New York: The Economist Books/Times Books/Random House, 1990.

Sowell, Thomas. *Say's Law: an Historical Analysis.* Princeton, N.J.: Princeton University Press, 1972.

Spurge, Lorraine, ed. *Portraits of an American Dream.* Los Angeles: The Knowledge Exchange, Inc., 1991.

Stein, Herbert. *The Fiscal Revolution in America.* Chicago: University of Chicago Press, 1969.

Stockman, David A. *The Triumph of Politics: Why the Reagan Revolution Failed.* New York: Harper & Row, 1986.

van den Haag, Ernest, ed. *Capitalism: Sources of Hostility.* New Rochelle, N.Y.: Epoch Books for the Heritage Foundation, 1979.

Wanniski, Jude. "The Mundell-Laffer Hypothesis—A New View of the World Economy." *The Public Interest.* No. 39 (Spring, 1975).

––––––. *The Way the World Works.* New York: Touchstone/Simon & Schuster, 1978.

Weber, Eugen. *France, Fin de Siècle.* Cambridge, Mass.: The Belknap Press of Harvard University Press, 1986.

Werner, Walter, and Steven T. Smith. *Wall Street.* New York: Columbia University Press, 1991.

White, Lawrence J. *The S&L Debacle.* New York: Oxford University Press, 1991.

Whitman, Marina v.N. "Global Monetarism and the Monetary Approach to the Balance of Payments." *Brookings Papers on Economic Activity.* Vol. 3 (1975).

Wolfe, Tom. *The Bonfire of the Vanities.* New York: Farrar Straus & Giroux, 1987.

Yago, Glenn. *Junk Bonds: How High Yield Securities Restructured Corporate America.* New York: Oxford University Press, 1991.

Acknowledgments

I owe two large debts: To my employer, *The Wall Street Journal* and Dow Jones & Co., not only for allowing me to make the time to write this manuscript, but also for sustaining me in the adventure it describes. And to my family—Edith, Beth, Susan and Katherine, who were exceedingly patient during the throes of draftsmanship.

I would also like to thank those who helped with the manuscript: Susan Lee and Irving Kristol read the entirety, and offered much encouragement and advice. At several key points, Peggy Noonan gave the words some punch. Various chapters were also read by Robert Mundell, Norman Ture, Jude Wanniski, Robert Barro, Daniel Henninger and Melanie Kirkpatrick. Dirk Reinhardt and Nicola Clark helped with research, and James Condon did the figures.

Finally, in this as in so much else, I owe a special thanks to my administrative assistant, Patricia Broderick, who chased facts, people, phone messages and lost files, and most important of all keeps me from being buried in the office avalanche.

Index